INSURGENCY

INSURGENCY

How Republicans Lost
Their Party and Got
Everything They Ever Wanted

★ ★ ★

JEREMY W. PETERS

CROWN
NEW YORK

Published in the United States by Crown, an imprint of Random House,
a division of Penguin Random House LLC, New York.

CROWN and the Crown colophon are registered trademarks
of Penguin Random House LLC.

LIBRARY OF CONGRESS CATALOGING-IN-PUBLICATION DATA
Names: Peters, Jeremy (Jeremy W.), author.
Title: Insurgency / Jeremy Peters.
Description: First edition. | New York : Crown, [2022] |
Includes bibliographical references and index.
Identifiers: LCCN 2021040114 (print) | LCCN 2021040115 (ebook) |
ISBN 9780525576587 (hardcover) | ISBN 9780525576600 (ebook)
Subjects: LCSH: Republican Party (U.S. : 1854-)—History—21st century. |
Trump, Donald, 1946—Influence. | Conservatism—United States. | Right-wing
extremists—United States. | United States—Politics and government—21st century.
Classification: LCC JK2356 .P38 2022 (print) | LCC JK2356 (ebook) |
DDC 324.2734—dc23/eng/20211019
LC record available at https://lccn.loc.gov/2021040114
LC ebook record available at https://lccn.loc.gov/2021040115

Printed in the United States of America on acid-free paper

crownpublishing.com

2 4 6 8 9 7 5 3 1

First Edition

Book design by Victoria Wong

For my mom and dad

Contents

A Note on Sourcing

Insurgency draws on interviews with more than three hundred people, the vast majority of which were conducted during the four years that Donald Trump was president. Many of them were conducted on background, under the condition that the author not reveal the source. But many were also on-the-record conversations that often lasted several hours and occurred in multiple sittings. Where the quotes are rendered in present tense—*Buchanan says* or *Cantor recalls*—that indicates material from interviews conducted with the author on-the-record. Scores of the senior-most elected officials and top strategists in the Republican Party agreed to speak for this book, as did some of the most powerful figures in conservative media. This includes members of the Trump cabinet, staff of both Trump presidential campaigns, several former chairmen of the Republican National Committee, current and former governors, senators, House members, and Trump himself. They provided a wealth of private communications, including confidential memos, personal emails, contemporaneous notes of meetings, and memoirs they never published. Quotes in the past tense are typically taken from other journalistic accounts of the events described or are reconstructions of conversations explained to the author under the condition that the source not be named. Where the author has cited scenes, events, documents, and other information from outside journalistic sources, those are credited in the notes at the end of the book. For a more specific accounting of the journalists whose work the author relied on most frequently, please see the acknowledgments at the end of the book.

Introduction

"This Isn't Their Republican Party Anymore"

I have the tough people, but they don't play it tough—until they go to a certain point. And then it would be very bad, very bad.
—President Donald J. Trump, in an interview
with *Breitbart News,* March 13, 2019

Adam Kinzinger had a higher threshold than most for danger. But something about January 6, 2021, made the forty-two-year-old Air Force veteran uneasy as he got ready to go into work. As a combat pilot, he had flown missions in Iraq and Afghanistan during the wars. When he was in his twenties, he helped apprehend a knife-wielding man in downtown Milwaukee who'd just slashed a woman in the face, chasing the man down and pinning him to the ground until police arrived. Kinzinger was one of eighty-seven Republicans swept into the House of Representatives in 2010 with the help of the Tea Party—that anvil of resentment and rage that promised to flatten Washington and "Take America Back," as a popular slogan at the time summed up the movement's animating spirit. Kinzinger believed that the country was a pretty dysfunctional place then.

The federal government was saddled with more than $13 trillion in debt and on the verge of implementing a costly new government-run healthcare system. Kinzinger, like many of his new colleagues, ran on a message that the Democrats and their new president, Barack Obama, were gambling with the country's future by spending so much money. He won Sarah Palin's endorsement, one of most coveted imprimaturs of maverick conservative authenticity. Kinzinger sometimes shook his head when he thought about his generation—the generation that would soon be in charge—with a "kids these days" sense of apprehension.

At first, many of Kinzinger's fellow freshman Republicans struck him as the solution. They were willing to fight for their country, if not physically like he had, then on the field of representative democracy, which he considered the next best thing. They showed up for work in the U.S. Capitol with their foam mattresses and toothbrushes, saying they would rather live in their offices than rent an apartment and lay down roots in the swamp that was Washington. Like a liberating army, they would secure the place and then be gone. But it didn't take Kinzinger long to see an ugly, irrational side to many of his Tea Party allies. They scorned him for siding with Republican leadership in debates over spending. Fiscal hawks like Paul Ryan, a forty-one-year-old rising star from Wisconsin, were calling for enormous cuts to social programs, and yet hard-right Tea Party members wanted to cut even more. In an attempt to punish Kinzinger for the perceived betrayal, activists leaked his cellphone number online along with the numbers of other members who had gone along with the smaller cuts. Looking back on the incident years later, he realized that was when he could see the movement was more reactionary and vindictive than what he had signed up for. "The beginning of the new Tea Party," he says. Whether it was the portent of something new or the moment the pretenses about the Tea Party's true character fell away, Republicans like Kinzinger could no longer deny that the insurgency they rode to power was turning on their party from within.

Kinzinger had grown alarmed about what might happen on January 6 as it became clear that President Donald Trump and his supporters would not accept defeat. He saw how Trump's most devoted followers weren't becoming less enamored with him. Instead, they were taking up his latest rallying cry—STOP THE STEAL—just as they had with his others like BUILD THE WALL and LOCK HER

UP.* After multiple people were stabbed at a pro-Trump rally in Washington in December, Kinzinger thought the president's insistence that he had been cheated of victory had gone beyond self-indulgent delusion. It might get someone killed. And the rally scheduled for the sixth, billed as the "Save America Rally," seemed like the place Kinzinger thought it might happen, since that was the day the United States Congress would make official the reality that Trump and his followers refused to accept. *Is it really that crazy to think that one or two of them will take the law into their own hands when you have the first, second, and third in the line of succession to the presidency within a few feet of each other?* he thought. He also worried that some of his Republican colleagues were inflaming the situation by lending credence to Trump's lies about votes that were supposedly flipped by hackers or cast by dead people. Almost one hundred forty of them in the House had already decided they would object to declaring President-elect Joseph R. Biden, Jr. the winner. "Look, you guys need to stop this shit," Kinzinger had chastised his fellow Republicans on a conference call as the certification vote loomed. "There is going to be violence." The Republican leader, Representative Kevin McCarthy of California, was not eager to open the floor up to a debate over Kinzinger's concerns. "Thanks, Adam," McCarthy responded. Then he asked the operator to patch through the next member in the queue.

Kinzinger's wife had asked him about joining him at the Capitol to watch as Congress and the vice president, in his constitutional role as the president of the Senate, carried out their formal duties in the process of finalizing the election. They were to begin the process of counting the electoral votes from all fifty states and the District of Columbia at 1 P.M., after which they were expected to affirm that Biden had won a majority. This procedure had gone off with only minor hiccups since Congress started doing it in the mid-twentieth

---

* The phrase wasn't new to Trump. His most enterprising co-conspirator in claiming he'd been cheated, Roger Stone, had used it in 2016 in a campaign that accused establishment Republicans of trying to deny Trump the nomination.

century. But Kinzinger told his wife to stay home. He also told his staff not to come in to the office. And he packed his pistol, an older .38 caliber Ruger LCP, before leaving. Like many who were there that day, Kinzinger recalls an almost bestial energy hanging in the air. "I felt a real darkness over the place that I've never felt before," he says. Later, after speaking to law enforcement officers who were on the scene, he recalls that one told him, "We felt a lot of evil out there."

The chaos that had been building up gradually over the course of the morning erupted around 2 P.M., less than an hour after Trump closed out his speech by telling the crowd to join their president and march on the Capitol. "Let's walk down Pennsylvania Avenue," he said. And together they would give the Republicans he called "weak" a dose of courage: "The kind of pride and boldness that they need to take back our country," he said. The United States Capitol Police estimated that between twenty-five thousand and thirty thousand people gathered at the Ellipse waiting to hear Trump address the crowd. But already by 11 A.M., police were on edge about the reports coming in from officers on the Capitol grounds, where about two hundred members of the Proud Boys were gathering. Members of the group, which preached about the supposed supremacy of Western culture, were like a rag-tag far-right paramilitary unit. They were known for showing up at political events armed with clubs, bats, and pepper spray. Concerned citizens called 911 to say they had seen suspicious packages and demonstrators brandishing firearms. From the Washington Monument to the top of Capitol Hill, marchers waved banners that spelled out T-R-U-M-P in large letters and superimposed his face onto the body of a machine-gun-toting Rambo. They flew the Gadsden flag. They hoisted up banners that said STOP THE STEAL and DON'T TREAD ON TRUMP. At the foot of the West Front of the Capitol, someone had erected a makeshift gallows out of wood and hung a noose from it.

Kinzinger was on the floor of the House chamber just before 1 P.M., when a group of demonstrators near the Capitol's reflecting pool picked up one of the movable metal bike racks that police had set up as barricades. They used it as a battering ram against the officers standing patrol, who eventually could no longer hold the mob back. People started pouring through the opening and rushing toward the building—the first breach of the Capitol's outer security perimeter that day. Like his fellow members, Kinzinger was unaware of the deteriorating scene unfolding just a few hundred yards away. Inside, debate over counting the electoral votes began after Vice President Mike Pence banged the gavel to open the joint session of Congress at 1:03 P.M. Kinzinger still felt uneasy being there and decided to return to his office across the street in the Rayburn House Office Building. He took the underground tunnels to avoid the crowds, which by then had advanced closer to the Capitol.

He had not been in his office long when a chilling alert from the Capitol Police landed in the email inboxes of members and congressional staffers. Time-stamped at 2:18 P.M., it said there was a threat inside the building. Everyone should close, lock, and stay away from external doors and windows. "Remain quiet," the email continued, ordering them to silence all electronics. "No one will be permitted to enter or exit the building until directed by USCP."

Kinzinger barricaded himself inside his office and took out his gun.

Click, click, click. Representative Ronny Jackson looked up from his seat on the floor of the House as Capitol Police officers were hurriedly closing and locking the doors to the chamber. He saw Speaker Nancy Pelosi's security detail hustle her out of sight. He heard someone mutter something about a bomb threat. It was only his fourth day on the job. As a military doctor who had served in Iraq, Jackson knew that the police wouldn't be locking them inside a place where members of Congress would be sitting ducks. He had been elected to represent the Texas panhandle in November despite having never held office. He did, however, have Trump's endorsement. And that was enough to vault him past a rival candidate in the Republican primary who was supported by the veteran member of Congress vacating the seat. Jackson, the former White House physician, was one of the few freshmen who knew Trump personally. But he had earned the president's support the way every other Republican law-maker had to: by displaying the deference and fealty that Trump demanded. During his campaign, Jackson adopted his boss's delusions and grievances as his own. Though Jackson had been President Barack Obama's physician for eight years, that didn't stop him from calling his former patient "a Deep State traitor." And when Jackson came under fire for it, he doubled down, insisting he would "never apologize for standing up to protect America's national security interests."

Jackson's experience—not Kinzinger's—was the new norm for Republicans. In the five years since the insurgent president had steamrolled over the party leadership, most Republicans had learned that denying or resisting his power to sway their voters, and ultimately to determine their fates in elections, was largely futile. They had to defend his most indefensible conduct, or at least not be caught criticizing it in anything but the most gentle and deferential terms. Trump's enemies had to become theirs. Trump's allies became theirs too, no matter how far on the political fringes they came from. This was the simple, prescribed path to public office as a Republican in 2020 and to power in Trump's Republican Party for the foreseeable future. Jackson evidently thought so little of the warnings of Republicans like Kinzinger that he attended the "Rally to Save America" as a VIP guest. His passes gave him access to seats just a few feet from the stage where Trump would speak. Before the speeches began, he mingled with dignitaries from Trump's orbit like James O'Keefe, the right-wing saboteur who employed hidden-camera schemes to try to entrap Democratic activists and mainstream media reporters. Right before heading up to the Capitol for the Electoral College debate, Jackson posted a Trumpian battle cry to his Twitter account. "We're out here FIGHTING FOR TRUMP and for our election integrity! American Patriots have your BACK Mr. President! We will FIGHT for YOU and we will fight for OUR country!!"

Soon, he would discover how literally some Trump supporters took words like that. The *click, click, click* of the House chamber doors sent Jackson into fight-or-flight mode. By chance, Jackson was sitting with two other freshman members of the Texas delegation who also had military training. Tony Gonzales, a Navy veteran, and Pat Fallon, a former Notre Dame wide receiver who served in the Air Force, were also Republicans. They were all now faced with wondering whether they would survive an attack from people they thought they were representing. The three men grabbed whatever they could to fashion makeshift weapons. They broke legs off chairs to use as clubs and ripped the base off a hand sanitizer dispenser stand to wield as a baton. They picked up whatever furniture that wasn't bolted down—desks, cabinets, chairs—and piled it up in front of the doors. The voices they could hear on the other side of those doors grew louder and louder. "This is our house!" a man outside shouted. Another intruder smashed a window, sending glass bits flying inside. Officers drew their guns and aimed them at the jagged holes where the glass had been punched out. Then the doors started buckling.

Jackson took off his necktie. If the mob did get inside, he told himself, it was best not to give them something to strangle you with. His mind flashed to a war zone in the Middle East. *This should not be happening in Washington, D.C.*, he thought. Gonzales had a similarly disturbing thought: *Wouldn't this be something? I fight in Iraq and Afghanistan just to be killed in the House of Representatives.*

Like most Americans, I experienced the shock of January 6 on television. I was sitting in my apartment in New York, watching the "Save America" rally, toggling between Fox News and a web stream of the speeches that were only being broadcast online. Had you just seen what the cable networks were showing of the event, you would have missed the full panorama of Donald Trump's Republican Party in those final, delirious days of his presidency. Trump's warm-up acts that morning were a fitting representation of the fringe figures he had empowered over the course of his short time in national politics, and a jarring reminder of how distant he was from the party's other recent standard bearers like Mitt Romney, John McCain, and both George Bushes. The speakers at the rally included opportunists, sycophants, oddballs, and some who displayed such a severe detachment from reality they seemed on the verge of psychosis. Rudy Giuliani, the former Republican mayor of New York, howled from the stage about how Trump's enemies had programmed voting machines to steal his votes. "If we are wrong, we will be made fools of," Giuliani said. He didn't linger on this thought for too long. The fact was there was almost nothing Trump or anyone else could do now to make him seem like a fool in the eyes of his most devoted followers.

Tens of thousands of them filled the National Mall for the rally, their presence a testament to the peculiar power Trump had to make his voters see the world as he wanted it to be, not as it actually was. Amid the spew of lies and distortions uttered on the stage, one remark from Trump's oldest son, Donald Trump, Jr., stood out to me as one of the few incontestable statements made. He was attacking Republicans in Congress for disloyalty, insisting they hadn't done enough to stand behind his father's illegitimate claim to a second term. He was incredulous: *After four years, don't they get it?* "This isn't their Republican Party anymore," Trump Jr. shouted. "This is Donald Trump's Republican Party."

Indeed, it was. In many ways, the GOP had been Donald Trump's for decades. And that is the idea at the heart of this book.

Trump, for the most part, didn't bring anything inside the Republican Party that wasn't already there. He just validated the suspicions and fed the anxieties of tens of millions of Americans who had long feared they were one presidential election away from losing their purchase on social and political power. They organized under different banners and followed a variety of magnetic personalities over time. Through the years they tended to share a consistent belief that the establishments of both political parties were threatening to take away what little they had left—if not in a literal or financial sense then by devaluing whatever cultural supremacy they believed they had as Americans. As a reporter for *The New York Times* whose assignments over the last decade have included covering the conservative media, the rise of the Tea Party and right-wing populism, and the last three presidential campaigns, I have gotten to know many of the players who organized and profited from the insurgency inside the GOP. I also got to know the politicians and strategists who saw it as their mission to crush these insurgents. In this book, I aim to chronicle the tensions between those two wings of the Republican Party and show how unnatural and unworkable their alliances always were.

Elements of Trumpism were never far from the surface. In the Cold War era, similar fears flourished among the well-heeled suburbanites who joined the arch-conservative John Birch Society. The organization taught its members they weren't wrong to suspect that communist revolutionaries were burrowing themselves deep into American society, infiltrating the highest levels of the government and using the civil rights movement as their Trojan Horse. Like many others who considered themselves conservative, they favored quick, blunt demonstrations of force to quash problems foreign and domestic. *Russian troops moving into Cuba?* Nuke them. *Rioters and looters in major American cities?* Shoot them. They put bumper stickers on their cars with slogans like SUPPORT YOUR LOCAL POLICE. They flew the Gadsden flag as their banner, with its menacing-looking, coiled-up rattlesnake and testy admonition: DON'T TREAD ON ME.

In the 1990s, right-wing populism under Patrick J. Buchanan was less conspiratorial but just as nationalistic. Buchanan, a former Nixon speechwriter and cable television commentator, built a movement around a policy agenda he described as "America First." He said he would build a fence along the southern border to keep immigrants out. He vowed to confront nations like China that profited from relaxed trade policies with the United States while freezing out American competition in their own economies. His devotees considered it a badge of honor when critics compared them to a mob of pitchfork-wielding serfs. To this day, he keeps a pitchfork in a glass case in his home in McLean, Virginia, a gift from his followers that's inscribed with the nickname they adopted: The Buchanan Brigades. Though Buchanan is most associated with his proto-Trumpian barrier along the border and his opposition to large-scale immigration from Latin American countries, it is often forgotten that his first of three presidential campaigns, in 1992, was an indicator of how ripe racial tensions were for a presidential candidate willing to risk inflaming them. And many voters responded to his message that liberals were exaggerating racial discrimination and then overcorrecting for it with affirmative action programs that disadvantaged white Americans. I spent hundreds of hours interviewing Republicans like Buchanan and many others for this book. They provided me with their strategy memos, emails, early drafts of speeches, unpublished memoirs, and other documentation. During our conversations and emails, Buchanan used a metaphor to describe the combustible environment building up before Trump that I thought also aptly described many of the scenes in this book. "I tell you—this had been building. It was out there. It's one of those things where you don't realize there's explosives all over the ground," he told me.

One speaker at the rally on January 6 had enough of a background in conservative organizing to trace a line through the various iterations of populist upheaval on the right. Amy Kremer, a former Delta flight attendant, was a well-known activist long before Trump started making inroads with her people. She helped co-found and lead two major Tea Party groups, leaving the first, Tea Party Patriots, and sparking ugly legal battles after her partners accused her of taking too much credit for their work. Kremer had become a leading figure of the Tea Party thanks to her awareness of and eagerness to exploit the vast distance that had grown between conservatives like her and the Republicans they sent to Washington.

Mainstream Republicans considered people like Kremer gadflies and grifters—and not always without justification. (She turns up in a later chapter as something of a Cassandra whose thoughts on the kind of leader the GOP needed were ignored and long forgotten until one of my sources found them in an old notebook.) As an activist, Kremer was constantly reinventing herself with her antenna tuned to the zeitgeist of the populist right. She hitched herself early on to Trump as his star rose. And by 2016 she had ditched the Tea Party banner and co-founded a group called Women Vote Trump with Roger Stone's ex-wife, Ann. To help with his reelection campaign four years later, she started another group with her daughter, Kylie, called Women for America First. Kremer had also run for Congress in Georgia in 2017. She earned attention from right-wing media stars like Sean Hannity, who featured her on his radio show and endorsed her candidacy. And she made headlines in the mainstream media when she sent out a fundraising solicitation that offered an AR-15 rifle as a prize for one lucky donor. "We Will NOT Go Quietly into the Night!" her pitch said. She didn't win, leaving her more time to make a career out of being an activist-entrepreneur in the Trump movement, where she went back to build up her base of donors and supporters, antagonizing the GOP establishment.

Before she ended her speech on January 6, she beseeched the crowd to stand its ground for Trump. "Let Republicans know: We're coming for you," Kremer said.

Like Buchanan said, the explosive charges already littered the landscape. And then *boom*.

All morning, Vice President Mike Pence could sense that the Secret Service agents protecting him were unusually tense. Shortly after 2 P.M., he learned why, after the first group of demonstrators breached the Capitol by smashing through a window on the first floor of the building's south side, creating a hole big enough for them to climb through. Two of them kicked open a nearby door, making way for more to stream inside. Pence, as the president of the Senate, was seated at the rostrum in the front of the chamber at that moment.

Many in the crowd outside the Capitol had just learned that Pence would not accede to Trump's demand that he attempt to interfere with the formal congressional process of counting Electoral College votes. One man, who had been following news coverage of the demonstrations on his phone, called out to the people nearby what he'd just seen on *Breitbart*. As word spread across the Capitol grounds, the crowd erupted. "He has betrayed us! Mike Pence has betrayed us!" someone shouted. Two young women started chanting: "Hang Mike Pence! Hang Mike Pence!" Another: "Mike Pence is a bitch." Another: "May he go under the gallows." Another: "Mike Pence? We're coming for you too, fucking traitor."

On the floor of the Senate, Pence's Secret Service agents moved fast. They hustled him out of the chair and into an office just outside the chamber. They told him they needed to leave the building immediately—for his safety and the well-being of his staff and his family, who had accompanied him to the Capitol to witness the proceedings. As the Senate went into recess at 2:13 P.M., stunned lawmakers were left wondering what they had just witnessed. Senator Pat Toomey of Pennsylvania first thought that Pence was doing what he'd almost always done: acquiesced to Trump. The hasty exit, Toomey assumed, was the vice president's way of ducking out so he wouldn't have to defy Trump and preside over the vote counting that would show Biden had won. Senator Mitt Romney was one of the first to see the news, and he announced it to his colleagues as soon as he read it on his phone: The Capitol had been breached. Hearing this, Senator Tom Cotton of Arkansas turned to a member of his staff with an urgent demand: *Go retrieve my LederMann bag. It has a weapon inside, and I want it in case I have to defend myself and my fellow senators.*

Inside the office where the Pences were, additional Secret Service arrived to stand guard as backup. But Pence refused to agree to leave because he knew the image of his motorcade fleeing the Capitol in distress would send the message that the mob had succeeded. Eventually, he settled on a compromise with the agents. They would move him down into a lower level of the sprawling Capitol complex where they would be at a safer distance from the rioters, who were already outside the chamber. Security cameras captured him and his family being rushed down a flight of stairs to safety. Once they were downstairs, the agents made another plea for the vice president to get inside his armored vehicle. But he refused this too, telling them he knew they could drive off at any moment. In the distance, they could hear the clamor of the intruders.

The humiliation of Mike Pence that day represented a stunning casualty for the old Republican Party at the hands of the insurgency. He became another dyed-in-the-wool Republican that Trump ran off like Reince Priebus, the former party chairman, and Paul Ryan, who had styled himself as the face of a gentler, more inclusive GOP. It was also one of the starkest examples of the kind of miscalculation that Republicans like Pence made all along in how they understood the balance of power between themselves and renegades like Trump. Since populist candidates rarely succeeded without some help from the party establishment, which controlled the barriers to entry in politics, Pence and many Washington Republicans saw the relationship as a true partnership where they still held most of the cards. Without Pence on the ticket in 2016 to reassure social conservatives and evangelical Christians, after all, Trump might never have been elected. Pence had been a doting, unwaveringly loyal partner to Trump, no doubt helping to keep conservatives in line through the transgressive president's innumerable affronts. But Pence had not only been a symbolic factor in Trump's success. A political veteran with deep relationships inside Washington's network of conservative activists, he helped Trump staff the federal government and fill his cabinet when Trump and most of his campaign staff were clueless about the workings of the executive branch. "After all the things I've done for him," Pence fumed to Senator James Inhofe of Oklahoma on the day of the attack on the Capitol.

But it had also been true for decades that establishment Republicans needed votes from people who far preferred candidates who vowed to topple the establishment. These voters saw their support for mainstream politicians as a compromise they were forced into accepting. But once these voters were empowered—first through the Tea Party and then through Trump—they saw no reason to accept any political outcome that looked to them like an establishment capitulation. This was hardly a new phenomenon. Lee Atwater, the architect of George H. W. Bush's election in 1988, once reportedly observed, "The problem with conservatives is that you can get 99 percent right with them. But if you're 1 percent wrong, they want to eat their own." Few politicians had been as cautious and purposeful as Pence had about maintaining good standing with the various camps of the Republican Party. As a former congressman, a governor of Indiana, and the outgoing vice president, Pence had connections everywhere. He was an evangelical Christian who was adored by religious conservatives and antiabortion activists. He was a free-market libertarian who had partnered with the Koch family's political operation on tax policy and deregulatory issues. And he was Trump's faithful defender. Pence's allies and advisers assumed that this kind of full-spectrum credibility in the party would serve him well if he decided to run for president someday. And they had worked assiduously to keep his relationships with conservatives strong, hosting regular gatherings with activists in his offices in the Eisenhower Executive Office Building and at the vice president's mansion at the United States Naval Observatory.

A baton pass from Trump to Pence or anyone vying to be his heir may never have been in the cards. As is the case with many political revolts, what happens once the revolution is over isn't really the point. And that was certainly how many of Trump's followers understood his victory. "The point of the revolution is the revolution," observes Stephen K. Bannon, Trump's White House chief strategist during his first year in office and the third and final chief of his 2016 campaign. That's not to say that Trump doesn't care about his legacy or how he is written about in the historical record. But he is not one to spend much time thinking about a successor to inherit the Trump movement—*his* movement. "Trump doesn't give a shit. He's not looking to nurture. He's not looking to mentor guys," says Bannon. "Do you think Trump wants a guy to win after him?" Bannon asks. Then he quickly answers his own question. "No way. He's Donald Fucking Trump: The only guy who could do it. He wants the guy following him to lose by forty."

When I spoke to Trump during our interviews for this book—the first of which took place at Mar-a-Lago eight weeks after January 6 and the second over the phone in late July 2021—he made it clear that he sees himself as the sole figure responsible for the political and popular success the GOP had during his time as the party's leader. He is not interested in talking about which Republicans might do well in 2024. In his mind, there will be no succession, because he seems to genuinely believe that he will avenge his defeat in 2020 by running and winning in 2024. "There is more anger now than there ever has been," he says, urging me to consider his political instinct, which he assures me is singular in the history of American politicians, before I object. "In my opinion, the single biggest issue today is not the border. It's the scam election of 2020." I ask if he would commit to putting Pence on the ticket again. He won't. "We'll see what happens," he says. But he does offer an unsolicited observation about Pence's future in politics after rebuffing his demand to object on January 6 and stop Congress from counting the electoral votes. "There was no downside," Trump says. "So Mike could have done that. And I wish he did. I think it would have been much better for the country. I also think it would have been better for Mike."

He expresses little interest in revisiting what harm might have befallen his beseechingly loyal lieutenant of four years. I ask if it troubled him to hear his supporters threatening to execute Pence as they marauded through the halls of the Capitol. "Yes, it did bother me. I didn't like it," he says. But he doesn't dwell on this thought for very long. He quickly dismisses the idea that Pence was ever in any real danger. The rioters, whoever they were, weren't being literal with their calls to send the vice president to the gallows, he says. Rather, he insists that their threats were more like a figure of speech. "I think it was an expression. I don't think they would have ever thought of doing it."

Though the GOP was in many ways Trump's party culturally well before he took an interest in conservative politics, it was also very much the party of Roger Ailes, Sarah Palin, Phyllis Schlafly, and Rush Limbaugh. Trump borrowed from all of them. Schlafly, the matriarch of the modern activist right, used the language of theft and expropriation to describe how establishment Republicans had conspired to shut out conservatives like her since the 1930s. One of the chapters in her seminal 1964 book, *A Choice Not an Echo,* was "The Big Steal: 1952," a reference to the defeat of Senator Robert Taft, a conservative hero, at the GOP convention that year. Limbaugh, the titan of talk radio from the late 1980s until his death in 2021, built a following of tens of millions not because he was a devoted conservative ideologue but because he paid obsessive attention to what his audience did and didn't want to hear. His listeners felt they were getting a political education they couldn't get anywhere else because he told them that just about everyone but him was lying to them.

Trump cultivated relationships with all of them and got to know them personally, as this book will detail. Watching them was how he understood that the Americans who were his most enthusiastic supporters saw politics as a good-versus-evil struggle and believed their enemies would stop at nothing to deny them a voice. It was practically a given that he would embrace a conspiracy theory about what happened on January 6—and that his backers would accept it as their truth—from the moment the rioters broke that first window in the Capitol. The effort to rewrite the history of that day and replace it with a sanitized version of events had already made its way to the House floor that night—where just a few hours earlier Republicans like Ronny Jackson thought they might die in an attack perpetrated by people wearing tactical gear and hats with the slogan Trump had borrowed from Ronald Reagan and then officially trademarked for himself: MAKE AMERICA GREAT AGAIN. Representative Matt Gaetz of Florida, one of Trump's most loyal backers in Congress, repeated the lie in his speech objecting to the Electoral College count. "They were masquerading as Trump supporters," Gaetz said, eliciting groans and jeers.

Trump had been showing them for five years how do this. Long before January 6, he had conditioned his most faithful fans to believe that any difficulty or resistance he encountered was part of a plot against him. If Trump didn't win, the only possible explanation was that the other side had cheated. This was how he often told the story of his career, such as when he was starring on *The Apprentice* on NBC in the 2000s and complained that the show had never won an Emmy. The awards, he said, were "a con game." He applied the same victim's logic to politics. Before he won the Republican nomination outright in 2016, he smeared the rivals who stood the best chance of beating him as cheaters and liars—"Lyin' Ted" Cruz, "Crooked Hillary" Clinton. "Our Republican system is absolutely rigged. It's a phony deal," he declared when Cruz supporters attempted to organize to stop him at the Republican National Convention.

On Fox News on the night of January 6, Sarah Palin claimed in an interview that she had been sent pictures of people arrested that day who were also at the nationwide Black Lives Matter protests against racial injustice and police brutality the summer before. "We don't know who all were the instigators in this, of these horrible things that happened today. I think a lot of it is the Antifa folks," she said. "There is a lot of questions out there, and I wish that we could trust the media to do its job to do the research and report who all these people are," Palin added.

Of all the conservative populists who were antecedents to Trump, Palin was his closest contemporary—the first of "the deplorables," to borrow Hillary Clinton's condescending term for Trump supporters that they in turn appropriated. As governor of Alaska, Palin took her attacks on the media to a place even most conservatives didn't go, accusing journalists of outright fabrication and demanding that they "quit makin' things up." It was "fake news" by another name. She wasn't one to let facts stand in the way of a useful line of attack, as she showed when she doubled down on her false claim that Obama's healthcare bill included "death panels" that would decide if vulnerable populations could receive treatment. She used social media at a time when few politicians understood it, discovering that she could post something on Facebook that would move news cycles without her ever having to grant an interview to the mainstream media. She built up her political brand by speaking directly to conservative voters on Fox News, where Ailes brought her on as a contributor because he saw her as someone with the star power to draw big ratings, just as she had drawn big crowds as John McCain's running mate in 2008. She proved to be more in step with the Republican base than party leaders were on issues like military intervention, which she rejected in part because she saw the mental toll that combat took on her son Track. She attacked the Bush family as "blue bloods" who wanted to interfere in the Republican presidential primaries so they could "pick and choose their winners instead of allowing competition." She relished the criticism she often heard from the people she dismissed as "elites" in both political parties and in the media. And often these critics misunderstood how negative stories about Palin would be received by her fans. News that her unwed teenage daughter was pregnant didn't dent her image with social conservatives, as many pundits had predicted. And when she couldn't answer a question from Katie Couric of *CBS News* about which news publications she regularly read, her supporters turned on Couric for asking one of the "gotcha questions" that Palin often complained about.

She is the best place to start when answering the question that her former Fox News colleague Brian Kilmeade asked on *Fox & Friends* on the morning of January 7.

"So, how did we get here?"

INSURGENCY

CHAPTER 1

The Tip of the Spear

Sarah Palin and the "Dennis Miller Republican"

I will put Alaskans first.

—GOVERNOR SARAH PALIN, inaugural address, December 4, 2006

A ir Force One broke through the dense layer of clouds over Fairbanks on its descent into Eielson Air Force Base, a sprawling, remote outpost in the most remote state in the union. In what would be one of the last international trips of his presidency, George W. Bush and First Lady Laura Bush were on their way to Beijing for the opening ceremony of the summer Olympics. But first they would stop at Eielson to refuel and to meet with troops and their families stationed at bases across the vast forty-ninth state.

One in twelve people in Alaska were members of the military or their dependents. The state had shouldered a disproportionate share of the losses and casualties from the nation's engagement in the Middle East, which was about to enter its seventh year. More than two hundred airmen from Eielson were currently deployed in Iraq, Afghanistan, and other countries around the world. Scores from other Alaskan bases would soon join them. Bush was there to be the grateful commander in chief: to deliver a pep talk, thank them for their sacrifices, and assure them that deployments weren't going to be open-ended. In military communities like these across the country, a new reality had set in. Many people had long gotten past the shock of the September 11 attacks and the swell of patriotism that followed. They weren't convinced the wars in the Middle East were a conflict Americans should be fighting in anymore. Bush would acknowledge the fatigue when he spoke. "These have been tough times on our families," Bush said. He reminded his audience that their sacrifices were in the interest of America's mission to keep the homeland safe, and to export the "transformative power of liberty" to places that needed it most. "The terrorists will be denied a safe haven, and freedom is on the march," the president said, framing the issue in the rhetoric of black-and-white moral clarity he preferred. "I know free societies yield the peace we all want."

But it wasn't just the American heartland that had grown weary. The consensus in the Republican Party that Bush was keeping America safe by maintaining a robust military presence in the Middle East had considerable cracks in it. Republicans in Congress were concerned that the public's impatience with these two costly wars was setting them up for an even bigger defeat on Election Day than the "thumping" they saw—a Bush colloquialism—in the 2006 midterm elections. Some had insisted that future funding for the war be tied to certain benchmarks that the Iraqi government would have to meet. No more blank checks, no more open-ended timetables for troop deployments.

There was one military mother in the crowd that day, August 4, 2008, who was typical in many ways of the family members of the enlisted. Her nineteen-year-old son was set to ship off when he finished his training in a few weeks. She was conflicted—apprehensive but also proud and idealistic about the higher calling he would serve. As a Republican, she was committed to the idea that keeping the country safe meant bringing the might of the American military to the enemy, wherever the enemy tried to hide. She had ambition, agency, and desires of her own. And when the White House reached out to see if she and her family would like to meet the president at Eielson, she said yes right away.

Before Bush met with her and the other military families, he scanned his briefing materials on Air Force One and committed to memory any relevant or unique biographical details about them. But this one mother's last name stopped him. Never known for his mastery of the tongue, Bush wasn't sure how to pronounce it. He turned to Laura and asked what she thought.

"Is it *Pal*-in?" the president asked, sounding the name out as if it rhymed with "gallon." The First Lady jumped in to the rescue: "It's *Pay*-lin."

Bush, the self-styled "compassionate conservative" who campaigned on the promise that he was "a uniter, not a divider," had no idea when he stepped off the presidential 747 that afternoon that he was meeting the woman who in one month would be the biggest star in Republican politics—a hybrid celebrity-politician who would torch the model of noblesse oblige leadership that he and his family had personified during three generations in public service. While Palin and Bush were members of the same political party, they were from entirely distinct worlds that were pulling ever further apart. She hadn't yet experienced the bitterness of being elevated to the national stage only to have some of the GOP's most powerful figures trash her anonymously in the media as a "whack job" and a "diva." She didn't yet know how many Republican voters would see their own aspirations and resentments reflected in her experiences. And she hadn't yet met the "hardened" version of her son she would describe when he returned home from war for good several years later.

The Republicans who thought she was just the populist spark Senator John McCain needed to invigorate his presidential campaign hadn't yet seen how they were entering into a Faustian bargain and enabling the vehicle for their own destruction. The forty-third president was vaguely aware of the chatter about Palin as a dark horse vice presidential contender for McCain. But he hadn't given it much thought beyond the attempt he made at a humorous ice-breaker when he met her that afternoon.

"Madam Vice President!" Bush exclaimed, extending his hand.

Sarah Palin was only thirty-two when she was elected mayor of Wasilla, the small city where she had spent most of her childhood. It sits in Alaska's Mat-Su Valley, where glaciers and wilderness meet the exurban sprawl of Anchorage, about forty-five minutes to the south. The area was known for its high concentration of evangelical Christians, earning it the nickname "the Bible Belt of Alaska." It had higher poverty rates than its big-city neighbor. The location and demographics were not incidental in the creation of Palin's political identity. In certain crowds, saying someone was from "The Valley" carried a class stigma that many of its residents didn't appreciate. And that tension was never far from the surface in local politics. Memorably, it erupted in a messy episode in 2004 when the son of Senator Ted Stevens, a towering figure in the state who had represented Alaska in Washington for four decades, called a woman from Palin's hometown "valley trash" in an email. The woman leaked the correspondence to the local media, igniting a backlash from outraged Valley denizens. They didn't take the slight lying down, and some even tried to reclaim the label with T-shirts that said PROUD TO BE VALLEY TRASH. Outwardly, Palin wore her "Valley Trash" identity with pride. Inside, she resented it. "Rightly or wrongly, the chip on her shoulder was always from the sense that 'You guys look down on us,'" says Lindsay Hayes, who worked for Stevens and later joined Palin's speechwriting team when she became the vice presidential nominee. She reserved much of her disdain for those she believed wanted to stop people like her without the right background and pedigree from advancing in state politics—none more so than the "good ol' boys" she antagonized in the Alaska GOP. "She felt, 'We're the ones who do all the work. You're corrupt. You're making money hand over fist. Who the hell do you guys think you are?'" Hayes adds.

One morning in April 1996, the year she was elected mayor, Palin told her husband that she was going to Costco. Instead, she drove to the JCPenney in Anchorage to meet Ivana Trump, who was on tour promoting her fragrance line. The names Trump and Palin would go on to have much greater significance in American politics. But at that moment, their convergence represented how people like Palin saw something at once aspirational and attainable in the Trump family's wealth and privilege. More than five hundred people waited in line with Palin that day. As Palin would explain to a reporter from the *Anchorage Daily News* who caught up with her there, the ex–Mrs. Trump was someone to look up to, even if the circumstances of Palin's own life seemed more limited than she'd like. "We are so desperate in Alaska for any semblance of glamour and culture," Palin said. That little bottle of "Ivana" perfume represented another world, one where the stubborn odor of salmon didn't cling to her all summer—which she admitted to the paper was a bit of a drag. Her victory in the Wasilla mayor's race later that year was her first step toward proving to her critics that they were no better than she was. She ran against the incumbent mayor and won on a platform of shaking up the status quo. She championed Christian values and Second Amendment rights, bringing the country's culture wars to the doorstep of Wasilla City Hall at a time when most other local politicians seemed content to leave those questions to people in higher office. Her opponent, John C. Stein, accused Palin of gratuitously playing up her faith and suggesting that the city needed to have its "first" Christian mayor. "I thought: 'Holy cow, what's happening here? Does that mean she thinks I'm Jewish or Islamic?'" Stein, who was raised Lutheran, told *The New York Times.* Soon after taking office, she started cleaning house. She promptly fired the police chief, saying she doubted his willingness to help her govern. But he also hadn't supported her for mayor, and critics accused her of retaliation.

She served two terms. Prohibited by law from running for a third, she was approached by Senator Frank Murkowski, a fellow Republican. Murkowski was in a unique position. In the middle of his fourth term, he decided to run for governor and won. As governor, he would be able to appoint someone to the Senate seat he was about to vacate. And he put Palin on his list of potential candidates. She was intrigued about the opportunity and even rented the classic Hollywood film about corruption-fighting senator, *Mr. Smith Goes to Washington,* from her local video store. But when Murkowski pared down his list to six, she did not make the cut. Palin, with no clear path forward in the Alaska GOP, said she was ready to get on with her life. She returned the movie. But Murkowski unwittingly gave her all the room she needed. He picked his daughter, Lisa, a state legislator, to serve out the remaining two years of his term—

handing Palin and his other critics a perfect example of the kind of "good ol' boys" cronyism they said needed to be excised from state government. But Murkowski also had a job in mind for Palin and appointed her to a state commission that oversaw the oil and gas industry. Soon, she set her sights on a fellow member of the commission who was also the state GOP chair, Randy Ruedrich. Palin accused Ruedrich of conflict of interest violations and various other abuses of his office, eventually forcing him to resign from the commission but not from his position in the party. Palin claimed the Republican machine had tried to silence her and told her to tone it down. "I'm being attacked," she said to a journalist, claiming that if the governor expected her to keep her eyes closed to the corruption she saw, he had picked the wrong woman. "I'm the same person now as I was then, the same person who Frank appointed."

Only now she was angrier. In 2004, when Lisa Murkowski was up for reelection, Palin let it be known through back channels that she was willing to help the Democratic candidate, Tony Knowles, though it was not widely known at the time. "She had been super helpful. . . . It was all behind the scenes," recalls Anita Dunn, a Democratic strategist who was working for Knowles and would later go on to work for Senator Barack Obama on his presidential campaign. Dunn, seeing Palin's potential to be a national star, was one of the Obama aides who encouraged the campaign to track her as a possible running mate for the eventual Republican nominee. Knowles didn't win the Senate seat. But Palin's belief that Alaskans would punish the Murkowskis for self-dealing would ultimately prove correct. "I had a healthy respect for her political skills," Dunn adds, "having watched her beat the Republican Party in Alaska."

Two years later, she came for Governor Murkowski. She ran against him in the Republican primary and beat him by more than 30 points. Their differences as candidates reflected the emerging divide in the Republican Party. In her victory speech, she declared "politics as usual" over in Alaska. The us-versus-them populist angst she embodied coursed through the crowd. "Let's take Alaska back!" someone called out as Palin spoke. Palin, with her irrepressible disdain for the wait-your-turn deference that had kept the GOP hierarchy mostly off limits to people like her, was a leading indicator for the trends upending American politics in that moment. Murkowski represented what had always worked for Republicans. His inclination was to make allies of the "Big Three" oil companies in Alaska and incentivize them to do more business in the state by giving them tax breaks. Her inclination was to mistrust big business and to threaten to end those tax breaks. He cut social service spending, including a popular state program that made cash payments to seniors. She said she would restore it. She didn't have an extensive résumé in government or a career as a successful businesswoman. Her supporters described her as a different kind of politician—"one of us," a straight shooter who was "much more likely to call them as she sees them," an outsider who was "doing it her way," they said. Palin's fans were among the most passionate and devoted of any politician in the state—sometimes to extremes. Three months before the November general election, a scuffle broke out in an Anchorage park between a group of Palin supporters and a well-known Republican Party lawyer. It escalated, according to a report by the journalist Amanda Coyne, when a sixty-nine-year-old female volunteer jabbed her sign at the lawyer. The Palin crowd had been taunting the lawyer, calling him a pawn of the "machine." The volunteer apparently took the Palin campaign slogan on the sign—TAKE A STAND—quite literally. The lawyer shot back with an epithet that seemed appropriate to him, given who his antagonists were. They were a bunch of "brownshirts," he shouted, invoking the nickname of one of Hitler's feared paramilitary organizations.

She easily won on Election Day, finishing seven points ahead of her closest rival. In her inaugural address, she spoke of the danger of being "beholden to outside interests" and decried a system that "favored a privileged few." Her remarks stood out for the suspicion she expressed about outsiders and her mistrust of powerful institutions—many of them big businesses such as the large energy corporations but also fisheries she said had depleted Alaskan waters, and the state and federal interests she said put their bottom line ahead of what was best for ordinary people. She ended the speech with a promise to protect the home front above all else: "I will put Alaskans first."

Alaska's first "lady governor"—Murkowski's infelicitous choice of words for Palin on the evening he conceded the race to her—enjoyed a burst of modest national media attention. And in the weeks before Bush's visit in August 2008, she and her staff had been juggling a number of requests and invitations from the Lower 48. Nationally syndicated conservative talk show hosts Glenn Beck and Laura Ingraham wanted her on their radio programs; Neil Cavuto was trying to book her on his Fox News show. *People* magazine wanted to interview her about what it was like raising a baby with special needs. She was working through drafts of a speech she planned to give to an antiabortion group that was honoring her at their gathering at the Republican National Convention in Minnesota, which was just a few weeks away. It wasn't exactly a prime-time address from the convention's main stage. But she understood that it was good national exposure for her with grassroots conservative activists.

There was also a query from the McCain campaign. Aides to McCain, the Arizona senator and soon-to-be Republican presidential nominee, had asked Palin to participate in a national media call on energy policy. That was about as close as she expected to get to his campaign. She was aware of the faint chatter that, in their longest of long-shot scenarios, Republicans close to McCain had floated Palin as a possible running mate. She didn't discourage the speculation. But she knew these were just rumors, and likely little else. No one from McCain's staff had approached her about doing any serious vetting of her and her family, which surely they would have started by early August if she were a legitimate contender for the number two spot on the ticket.

The fact that Palin was under consideration as a vice presidential contender at all showed the degree to which there was concern at the highest levels of the Republican Party that its presidential nominee was out of step with rank-and-file Republican voters. The base of the party had never been very comfortable with John McCain. And he had never been very comfortable with them. In fact, he seemed downright hostile at times. He had once famously called leaders of the religious right "agents of intolerance." He had butted heads with conservatives by championing a plan with Senator Ted Kennedy of Massachusetts, the Democratic Party's liberal standard bearer, that would have given legal status to millions of undocumented immigrants. When McCain talked about "my base," he often meant it as a joke about the national media, with whom he enjoyed a chummy relationship.

For the first half of August, all but a handful of national polls showed McCain losing to Obama. When McCain's attention turned in earnest to the selection of his running mate, some on his senior staff initially floated Palin—not as a serious suggestion but as a mechanism for getting McCain to see how deep their deficit in the polls was and the magnitude of the bombshell required to overcome it. "It was an example of how far he needed to think," recalls Fred Davis, who made ads for McCain and was one of the relatively few national Republicans who already knew the Alaska governor well. "She reminded me of my aunt Jo," says Davis, who was sent to Alaska in the summer of 2006 by the Republican Governors Association to film Palin and produce commercials that would sell her as a "bright, fresh face with new ideas." Aunt Jo, explains Davis, was his mom's sister. She was no shrinking violet. "Pick a subject. She had an opinion. She would tell you that opinion," Davis says. "And then she'd call you the next day to make sure you remembered her opinion. That's what I saw in Sarah." He recalls how she had media savvy and an instinct for being in front of the camera that he found surprising. He was prohibited by law from directly coordinating with her as a consultant outside the campaign. Relegated to observing her from a distance, he watched old news clips and read about her political ascent. He tracked the public schedule her office released and sent his camera crew to set up across the street from where Palin planned to be so he could get shots of her coming and going. Palin spotted the camera crew, a conspicuous presence in downtown Anchorage, and it was like a switch flipped. She marched with purpose, back and forth until Davis's team had enough for the shot they needed, he recalls. She was, he says, "a showman."

Another national party figure who was one of the few to see Palin up close then was Michael Steele, the future RNC chairman. A friend had called him with a request: Could Steele drop everything and fly to Alaska to mediate a dispute between the new governor and the state party chairman? Steele, the former lieutenant governor of Maryland who had run unsuccessfully for United States Senate in 2006, was in charge of running GOPAC, a national group that helped recruit and train up-and-coming Republican stars. He knew almost nothing about Palin. But he got an earful as soon as he stepped off the plane. "This woman, she doesn't know what she's doing. She doesn't know how to run the party," Steele recalls. "And I was like, 'But she beat all the boys to get the job. She must know something.' " Yes and no, Steele soon discovered. When he met with her, Palin struck him as full of raw political talent. But when he shared with her what he thought was useful advice on taking a more measured approach with her nemesis Ruedrich, who still had solid support inside the state party, she was undeterred. "She, of course, decided not to follow that advice, and she got her clock cleaned," Steele says. Palin and her allies tried to force a vote on a resolution calling for Ruedrich to step down and failed. Ruedrich remained chairman of the party for another four years. Still, Steele says, "Her ballsiness was impressive."

McCain liked that Palin seemed like him—a self-styled maverick. But he kept coming back to Senator Joseph Lieberman of Connecticut as his top choice for a running mate. Lieberman, while technically a political independent, had been a registered Democrat for years and the party's nominee for vice president in 2000. He was also pro-choice. The Republican base would revolt if McCain picked him. When his preference for Lieberman leaked to the media, conservatives were predictably outraged and saw it as another sign that establishment Republicans didn't care what they thought. McCain's reasoning had logic to it, as it was in line with decades of prevailing political science wisdom. Moderation wins presidential elections, the theory goes. And the partisan bases will mostly, if begrudgingly, accept their party's ticket rather than risk the chance that the other side could win. The idea was also who McCain was at heart: an idealist who thought the partisan extremes in American politics were destructive and dangerous. And as the putative Republican leader, he believed he could put his foot down, name Lieberman, and start lowering the temperature.

In the end, he decided to go where the voters were. He called Palin himself, reaching her on her BlackBerry while she was walking around the Alaska State Fair with her seven-year-old daughter, Piper. Palin said she would be on the next plane. At the ranch, Palin and McCain went off in private to speak, because he wanted to be sure she was the one. They were alone together for an hour—no staff, no family. "Nobody will ever know what they said—for the ages," says Steve Schmidt, who was McCain's senior strategist. When they were finished, McCain asked several members of his senior staff and his wife, Cindy, to join him on a walk.

They knew Palin's résumé had more than a few red flags, chief among them that she did not have the depth of experience that would make voters see her as an able and qualified number two. With McCain's age—he was about to turn seventy-two—and known history of melanoma, the credentials of his number two weren't just a matter of checking boxes for the media. They would be scrutinized by voters who actually had to consider the question of presidential succession.

"What do you think?" he asked them.

Mark Salter, a longtime aide to McCain, cautioned him that voters could see a Palin pick as discordant with the message of readiness and experience that the campaign had been focusing on as a contrast with Obama, a forty-seven-year-old first-term senator. "There's worse things, John, than losing an election. You could lose your reputation," Salter told him. Schmidt also thought Palin was a risk but said maybe it was one worth taking. He told McCain he should consider whether it would be worth it if he chose Palin and lost, but also knew in the end that he'd lost because he did something bold. "What you've got to decide," Schmidt told the senator, "is would you rather lose by seven going for it?"

McCain turned to his wife, Cindy. "John, it's a gamble," she said. This made McCain's face light up. "Well, I wish you hadn't said that," he said. McCain, an avid craps player, balled up his fist and blew on it, then shook it like he was about to roll a pair of dice.

"Fuck it," he said. "Let's do it."

The ascendancy of Palin-style populism was not confined to Alaska in 2006. But few Republicans were ringing the alarm about why their voters were drifting away from conventional politicians and their stale policy offerings of laissez-faire capitalism, robust military spending, and rising-tide-lifts-all-boats economics. One of the exceptions was Tony Fabrizio, a Republican pollster who caught an early break in his career working with Pat Buchanan on his 1992 primary challenge to President George H. W. Bush. In the years since, Fabrizio had become one of the most successful pollsters in the GOP, trusted by candidates for his accuracy and seen as a sage for interpreting the political impulses of the white working class. Fabrizio had grown up in a large Italian family in Massapequa Park on Long Island in the sixties and seventies, surrounded by people that his future boss Buchanan believed were the key to Republican electoral success: "white ethnics," Buchanan, a Catholic, called them. Their ancestors emigrated from less affluent European countries like Italy, Ireland, and Poland, and didn't always integrate easily into privileged WASP society. Many of them, like Fabrizio's father, worked construction or other blue-collar jobs. Despite Fabrizio's professional accomplishments, some in his family weren't terribly impressed that he worked for some of the most prominent politicians in the country. He liked to joke that his father never really considered him a success until he took on a new client in 2016: Donald Trump.

Fabrizio could see how the white ethnic sense of displacement had grown over the years, especially as non-white ethnic populations started to multiply around them. These people resented the government because they thought it used its power to pick society's winners and losers. They often saw themselves on the losing end, disadvantaged by social programs like affirmative action, trade policy that made it more profitable for manufacturers to make products overseas, and immigration laws that allowed noncitizens to do jobs they thought should go to Americans first. Even if the truth was more complicated—colleges employed their own affirmative action programs that disproportionately benefited white children of alumni, for example, or shortages of able or willing American workers meant companies needed immigrant labor—these Americans were angry.

In 2003, when the new Republican president, George W. Bush, proposed a plan to deal with the millions of undocumented immigrants in the country by offering them legal status, the voters Fabrizio was surveying saw it as an affront. The Bush White House was focused on making the Republican Party a more natural and welcoming home for Latinos, as Bush had done as governor of Texas. But Fabrizio could see that the response from many Republicans was "Why should these people get to break the law?" Where Bush saw a humane, sensible, politically smart policy, many of his voters saw a Republican president who seemed more concerned about rewarding people who were breaking the law than he did about helping them.

By 2007, Fabrizio had concluded in his research that there were enough of these voters in the Republican Party that they should be their own subcategory. He called them Dennis Miller Republicans. Miller, the stand-up comedian and former host of *Saturday Night Live*'s "Weekend Update" who was famous for his breathless rants, was the ultimate aggrieved white alpha male. He could be coarse and cynical and was always politically incorrect, like a modern reboot of Archie Bunker if Bunker had a college diploma and a bigger vocabulary. Miller wasn't so much a conservative as he was an antiliberal. And he intended to offend. He told jokes about immigrants with bad hygiene and mocked environmentalists. Bill O'Reilly, cable news's ultimate alpha male outrage machine, gave Miller a regular segment on his 8 P.M. Fox News program called "Miller Time," during which the two men bantered about subjects that amused or rankled them, like a pair of male penguins who were apparently a couple. "Listen, Billy. How do you even know when a penguin's gay? Is their corner of the penguin habitat inordinately tasteful?" Miller said in one exchange that was typical of their style of humor. O'Reilly responded dryly: "No, they wear tight T-shirts."

Fabrizio's experience with Buchanan, working for him in 1992 and then against him in 1996, was instructive in what it revealed about the insurgent tremors that were destabilizing the GOP. Ultimately, Buchanan couldn't overcome Bush and the full force and fury of the Republican Party's national campaign apparatus. But his surprisingly strong showing—he came within 16 points of beating Bush in the New Hampshire primary in 1992—was a startlingly close call for a sitting president. It foreshadowed defeat for Bush that November and hinted at the weakened role the party's leadership would have in choosing presidential nominees going forward.

Four years later, when Fabrizio went to work as the chief pollster for Senator Bob Dole's presidential campaign, his job was to help defeat an emboldened Buchanan. Buchanan won the first and second contests in Alaska and Louisiana, respectively, and then the crucial New Hampshire primary. But Dole eventually won the nomination, in no small part because Fabrizio and the rest of the campaign's high command understood that the mood among voters that year was favorable for an outsider candidate, and not for Dole. As the majority leader of the Senate, Dole was the consummate insider. So his path to victory, as Fabrizio saw it, was "to kill the outsiders." They eventually did just that—dispatching the publishing scion Steve Forbes, Senator Phil Gramm of Texas, and finally Buchanan. The strategy required Dole to adopt positions that were far to the right of where he was comfortable, which meant having to make the kind of public reversals that voters often find insincere. He endorsed a conservative proposal in California to deny public education to undocumented immigrants and repudiated affirmative action programs he had once backed, insisting it made no sense to fight "the evil of discrimination with more discrimination." Both were issues that Buchanan stressed repeatedly as Dole's rival. But in the end, it didn't work. Dole struggled to unite conservatives and lost the election to President Bill Clinton by almost 9 percentage points.

Fabrizio's 2007 analysis of the shifts in public opinion among GOP voters was a ninety-two-page presentation he called "The Elephant Looks in the Mirror 10 Years Later." And it foretold the end of the line for candidates like Dole in a party that was getting angrier and more conservative. Self-described conservatives were squeezing moderates out, he found. Only 55 percent of Republicans had described themselves as conservatives when Fabrizio polled in 1997. Now that figure was 71 percent. In his past postelection analyses, Fabrizio usually included a pie chart depicting the various ideological segments of the party on a left-right scale, with progressive Republicans representing a small but statistically significant slice of between 5 and 10 percent. But there were so few Republicans who identified as progressive now that Fabrizio had no reason to assign them any space on his chart.

Fabrizio draws a fairly straight line from the emergent "Dennis Miller Republican" to Sarah Palin's breakout as a national figure. "The tip of the spear," he says. Though a conservative populist eruption of some kind "was going to happen with or without her," he adds. The Dennis Miller Republicans were on the leading edge of several trends that were reshaping the Republican electorate. They weren't necessarily people who had been Republicans all their lives. About 36 percent of them said they had been Democrats or independents before switching. McCain was not their first choice for president. They liked Rudy Giuliani, the no-nonsense, tough-on-crime former mayor of New York whose battles to get rid of the most visible signs of blight and lawlessness in the city—like the "squeegee men" who would wipe down windshields of idling cars and demand payment—resonated with voters who believed the whole country was in need of a cleanup. The conservativism these voters adhered to was not defined by moral or economic issues—traditionally the two largest self-identified groups within the party. It was rooted in cultural grievance. They believed that American society devalued them while letting less deserving people—immigrants, underachieving minorities, women—skip ahead in line. When given the choice between two statements about government assistance—"People should try to make it on their own, but government should be there with a helping hand" or "People should always make their own way in life and not look for a handout"—76 percent of them chose the latter. Other categories of Republicans were much more evenly split over the issue, Fabrizio found. The Dennis Miller Republicans were upset about illegal immigration and resentful that politicians in both parties wanted to "reward" immigrants by giving them the opportunity to become citizens. More than a third of them said the government was doing too much to help the homeless, compared with 22 percent of Republicans who felt this way overall, Fabrizio found. Overwhelmingly, they did not believe healthcare should be a guaranteed right for all Americans. They were more likely than other Republicans to be male, own guns, and live in the South and the West. The Dennis Miller Republicans were harbingers of another shift: the degenerating norms and standards of conduct in Republican politics. As the popularity of Miller's political and social commentary showed, people didn't mind the offensiveness as long as they believed the person delivering the message was on the home team, helping them battle the left.

But most of all, the Dennis Miller Republican was disgruntled. "They were angry about everything," Fabrizio explains.

In the summer of 2004, a young state senator from Illinois delivered a speech that vaulted him to a new level of political fame. Barack Obama, then a candidate for United States Senate, spoke of the transcendent nature of America as an idea and rejected the premise that its people were naturally segregated by their racial or political identities. "My presence on this stage is pretty unlikely. My father was a foreign student, born and raised in a small village in Kenya," Obama said. "My parents shared not only an improbable love, they shared an abiding faith in the possibilities of this nation." The most memorable line of the speech, the one that would be played endlessly on cable news in the years to come, was his rejection of a nation divided against itself. "There is not a liberal America and a conservative America—there is the United States of America. There is not a Black America and a White America and Latino America and Asian America—there's the United States of America," Obama said. Palin was watching and would later tell friends how compelling she found Obama. "Impressive," she declared.

But by the time Obama became a plausible presidential candidate three years later, there were troubling signs that his ascendance was atmospherically unsettling, like a lightning storm over a dry, brittle prairie. A massive fire could break out any minute. Rumors that questioned his patriotism started spreading on email chains. *Here is a picture of Obama refusing to put his hand on his heart when reciting the Pledge of Allegiance.* The picture was actually taken while the national anthem was playing. *He put his hand on a Koran when he was sworn in as a senator instead of a Bible.* Keith Ellison, a Black congressman from Minnesota who actually was Muslim, did this in 2007—not Obama. Right-wing commentators repeatedly referred to him by his full name, Barack Hussein Obama, emphasizing the Arabic middle name. Others were more menacing. "Obama, he's a piece of shit. I told him to suck on my machine gun," the right-wing rocker Ted Nugent howled to an audience in California.

Smears and disinformation didn't stay on the fringes of the right for long, migrating from emails to obscure websites, and then to talk radio and Fox News like a contagion. A few weeks before Obama formally announced his campaign for president in February 2007, *Insight,* a magazine owned by *The Washington Times,* published a false report saying that the school Obama had attended as a child in Indonesia taught a radical version of Islam. Follow-up reporting showed that the school was both a public institution and non-religious, but Fox News picked up the story anyway, as did another Rupert Murdoch–owned outlet, the *New York Post.* Some conservatives let the racial subtext go unsaid. Others saw no need for subtlety. Rush Limbaugh, who had the largest non-satellite talk radio audience in the country, accused Obama of being antiwhite. "It is clear that Senator Obama has disowned his white half, that he's decided he's got to go all in on the black side," Limbaugh declared.

Fox News, which treated Democrats as effete and anti-American, was veering into new territory with its insinuations that Obama was not only insufficiently patriotic but overtly sympathetic to terrorists. Liz Trotta, a former *Washington Times* editor and a contributor to the network, referred to Obama as "Osama" and joked about how someone could "knock off" both of them. The week that Obama became the first African American man to win the nomination of a major political party, a Fox News anchor described an affectionate gesture the candidate and his wife had made to each other as a "terrorist fist jab." After an uproar, Fox took the anchor off the air.

David Axelrod, Obama's chief strategist, didn't need to think very hard about whose handiwork was all over many of these attacks. He had seen this kind of play before from a consultant he worked against in a Senate campaign in Illinois in 1984: Roger Ailes, the chairman of Fox News. That year was something of a watershed for negative campaigning, when, as *The New York Times* reported, "the intensity and proliferation" of attack ads became "more noticeable after a period of relative restraint." Ailes's clients had some of the most boundary-pushing ads of them all, including a radio spot for a Senate candidate in Texas that accused the Democrat in the race of attacking family values for hosting a fundraiser that used male strippers. But accusing his opponents of anti-patriotic tendencies was a favorite theme for Ailes, in the campaigns he consulted on and later on his network, where graphics of animated American flags rippled across the screen and musical guests on the morning show *Fox & Friends* performed patriotic songs. For a time, a hot topic for Fox hosts was the lack of an American flag pin on Obama's lapel, which most members of Congress wore. Obama said he didn't because he considered it an empty gesture. This was vintage Ailes. As a media consultant for George H. W. Bush, Axelrod recalls, Ailes once persuaded the candidate to appear at a factory where American flags were made in an attempt to appear more patriotic than his rival, Michael Dukakis. "Disproportionately, Fox viewers were inclined to say Obama wasn't an American. That he was a Muslim," Axelrod says. Obama's aides were growing increasingly concerned that Fox's coverage was not just reinforcing false stereotypes about him but helping the misinformation metastasize and reach a much broader audience in a way that most Americans—especially Democrats—did not fully appreciate. "This Fox alternative universe had started to take shape in a really meaningful way, and people who didn't watch Fox didn't realize what it was," says Anita Dunn.

There was always a delicate alchemy to a winning conservative co-alition. And the connective tissue between the GOP's elite and activist wings was the country's culture wars. That's where Bill Kristol saw an opening for Sarah Palin. Despite Palin's record as someone who thrived on antagonizing the Republican establishment—a record that he would be instrumental in bringing to the attention of Washington conservatives—Kristol saw her much in the same way Frank Murkowski had. Bring her inside, he thought, and Republicans could win with the disaffected voters who saw some of themselves in her, but not in McCain. "There was a populist moment coming. And one way to take account of it—but not yield to it—was to pick her," Kristol says, explaining why he urged McCain to name Palin, both privately and publicly in television appearances and newspaper columns.

Of all the Republicans who helped broker Palin's introduction to Washington's high-powered conservative circles, Kristol seemed like an unlikely emissary. He was a picture of East Coast privilege: raised by professional intellectuals on the Upper West Side, educated at the prestigious Collegiate School and then Harvard, where he earned a Ph.D. in political science. His father, Irving, was a leading voice of twentieth-century American conservatism; his mother was a highly regarded historian of Victorian England. Kristol worked in two Republican administrations, first in the Department of Education during the Reagan years and then as the chief of staff to Vice President Dan Quayle while George H. W. Bush was president. While he and Palin diverged in their upbringing, Kristol could grasp the motivational power of a brawling us-versus-them culture war clash. He had helped instigate one of the most memorable face-offs of the 1990s: Dan Quayle vs. Murphy Brown.

In the spring of 1992, Quayle, with Kristol's encouragement, took up a public campaign against Brown, a fictional broadcast journalist whose eponymous prime-time show on CBS hit a nerve with social conservatives after Brown became pregnant and decided to raise her son as a single mother. Kristol understood that Quayle, a member of a wealthy newspaper publishing family that once owned *The Indianapolis Star* and *The Arizona Republic,* was an imperfect messenger. But he was the more convincing half of the Bush-Quayle ticket to sell voters on the idea that the 1992 campaign was a war between two Americas, and that Republicans were fighting for the people patronized by the cultural and political elite. Kristol worked with two speechwriters who were among the best in their business. One was John McConnell, a young Yale Law graduate who scripted the most memorable of Quayle's lines about the criticism he received for going after Brown: "I wear their scorn like a badge of honor." The other was Matthew Scully, who had a less ivy-specked background. He had gone to Arizona State University but never graduated and was pleasantly surprised to find that Kristol didn't seem to care. The feud captured the nation's attention. And when *Murphy Brown* addressed the controversy in an episode that fall, it drew 44 million viewers. Sixteen years later, Scully would revisit the same "two Americas" themes as the speechwriter on the McCain campaign who was responsible for drafting Palin's public remarks.

Kristol was only vaguely aware of a new Republican governor in the nation's forty-ninth state when an Alaskan women's club reached out to him in the spring of 2007 with an invitation to meet Sarah Palin. Kristol and some of his colleagues from the conservative magazine he helped edit, *The Weekly Standard,* were scheduled to pass through Juneau on a seven-day cruise up the Alaskan coast in June. He and his co-editor, Fred Barnes, both regulars on Fox News, were the star attractions on the ship, nicknamed the S.S. *Standard.* And Palin, as Jane Mayer of *The New Yorker* has documented, was eager to develop a higher profile in national politics now that she was governor. She had hired a stateside public relations firm to pitch stories about her to East Coast media, according to Mayer, and had reached out to *The New York Times* and *The Washington Post*—the same elite media Palin would soon be at war with.

Kristol and his *Standard* colleagues arrived at the governor's mansion in Juneau thinking that the occasion was more of an informal meeting than a coming out. Kristol brought his wife and one of his daughters; Barnes brought his wife and his sister. They were both struck by how such a petite woman filled the dining room of the stately governor's mansion with her presence. "Quite impressive and likable and smart and pretty," Barnes later observed. (Barnes was no outlier here in making note of Palin's looks; men were always commenting on them.) "I won't pretend she read every issue of the magazine," Kristol says. But she seemed like a real person—a mother juggling the responsibilities of governing and child-rearing, as they would learn when her young daughter Piper kept popping in and out of the dining room as they ate. The *Standard* hadn't intended to publish anything about Palin before the lunch. But when Kristol and Barnes returned to Washington, they agreed they should do something to alert the GOP to this rare and raw political talent in their midst. Barnes arranged to interview her twice more by phone. And in July, the magazine published his piece, which was titled "The Most Popular Governor; Alaska's Sarah Palin Is the GOP's Newest Star." It read like Palin's debutante announcement in the society pages of Washington's conservative elite. The Republican wipeout in the midterm elections in 2006, which cost the party control of the House and the Senate, obscured Palin's victory in the Alaska governor's race. And Barnes thought she was a reason for the party to buck up. "They've overlooked the one shining victory in which a Republican rising star was born," Barnes wrote. He included quotes about the scrappy young governor from interviews with friends and local observers who described her as Alaskan through and through—a "hockey mom" with an NRA membership who rode snowmobiles and loved moose stew. One pollster told Barnes, "The landscape is littered with the bodies of those who crossed Sarah."

Mistakenly, he and Palin's other champions were operating under the assumption that she and the voters who found an agitator like her appealing were content with the arrangement that had endured for decades in the GOP. It usually called for the insurgents to take a backseat while the Republicans who fit a more traditional, patrician mold of leadership ran the show. Both sides learned they often had more power through unity. And sometimes the insurgents even became the establishment. Kristol's friend John McCain had done this, after all. McCain was the maverick who challenged the powerful Bush wing of the party for the Republican nomination in 2000. The 2000 insurgent McCain ran on a platform of crushing what he called the "iron triangle" of influence in Washington: money, the lobbyists it paid for, and the legislation they wrote. Kristol and other writers at the *Standard* cheered when McCain defeated Bush in the New Hampshire primary. For this reason alone, they should have understood that a partnership with Palin was risky. The *Standard* had presciently observed in 2000 that if McCain didn't prevail that year, someone else running against the old guard eventually would. "The establishment's weakness has been exposed, and some other insurgency will eventually take advantage of it," wrote Kristol and his colleague David Brooks. Recalling his lunch in Juneau, Kristol remembers that while Palin's political beliefs may have been inchoate, she didn't come off as someone who considered herself a different breed of Republican. "It wasn't like, 'Oh, that's a different part of the Republican Party,'" he says, imagining how Palin saw him and Barnes as members of the same tribe. "It was, 'I'm a Republican governor. These are Fred Barnes and Bill Kristol. I'm going to have them to lunch.'"

Kristol says he believed at the time that Palin would merely "accent" McCain's message. What he didn't count on was that Palin's accent wasn't the issue. She was speaking an entirely different language.

There is a paradox at the heart of the story of Palin's meteoric rise that has been glossed over in most accounts of the ten weeks she spent as McCain's running mate. When McCain picked her, she instantly connected with a particular type of American who wasn't used to seeing someone like her represented at the pinnacle of power in the Republican Party. These were people who usually voted Republican but had started calling themselves independents in larger numbers as their disenchantment with the party and its candidates grew. They often described feeling socially and economically distant from the politicians they were asked to vote for—people who had more money, more education, and seemed to inhabit a different cultural universe than they did. They considered themselves to be in conflict with the Republican Party as much as with Democrats. And Palin was one of them.

But Sarah Palin the national conservative icon was also largely a product packaged by the Republican establishment—specifically by a group of highly successful, media-savvy political professionals who had worked for Bush and then went to the McCain campaign. They took the "Valley Trash" grievances she spoke to in Alaska and wrote them into a script that worked in front of a national audience. They empowered her and her supporters by giving her tell-it-like-it-is, no-apologies voice a sharper edge—all the while testing the boundaries of what a white candidate could say about a Black rival. She became a political phenomenon using the tools they had given her. "Everyone said, 'She went rogue,'" says Brooke Buchanan, an aide to McCain who was at his side during the final phase of the campaign. "I think people are trying to rewrite history." Buchanan recalls isolated incidents when Palin did push the boundaries. After being ordered by senior McCain aides to drop the subject of her pricey wardrobe for the convention after it leaked to the media, for instance, she insisted on defending herself publicly because she had only picked out clothes the campaign offered her and was devastated thinking about how the story would play back home. "Don't get me wrong. There were certain things where we said, 'This happened?' But it wasn't 'rogue,'" Buchanan adds.

From the moment of her introduction to the nation in her speech at the Republican National Convention, Palin was reading from the script the McCain campaign tailored for her. McCain chose Scully, a veteran of both Bush White Houses, to write the speech for his number two even before he knew who he was going to pick. And Scully had written much of the speech before he knew it would be Palin, including what ended up being one of the most memorable culture war broadsides: "We tend to prefer candidates who don't talk about us one way in Scranton and another way in San Francisco." Scully's intuitive sense for capturing the voice of anti-elitism told him the line would push the right buttons in almost any nominee's voice, given the indignant mood of the Republican electorate. Palin added only one line herself, which she wrote into the margins of the draft she practiced reading through thirteen times. She asked what the difference was "between a hockey mom and a pit bull?" Her answer: "Lipstick."

Pat Buchanan, who watched Palin's speech from his hotel room in Minneapolis while he was between appearances on MSNBC, was blown away by Palin and the speech. He grabbed his laptop and started to tap out his impressions for a column. He couldn't fit everything he had to say about her into one, so he wrote two. "The American Right has just died and gone to heaven," he said. He wasn't alone. Palin invigorated the campaign to a degree that stunned McCain's advisers and Republicans in Washington. Charlie Black, a Republican operative and longtime friend of McCain's who sometimes traveled with him on the campaign trail, says that Palin's ability to turn people out where McCain couldn't was something they treated as a joke at first, using it to tease the senator. "The days we were campaigning with her, the crowd would be double, triple," Black says. If there were ten thousand people at an event, Black remembers turning to McCain and ribbing him, " 'Two thousand came to see you, John, and eight thousand came to see the governor.' . . . We'd all laugh it up, you know. But it was true," Black says, adding, "I haven't seen anything quite like it." Charlie Dent, a Republican congressman from Pennsylvania who often had an uneasy relationship with the activists in the party, recalls how before Palin was announced, the volunteer hubs where people would gather to make calls and canvass neighborhoods for McCain were lacking energy. "Once he selected Sarah Palin, the number of people who started showing up exploded," Dent says.

Her rallies filled up with superfans who wrote on their signs in lipstick instead of marker. They called themselves "Dudes for Sarah" and "Palin's Pit Bulls." They gushed to reporters about why they loved her. "She's more like one of us than the Washington crew," said Al Sandelli of Bucksport, Maine, speaking to the *Portland Press Herald* at one Palin rally. "The most refreshing thing I've seen in politics in twenty-five years," said Lorna Hoff of Reno, Nevada, to the *Las Vegas Sun*. Hoff was one of five thousand people to see Palin at a rally in Carson City. In Coral Springs, Florida, Tami Nantz started a blog, *moms4sarahpalin.blogspot.com,* to sing Palin's praises and defend her from criticism. "Sarah Palin is just a real woman. A real chick. She's one of us," Nantz told the South Florida *Sun-Sentinel*. Buzz Jacobs, an aide for McCain, offered another possible explanation for Palin's magnetism in middle America. "I even heard she's a Mary Kay lady, but I'm not sure if that's true. If it is, there's another reason people will connect with her," Jacobs said. She was whatever version of normal and authentic that voters wanted her to be—even a Mary Kay lady. She was connecting with voters in a way that McCain couldn't himself.

She asked for more input and independence. But the dismissiveness of the McCain team—some of whom disparaged her in the press anonymously as an entitled know-nothing, a "diva," or a "whack job" in separate, anonymously sourced reports—enraged her and her supporters. It was another slap in the face from the Republican "good ol' boys." It was like being called "Valley Trash" all over again.

Tellingly, one of the most indelible and controversial episodes from her time on the campaign trail was choreographed by the McCain campaign, complicating the picture painted by many of his advisers after the election that Palin was an egotistical insubordinate who freelanced against the better advice of headquarters. On October 4, Palin delivered her most searing attack on Obama yet, mainstreaming the kind of smears on his character and background that had proliferated until that point largely online and on Fox News. "This is not a man who sees America as you see it, and how I see America," Palin said at a fundraiser in Englewood, Colorado. "Our opponent, though, is someone who sees America, it seems, as being so imperfect that he's palling around with terrorists who would target their own country." He wasn't just the elitist, unpatriotic leftist who refused to wear an American flag pin and looked down on the "Joe Six Pack" types like her, Palin seemed to be saying. He was a dangerous man who had sympathies for the enemies who seek to harm Americans.

She delivered the words so crisply and convincingly, they sounded as if they could have been hers. But in fact, they had been written into her speech by members of the senior campaign staff at headquarters in Crystal City, Virginia, who were executing on Palin's insistence that they attack Obama in a more aggressive way. Palin had been pushing McCain and his top advisers to embrace a story line that was popular in conservative media at the time about Obama's relationships with a variety of people who had espoused radical anti-American views. McCain rejected Palin's first suggestion, which was to tie Obama to Jeremiah Wright, the pastor who had married him and his wife and baptized his two daughters. Wright, who was Black, had harshly criticized the American government for historically marginalizing and disenfranchising Black Americans and blamed American foreign policy for instigating the September 11 attacks. In one clip that circulated widely in right-wing media, from a sermon Wright delivered in 2003, the pastor thundered, "God damn America!" McCain nixed the idea, concerned that it was too racially loaded. As an alternative that would prove no less racially inflammatory, McCain aides in Crystal City came up with the "palling around with terrorists" language as a way of linking Obama to Bill Ayers, a onetime leader of the militant group Weather Underground. Ayers, who was white, was involved with the group when it was responsible for several bombings at public buildings in protest of the Vietnam War. But that was two decades before Ayers met Obama. The two were casually acquainted as neighbors in Hyde Park, Illinois, and had worked on education reform initiatives together when Obama was a local activist and state senator.

On the day of the speech, Palin and her traveling aides received an email containing the remarks while she was still in an airport hangar in Colorado, waiting to go to the fundraiser. Few words she spoke during the campaign would do more to cement her status as the voice of the Obama opposition. And over the next several days as the comments generated considerable controversy and coverage, neither she nor senior McCain staff made attempts to back away from the comments. Rather, they leaned into them.

Scully, the speechwriting team, and campaign brass discussed over email ways to make the attack more potent. They debated whether Palin should level a broader accusation and question Obama's honesty about his past. Included on the emails were Tucker Eskew, a senior communications consultant, and Matt McDonald, another communications aide. Also copied were Schmidt and Nicolle Wallace, both alumni of the Bush White House who would later publicly question Palin's professionalism and lament her influence on the increasingly shrill tone of the nation's political discourse. Two days after Palin first delivered the remarks, the *Washington Post* columnist Dana Milbank reported that after Palin mentioned Obama and Ayers at a rally in Clearwater, Florida, someone shouted, "Kill him!" Milbank also reported that another person hurled a racist epithet at a Black cameraman, telling him, "Sit down, boy." Then McCain added fuel to the fire himself at a rally in Albuquerque the same day, asking "Who is the real Barack Obama?" Someone in the audience called out, "Terrorist!" according to *The New York Observer.* "McCain grimaced," the paper wrote, "but kept going."

By noon the day after those incidents—which were receiving widespread coverage in the media—McCain's team was still discussing how to make the language stronger. And one of the suggestions floated was to nod to an opinion piece by the conservative writer Thomas Sowell, who had criticized Obama for "repeatedly allying himself over the years with people who make no attempt to hide their hatred of America." (Dan Balz and Haynes Johnson, in their comprehensive account of the 2008 election, *The Battle for America,* have also reported on the involvement of the McCain campaign's high command in crafting the remarks.) Palin's traveling speechwriter, Lindsay Hayes, recalls receiving instructions from headquarters immediately after she gave the speech on October 4 not to change any of the language in the text unless it was to add a passing reference that the local audience would recognize. "It was locked into the speech," says Hayes. "I was basically told, 'This is part of the stump now.'"

At first, Palin had been uncomfortable with all the attention. Jason Recher, a campaign aide who started traveling with the Palin family not long after McCain picked her, noticed within her first few days on the road that the schedule demanded of the Republican Party's newest and biggest celebrity was taking its toll on her and her husband, Todd. After a fundraiser one evening, Recher tried to cheer them up. "You guys, you just raised eight and a half million dollars," Recher told the couple. Their jaws dropped. At a wildly successful fundraiser in Alaska, maybe she would raise five figures. A high-seven-figure sum was not just out of the realm of normal for the Palins, it was unfathomable.

"Is this normal?" was the question that Palin started asking repeatedly of the people around her. Was it normal that the crowds were so big? Sixty thousand in The Villages, Florida; seventeen thousand outside St. Louis; seven thousand in Salem, New Hampshire, only two days after Joe Biden visited nearby Manchester and turned out six hundred. Was it normal for people to linger a half hour afterward to see if they could catch a glimpse up close or maybe even get an autograph from a vice presidential candidate? Was it normal that some of those people would start crying when they met her? Was it normal that sometimes men from the crowd would grope her as they leaned in for a picture? She didn't get the concept of not being able to carry her own bag off the plane, a task typically delegated to young, low-level campaign staff so candidates aren't photographed awkwardly holding a carry-on with one hand and waving with the other. "I can carry my own bag," she objected.

But when she saw the crowds, it gave her an enormous emotional boost. And she kept going. "It almost gives her her confidence back. That's what it looked like to me," says Maria Comella, who was assigned by the McCain campaign to work alongside her in the beginning. But as the crowds and her confidence grew, so did the vitriol. "It unleashed some of our base's worst instincts and fed it. And we never really came back from that," Comella concludes. Some conservatives remember a much darker undercurrent to Palin's support than they could remember with other populist candidates, like Buchanan. When the syndicated columnist Kathleen Parker wrote that Palin should step aside because she was in over her head and unfit to be a heartbeat away from the presidency, Parker received twenty thousand emails. Sixty percent, she says, were hate mail. People called Parker a traitor, told her to kill herself, and said her mother should have aborted her. The other 40 percent, Parker recalls, expressed a sentiment of relief—"Thank God someone said it." Parker, who was initially impressed with Palin after her convention speech but changed her mind after watching the governor struggle to answer basic questions, says she had scheduled a meeting at the White House before her piece ran. Given the backlash, she worried that she might be persona non grata. But when she showed up and joked that she wasn't sure she'd be welcome, an administration official told her, "Are you kidding? We were waiting for someone to write that."

But that wasn't the message Parker was getting elsewhere. Within a few days, she couldn't bear to look at her email anymore. The Heritage Foundation canceled a speech she was scheduled to give. The *National Review* dropped her column. The outrage seemed to erupt from the deepest feelings of resentment and insecurity among people she assumed she had a lot in common with. She also assumed people would value preparedness and thoughtfulness in a leader. And when that leader proved to have deficiencies that were obvious to her, she assumed that people could admit that. Instead, they accused her of attacking them. "You can't critique her honestly because that is basically an insult to a whole swath of America," Parker says. "You have to hate the Republicans for putting us in that situation," she adds. "They threw something foul in the punchbowl, and we had to drink it."

Journalists covering Palin's rallies kept documenting the vitriol that was erupting from her crowds, some of it so ugly that the Secret Service had to look into one incident as a precaution. Reports documented people shouting "Obama bin Laden," "Treason!" and "Off with his head!" And when McCain attempted to correct a woman at one of his events who said she heard that Obama was "an Arab"—"No, ma'am. He's a decent family man," McCain said—the crowd booed him.

There was nothing normal about that.

CHAPTER 2

Winning Is Losing

If I set myself on fire for you guys, you would actually complain
that the temperature of the fire is not hot enough.
—Congressman Charlie Dent (R-Pennsylvania)

Dede Scozzafava, a state assemblywoman from Upstate New York, started her career in Republican politics just like Sarah Palin did. She was only twenty-nine when she ran for and won a seat on the board of trustees for her village, a tiny working-class hamlet in the state's rugged North Country called Gouverneur. Within four years, she was elected mayor. She thought it would be rewarding to play in the higher-stakes game in Albany, and won a race for state assembly in 1998. Scozzafava's middle-of-the-road politics reflected the sensibilities of the GOP in New York State, where the governor for most of her time in office, George E. Pataki, was a moderate Republican and shared Scozzafava's liberal positions on abortion and gay rights. But unlike Palin, Scozzafava's career advanced because she played the insider Republican game. Instead of antagonizing party leaders when she arrived at the state capitol, she tried to work with them in spite of the differences she had with many of her more conservative colleagues. Eventually, she accumulated enough seniority and goodwill to become the minority leader pro tempore, a high-ranking position that allowed her to run legislative debates on the assembly floor. She drove a blue Buick and had a warm, gentle way about her that made her a maternal figure to members of both parties in Albany. And in early 2009, after a decade in the state legislature, Scozzafava felt the urge to try something new in national politics. Her intellectual curiosity had been pulling her toward foreign affairs, and Congress seemed like the best place to see that through. She jumped in the race when a seat opened up in her district, New York's Twenty-third.

Scozzafava (pronounced skoze-ah-FAV-uh) was a textbook public servant in many ways. But she was hopelessly mismatched for the moment of upheaval that was transforming her party. She was part of the long but declining tradition of Rockefeller Republicans in the Northeast. The label originated with the pragmatic, centrist former governor of New York during the 1960s, Nelson Rockefeller, who charted a separate course from his party's hard right by championing civil rights, the state university system, and the spending of massive sums of public money on infrastructure and housing for the poor. The feeling among activist conservatives was that moderates like Rockefeller didn't respect them or the large bloc of engaged voters they brought with them. He irked the GOP right flank so much that they formed their own splinter party in protest, the Conservative Party of New York State. Because hard-liners usually struggled in congressional races in New York State, conservatives in Washington tolerated candidates like Scozzafava as a necessary cost of preserving their power. Newt Gingrich, the former Speaker of the House, was among her endorsers, calling her "responsible and principled." But being "responsible" was not what many Republican voters were interested in by 2009. In fact, it was almost disqualifying. The attributes of candidates like her—who respected civil service experience, preached moderation, and rejected ideological purity tests as self-defeating and wrong—had been rapidly devalued in the year since Palin's debut and Obama's election.

The special election in New York's Twenty-third District has been relegated to a footnote in the historical accounting of the infighting that would define the GOP for at least the next decade. But due to a unique set of circumstances—an early exit of an incumbent Republican who joined the Obama administration; the sense of discontent and cultural displacement simmering among white working-class Americans who saw the government bailing everyone out but them; the rise of an insurgent political movement with electrifying new leaders; and a widely watched cable news channel that was aggressively redefining itself as the voice of the Obama opposition—the race in the North Country was the first to put the country on notice about the disruptive power of the Tea Party.

It had been a year since McCain lost to Obama. The magnitude of his defeat had been so staggering that it left Republicans wondering whether the party as they had known it was fading into obsolescence. "Conservatives woke up, and it was all gone," says Henry Olsen, an author who has studied American populism and its impact on the GOP. Olsen wasn't being hyperbolic. The half-trillion-dollar bailout that Congress passed before Bush left office to avert the collapse of the financial markets seemed to suggest that the very brand of conservatism that had undergirded the modern Republican Party—with its devotion to a minimalist government and a belief that big spending was often the cause of, and not the solution to, society's ills—was dead. "GOP R.I.P.," declared the conservative radio host John Batchelor, who warned Republicans not to deny their fate expressing an opinion that was typical on the right and left at the time. "I can hear you doubting that this could truly be the end. The final stage of grief is acceptance," Batchelor wrote.

Obama had received nearly ten million more votes than McCain, a margin that lifted him to victory in states like Indiana and North Carolina that hadn't voted Democratic in decades. In congressional races, the Democratic Party added to its majorities in the House and Senate. But the most telling gains were in the Senate, where it seemed a political realignment was underway, thinning Republican ranks on the coasts and hastening the solidification of Democratic power in New England and the Pacific Northwest. This was supposed to be the kind of shift in the balance of power between the two political parties that most people alive had only read about in political science textbooks. North Carolina and Virginia both had new Democratic senators, illustrating the shifting demographics of the New South, where conservative candidates were having a harder time in the suburbs of Washington and the exploding academic research hubs around Raleigh and Chapel Hill. In Oregon, Senator Gordon Smith lost the seat he had held for two terms, leaving Alaska as the only state on the geographical West Coast with any Republican representation in the Senate. But even Alaska didn't look like a safe haven anymore. Mark Begich, the mayor of Anchorage, beat Ted Stevens, a fixture of the state's Republican machine who had been in the Senate since 1968. Once the outcome of the contested race in Minnesota was settled in June, with the former *Saturday Night Live* star and writer Al Franken overtaking the Republican incumbent, Democrats would have the sixty votes necessary to overcome a Republican filibuster, that vexing procedural blockade that the political minority had used since the nineteenth century to kill landmark legislation. This meant that under Obama's leadership, the alarmist scenarios that Republicans like Palin had told voters about suddenly seemed more than just hypothetical: Socialism, or something just as foreign and un-American, was taking root in America, they warned.

Those who considered themselves Republicans in 2008 had lived for almost an entire generation in which their party was in control of at least one of the major levers of power in Washington. The thinking inside the office suites of congressional leaders and the consulting firms that were paid handsomely to advise them was that success would essentially require building something like the broad political coalition that Obama put together. Eric Cantor, who would eventually become the number two Republican leader in the House, recalls stepping out onto the West Front of the Capitol to watch Obama's inauguration and being struck by the enormous crowd, estimated at about 1.8 million people. Cantor had two thoughts. First was the realization that he was witnessing something historic in the swearing-in of the first Black president and the shattering of one of the most formidable racial barriers in American politics. "I was amazed," Cantor says, recalling what he felt when he saw so many people on the National Mall. "It was an exciting moment for so many in this country, obviously," he adds. Then his brain switched over to political survival mode. "But I also thought, as a Republican, that we needed to provide an answer or alternative if this very popular new president was going to have an opposition that was going to be effective in influencing the outcome of policy." Cantor had worked in his family real estate business and started his own mortgage brokerage before being elected to the Virginia House of Delegates in 1991, and then to Congress in 2000. Along with Representatives Kevin McCarthy and Paul Ryan, Cantor would lead the "Young Guns" of the Republican conference in the House, a moniker that described both a new generation of conservative lawmakers who styled themselves as forward-looking and entrepreneurial, and the idea that the GOP needed to do a better job at being more appealing to a younger, more diverse coalition of voters.

Cantor, who had a thick black mane of hair and a deliberative, almost patrician style of speaking, was happiest when dealing with the policy aspects of public office. The populist anger that was rising in the party—which seemed to be shouting no to just about everything—wasn't just counterproductive in lawmaking, he believed. It was going to make it even harder for Republicans to win again. The answer, as he and many other Republicans saw it, was to "broaden our appeal in an increasingly diverse country." After all, he says, "It just sort of makes common sense that a party would like to be as appealing to as many voters as possible." Ideas would be at the center of that approach, not obstinacy. "You just really are not going to be able to attract that many more people by only being negative. You had to inspire," he recalls—just as Obama had.

But many Republicans in Congress had no interest in emulating a president they were attacking as dangerous and anti-American. By that point, Republican leaders had already survived one brush with catastrophe that revealed how eager some of their members were to push the limits. On Thursday, September 18, 2008, with the nation's banking system on the verge of a catastrophic failure, Treasury Secretary Henry Paulson walked into the room in the basement of the Capitol where Republican House members gather for their regular conference meetings and dropped a bombshell. Overly lenient lending practices had saddled banks with mortgages that weren't being repaid, he said. And if the banks didn't get relief, they would collapse and take the entire economy down with them. Paulson's ask of Congress was enormous: *I need $700 billion, and I need it by Monday*. The Capitol switchboard jammed up with calls from Americans who said they opposed letting Wall Street off the hook for making bad bets on mortgages while the homeowners who actually had to pay those mortgages got no assistance. Eleven days after Paulson's visit when the bank bailout package came to a vote, House Republicans defeated it, rejecting pleas from President Bush, John Boehner—the Republican leader—and Cantor. The Dow Jones Industrial Average plunged almost 7 percent. Some lawmakers noticed how many people were strangely approving of the havoc being wrought on the nation's financial institutions. They seemed content watching as the entire system crashed and burned. That included a surprising number of Republicans in the House—133 of them, or two-thirds of those who voted that day—even though they had been warned of the consequences by the Republican Treasury secretary. It also seemed to carry little weight with these Republicans that Paulson had as prestigious a pedigree as one gets on Wall Street: He was the former chief executive of the investment bank Goldman Sachs.

"I remember hearing some of these folks saying in 2008, 'We've got to just burn it all down,'" says Charlie Dent, a moderate Republican who represented Pennsylvania's Lehigh Valley at the time. "They thought it was good to have this kind of crisis, and then out of the ashes we would miraculously build this conservative majority. The whole thing struck me as bizarre." Dent was quick-witted and good enough at turning a phrase that reporters on Capitol Hill sought him out often for the kind of candid analysis of intra-Republican dynamics that few other members were willing to offer on the record. He, like Cantor, found the attitude of many Republican insurgents self-immolating. "If I set myself on fire for you guys, you would actually complain that the temperature of the fire is not hot enough," Dent says.

The victory of a candidate like Scozzafava would, in theory, help prove the case that Republicans like Dent and Cantor were right that their party could be competitive if it offered voters something more than just antipathy and resistance to the new president. The situation was especially dire in New York, where only three of twenty-nine congressional districts remained Republican. Scozzafava was relying on a message that was more optimistic and inspirational than many others in her party were. "The politics of fear, it's not going to work," she said as she campaigned that summer. "And we can't be the party of 'no.'" She insisted that her views on marriage and abortion were fundamentally conservative, rooted in firm convictions about individual rights and liberty that she said too many Republicans preached but did not practice. "If these parties really believe in less government, I think they have to believe in it across a broad spectrum," she insisted. Scozzafava visited Washington to meet with the men and women she hoped would be her new colleagues. And when it came time to introduce her to the entire Republican conference, Dent was asked to do the honors. He didn't think that was a coincidence, given that they were both moderates—a label that was now practically a slur in their party. And he sensed that the Republican leadership wanted some distance from her. "'Let Dent do it,'" he says. "Keep their fingerprints off it in case it goes badly, which it did."

Scozzafava had been a Republican all of her life. Even though she considered herself pro-choice and had voted twice in the assembly to legalize same-sex marriage, she never considered becoming a Democrat as her views became increasingly uncommon in her party. She had the endorsement of the National Rifle Association. She opposed Obama's plan to repeal the Bush tax cuts and his legislation to implement a government-run healthcare system. But now she was being told she wasn't really a Republican—at least not according to the standards set by activists on the right who appeared to be calling the shots. She found it all disorienting. One day she was driving in her car, listening to Rush Limbaugh. She was stunned to hear him attacking her. He kept calling her "a RINO," which she didn't think made any sense. *Why is the biggest name in conservative radio calling me a rhinoceros?* Had she been better versed in the lexicon of the new hard right, she would have understood that it was an acronym: Republican in Name Only. Limbaugh wasn't the only one going after her. Glenn Beck, the Fox News host and talk radio star who had one of the fastest-growing audiences in conservative media, covered her as a recurring story on his shows. "The Democrat is basically the same as the Republican," Beck complained in one monologue that was typical of his complaints about Scozzafava. "Haven't we tried this formula before?" Robocalls in the district referred to her as a "lesbian lover" and a "child killer."

Scozzafava had known she would encounter resistance from the right. She started putting feelers out that she was interested in running not long after she learned that the seat would be opening up because the Republican incumbent, John McHugh, had been nominated by Obama to be secretary of the Army. She won the nomination from the local GOP, but the way it happened only validated the complaints from her critics that she was out of touch. Because it was a special election, a regional committee of eleven county party chairs, not primary voters, selected her. They made their decision in secret, at a pizzeria in Potsdam in late July, and cited her "tradition of service and commitment to the people of the 23rd Congressional District." But soon other doors were slamming shut in her face. Conservatives who had supported her in previous elections were telling her through intermediaries that she wouldn't get their backing this time. A mutual friend brokered a meeting between her and the powerful leader of New York's Conservative Party, Mike Long. But when they sat down in Lake Placid, Long told her there was no way she could win the party's endorsement, a snub that could cost her thousands of votes. Long told her that her votes for same-sex marriage were the deal-breakers.

The arrival of the Obama administration in Washington along with unified Democratic control of Congress felt like the beginning of a long period in the political wilderness for most Republicans. But for social conservatives, the future seemed especially dire as they looked at a political landscape where they were losing power and a culture that was leaving them behind. In the spring of 2009, lawmakers in Maine, New Hampshire, and Vermont all passed laws allowing same-sex couples to wed, a falling domino–like pace of social change that had been almost unfathomable a few years earlier. (The pace of change was so fast that even Obama did not publicly support legalizing marriages of gay men and lesbians until 2012.) LGBTQ rights activists were pushing to make the next state New York, which had come one step closer in May when Scozzafava joined four other Republican colleagues in the State Assembly to pass marriage equality legislation. If it were to get through the more conservative State Senate, same-sex marriage would become legal in the nation's fourth-most populous state—a crushing prospect for social conservatives. Long vowed "to do everything we can possible" to stop it. And that included taking out a Republican on the wrong side of the issue, if necessary. Says Scozzafava, "It became clear that they needed to make a statement, make a point to show any other Republicans" that they couldn't buck the party on marriage or other issues that the party base considered bedrock. But apart from marriage, Scozzafava's views on the issues weren't much different from McHugh's. To her, it didn't seem like she'd changed anything about her politics to earn such reprobation from conservatives in her party. It was the party that had changed. "I feel like the party left me," she says.

She never counted on becoming the most vilified woman in all of the Republican Party, which is exactly what she became for a few months in late 2009. The opposition to Scozzafava seemed to spring up out of nowhere—an ad hoc coalition of national conservative activists and right-wing media personalities who descended on the North Country because they believed there was no greater cause at that moment than to stop her—even if it meant Republicans ended up splitting their votes between her and a more conservative rival, delivering the seat to a Democrat instead. The flood of money and manpower from the outside working to defeat her was a juggernaut. The Susan B. Anthony List, an antiabortion group based in Virginia, and the National Organization for Marriage, which was fighting marriage equality campaigns in several states, relocated to a Days

Inn in Watertown, a former industrial center outside Fort Drum not far from where Lake Ontario connects with the St. Lawrence River. From a musty hotel suite, they commanded a small battalion of activists who roamed the district with the goal of stuffing eighty thousand anti-Scozzafava leaflets into mailboxes and doorways before the November election. "The No. 1 victory will be to defeat Dede," declared Marjorie Dannenfelser, president of the Susan B. Anthony List. Based on what it learned in the Scozzafava race, the Susan B. Anthony List would expand its work to purge the GOP of pro-abortion-rights candidates into a national movement with a budget of tens of millions of dollars over the next decade.

How defeating Scozzafava—a woman none of these activists had ever heard of until she announced, and whose name most of them couldn't pronounce—became a cause so urgent that people would uproot their lives and move into a motel to achieve it is the story of the first crack in the dam that eventually broke open, exposing how Republican leaders in Washington could no longer withstand the pressure from their activist flank that they had tried to suppress and deny for years. After Obama's victory, many of these activists felt they had nothing left to lose. So losing again—if it sent the right message about the need for ideological conformity in their own party—didn't feel like much of a sacrifice. They began to see it as a way of rebuilding their party from the ashes of its historic defeat. And if they succeeded, it would send a powerful signal to establishment Republicans everywhere: Moderate politics are dead, and we buried them right in Nelson Rockefeller's backyard.

On January 30, 2009—ten days after the first African American was sworn in as president—Republicans met in Washington and chose the first African American to lead their party, Michael Steele, the former lieutenant governor of Maryland. Steele, a frequent cable news talking head with degrees from Johns Hopkins and Georgetown, impressed crowds with his quick wit and irreverence. In one of his more memorable moments, he put his skills to use during his speech at the 2008 Republican convention when he introduced the country to the phrase "Drill, baby, drill" when talking about the need for less restrictive energy exploration. (It would later be erroneously attributed to Palin because she adopted it as part of her arsenal of zingers on the campaign trail.) But from the moment he was elected and declared in his victory speech that it was "time for something completely different," Steele says he knew that many Republicans weren't interested in the kind of shift in tone and style that would make the party more appealing to non-white voters and others beyond its base. As he celebrated his election, Steele says that a woman who was an elected member of the party's 168-member governing body approached him and told him excitedly, "I'm glad you're chairman now because Blacks will join the Republican Party." Steele smiled politely but knew how the comment reflected the lack of understanding in his party about why Black voters were turned off in the first place. "I don't pretend that I don't know why a lot of these members voted for me. They looked down the street at 1600 Pennsylvania Avenue, saw Barack Obama, and went, 'Oh shit,'" he adds. "I got it."

It was only a taste of what was to come. Steele had barely set up his office at the RNC headquarters on Capitol Hill when he started getting pressure from the committee's political staff to take a harder line on Obama. He was uncomfortable with what he saw as pressure to be "the good negro," he explains. RNC staff pressed him about using the conspiracy theory about Obama's birth certificate as a way to raise money. One day, one of Steele's deputies let his guard down and told the chairman why he thought Republican voters were so mad: "They lost in 2006, and they just got their clock cleaned by the Black guy." It made Steele realize something he found incredibly depressing: If this is what they said to his face, what were they saying behind his back?

In a way, he already knew. One member of the RNC, a party operative from Tennessee named Chip Saltsman, had come under fire a few months earlier for sending out a CD of holiday tunes to party officials that included a song called "Barack the Magic Negro." Set to the tune of "Puff the Magic Dragon," the singer, an Al Sharpton impersonator, says Obama was only successful because he "made guilty whites feel good." He continues, "They'll vote for him and not for me / Cause he's not from the 'hood." The title of the song was taken from the headline on an opinion piece in the *Los Angeles Times* by David Ehrenstein, a Black writer who argued that Obama was similar to popular Black movie stars like Morgan Freeman and Sidney Poitier who satisfied white audiences' desire to see "a noble, healing Negro" on screen. Conservatives in the media like Rush Limbaugh, who played the song on his show in 2007, had been getting bolder about pushing these kinds of racially motivated attacks on Obama into the mainstream. They would say something that could easily be seen as racist and then deflected by blaming the backlash on the hysterical overreaction of liberal hypocrites. "This columnist is black, by the way," Limbaugh told his audience, declaring it entirely appropriate. "So we're just highlighting what the left says."

After only a month on the job, Steele had his own rude awakening about the extent of Limbaugh's power in the Republican Party. Steele went on a talk show hosted by D. L. Hughley, a Black comedian. Hughley asked Steele what he thought about a recent comment of Limbaugh's that he hoped Obama would fail, considering that Limbaugh was, in Hughley's description, the "de facto" leader of the party. The remarks from Limbaugh's show on January 16, 2009, are worth considering at length because the host was a careful, studious reader of the feedback he received from his audience. As he told people when they asked him to tone it down, Limbaugh's commentary usually reflected what his listeners were telling him in phone calls and emails. He was merely channeling them, he liked to say. "Why do we have to accept the premise here that because of the historical nature of his presidency, that we want him to succeed?" Limbaugh asked his audience. He went on:

> This is affirmative action, if we do that. We want to promote failure, we want to promote incompetence, we want to stand by and not object to what he's doing simply because of the color of his skin? Sorry. I got past the historical nature of this months

ago. . . . We're talking about my country, the United States of America, my nieces, my nephews, your kids, your grandkids. Why in the world do we want to saddle them with more liberalism and socialism? Why would I want to do that? So I can answer it, four words, "I hope he fails."

Steele responded by reminding Hughley that he, not Limbaugh, was the leader of the party. Limbaugh's rhetoric, he said, was sometimes "ugly" and "incendiary." But Limbaugh was ultimately an entertainer, Steele explained, and this is what entertainers do.

The comment almost cost Steele his job. It mattered little that Limbaugh had described himself many times in public as a broadcaster whose job was to get as many people as possible to listen to his show. Steele, who was friendly with Limbaugh, had in fact heard Limbaugh say this before. But that was of little comfort to the legions of Limbaugh fans who were active Republicans. Steele says that donations to the party plunged 30 percent over the next three weeks. One member of the RNC called on him to resign. Limbaugh agreed, saying the GOP was in such a sorry state that maybe Steele should quit. Steele called the host directly to try to calm the fury. And when Steele reached him on his cellphone, Limbaugh started laughing. "Michael, I know what you said," Limbaugh assured him, insisting that everything was fine. It struck Steele that Hughley was right after all about who was in charge.

The earliest news coverage of the political protests that started erupting across the country in the weeks after Obama's inauguration often gave marquee billing to people who said they weren't partisan. They claimed to have been apolitical or independent and were compelled to speak up because they were concerned about runaway federal spending. This left an impression, which professional activists and politicians encouraged at the time, that the uprising was an organic mix of disgruntled Americans spread out across the political spectrum, left, right, and center. It was an appealing but inaccurate narrative. And at first, many who were drawn in believed that was what they were signing on to. Early adherents included Mark Sanford, the governor of South Carolina, and Jeff Flake, a congressman from Arizona. Followers convened at "tea parties"—named so in an homage to the colonial rebellion against the British when they still ruled America as a colony. "We are at a truly frightening tipping point with regard to federal spending," Sanford declared at one event in the spring of 2009. The crowd chanted his name; some called out to him to run for president.

The "tea parties" kept getting bigger, with the largest outpouring yet taking place on April 15, Tax Day. In Austin, Texas, a thousand people cheered as Governor Rick Perry accused the Obama administration of attacking states' rights. In Salt Lake City, demonstrators jeered Governor Jon Huntsman for accepting federal stimulus money. In Bakersfield, California, as many as two thousand people showed up at the plaza downtown where there is a replica of the Liberty Bell. The event included two VIP guests who were curious about this new wave of activism: the House Republican leader, John Boehner, and Kevin McCarthy, the local congressman and a rising star in the party. But in a sign of the low regard Tea Party followers had for Washington Republicans, the crowd booed at the mere mention of McCarthy's name. When Boehner returned to Washington, he told colleagues not to fear the Tea Party but to embrace it and bring it inside the GOP tent. "Something's going on out there," he would say, recalls a former aide. "You may not agree with everything. But if you ultimately want their help come 2010, you need to engage with them." Boehner's conclusion was that the good outweighed the bad. "Their heart is in the right place," he told his members.

But Republican leaders sometimes didn't know whom or what they were engaging with. Steele still had the Limbaugh rebuke fresh in his mind when he decided to take a few dozen Tea Party activists up on their request to meet with him at RNC headquarters. The messages he had been getting from his staff about the souring mood in the country that spring made him share Boehner's view that this was a political force of nature they shouldn't fight but embrace. On the day of the meeting, the activists joined Steele in a conference room overlooking Capitol Hill. They unloaded on him and his staff. *Why weren't all these big-government Republicans in Washington doing enough to stop out-of-control spending and tame soaring deficits? Had they forgotten what was in the Constitution?* At one point, Steele asked what he thought was a simple question: How could he get in touch with "the Tea Party" in the future? He assumed they had a central leadership committee or a head organizer or someone in a dedicated position to communicate with top party officials like him.

"We're not an organization," one of the activists told Steele. They were a loosely affiliated network of state and local chapters, the activist said, some with five members and others with five hundred. "We're a group of people who call ourselves 'tea party.'"

Some leading movement activists soon became disillusioned about what they were seeing inside their own organizations. Rob Neppell helped found Tea Party Patriots, which became one of the fastest-growing groups in the movement. Neppell, a computer scientist and blogger, was drawn in because he thought his knowledge of internet technology could help the fledgling Tea Party reach a larger audience online. So he joined with a handful of other activists who were newer to politics, one of whom was Amy Kremer, to create a group that intended to connect people who wanted to participate in—and donate to—the disparate and disorganized movement. Neppell says he didn't have a radicalizing moment in his life that made him take up the cause. He worried about the country's ability to rebound from the Great Recession. He wanted to help people he believed shared his beliefs that the government was spending beyond its means. "'No kings and queens' was something we said a lot," Neppell recalls. He believed the Tea Party was better off if no single person or group tried to play the leading role. It was supposed to resemble a federalist model, with groups like Tea Party Patriots acting as facilitators inside a decentralized network.

But he says that some colleagues had grander visions for their roles that seemed to have little bearing on the group's stated mission as a "grassroots movement of Americans who favor free market economics, fiscal responsibility, and limited government." Neppell says,

"Amy literally wore a tiara at one of our Tea Party rallies. I was like, 'Arggh! Didn't we have this conversation?' " Kremer was pushed out of the organization after less than a year and joined the leadership of a new group, Tea Party Express. He says he came to see that what began as a cause "ends as a racket." He left the group in December 2010. After the January 6 riots, he fished out an old photo of himself and two other Tea Party Patriots founders and posted it on Twitter alongside one of the signature images of the attacks: a bare-chested man wearing a horned, fur-trimmed hat standing inside the Capitol. He captioned it "how it started/how it's going."

In Upstate New York, the Tea Party insurgency was coalescing around an unlikely challenger to Scozzafava. Doug Hoffman was certainly no one's idea of a revolutionary. He was a managing partner in an accounting firm and looked every bit the part. His boyish face, neatly parted blond hair, and rimless oval glasses recalled the archetypal young Republican Alex P. Keaton, not a grown man in his fifties. He spoke slowly and haltingly in a monotone voice. His political consultants found him to be such an underwhelming spokesman for the animating issues of his campaign—limited government, fiscal responsibility, traditional family values—that they used hired narrators instead of featuring his voice in his ads. But as a candidate whose conservative positions could be listed on campaign flyers alongside Scozzafava's more liberal record, Hoffman was the conservative ideal.

Stilted as he was, Hoffman could channel the indignation of Republican voters in the district and far beyond who saw Scozzafava as the kind of politician whose time was up. He villainized "the bosses" who had looked at Scozzafava's long record of service and blessed her candidacy. He wore his lack of political or government experience as a badge of honor. He talked up his small business background and declared himself fed up with the ever-expanding government. He was self-deprecating about his awkwardness. "If you want polish and pizzazz, I'm not your guy," he told voters. For the location of his campaign headquarters, he chose a site that used to be the service station where he pumped gas as a teenager. In a much earlier era, he might have been the farmer who puts down his plow and enlists in the war, as one of the consultants who worked on his campaign described him.

The Conservative Party's imprimatur alone would not be enough for Hoffman to beat Scozzafava. But it did mean that he was guaranteed a spot on the ballot as the party's nominee in the Twenty-third District. And it opened doors in Washington that would provide the financial backing, advertising, and consultants he would need to wage his war on the Republican Party. One of Hoffman's stops on a trip to Washington in the summer of 2009 was at the Club for Growth, a major source of outside cash for Republican candidates that attracts donors for its hard-nose tactics to push Republicans further to the right on issues of fiscal austerity, taxes, and free markets. The club had no plans to get involved in the New York race because it was focusing on preparing for the midterm elections the next year. But once they heard Hoffman's pitch, they decided to make his race a dress rehearsal for 2010. He talked about opposing Obama's stimulus package and how he favored slashing taxes and spending simultaneously to help spur the economic recovery the country badly needed. He said he opposed the Obama administration's "Cash for Clunkers," which incentivized people to purchase new, more-fuel-efficient cars by giving them cash vouchers when they traded in their older models. Hoffman struck his audience at the club as "a little goofy," as one of the group's longtime strategists, Andy Roth, put it. But they thought he was worth an investment. "Our Spidey sense was tingling," Roth says. "He was definitely conservative, and he was definitely challenging the establishment." The club, which would become a major player in Tea Party races over the next year, commissioned a poll in the district. And when the numbers came back and showed that Hoffman had a shot at winning, they decided they would back him.

Congressional Republican leaders and their strategists were watching Hoffman's rise with a growing sense of alarm. And they retaliated by trying to reassert their dominance and freeze Hoffman's backers out. Nelson Warfield, a veteran Virginia-based consultant who had worked with the Club for Growth on other campaigns, heard the group was backing Hoffman through a friend and agreed to sign on as a senior strategist for his campaign. Then a threatening message from someone at the National Republican Congressional Committee arrived in his email inbox. "If you proceed in this, you're never going to work on a Republican campaign again," Warfield recalls. He thought the arrogance validated Hoffman's entire premise for running against the party and perfectly captured the reason that so many conservative activists were rebelling. What strategists like Warfield and Roth then set out to do was to take as much as they could in Scozzafava's public record—the way she had won the nomination with the consent of local party officials in a closed-door meeting, how she had voted with liberals in the legislature, how she responded to criticism when asked about those votes—and match it to the mood on the insurgent right. "There was a detachment and a sense of entitlement that she had been in the legislature and was entitled to respect and deference because she was a person of substance," Warfield says.

There would be none of that. Using Hoffman as a messenger was a challenge, given his limitations as a public speaker. But that didn't seem to affect how voters saw him. He was a mere vessel. Voters poured into him all their boiling resentment of Obama, the Democrats, and the bailouts. In its message testing, the Hoffman campaign discovered that if they mentioned Scozzafava in the context of the federal economic rescue efforts, voters had a powerful negative reaction. Warfield describes the response: "Everybody is getting something except me. . . . The banks were getting bailed out, the car companies are getting bailed out. Nobody in the Tea Party thought they were getting bailed out."

Roger Ailes, the irascible and domineering chairman of the country's most viewed cable news network, did not see his role in the post-Bush years as especially complicated. If Americans were dumb enough to elect Obama as president, Ailes told his colleagues that the most effective thing he could do was to fill as many hours of programming as possible with voices that reminded them what a terrible mistake the country had made. In his quest to drive ratings ever higher, Ailes understood that the Obama presidency could be a godsend. He had obvious problems with the new president's politics, which he believed were not only socialist but pure patronage for Democratic constituencies like Black people and the poor. He also thought Obama's biography was suspiciously thin for someone who'd risen so high, so fast. He insisted that there had to be someone putting up the money and pulling the strings, like Valerie Jarrett. But it was no secret inside the network that Ailes always preferred a Democrat in the White House. "The reporters understood management was concerned that if there was a Republican president, Fox would be ignored by the White House," says Carl Cameron, who was with the network from its debut in 1996 and served as a senior political correspondent until 2017. "Whereas if the Republican lost the election, Fox could just let loose the hounds on whoever the Democratic president was for the next four years." After two terms of George W. Bush, Ailes was feeling bored, neglected, and eager for a change in programming. Inside the network, the joke about its irrelevance during the Bush years became "the Bush White House treats Fox News like the Democrats treat the NAACP. They ignore us." Being in the opposition was also more suited to Ailes's way of operating, which the political operative Lee Atwater once described as having two speeds: "Attack and destroy."

He hired the radio personality and CNN Headline News host Glenn Beck and gave him an hour-long 5 P.M. show that debuted the day before Obama's inauguration. Beck loved the symbolism of Doug Hoffman's campaign, and the race became one of his biggest story lines in his first year on the air at Fox. He framed it for his audience as a *Mr. Smith Goes to Washington* story of "the average guy" who wages an against-all-odds battle against a political machine. His support was essential to Hoffman's rise as a national Tea Party star. Beck's program was drawing close to three million viewers at the peak of its success in 2009. During their conversations on radio and television, Beck usually did most of the talking. The taciturn Hoffman would smile uncomfortably at the softball questions like "Do you like Karl Marx?" Beck sketched out for his viewers how a Scozzafava defeat would be the moment the political world would have to take the conservative movement seriously. "Do you think if you win, the parties will begin to see that this movement is real?" he asked Hoffman in late October. Hoffman answered that he did and captured in a few words how he and people like him saw the race as something much larger than a single seat in Congress: "I'm fighting for the heart and soul of the Republican Party."

Beck, a former FM radio disc jockey, was famous for his ponderous, stream-of-consciousness monologues and sinister insinuations about the motives of people he considered unpatriotic. In 2006, Beck demanded that Keith Ellison, a Black Muslim who had just been elected to Congress in Minnesota, demonstrate his loyalty to America on the air during their interview. "Sir, prove to me that you are not working with our enemies," Beck said. He borrowed heavily from the anticommunist tradition of American conservatism in attacking Van Jones, an adviser on clean energy who was Black, and other Obama administration figures as radicals who were hiding anti-American views. Beck's fusillades against the Obama White House often involved Black members of the administration, notes Anita Dunn, who went from the Obama campaign to serve as White House communications director for part of the first term. "Valerie was on that whiteboard a lot. And so was Van Jones," she says, referring to the prop Beck used in his studio to visually connect all the conspiratorial dots he drew for his audience.

Beck's show quickly grew into a platform for conservative candidates in the Tea Party era because of how closely he tied his political brand to the nascent uprising. When Tea Party organizers declared April 15, Tax Day, a national day of protest against government spending, Fox sent Beck to broadcast his show live from the Alamo, where he hosted Ted Nugent—the rock singer who had told Obama to "suck on my machine gun." The involvement of media stars like Beck represented a new phase in the symbiotic relationship between Fox News and the American right. Beck's vast reach gave him a unique ability to elevate candidates, rivaled perhaps only by Sarah

Palin at that time, whose own professional relationship with Fox as a $1 million per year on-air personality would begin in January 2010.

Palin, who had accrued more than $500,000 in legal bills while fighting numerous ethics complaints lodged against her as governor, resigned the office in July 2009. Alaska's liberal ethics laws gave any state resident the right to file a complaint, and the volume of charges leveled at her after the election increased dramatically. It was a waste of too much money and time—hers and the state of Alaska's, she said. But the timing was advantageous for someone who sought to establish herself more firmly as a conservative brand at a moment when the leaderless Tea Party movement was just taking off. She brought on a small group of staff to help her with her growing list of projects, which included writing her first memoir for HarperCollins, *Going Rogue,* and to deal with the deluge of media requests. Palin chose to communicate in those days primarily through her Facebook page because her team, which now included Rebecca Mansour as the lead author of her public statements, convinced her she could bypass the mainstream media and speak directly to people in their feeds. "She had a website," Mansour says, explaining how she prevailed on Palin to see the power in social media. "Instead of having all these people come to you, you're going to go straight to them." Palin agreed. And the first fire she lit was a doozy. When Palin was in San Diego in August, working on the manuscript for *Going Rogue,* she sent a draft of a post criticizing Obama's healthcare proposal to Mansour. Mansour read it over and deleted a phrase she thought was unnecessary: "Obama's death panel." She sent it back to Palin, who insisted that Mansour restore it. Her reasoning, based on a false claim that critics of Obama's had spread that summer, was that she'd be damned if her baby with Down Syndrome was going to have his healthcare withheld by some board of Obama's bureaucrats.

Before Palin's post, most Americans had never heard the phrase "death panel." A *PolitiFact* analysis, which rated the claim false, found no previous instances of it in news accounts of the healthcare debate. But Palin gave it a place in the American political lexicon, making it synonymous with the pernicious brand of right-wing mis-information that Obama's critics hurled his way. Rumors of these nonexistent death panels got so out of hand that Obama had to re-fute Palin's words in an address to the nation a few weeks later, call-ing it "a lie, plain and simple." This pleased Palin. "Obama had to call a joint session of Congress to address it," says Mansour, noting how far a simple Facebook post could go. For Palin, the lesson had nothing to do with being labeled a liar by the president or having her words picked apart by fact-checkers at a website she didn't read. She learned that social media could be her workaround with the networks and newspapers that she wanted nothing to do with.

Before Hoffman, Palin had never endorsed a candidate for office in her new capacity as the darling of the right. On October 22, she wrote a simple Facebook post that gave Hoffman the single biggest day of fundraising of his campaign. So many donations flooded his campaign website that it crashed. "Best of all," she wrote, "Doug Hoffman has not been anointed by any political machine." Along with Beck's coverage on Fox, Palin's support, and the backing of conservative groups like the Club for Growth, which steered more than $1 million to him in ads and direct financial support, all the machinery of the new right was clicking into place for Hoffman. "It was a coalition," Warfield says. "Maybe not a structured coalition, but it reflected the right-of-center consensus emerging."

One of the biggest players in this new coalition wasn't supposed to be there at all. As an unwritten rule, Tea Party activists did not talk about social issues. The large groups and smaller local outfits that comprised the movement's disparate national network often didn't agree on much. But as a general principle they agreed to steer clear of issues like abortion and same-sex marriage, at least in their offi-cial messaging, because including them would have compromised the movement's self-declared identity as politically independent. That made the arrival of three socially conservative groups—the Susan B. Anthony List (SBA List), the American Principles Project (APP), and the National Organization for Marriage—audacious.

In late October, a dozen staffers set up a command center at the Watertown Days Inn. Maps of the Twenty-third District covered the walls. Empty styrofoam coffee cups littered the tables and dressers. In one corner, a few Scozzafava signs were conspicuously leaning up against the wall, pilfered from front yards by an overzealous staffer. A small picture of Jesus and the Virgin Mary rested on top of the television. From here, they set out to visit area churches and the local chapters of antiabortion groups to recruit volunteers for a door-knocking operation.

The feeling of being unwanted was nothing new for people like Marjorie Dannenfelser, the Susan B. Anthony List's president, or Frank Cannon, a veteran social conservative activist who mentored her and wore two hats as the strategist for both the SBA List and APP. He looked at the election in New York's Twenty-third District as a chance to demand what he believed was long overdue recognition for the political muscle that social conservatives could flex. Cannon, a stout toadstool of a man with jet-black hair who puffed cigars constantly, describes the attitude most Republicans held toward pro-life activists for most of his career as generally dismissive. "We set the priorities. You're part of the coalition, and your job is to elect us," he says. He saw his fellow social conservatives as hopelessly stuck on defense, he explains, with "no plan to go from being the bastard stepchild of the movement to a constituency that would matter. This was really a shot across the bow."

New York's Twenty-third District offered a prime opportunity. They could send a message to the national party that there would be a cost if they continued to back candidates who were not pro-life. "If the party was not going to be serious about this, we were not going to acquiesce," Cannon explains. He convinced Dannenfelser and other allies that they should invest in a new kind of strategy that borrowed from the strong-arm tactics of the right's model for stick-over-carrot political enforcement: the National Rifle Association. "You have to make it politically painful for people who are going to betray you," Cannon told his colleagues. "She's got to lose." For the first time they were targeting Republicans who were blessed by the national and local party, and gambling that their campaign wouldn't cause conservatives to split the vote and hand the election to the Democrat. But if it did, that would be fine as long as it advanced their larger ambitions. They were moving their organizations in line with the culture of the Tea Party. And the Tea Party aimed to punish. "This was a punitive expedition against the liberal Republicans," says Warfield.

Dannenfelser, a forty-three-year-old mother of five young children, did not start out in politics aiming to be a renegade Republican. She wasn't against abortion when she joined the College Republicans at Duke University and recalls arguing the pro-choice side in a mock debate once because it was what most other Republican women she knew believed. She was raised in the Episcopal Church, hardly a hotbed of fiery social conservatism. But her politics started leaning harder to the right after she spent a summer in Washington working for the Heritage Foundation as an intern. The program exposed her to the more orthodox side of conservative ideology that was ascendant during the Reagan years. When Dannenfelser graduated in 1988, she got a job working in the Capitol Hill office of Alan Mollohan, a congressman from West Virginia who was both a Democrat and a member of the House pro-life caucus, which appealed to her newfound political and religious sensibilities. She converted to Catholicism. (Two decades later, in a full-circle moment that underscored her and the anti-abortion movement's transformation, Dannenfelser would use the SBA List's resources against Mollohan and help defeat him for voting for Obama's healthcare plan because it contained provisions that funded some abortions.) Dannenfelser was immediately struck by the gender divide between the pro-life lawmakers and those who were pro-choice. On her side, she says, "It was all men." On the other side there were women— empowered and confident women whose politics she disliked but whose station and success she couldn't help but envy: Pat Schroeder, Nita Lowey, Barbara Boxer. As Dannenfelser sat in on committee meetings for hours at a time, the imbalance gnawed at her. "It was just so unbelievably frustrating. They owned that. No matter how good or how smart the women on our side were, they couldn't have equal standing." She suggested starting a caucus for pro-life women but says that Republicans balked, telling her, "We don't do identity politics."

Dannenfelser left Capitol Hill after a few years to join the SBA List as it was just getting its footing as an emerging political player. The group's name was an indication of the hard-nosed politics it was capable of engaging in. The "list" part was an intentional echo of the influential pro-choice political group Emily's List. And appropriating the name of the famous suffragette and feminist icon was pure audacity. The SBA List's founders ignored the fact that Anthony's views on abortion were, at best, disputed, claiming that she had revealed her true beliefs in an anonymous article from 1869 whose author had signed with the initial A.

The anti-abortion movement of the early 1990s was not yet the fearsome and sophisticated political machine it would become, capable of elevating candidates it supported and defeating those it didn't. While it was energized and large, its focus was on civil disobedience and attention-grabbing protests. This was the heyday of groups like Operation Rescue, whose members threw themselves down in abortion clinic driveways and formed human chains to block women from going inside. Congress made blocking clinic access illegal in 1994. And that's when Dannenfelser says she realized how truly outmatched the pro-life forces were. She recalls watching other lobbyists operate during her time on Capitol Hill. All of them, even the dairy lobbyists, she says, "took themselves so seriously." And she asked herself, "How do we do that too?"

Scozzafava felt boxed in as the opposition to her from the right multiplied. Anti-tax activists had been badgering her for weeks on social media to sign Grover Norquist's pledge not to raise taxes. She didn't like the inflexibility of a pledge that committed candidates to hold the line on any issue in perpetuity. It was another way that the demands of conservative activists were making the Republican Party more doctrinaire, she believed. In October, when she visited Representative Pete Sessions, the chairman of the House GOP's political committee, he raised the issue and said it was becoming a problem.

"You really need to sign this," he told her. She tried to resist and asked him to explain what the pledge meant and why it was so important. Ultimately she relented. And then they made her sit for a photo shoot as she scrawled out her signature. "They got out the ceremonial pen and the cameras," she recalls.

On the Friday before Halloween in 2009, Scozzafava received the first batch of numbers from the final poll her campaign would conduct. The results were so bad that she decided she would quit the race. She couldn't wait four more days until the election—or even twelve more hours before the rest of the data from the poll was analyzed by her strategists. She talked her decision over with her husband as they sat in the parking lot of a Stewart's, the gas station and ice cream store chain that's ubiquitous in the uppermost parts of Upstate New York. She was upset but relieved, seeing no conceivable path to victory and badly wanting it all to be over. She didn't tell anyone on her staff about her decision that night. She had not decided then whether she should do what many of her fellow Republicans were pressuring her to do and endorse Hoffman. She also did not rule out endorsing the Democrat, Bill Owens, a well-known lawyer she thought would be perfectly capable in the job. Senator Chuck Schumer called and implied that her support would be greatly appreciated. Owens called her as well. But Hoffman never did.

It was a different phone call over the weekend that helped Scozzafava make up her mind about whether she wanted to capitulate and throw in with the Tea Party, which would have been the politically smart thing to do as a Republican. But she was thinking as a mother first. Saturday had been painful. Her campaign made the official statement announcing her withdrawal in the morning. Later, when a local television reporter caught up with her outside her office, she was still so overwhelmed that her eyes welled up with tears as she spoke. She drove herself home and sat in the driveway for a minute. Her phone rang and it was her twenty-year-old daughter, who was away at college. "Mom, I'm so proud of you," she said. Then she revealed why: She was a lesbian. "Honestly, I had no inkling," Scozzafava says. She barely registered the news before moving on. "Oh, that's nice. What else is going on?" But as she sat in church the next morning, which she did every Sunday but chose not to draw attention to while campaigning, she came to the realization that she had to endorse Owens.

Hoffman lost on Election Day by about forty-three hundred votes. Owens became the first Democrat elected in that region of New York since the nineteenth century. It was a defeat for Republicans on what was otherwise a good night. A federal prosecutor in New Jersey, Chris Christie, would be the next governor. Robert McDonnell, the state attorney general in Virginia, won the race for governor. Steele declared the results that night a sign of a "Republican renaissance" and dismissed concerns over whether the fight in New York was a prelude to a longer, more destructive civil war in the party. "This is healthy in that it exposes the fault lines that we can learn to avoid," Steele said.

But conservative activists came away with a different lesson, and conflict avoidance had nothing to do with it. Cannon, Dannenfelser, and other Hoffman supporters declared victory in defeat. Dannenfelser said, "It might be a blow to some people, it's not a blow to us." The head of the National Organization for Marriage, Brian Brown, insisted the movement had achieved its goal, which was always "to make clear that the Republican Party cannot take someone as liberal as Dede Scozzafava and thrust her out on the voters and expect the voters just to accept it." Marilyn Musgrave, a former congresswoman from Colorado who worked with Dannenfelser on the Hoffman-Scozzafava race, declared a breakthrough moment for social conservative activists after decades of being patted on the head by the national party. "This is probably the most amazing coalition-building I've seen in a long time—probably decades," she said. The lesson Republicans should take to heart in Washington: "Don't just assume we're yours," Musgrave said.

CHAPTER 3

The Popularist

If you think the guy is crazy, he's not.
He's doing what's always worked for him.
—HANK SHEINKOPF, referring to Donald Trump

A s the spasm of political protest sweeping the country built toward a full-blown escalation in the culture wars by the end of 2009, Feisal Abdul Rauf had reasons to be optimistic. It had been eight years since 9/11. And Muslims like Abdul Rauf, a prominent imam from the New York City area, saw that many Americans were willing to separate their religion from the radical strains that inspired terrorism. An idea came to him when he was traveling the country in the weeks after the attacks, speaking to audiences at universities, think tanks, and churches. Often people asked him a version of the same question: Why did the hijackers commit such a violent act in the name of his religion? He found these conversations cathartic, if occasionally frustrating, and eye-opening. Then during one trip to a church in Greenwich, Connecticut, someone asked him a question he had never heard before. A woman—"a lovely lady," he recalls—said to him, "What can I do, as a Christian, to help?"

Abdul Rauf, sixty-one, who wore a closely cropped white beard and had a slight build, thought it was such a profound question that he would devote the rest of his career trying to answer it. He realized that Muslims like him and Christians like the woman in Greenwich did not spend a lot of time thinking about ways to bridge the cultural gaps between them. He decided that he wanted to dedicate himself to facilitating a new kind of openness between faiths—a way, he says, to help people "talk through those issues where religion was deemed to be a factor in the conflict." This was the mission of a nonprofit organization he founded in 2004 called the Cordoba Initiative, named after an ancient city in Spain where Muslims, Christians, and Jews lived side by side in relative harmony. After several years of looking for a permanent home for the organization, a thirty-six-year-old real estate developer named Sharif el-Gamal presented the imam with an attractive offer to build on a parcel of land in Manhattan, two blocks from Ground Zero. El-Gamal worshiped at a nearby building he found to be depressingly cramped and wanted to find a new place for the community to pray. He had been looking into the shuttered Burlington Coat Factory at 45 Park Place between West Broadway and Church Street. The neighborhood left a lot to be desired. There was a strip club, a betting parlor, and a porn shop all nearby—not to mention incessant noise and dust from the ongoing construction at the World Trade Center site. And the building itself was not in the best shape, having been damaged on September 11 when a piece of landing gear from one of the hijacked planes fell through the roof. A few blocks away on Warren Street, there was a mosque that had been operating for years, its presence unremarkable and uncontroversial. Abdul Rauf thought it was a fine place to build what he conceived of as the Muslim equivalent of a YMCA or a Jewish Community Center—a gathering place inspired by his religion but where people of all faiths would feel welcome.

El-Gamal rounded up $4.85 million to pay cash for the building—a price well below what the owners had once been asking. City records documented the sale on July 16, 2009, and listed "community center" as the use for the property. Abdul Rauf was not naïve about the optics of building so close to the hallowed ground where more than twenty-six hundred people had been murdered by Islamic terrorists. He sought out leaders of different faiths in New York and local politicians, whom he found to be supportive. And by the time he was ready to announce the plans, he had lined up the support of

Mayor Michael Bloomberg's administration. "We as New York Muslims have as much of a commitment to rebuilding New York as anybody," declared Fatima Shama, the city's director of immigrant affairs when Abdul Raul unveiled his plans. Abdul Rauf believed that building on a spot that still bore physical scars from the September 11 attacks was a powerful rejection of what the terrorists did that day. And when he went public with his vision in *The New York Times* in early December 2009, he insisted that Cordoba House "sends the opposite statement to what happened on 9/11." Plans for Cordoba House called for amenities like a pool, a basketball court, a restaurant, and a five-hundred-seat performing arts center. In the basement of the fifteen-floor complex would be a space where Muslims could pray.

There was little backlash. But one objection to the project hinted at the fury on the horizon. It was small but immediate. Pamela Geller, a New Yorker and occasional right-wing media talking head who published a right-wing blog, *Atlas Shrugs,* from her Upper East Side apartment, saw the *Times* article when it went up on the paper's website on December 8 and immediately registered her disgust. "I don't know which is more grotesque . . . jihad or the NY Times preening of it," Geller wrote in what would be the first of many articles, press releases, and statements on Cordoba and the imam that she would disseminate to the wider right-wing media universe. Geller, fifty-one, was a well-to-do former executive for *The New York Observer.* She had developed a fixation on Islam after September 11, coming to believe that the religion was inherently violent and impervious to moderating influences. She became a regular commenter on websites that, according to a 2010 profile in *The New York Times,* "focused on Islamic militancy." She referred to Muslims as savages, insisted there were Islamic conspiracists working in the American government, and once posted a video online of herself prancing around in a bikini—in an apparent show of defiance against her perception of strict Islamic dress codes for women. She was also an early peddler of the "birther" lie about Obama's upbringing. Some of the disinformation she spread sounded downright delusional. One piece Geller posted to her blog in July 2008, written by someone using the pseudonym Techdude, claimed that the birth certificate Obama released to the public was actually an elaborate forgery, soaked in ink-erasing solvent so Obama's details could be filled in the blanks.

But that didn't stop conservative media heavyweights from taking her seriously. Geller was a pipeline into some of the biggest outlets on the right, with connections to Sean Hannity's producers, writers at the *New York Post,* and the editors of *Breitbart News,* a new player that was unsettling the media landscape. *Breitbart* brought Geller on as a contributor in late 2009 after the website's namesake founder, Andrew Breitbart, heard about her from his friend Stephen K. Bannon, a former investment banker and producer of conservative political documentaries. Bannon had read her blog and told Andrew that Geller was "a great lounge act" that could be much bigger. He agreed, and gave Geller a column she used to tell *Breitbart* readers of Muslims who were "sharpening their machetes for the beheading of the Jewish state." She attacked the Cordoba development as an act of "Islamic supremacism" perpetrated by Muslims who were "doing a victory dance on the hallowed burial ground of Ground Zero."

And up the right-wing media food chain the story went, from the *New York Post* to Fox News and eventually to Donald Trump. The public campaign Trump waged against the project is not a widely examined piece of his past. But his involvement in the "Ground Zero Mosque" controversy in the summer of 2010 was a formative chapter in his development as a politician and a prequel to his 2016 presidential run. It offered an early glimpse of his instinctual feel for identifying and inflaming culture war battles that resonated with the people who would become his political base. And it showed him how antagonizing powerful enemies was crucial to building that base.

But as much as the episode previewed the emotions and ideas that would energize the Trump movement, it also brought together many of the key players who would be instrumental to his rise. More than a half dozen of the conservative activists who assisted the campaign to stop the development from going forward would become major figures in the planning and running of Trump's 2016 race or crucial allies during his presidency. They included Bannon, chief of his first campaign and White House strategist; David N. Bossie, a senior strategist on both campaigns; Roger Stone and Sam Nunberg, two early advisers who influenced him as he decided whether to run; Jay Sekulow, his lawyer during his first impeachment trial; Hannity, his go-to Fox News host and friend; and Robert Mercer, one of his biggest financial backers. Many of the people opposing the project saw their fight in the same vein as they would see Trump's victory, and used the same David-versus-Goliath framing to describe it. "The Ground Zero Mosque story," as Geller wrote in an essay for *Breitbart,* reflecting on it years later, "is a story of ordinary Americans defeating powerful and moneyed elites." And there was Trump himself, who attempted to halt the development by offering to buy the property for more than the developers paid. Caught in the middle were establishment Republicans, who saw the potency of the issue and attempted to exploit the anger around it but discovered that it was pulling them toward an undeniably dark side of the burgeoning Tea Party movement.

The raging national debate over the project was sustained by coverage from the conservative media, which was entering a new phase of its evolution, pushed ever harder to the right by the same activist disruptors who were destabilizing the Republican Party. One veteran New York public relations consultant who was brought in by the developers to help contain the controversy, Hank Sheinkopf, recalls how Trump put the story on steroids. "It changed everything," he says.

And Trump, who recalls the episode wistfully, saw how easy it was as a celebrity to insert himself into one of the most combustible issues of the day and overtake the news cycle. "I've always gotten an inordinate amount of coverage, for whatever reason. And you ought to see this thing. It blew up," he says, offering a simple explanation for why he got involved. There wasn't anything especially ideological about it. He saw the polls showing a lack of public support for the Cordoba House and knew he was on the right side. "The politicians just weren't listening. And that included everybody. I mean, they would just try to be so politically correct." It was how Trump developed more confidence in his instincts about popular opinion—and what divides it—before he would test them on the national political stage. "He's always had one thing that's worked for him. And that's an intuitive sense of what his audience wants to hear," says Tony Fabrizio. "*His* audience. Not everyone."

Between December, when the *Times* ran its initial story, and early May, when the Cordoba House received a favorable nod from a local community board, there wasn't much commentary about it in the media, pro or con. Then the *Post,* via Geller, got wind of the story. Columnist Andrea Peyser appears to have been the first to introduce the falsehood that the project was a "mosque" to the media beyond the blogosphere, first in a brief mention in a piece on May 10 and then three days later in a column headlined MOSQUE MADNESS AT GROUND ZERO. Peyser interviewed Geller and quoted her at length, calling the development "a stab in the eye of America." Hannity, an avid consumer of the New York City tabloids who had a habit of ripping articles he found interesting straight out of the papers and handing them to his producers, saw Peyser's piece and booked Geller for his radio show the same afternoon. Hannity also kept up with Geller's blog. And as the story exploded over the coming weeks, Geller remained in regular contact with Hannity and his producers, emailing them with her latest items and updates on the protests she was helping organize, including one planned near Ground Zero on June 6, to coincide with the annual commemoration of D-Day. Given Hannity's stature in conservative media—he had a prime time Fox News program and a talk radio show with a reach that only heavy hitters like Limbaugh and Howard Stern could beat—Hannity was essential to keeping the story alive. He would keep up with it for weeks, teasing segments with sensational claims. He purported to have "chilling details" about the money behind Cordoba and attacked Abdul Rauf, for instance. "This man is an extremist," Hannity declared on July 15.

But the story couldn't have gained the prominence it did without another crucial accelerant: the Tea Party. The story had a natural and receptive audience in the people who were drawn to the movement for its espousal of traditional, grievance- and identity-based wedge politics. Local and national Tea Party–affiliated organizations joined Geller and her opposition campaign, which extended far beyond New York. In Tennessee, Geller was invited to speak at an event in May that she described as the "inaugural statewide Tea Party Convention." As she and another anti-Muslim activist, Robert Spencer, recruited supporters, they partnered with local political groups like the Staten Island Tea Party as well as 9/11 first responders, family members of people killed in the attacks, and Republican candidates for public office. As distortions and misinformation about the development and Abdul Rauf's background circulated more widely, the anger grew. The New York *Daily News* reported on the palpable hostility toward Cordoba House at a Tea Party gathering in Manhattan in May, quoting a forty-four-year-old union construction worker named Andy Sullivan, who told the paper, "That place is going to be a house of evil where plans to kill Americans will be hatched." Tea Party symbols were common sights at anti-mosque demonstrations. Geller's event on June 6 drew a large crowd to a square about a block from Ground Zero. Demonstrators waved the yellow Gadsden flag. They wore FDNY-branded gear and construction hard hats. At one point, a fight almost erupted when some of the demonstrators heard an Egyptian camera crew speaking in Arabic and started taunting them. "Go home!" several in the crowd shouted, mistakenly believing they were Muslims. In fact, they were Coptic Christians and opposed Cordoba House, which they explained to a journalist who approached them after the police intervened and escorted them away to safety.

With the help of Fox and the *Post,* Geller had two of the most powerful organs of conservative media on her side. But a new media player on the right that aggressively aligned itself with the Tea Party movement was emerging as a crucial source of "Ground Zero Mosque" coverage: *Breitbart News.* Andrew Breitbart, its founder, was equal parts polemicist and performance artist. Husky, standing six foot one with a mop of curly sandy hair, neither he nor his mouth ever seemed to stop moving. He caught two big breaks that helped him turn his small news aggregator into a website that would eventually draw tens of millions of readers every month. He befriended the right-wing internet pioneer Matt Drudge, who hired him to help post articles to his eponymous website, *The Drudge Report,* during off-hours. Sometimes Breitbart would post links on Drudge's site that would direct readers to Breitbart.com, giving him an early foundation for an audience. Drudge introduced Breitbart to Arianna Huffington, who hired Breitbart as her researcher as she was establishing herself as a famous left-of-center political commentator. Huffington would later bring him back on as she was preparing to launch her own website, *The Huffington Post,* in 2004, allowing him to have hands-on experience with one of the most successful online journalistic ventures of the decade.

As a publisher in his own right, Breitbart lowered the barrier to entry in conservative news in a way that Huffington did with her small army of liberal bloggers, many of them unpaid, and helped erode the journalistic standards those barriers preserved. As he tore down those guardrails, he also made truth and reality more subjective for his readers, and gave conservatives a playbook for how to level racially charged attacks without expressing any remorse about it. The moment the mainstream media started paying serious attention came in 2009 when he published a story about a hidden camera operation carried out by a young conservative activist named James O'Keefe. O'Keefe gave Breitbart a series of videos he had secretly recorded inside the offices of ACORN, a federally supported community organizing group. O'Keefe and a friend had posed as a pimp and a prostitute seeking tax advice from ACORN workers who blithely offered to help as the couple explained that their business involved smuggling underage girls into the country. What O'Keefe did wasn't journalism, certainly not under any conventional definition of the profession. As *The New Yorker* described his work, the undercover sting–style operation bore "a closer resemblance to the methods pioneered by Sacha Baron Cohen." There was also a racial component to the story. Many of the people ACORN registered to vote and provided assistance to were Black, and depicting it as a corrupt entity that offered advice to pimps and prostitutes played into ugly stereotypes. But Breitbart didn't care about being called a racist by liberals and bet that his readers wouldn't care either. He liked to claim that liberals lazily and dishonestly accused conservatives of racism. And in 2010, when Representative John Lewis, a civil rights icon, claimed that Tea Party demonstrators had hurled racial slurs at him, Breitbart insisted the incident had never happened and offered to donate $10,000 to the United Negro College Fund if Lewis could prove it. The ACORN story made him a media celebrity in his own right. He started getting recognized in public and approached by strangers offering him story ideas. He would listen for a little while, get distracted, and then give them his personal email. "I'll forget all this. So email me at andrew@breitbart .com," he'd say. He got a book contract for a memoir and hired a young writer named Ben Shapiro as his ghostwriter. As the number of staff at his website site grew, Bannon let Breitbart use space in his office in Santa Monica. And a conservative hedge fund mogul from New York, Robert Mercer, invested $10 million in the site to help fund its expansion.

The Breitbart-Geller partnership was born of the unique cultural moment unfolding inside the American right, as newcomers like Twitter and *Breitbart* were elevating controversial people and ideas beyond the conspiratorial fringes of the blogosphere. *Breitbart*'s coverage of a story would soon have the power to force the more traditional gatekeepers in the media to pay attention. In 2011, it published details about the online sexual exploits of Anthony Weiner, the New York congressman, forcing him to apologize and eventually resign. And when Breitbart oversaw the Weiner coverage, he became as big a figure in the saga as the congressman. On the day Weiner held a press conference to discuss the allegations—spurred on by *Breitbart*'s publication of explicit photos Weiner had taken of himself— Breitbart commandeered the event by walking up to the lectern and taking questions from reporters. Cable news carried it live. *Breit-*

bart's confrontational no-boundaries style erased the lines between political activism and journalism. Breitbart himself was the model. He spoke at Tea Party events. Geller made him a featured speaker at one of her anti–Cordoba House rallies. Appearances like these elevated his visibility in right-wing circles and established him as an important ally of the Tea Party movement in a way that other conservative media like Fox News did not tolerate with its star hosts. In fact, Fox chief Roger Ailes forced Hannity to cancel his planned appearance at a Tea Party rally in April 2010 out of concern that it looked too cozy, demonstrating that there were at least some journalistic boundaries the network was wary of flouting so conspicuously.

No one would mistake Rick Lazio for someone with the fire of a Tea Party insurgent burning inside him. But in the summer of 2010, as the Ground Zero Mosque story exploded and Lazio looked for a way to supercharge his campaign for governor of New York, he had to try to act like it. He was a pragmatist and a professional politician—a former assistant district attorney and county legislator who went on to represent Long Island in Congress for four terms in the 1990s. He had a reputation of being nonideological and carefully attuned to the politics of his district, voting with conservatives to cut social services spending and with liberals on gun control. Sometimes he split the difference, like his vote to approve two of the four articles of impeachment brought against Bill Clinton. *The New York Times Magazine* found Lazio so bland and inoffensive that it once described him as "the candidate from 'Pleasantville.' "

Lazio recalls sensing that his politics might be mismatched for the maelstrom of 2010 when he was campaigning upstate and a conservative activist asked him to sign an unusual pledge. As governor, would he agree to slash 20 percent of the state budget? Lazio thought the idea was absurd. He had often voted with Republicans on budgetary matters, but also knew that taking such a huge bite out of money used to fund everything from public universities to the state police was not fiscally conservative. It was insane. "These were not people who were looking to find solutions through consensus or negotiation. They were confrontational, distrustful, and difficult to deal with," Lazio says. He understood where many of them were coming from, especially those who'd struggled in the depressed economy upstate. He explains that they thought that politicians from downstate, like him, "had forgotten about them, didn't care about them, and just imposed their will on them—which in their minds led to businesses closing, young people moving out, and a drain on their tax base. "That was like dry tinder," he says. As he campaigned across New York, activists continued asking him to sign several other pledges to eliminate various parts of the government he says he found to be "often wholly unrealistic."

The problem for Lazio was that his primary opponent was a wholly unrealistic guy, and many Republican voters liked that. In more ordinary times, Carl Paladino, a wealthy businessman from Buffalo, would not have stood a chance of winning the Republican nomination. He said his idea of cleaning up the state government was to "take a baseball bat to Albany." He talked about imprisoning the speaker of the State Assembly, Sheldon Silver, an Orthodox Jew from Manhattan, in a Roman cage and parading him around from town to town. One of Paladino's favorite shticks was repeating Howard Beale's cri de coeur from the movie Network—"I'm mad as hell, and I'm not going to take this anymore!" He told a newspaper that he wanted to turn state prisons into dormitories for welfare recipients, where they could work state-sponsored jobs and receive lessons in personal hygiene. He had been caught forwarding racist email threads about the Obamas. He suggested using the state police to arrest and deport undocumented immigrants. His advisers included Roger Stone and Tony Fabrizio. Running against someone so outrageous should be easy, Lazio thought. "We should debate him," he suggested to his campaign team. But one of his consultants, the veteran Republican strategist Arthur Finkelstein, warned him that might actually do Lazio more harm than good. There were plenty of voters who didn't think Paladino was such a clown, Finkelstein ex-

plained. And as someone who understood the fissures in the electorate and how to extract more votes from them better than almost any
consultant in the GOP, Finkelstein saw a way Lazio could get a clear
leg up on his opponent.

It was the Ground Zero Mosque. Finkelstein had looked at polling on the issue and saw that far more New Yorkers opposed than
supported it. If Lazio came out publicly against it, he said it would
help him with conservatives and Tea Party–affiliated voters. It was
also an issue that was attracting a huge amount of national media
attention. It was a no-brainer as far as Finkelstein was concerned.
Lazio wasn't entirely comfortable with it but trusted his adviser,
who had honed his craft since the 1960s by devising campaigns that
often appealed to the negative emotions of voters. Finkelstein was a
bundle of contradictions. Gay and a nonpracticing Jew, he worked
for candidates like Senator Jesse Helms of North Carolina, a hero of
the religious right. Finkelstein's protégés were scattered throughout
high-level Republican campaigns for national office, and included
Fabrizio (Buchanan, Dole), Stone (Nixon, Reagan), Charlie Black
(Reagan, McCain), Stuart Stevens (George W. Bush, Mitt Romney),
and Frank Luntz, the consultant who was well known for his televised focus groups with voters. Finkelstein preferred working for
candidates with rough edges over to-the-manner-born Republicans
like George H. W. Bush. "He was more respectful of the unwashed,"
says Craig Shirley, a historian and former Republican consultant
who studied under Finkelstein. Shirley says Finkelstein once told him
a story about refusing to even meet with Bush about a job on his
presidential campaign.

The foundation of Finkelstein's approach to campaigns was a
six-part theory on the divisions in the electorate, which broke down
mostly on a left-right scale. It would prove to be both enduring and
prescient. He thought that conservative Democrats were the most
important swing constituency, and that Republicans could win tight
races by appealing to these mostly blue-collar voters. And one way
to effectively do that, he believed, was by tapping into voter disillu-
sionment with candidates they saw as too far left. In 1994, he helped

George Pataki defeat Mario Cuomo in his bid for a fourth term with a memorable, alliterative one-liner: Cuomo had been "too liberal for too long."

Finkelstein took an expansive view of the truth in campaigning. Explaining how he viewed American politics in a lecture at an academic institute in Prague in 2011, he said that the most overwhelming factor in any campaign is "what people do not know." He dryly observed what "a wonderful business" politics was because of how easily it can be separated from reality. "In politics, it's what you perceive to be true that's true, not truth," he said. Starting with the fact that no mosque was going to be built at Ground Zero, Cordoba House was precisely one of those issues where perception eclipsed the truth.

Lazio thought that well-intentioned voters had sincere misgivings about the project, seeing it as insensitive to 9/11 victims. And he ultimately agreed with Finkelstein to make it a campaign issue. He focused on Abdul Rauf, raising questions of how he was financing the project. The imam had come under intense scrutiny from opponents of the development, who uncovered problematic comments from his past, including a *60 Minutes* interview from 2001 in which he claimed that American policies were "an accessory" to the 9/11 attacks. People started looking into the project's financiers and linked one of them to a charity that years earlier was found to have had connections to Hamas. In July, Lazio called on the state's attorney general and Democratic gubernatorial candidate, Andrew Cuomo, to investigate. The strategy put Paladino on the defensive. And Paladino responded by declaring that if he were governor he would use the power of eminent domain to seize control of the construction site.

When New York's Landmarks Preservation Commission put the issue on its agenda for review in July—opponents were now hoping to make another run at stopping it by arguing that the old Burlington Coat Factory building was a historically significant structure—Lazio decided to attend and speak out. About one hundred people showed up at the meeting, which was in a lecture hall of an Upper East Side college. Lazio, more measured than many in the crowd, made the case for a delay to allow for a more thorough investigation into the financing. When el-Gamal, the young developer, rose to speak, he was heckled. Some shouted "Liar!" and "Murderer!" at him. Others there called Cordoba "a citadel of Islamic supremacy" and "sacrilege on sacred ground." One compared the construction to defiling a battlefield where thousands of American soldiers were killed, saying that it was like "removing the sunken ship from Pearl Harbor to erect a memorial to the Japanese kamikazes." By the time Lazio left the meeting, it was clear to him that he hadn't fully appreciated how ugly things could get.

Abdul Rauf was slow to accept how heated the debate was becoming, and how he had become a target for some of the most hateful attacks. "It took me a while to see that it was part of a bigger picture of this battle of who we are as Americans," he says. He was traveling out of the country in July and August. When he returned, he found hate mail addressed to him depicting Muslims as cartoon pigs. Someone hurled a brick through a window of his house in New Jersey. He was sleeping four hours a night. Friends started telling him he should stay somewhere else until things blew over. And then one day, an official from the New York Police Department visited him with a chilling disclosure: They had received a credible threat against his life.

As activists from across the right mobilized that summer in opposition to the development, there was a convergence of groups and conservative leaders old and new. People who were part of the existing faith-based political network found common cause with the new Tea Party–aligned groups. Newcomers included national groups like Liberty Central, which was founded by Justice Clarence Thomas's wife, Ginni, and counted among its board members Leonard Leo, a senior executive with the conservative Federalist Society and the former head of Catholic outreach for the RNC under George W. Bush. Liberty Central organized a petition that claimed to have ten thousand signatures opposing the development. Franklin Graham, the evangelical leader and son of Billy Graham, gave an interview to *Time* in which he insisted that Muslims were marking the territory around Ground Zero so they could claim it as their own. "Everything within that area is now Islamic land, just like they claimed Israel as Islamic land," Graham said, calling Islam "a religion of hatred." The project had become a new land of opportunity for right-wing political entrepreneurialism. Sarah Palin weighed in on Twitter a few days after the Landmarks Commission meeting and urged "peace-seeking Muslims" to call for the project to be stopped. "It stabs hearts. Pls reject it in interest of healing," she wrote. Newt Gingrich sat down with *Fox & Friends* and equated the project to the Nazis putting up a sign next to the Holocaust museum in Washington.

Lazio's involvement in the mosque debate got him the bump he was looking for. *Meet the Press* booked him. Donations came pouring in after his appearance at the Landmarks Commission hearing. Robert Mercer, the eccentric New York hedge fund CEO who was one of many wealthy conservatives who'd doubled down on dumping their fortunes into right-wing political activities since Obama's election, agreed to help. He wrote a $1 million check to the Conservative Party of New York, which used the money to finance an ad campaign claiming that Abdul Rauf was a terrorist sympathizer. Another backer of conservative causes, Lawrence Kadish, contributed $75,000 to Lazio. But it wasn't enough. And he lost the GOP nomination to Paladino in September.

It wasn't the first time that an ugly fight over questions of national identity and loyalty erupted in nearly the same spot. Almost exactly forty years earlier, in the same part of downtown Manhattan, the "Hard Hat Riot" of May 8, 1970, broke out when hundreds of construction workers attacked a group of anti–Vietnam War protesters who had gathered on Wall Street. It was the day Richard Nixon's "silent majority" was silent no more—and it became one of the most indelible images of his presidency, symbolizing the class and generational divides that were ripping the country apart. The workers, many of whom stormed over from the unfinished World Trade Center, chanted "All the way, USA" and "Love it or leave it" as they punched and pushed their way through the crowd. Seventy people were injured. *The New York Times* described the scene on its front page the next day as a "a wild noontime melee." Nixon, who was grateful for the show of support and steaming with resentment about the mass demonstrations against his war policy, expressed his thanks by inviting leaders of the city's building trades and long-shoremen's unions to the White House. They presented him with his own hard hat, inscribed COMMANDER IN CHIEF. The hard hat would become the new totem for the aggrieved white working-class Nixon supporter. The marriage between Nixon's Republican Party and the blue-collar union worker would mark the beginning of a political realignment that would gradually unwind the Democrats' monop-oly with organized labor—one of the most enduring and successful political alliances of the twentieth century.

Kadish, a commercial real estate developer who helped found the pro-Israel Republican Jewish Coalition and provided funding for an occasional documentary of Bannon's, was involved in another proj-ect that summer relating to Cordoba. He had sought out Bannon and David Bossie, a longtime conservative activist, to make a film about the project and the debate it sparked. For the working title, Bannon recalls that he planned to use a historical reference to the expulsion of Muslims from Spain. Since Cordoba House had been named for a Spanish city with a rich Muslim history, Bannon wanted there to be no subtlety about his point: "We're running them out of New York," he says. As Bannon watched the protests, he recalls being struck by the rawness of the emotion. "The anger," he says. "Remember, 9/11 is years ago. . . . This is the most fire-breathing thing I've ever seen." And it struck him that while there were Tea Party elements to the demonstration, this wasn't a typical Tea Party crowd. "All the way down that street it is packed. And it's guys in hard hats, union guys."

As he was editing film one day that summer, Bossie, his frequent collaborator, called. Could he come up to New York to meet with Donald Trump, who was interested in discussing a possible presi-dential campaign?

"President?" Bannon asked. "Of what country?"

"You understand the Tea Party movement," Bossie, a hardened

veteran of the Republican wars with the Clintons during the 1990s, told Bannon. "Explain it to him." Bannon reluctantly agreed. He had never met Trump. Bossie told him it was best to keep his presentation as short as possible, so he prepared no visuals or written material.

Once they got to Trump Tower, Bossie ran through some of the potential trip wires that Trump's political opponents were sure to exploit, like his inconsistent voting record. "What voting record?" Trump asked, surprised they knew anything about what he had done in previous elections.

"The issue is, you don't vote," said Bossie, who had gone to the minimal trouble of looking up Trump's information in public records.

"Of course I vote. Every election. Every Republican primary. I voted for Rudy," Trump said. Bossie showed him the records, which proved Trump indeed had not. Caught in his lie, Trump asked worriedly, "Do you know how I voted?"

When it was Bannon's turn to speak again, he explained how the eruptions of anger happening across the country were part of a long tradition of populist tremblors in American politics. Populism, Bannon said, thrived under leaders like William Jennings Bryan, who empowered Americans to push back against political leaders who were seen as detached, unresponsive, and corrupt. Trump seized on one word. "A popular-ist. Yes, that's what I am."

Bannon corrected him: "No, you mean populist."

Trump repeated himself. "Yeah, a popular-ist. I'm a popular-ist." Bannon let it drop, seeing no point in trying to dissuade him. Trump also lit up when their discussion turned to the Tea Party, and he claimed to be a kindred spirit with the people he had seen on television wearing tri-corner hats and waving those yellow flags. "I love the Tea Party," he told Bossie and Bannon. "I am the Tea Party. They love me."

Bannon couldn't put Trump's "popularist" talk out of his head. Later, it occurred to him that while Trump surely hadn't intended to coin a term for his own school of political theory, he was unwittingly revealing what he understood politics was to be to him. "You know what? He was right," Bannon says. "He's about popularity. He is a popularist." Bannon notes that Trump's fixation on always taking the path he thinks will earn him the most public affirmation has upsides but also significant downsides. "He is the classic Greek tragic hero. His greatest weaknesses are also his greatest strengths. It's Oedipus. Everything you try to do to get yourself out of it just pulls you back in deeper."

When the 9/11 attacks derailed much of the domestic policy work George W. Bush had hoped to focus on, it forced his and the nation's attention to Iraq and Afghanistan and the threat of terrorism at home. Bush adopted aggressive policies, including approving the use of torture, that allowed for the surveillance and interrogation of Muslims suspected of aiding terrorist plots. But as much as those policies created outrage in Muslim communities, the Bush administration was also deeply worried about the possibility that the more than one billion Muslims in the world would view the United States as hostile to their faith. This was not just an ethical concern but a national security imperative for the Bush administration. Six days after the attacks, Bush visited an Islamic cultural center in Washington and declared, "Islam is peace." Three years later, on the opening night of the Republican National Convention at Madison Square Garden, the Bush campaign invited the Muslim chaplain of the New York City Police Department to deliver the invocation.

The Republican Party's work with minority outreach continued after Bush's reelection under Ken Mehlman at the helm of the Republican National Committee. Mehlman made it a mission to try to build ties to immigrant enclaves and minority communities across the country. His approach began with a basic supposition: If Republicans weren't physically present in certain communities, they would never win the support of those communities. So he personally visited them. Speaking to a Somali and Hmong audience in Minneapolis, he asked them to "give us a chance." At a gathering of the NAACP in 2005, he acknowledged the GOP's history of tolerating racism and formally apologized for its "Southern Strategy." It was one of the most explicit acknowledgments from a party official that Republicans had tried to exploit white prejudices. "Some Republicans gave up on winning the African American vote, looking the other way or trying to benefit politically from racial polarization," Mehlman told the civil rights group. "I am here today as the Republican chairman to tell you we were wrong."

Less than two years after Bush left office, inclusiveness was no longer a value that was overwhelmingly popular in the party. The person at the Landmarks Commission hearing who invoked the image of honoring Japanese pilots at Pearl Harbor was a young, aspiring conservative campaign operative named Sam Nunberg, who was the deputy political director at a Christian conservative legal group, the American Center for Law and Justice. The center's best-known figure and public face was its legal counsel, Jay Sekulow, a conservative lawyer and frequent cable news talking head. Sekulow had recently taken up the case of a firefighter who was at Ground Zero on 9/11 and wanted to sue to stop Cordoba from being built. And Nunberg, who was not exactly a Central Casting consultant for the religious right, was helping Sekulow out. He threw himself into the campaign to halt construction, by combing through old interviews Abdul Rauf had given and reading his published writings.

Nunberg was Jewish, lived in Manhattan, and loved professional wrestling and listening to Mark Levin on the radio. Eager to establish a reputation in the world of conservative operatives, he started emailing news articles and video clips of his work with Sekulow to more prominent consultants. One of them was Roger Stone, the Finkelstein protégé and Trump friend who was one of the GOP's most notorious practitioners of political sabotage. Stone was also close to Paladino, and one day, Stone wrote Nunberg back and asked if they could speak by phone. Nunberg passed along to Stone some of the research that he had done into the imam and his writings. Nunberg explained how he was helping organize some of the demonstrations at the construction site, where protesters were starting to gather in larger numbers. Intrigued by what Nunberg was telling him, Stone suggested that they get together in person. After a meeting at a bar in Manhattan during the New York State Republican

Party convention in June, they grew more friendly. And then, Nunberg recalls, one day Stone extended to him an invitation that he couldn't refuse: "I'm going to see Trump. Come with me."

When Stone and Nunberg went to see Donald Trump in his office on the twenty-sixth floor of Trump Tower that summer, the real estate developer had been a registered Republican for less than a year. Political parties were like wives to him—an attachment to be discarded every so often and eventually refreshed and replaced. He had registered as a Democrat in 2001. Before that he was a member of the Ross Perot–aligned Independence Party. And before that he was a Republican, which he became in 1987 right before his first flirtation with running for president. As was true with with many Trump endeavors—the Trump Shuttle airline, Trump hotels, Trump casinos—Stone was involved as an adviser when Trump traveled that year to New Hampshire to tease that he might get into the race.

Trump was more reserved than usual around Nunberg, whom he'd never met. But Nunberg warmed him up when he started talking about what he had been doing to stop Cordoba from breaking ground. He boasted that one of the displays set up by protesters across the street from the site was his idea: a pair of mock missiles, one of which had a mannequin wearing a traditional Arab headdress mounted on top of it. On the side in big letters, it read: "Obama: With a middle name Hussein. We understand. Bloomberg: What is your excuse?" Trump burst out laughing as Nunberg described it. Nunberg told him about the lawsuit from the firefighter who was being represented by Sekulow. He told Nunberg and Stone that he thought the project was a bad idea. "This can't be built," Trump said.

The Ground Zero Mosque was a story that appealed to Trump on two fundamental levels. First, it was a media frenzy. It was written about daily in the New York tabloids and talked about constantly on cable news, both of which formed the basis of his knowledge of current events. Second, Obama and other political leaders Trump disliked were supportive of the project. And Trump, who always liked to get behind winning issues and candidates, could see from the public polling that most people didn't like the idea of it. "Ground

Zero Mosque was an elite versus anti-elite issue. Bloomberg wanted it. Obama had endorsed it," Stone says, describing how Trump saw it.

Outside New York, the issue was exploding into an international crisis. An evangelical pastor in Gainesville, Florida, Terry Jones, planned an "International Burn a Koran Day." Jones called off his bonfire only after the secretary of defense, Robert Gates, personally telephoned him and told him that he was endangering the lives of U.S. service members stationed in the Middle East, where the pastor's plans had provoked a furious backlash.

For Trump, weighing in on such a fraught political debate was relatively new. He tested the waters with a series of public statements. Seeing that he was getting a lot of attention for each one, he kept going. He spoke to the entertainment program *Extra* in late August, saying that the project was "very insensitive, and it shouldn't be there." On September 1, he sat down for an interview on *The Late Show with David Letterman,* giving him his biggest audience yet on the topic. "I think it's not appropriate; I think it's insensitive; and it shouldn't be built there," he said, looking toward the audience. Letterman tried to get Trump to acknowledge that the Muslims who wanted to build near Ground Zero were not the same as the Muslims who planned and executed 9/11, but Trump held firm. "Somebody's blowing up buildings, and somebody's doing lots of bad stuff, David."

But it was ultimately a coincidence why Trump decided to make the move that drew the most attention and media coverage. At the most basic level, the Ground Zero Mosque concerned a real estate transaction—Trump's bread and butter. On September 9, two days before the ninth anniversary of the attacks, Trump released a letter to the media in which he responded the way that made the most sense to him: He offered to buy 45 Park Place for 25 percent more than the developers had paid for it—all cash, with an immediate closing. He said in his letter that he wanted to purchase it "not because I think the location is a spectacular one (because it is not), but because it will end a very serious, inflammatory and highly divisive situation that is destined, in my opinion, to only get worse." He was making the offer, he noted, "as a resident of New York and a citizen of the United States." He had managed to put himself at the center of the biggest story of the moment, where he preferred to be. But he also says that his feelings about the issue were shaped by seeing how frustrated and angry Cordoba's opponents were—the modern-day "hard hats," conservative Christians and Tea Party activists. "They were fighting it. And the politicians didn't hear them," Trump says.

Sharif el-Gamal, the developer, had no idea Trump's letter was coming and had no experience dealing with the kind of publicity that would ensue. "We weren't prepared for what was coming at us," he later recalled. He called Trump, but the conversation went nowhere. "He started going on the morning talk shows, calling me a sleazy developer, greedy, that he made me a fair offer," el-Gamal said, knowing he would never accept Trump's deal. He worried about the message it would send to his children about how American society valued Muslims. He hired Sheinkopf as a public relations consultant, who, by virtue of a long career in New York media, knew Trump's involvement in the story meant he could forget about bringing down the temperature. "He understands fear," Sheinkopf says of Trump. "What this guy understands better than anyone else is the energy of that crowd," he adds. "If you think the guy is crazy, he's not. He's doing what's always worked for him."

CHAPTER 4

The Paranoid Style

The problem with predicting the end of the world every day is
that sooner or later you have to deliver.

—ROGER AILES, as recalled by Chris Stirewalt of Fox News

Roger Ailes wrote the ad copy himself. "How did ABC, CBS, NBC, MSNBC, and CNN miss this story?" That question, printed in yellow block type, floated above a picture of tens of thousands of people marching on the Capitol. At the bottom of the page were the Fox News logo and a simple but misleading declaration: "We cover all the news." The ad ran in several of the country's top newspapers on September 18, 2009, and took up a full page. Its tenuous relationship to the truth made it a lot like the ads Ailes had produced when he was the Republican media Svengali who helped elect Nixon, Reagan, and George H. W. Bush.

The other networks hadn't missed the story at all. They'd devoted considerable resources and coverage to it. The demonstration on September 12 had been the biggest public outpouring of discontent so far of Obama's young presidency—and a major show of force for the budding Tea Party movement. It was a boisterous, impassioned, and sometimes ugly display aimed at the president and his fellow Democrats as they pressed ahead with an ambitious legislative agenda to expand the government's role in strengthening the economy and guaranteeing healthcare. Cries of "Liar! Liar! Liar!

Liar!" filled the air at the mention of Obama's name. Some demonstrators carried signs that showed his face superimposed over the visages of well-known Communists like Che Guevara. A few waved Confederate flags. It was such a big story that the *CBS Evening News* led with it that night, and CNN had four journalists broadcasting live from the National Mall throughout the day. *The New York Times* included a large photo of the protest on its front page.

That was incidental to Ailes, whose intention with the ad was to portray his network as the only trustworthy source for reporting on the Tea Party. The idea behind the ad, recalls one former colleague who was involved in discussions about it, was "We were the ones telling you the story." The message was, in essence, an encapsulation of the network's whole business model: *From Fox you will get the whole truth, nothing but, and the stories the mainstream media isn't telling you.* That made Fox stories seem like more than just news. They were a special commodity. If you were a loyal viewer, Fox's depiction of the country and its political system not only became your reality, it sometimes became a part of your identity. Viewers can buy cookbooks and historical nonfiction written by Fox anchors. They can outfit themselves and members of their family in red, white, and blue Fox-branded socks and boxer shorts and decorate their Christmas trees with Fox-branded ornaments. One longtime on-air personality recalls how a senior network marketing executive once described the unique relationship between loyal viewers and the network. "Fox is a lifestyle," the executive said, offering a Fox-themed community of manufactured homes as a hypothetical example of the kinds of products the network could be selling because its most die-hard fans would buy almost anything the network stamped its name on. The personality, who had been with the network almost from the day it debuted in 1996, was struck by the comment, unaware of how much network brass had apparently thought about ways to profit from the bond they had created with an ever-growing audience that was based on the false premise that Fox News was the only place for "Fair & Balanced" news.

But this model made the same assumption as Ailes's fallacious question from the ad: Fox News was calling the shots with its viewers and its hosts. The year 2009 was the beginning of the undoing of that premise. During Obama's first term, as Fox covered his presidency and the rise of the Tea Party, three personalities Ailes put on the air stood out for the way they gave voice to a particular kind of American grievance. There was Glenn Beck, whose show debuted the day before Obama's inauguration in 2009; and Sarah Palin, who joined as a network contributor a year later. And then, as Obama was preparing to ask voters to reelect him for a second term, Ailes turned to an old friend, Donald Trump, who agreed in early 2011 to appear on a weekly *Fox & Friends* segment called "Mondays with Trump." All of these stars initially delivered what Ailes was looking for: compelling television, good ratings, and content viewers could find nowhere else. All three also ended up growing into big enough political celebrities in their own right—one more popular and entitled than the next—that Ailes eventually lost his ability to control them. And he sometimes expressed regret about having given them a platform on his network. Christopher Ruddy, the chief executive of the conservative magazine and website *Newsmax,* recalls speaking with Ailes about the Tea Party early on and says that while the Fox News chief always liked the movement's use of patriotic language, its rebellious spirit and anti-elitism, he ultimately "saw them as a convenient grassroots group."

In that sense, Ailes was no different from the transactionally minded Republican leaders in Congress who looked at this energized group of voters and thought the same thing: *This is going to be good for business.* He thought the movement's rage and fervor could be incredibly valuable as the means to the end he cared about more than anything else: growing the size of the Fox News audience and the attendant profits that would fatten his annual bonus. Strictly speaking, Ailes was part of the establishment—the strategist who helped elect Nixon, Reagan, and George H. W. Bush, revered them, and didn't identify at heart with the GOP's insurgents. He thought the Tea Party was shrill and self-destructive. "Roger Ailes was an establishment guy," says Steve Bannon. "He used to say, 'Bannon, these guys are fucking crazy.' " Bannon, who was no less aware than Ailes that doing business with the Tea Party was a devil's bargain but more accepting of the possible consequences, recalls his response was essentially to shrug: "And, your point?"

The idea that Ailes could be a moderating force is almost irreconcilable with the image of him as a right-wing mastermind who manipulated Republican voters and candidates and preyed on the women whose careers he controlled. But that's not the full picture, as it fails to capture how Ailes was whiplashed by the Tea Party—and eventually by Trump—the same way the Republican Party establishment was. What neither Ailes nor the leadership of the GOP considered fully as they opened their arms to the movement was what would happen if encouraging and empowering it meant redefining the limits of acceptable political discourse, dropping the bar ever lower, and then discovering that they were helpless to reel it back in.

At first, no one did more to further Ailes's goal of converting the Tea Party movement's energy into ratings for Fox News than Glenn Beck. The license that Beck had from Ailes during his first year on the air set him free to produce one of the most surreal hours of television news ever broadcast. His racial dog whistles and fanatical attacks on Obama and members of his administration broke new boundaries for cable news. Often his commentary was downright conspiratorial nonsense. He gave credence to rumors that FEMA was building structures that would be used as concentration camps on American soil. He suggested that the Obama administration was, in his words, "setting up an Oklahoma City"–style attack to boost the president's popularity. He said that the government could try to prop up the value of the U.S. dollar by seizing land from private citizens. When he was called out for crossing lines, he deflected, Limbaugh-style, by insisting that he was a mere entertainer—a "rodeo clown," as he told the *Times* in early 2009. The only reason people were offended, Beck claimed, was that they weren't in on the joke.

One Beck outburst in the summer of 2009 in particular demonstrated how far Fox News would tolerate his pushing the limits. On

July 16, the raw, racialized anti-Obama anger of Tea Party sympathizers like Beck collided head-on with the country's fraught history of systemic discrimination in Cambridge, Massachusetts, when a white police officer arrested one of Harvard's most prominent scholars of African American history, Henry Louis Gates, Jr. Professor Gates had arrived home to find his door jammed, so he forced it open with the help of the cabdriver who was dropping him off. A white woman in the neighborhood saw them, assumed they were breaking in, and called the police. The responding officer claimed that Gates was "becoming disorderly" because he objected to being questioned about whether he was indeed in his own home. When Obama was asked about it at a press conference, a full-blown conservative media conflagration ensued, with Fox and Beck fanning the flames. The president had accurately pointed to what he described as the "long history" of law enforcement that disproportionately targets minorities in the United States—"That's just a fact," he said—and remarked that the police had "acted stupidly" in throwing the book at Gates.

Rush Limbaugh called Obama's response "the militant black reaction." Rudy Giuliani gave an interview to Sean Hannity in which the former New York mayor said Gates should just "shut up." But it was Beck who went the furthest. In an appearance on *Fox & Friends* a few days after the arrest, he said that the president's remarks had revealed his "deep-seated hatred for white people or the white culture." Then he added, matter-of-factly, "This guy is, I believe, a racist." Beck and Fox News immediately came under fire but refused to admit that he had gone too far. Ailes gave Beck his blessing partly because, as one Fox executive recalls, "Roger *did* think that Obama was a racist." But Ailes rarely, if ever, agreed to issue public apologies or utter any expression of regret whatsoever. He approved a statement through his public relations department, written under the name of the network's head of programming, Bill Shine, that defended Beck. "Glenn Beck expressed a personal opinion which represented his own views, not those of the Fox News Channel. And as with all commentators in the cable news arena, he is given the freedom to express his opinions," Shine's statement said.

The significance was hard to overstate. One of the biggest stars on the most-watched cable news network in the country said the country's first Black president hated white people. And Shine*, the executive directly responsible for overseeing Fox News's top personalities, said it was perfectly defensible. At the heart of many Beck complaints about Obama was the idea that his White House was a hothouse for radicals, including Communists. And his attacks on Van Jones, Obama's "green jobs czar," were revealing about the changing culture in conservative media and the Republican Party, even as they borrowed from Phyllis Schlafly and others who alleged that a Communist conspiracy was operating in the government in the 1960s. Beck smeared Jones as a "self-avowed radical revolutionary Communist," recalling the tactics of white opponents of the civil rights movement who tried to discredit the push for racial equality by claiming it was being manipulated by Communists. Beck claimed that Jones was only the tip of the iceberg. Dozens of administration czars with jobs that no one knew anything about could be hiding something, he declared. "Who are they? What do they believe? What are they advising the president to do?" Beck asked at the opening of a program in August 2009, not letting the question hang in the air too long before answering it himself. Jones, Beck said, had arrived at his first day of law school "wearing combat boots and holding a Black Panther bookbag."

By this point, many Democrats weren't aware how the network had constructed a damaging narrative about the new president and his administration that viewers found convincing and compelling. The twistedness of it all was clearest to her whenever the White House would push back and then Fox hosts would claim that the administration was using Obama's race as a crutch. "They constantly accused us of playing the race card," Anita Dunn says.

Sometimes Ailes was drawn to the most outrageous and provocative content because he knew the response it would provoke. "He used to say 'This will make their heads explode.' And he loved

---

* Shine would later serve as President Trump's White House communications director, a position he held for eight months.

doing that," recalls Chris Stirewalt, who covered politics for the network for a decade before being broomed out in a post-2020, Trump-friendly restructuring. But often, he believed the most outrageous conspiracy theories, especially when it came to Obama. At the White House Correspondents' Dinner in 2013, Obama asked Michael Clemente, Fox News's executive vice president for news, whether Ailes was a true believer or doing it all for the ratings. "Does Roger really believe this stuff?" Clemente answered, "He does."

As far as Ailes was concerned, Jones probably was a communist. He thought the word "czar," with its Russian provenance, was a tell—even though previous presidents as far back as Calvin Coolidge had given the term to officials they appointed, often ones that tackled complex, specialized problems, like an AIDS czar or a terrorism czar. David Axelrod, who kept an open line of communication directly to Ailes, recalls meeting in New York with the Fox News chief around this time and being baffled that Ailes was fixated on the Obama administration's czars. "Let me tell you what bothers me about your guy. He's hiring Communists," Ailes told Axelrod over breakfast in Midtown.

"What are you talking about, Roger?" Axelrod replied, not seeing that particular critique coming.

"That Van Jones. He's a Communist," Ailes said.

Axelrod tried to reassure him. "Roger, he's not a Communist."

"Well, you've got all these czars. What's with all the czars?" Ailes demanded to know.

The attacks eventually broke Jones. Conservative media started digging into his past and reported on incidents that confirmed their caricature of Jones the radical militant. Earlier in his career, the Yale-educated civil rights lawyer had helped organize support for a new trial for Mumia Abu-Jamal, a former Black Panther who was sentenced to death for killing a white Philadelphia police officer in 1981. Jones's name was also on a petition that claimed George W. Bush knew about the 9/11 attacks in advance and did nothing because he wanted a pretext for war. (He would later claim he was misled by the organizers and didn't know what the petition said.) And a video of him surfaced in which he is heard calling Republicans "assholes."

Republican lawmakers, especially those who were savvy about playing to the conservative media, condemned Jones. One particularly ambitious congressman from Indiana, Mike Pence, said he was deeply offended at such language. Pence criticized Jones for "extremist views and coarse rhetoric," saying that this talk had "no place in this administration or the public debate." Such was the Republican double standard of political conduct in the Obama era. Beck's behavior elicited no reprisal or reproach from party officials. But years-old statements, some of which Jones himself admitted were ill advised and apologized for, were grounds for dismissal from the White House. It all became too much of a distraction for the White House, and Jones resigned on September 6, 2009, after just six months with the administration.

But the Obama White House didn't publicly discuss Jones's race as a factor in these attacks, because the 2008 campaign had taught the president and his advisers a sobering lesson about what a Black man at the pinnacle of American politics still couldn't say. Cornell Belcher, one of Obama's pollsters, recalls how Obama the candidate and Obama the president had a default position when it came to talking about race: Don't. "I certainly did polling around racial attitudes and how it was impacting the contest—which of course we never talked about," Belcher explains. One of his most significant findings was directly applicable to Beck's insistence that Obama was a racist, and helps explain why he got away with it. Belcher saw in his research that there were plenty of white voters in battleground states who said that they believed the kind of anti-white racism that Beck described was a big problem. They usually described it as a form of "reverse discrimination" perpetrated through policies like affirmative action that advantaged Black people and other minorities over whites in education and hiring. And they often said, Belcher's surveys found, that it was a bigger issue than racial discrimination against Blacks and other minorities. "White Americans refused to think that racism was a big deal, that it was a thing," Belcher says. So Obama rarely wanted to go there.

As a political consultant, Ailes understood the power of television to make people see something that wasn't there. And his application of this strategy to his candidates made him one of the most successful media consultants in the Republican Party. He was Machiavellian, tempestuous, and predatory—yet beloved by many who either didn't see or chose to overlook his dark side for his brilliance and wit. His clients included future senators who weren't exactly compelling as candidates but seemed that way to voters once they'd seen Ailes's ads. He helped put Al D'Amato of New York in office, a candidate he found so hopelessly disagreeable that he once threatened to throw him out a thirtieth-story window, recalled Larry McCarthy, who worked for Ailes in the 1980s and would graduate to notoriety of his own for producing what became known as "the Willie Horton ad." To make up for D'Amato's deficiencies on camera, Ailes decided to cast the candidate's mother in a campaign spot, hoping that people would find something redeeming in him if they heard her saying kind words about her son. It worked, helping D'Amato beat Senator Jacob Javits, an aging institution of New York liberalism who had been in office for more than two decades. Without Ailes, there might not have been a Senator Mitch McConnell, whose 1984 campaign rebounded from a double-digit deficit in the polls after an Ailes-produced spot that featured a pack of bloodhounds searching for McConnell's opponent. The implication was that the incumbent senator, Walter "Dee" Huddleston, was missing important votes— even though he wasn't. According to a story Ailes told about the ad's provenance, the idea had come to him when he was watching television and saw a pack of dogs running in an advertisement for dog food.

At Fox, Ailes built a large fortune for himself and his boss, Rupert Murdoch, perfecting a simple but powerful formula for political messaging. He could rouse his audience's patriotic and aspirational impulses, mine their darkest fears, stimulate their sensual side, and confirm their wildest delusions. Ailes, who produced Broadway shows between political gigs in the 1970s, projected his dramatic sensibilities onto the decidedly staid look of cable news. Fox News followed the model of a theatrical production. Each hour had its heroes (often square-jawed conservative men), villains (any disheveled-looking liberal or Black activist would do), and a chorus (an ensemble cast that usually consisted of attractive blondes). Colorful graphics popped off the screen—a riot of brilliant blues and fire engine reds. Animated American flags rippled in the background. Women wore cocktail dresses or miniskirts, even at 6 A.M, and were asked to put on open-toed shoes—"Because Roger prefers them," producers explained to the guests. Fox's makeup room was like a factory assembly line running at full capacity. Teams of cosmetologists glued fake eyelashes on guests and used high-pressure sprayers to layer on thick coats of makeup.

The centerpiece for his vision was *Fox & Friends*—three hours of sex and red meat starting every morning at six. People inside the network nicknamed the show "Roger's daybook" because of how involved he was in the programming. There were segments with visits from Hooters waitresses on the "Let Freedom Wing" USO-style tour; debates about whether parents who gave children large allowances were creating an entitlement society; segments on the killing of bald eagles; performances of "God Bless the USA" by Lee Greenwood. The hosts asked snarkily why Occupy Wall Street protesters were beating on bongo drums all day instead of looking for jobs; accused Transportation Security Administration agents of willfully violating grandmothers and toddlers; and waged battle after battle in Ailes's favorite holiday tradition, the "War on Christmas." (Explaining once why he felt so strongly that "Christmas" had been turned into a bad word, Ailes said it all started when he saw his son's school had something called a "friendship tree" in place of a Christmas tree. He snapped at the headmaster, "What the hell's a friendship tree?")

When Ailes worked for Nixon, he urged him to accept the importance of television in a modernizing world where voters needed to see a presidential candidate to trust him. But Ailes wasn't just a political strategist, he was a "hard hat" at heart. He thought that liberals coddled criminals ("We're too worried about the terrorists' feelings," he complained). He accused Democrats of cheating by giving free things to voters like Obamacare ("A voter registration plan," he called it). He thought that the younger, more multicultural generations behind him did not place enough importance on values like patriotism and were too entitled. He once told a group of college students that everyone their age was "still waiting for their trophy because they think they won something." He explained that Fox programmed for the middle of the country, not the coasts. "A lot of what we do at Fox is blue-collar stuff," he once said.

Under Ailes's leadership, Fox News helped spread a particular strain of misinformation about Obama, spawning a series of rumors about the president's background that became accepted as fact among many on the right, and would never really die. In this version of the Obama story, his rise to stardom was too meteoric to have happened entirely on its own. Obama—and those around him like Van Jones—had to be hiding something in their past, the story went. Ailes believed Obama wasn't being honest about his background, former colleagues say. He couldn't wrap his head around the idea that a relatively young politician could get so far, so fast, without something being corrupt about it. "He just couldn't believe that this Black guy, a one-term senator who wasn't really on anyone's radar, became president," said one Fox journalist who worked closely with Ailes and spoke extensively with him about Obama. "Jesse Jackson, he could deal with that. Al Sharpton, he got that. He knew where they came from. But not Obama. He believed that somebody's got to be putting up the money."

Part of what made this story line so appealing to Ailes was its villain: a fawning mainstream media that was so weak-in-the-knees about Obama that it didn't properly vet him. In news meetings, staff recall how Ailes would demand to know why the network wasn't digging more into rumors he had heard about Obama's life before politics. *Why wouldn't he come clean about his associations with known leftist radicals? Why did he like the Muslim Brotherhood so much?* "Why don't we know about Obama and the coke and the gay boys?" Ailes growled more than once in editorial meetings with network producers and personalities. He was always fascinated with the most lurid and laughably fabricated stories about the president, including one old canard pushed by Jerome Corsi and others that Obama had a secret gay life. Recalling his interactions with Ailes over the years, Axelrod says he recognized a pattern of thought that Richard Hofstadter captured in his seminal 1964 essay, "The Paranoid Style in American Politics." Hofstadter described paranoiac tendencies that many Americans harbored: "heated exaggeration, suspiciousness, and conspiratorial fantasy."

Adds Axelrod, "That was Roger." And that was what he would bring to the forefront of mainstream Republican politics.

Similar to the way CNN had the first Persian Gulf war to thank for establishing itself as a household brand name in the early 1990s, Roger Ailes had a war to thank for the record-smashing success of Fox News at the end of the 2000s: his network's war on Obama. Its coverage of the 2008 election led to the highest ratings the network had ever recorded in its twelve years of existence. It made Ailes extremely wealthy. He earned $19 million that year. As a candidate, Obama directly confronted Ailes about the misinformation that Fox was responsible for spreading about him. But he found that Ailes didn't want to hear the truth.

In June 2008, once Obama had secured the delegates he needed to foreclose any possibility that Hillary Clinton could still win the Democratic nomination, Obama got on a plane to New York to see Ailes and Rupert Murdoch. Two rooms at the Waldorf Astoria were booked for the occasion. The larger of the two was where Murdoch would meet with Obama first, without Ailes. The second was a holding room down the hall where Ailes would be waiting, unaware that his boss had stashed him away so he could talk to Obama one-on-one first and break the ice. For about thirty-five minutes, Obama and Murdoch chatted amiably. Looking on were two senior campaign aides, Axelrod and Robert Gibbs. Also in the room was Murdoch's communications chief, Gary Ginsberg, a former Clinton White House lawyer who was the unofficial Murdoch envoy to the Democratic Party. Satisfied that the meeting was going well—Murdoch seemed to grow more enamored with Obama by the minute—Ginsberg asked if it was time to bring in Ailes. Obama's face lit up.

"Yes," he said, making it clear to the rest of the room how much he had been anticipating meeting his tormentor.

Ginsberg led Ailes down the hall. And as soon as they walked through the door to the suite where Murdoch and Obama were, Ailes could see that Murdoch had started without him. And to his apparent annoyance, they actually seemed to be getting along quite well. Ailes immediately understood that he had been played. "I guess I'm the crazy uncle," he said. But his self-deprecating joke was also the truth: He was the relative no one wanted to invite to Sunday dinner.

Obama complained about Fox's promotion of conspiracy theories about his citizenship and his religion. Anchors and other on-air personalities were by now routinely spouting off on Obama's supposed socialist leanings, sympathy for Islam and Black nationalists, and friendships with 1960s radicals. Hosts were particularly harsh toward Michelle Obama. They constantly replayed remarks that made her sound unpatriotic, as when she said that her husband's political success had made her proud of her country "for the first time in my adult life."

"You've got to knock this off," Obama told Ailes, his tone growing less friendly by the second. "I am a Christian. I go to church." But Ailes had no intention of knocking it off. He didn't believe Obama, and he saw no reason why Murdoch or any Fox viewer should either. The only effect their meeting seemed to have on Ailes was that now his antipathy toward Obama had a personal dimension to it. At one point, the exchange between them deteriorated so badly that Ailes all but called Obama a liar, accusing the senator of misrepresenting his true views on national defense.

The reason, which Ailes later explained to his authorized biographer, was a viral video that had been publicized by Corsi, a notorious promoter of anti-Obama conspiracy theories. Ailes's knowledge of the video—and the impression it left on him—demonstrated the extent to which he wasn't just a successful purveyor of far-right, fringe ideas. He was also a believer and an avid consumer of them. Ailes questioned Obama about the video, a fifty-two-second clip that shows Obama describing his vision for peace. He says that he would de-escalate the nuclear arms race and cut waste from the defense budget, and that one day there could be a world without nuclear weapons. Obama told Ailes he had no intention of cutting the military's nuclear arsenal. Ailes was incredulous. "Senator, I just watched someone say exactly that on my computer screen before coming over here. Maybe it wasn't you, but it sure looked like you and sounded like you," Ailes said. "It was as good a lie as anyone ever told me," Ailes would tell his biographer, describing how he had observed Obama's eyes and body language like a detective would— "He never dropped his gaze, which is the usual tell," Ailes said—and understood exactly what kind of man he was dealing with.

How did these ideas make their way to Ailes? One answer is Corsi, the man who is probably most responsible for popularizing the conspiracy theory about Obama's birth certificate. Corsi found the Obama video to be so revealing about the danger he would pose as president that he quoted a nearly verbatim transcript of it in the introduction to his book *The Obama Nation: Leftist Politics and the Cult of Personality*. It came out in the summer of 2008 and purported to detail Obama's "extensive connections with Islam and with radical racial politics." Corsi had turned his attention to Obama before the 2008 election when the Illinois senator was expected to run for president. As part of his research, he started visiting the Senate press gallery, where he observed the freshman senator interact with colleagues. "A smooth operator," he says, a hint of condescension in his voice. One day, he recalls being in an elevator in the Russell Building when his subject stepped inside. "In comes Obama, and he has two of his Black Muslim body guys," Corsi says. How he pegged them as Muslim without speaking to them, he explains, was because of their suits and ties—presumably because the most logical reason a Black man would be wearing a suit and tie in the Capitol was because he was a member of Louis Farrakhan's Nation of Islam.

When the book came out, Corsi was asked to come on Fox News to promote it. He had a history with Sean Hannity, whom he'd relied on to help sell his first book about John Kerry. "I believe my first radio interview was with Sean Hannity," he recalls. One of Corsi's collaborators and the editor of *WorldNetDaily*, Joseph Farah, would also boast of his Hannity connections. "I literally chat with Hannity online every day," Farah once claimed. On August 15, 2008, Corsi appeared on *Fox & Friends*. But by then, his attention had moved on to the birth certificate, a story that most major news outlets, including Fox, had largely ignored up to that point. "There's been good analysis of it on the Internet, and it's been shown to have watermarks from Photoshop. It's a fake document," Corsi told the host, Steve Doocy. The "analysis" Corsi was referring to had just been published on Pamela Geller's blog, *Atlas Shrugs,* and was written by the anonymous writer who claimed to have expertise in document forensics and falsely claimed that Obama's details had been filled in on a birth certificate that initially belonged to someone else.

Corsi often published on a website whose articles Ailes was known to cite in meetings: *WorldNetDaily*. It was the kind of publication that would run a six-part series on the evils of soybeans ("Soy Is Making Kids 'Gay,' " one story claimed) and spread false rumors about Bill and Hillary Clinton's involvement in the suicide of their friend and deputy White House counsel, Vincent W. Foster, Jr. On paper, Corsi did not seem like the kind of writer who would indulge in such wild right-wing fantasies. He had a Ph.D. in political science from Harvard—a fact that anyone meeting him for the first time would likely learn from him a few minutes into conversation. He started out in banking and did well enough to indulge himself in high-end New York establishments like the Plaza in Manhattan, where he sometimes exchanged small talk with its owner, Donald Trump, in the 1980s. "I practically lived at the Plaza," he says. "I was a VIP guest." Years later, Corsi says, Trump would call him four times to ask questions about his research into Obama.

By 2004, Corsi had left banking to pursue writing and researching full-time. He describes himself and his work as "fact-based," appropriating the language of mainstream journalism in a way that lends his work the patina of credibility to people who want to believe it. He was shrewd about getting his writing injected into the bloodstream of the mainstream media where he wanted it. He reasoned that even if reporters there covered it as nonsense—which they almost always did—he was still getting it out to a wider audience via network newscasts and major newspapers. Before the 2004 presidential election, he published the accounts of men who questioned Senator Kerry's record in the Vietnam War in the book *Unfit for Command: Swift Boat Veterans Speak Out Against John Kerry*. It questioned Kerry's truthfulness about the atrocities he claimed to have seen and raised doubts about his bravery and his leadership. Several people who served with Kerry refuted the claims. Most media savaged Corsi's reporting in their coverage. But that wasn't the point. "Mainstream media is going to catch on to controversy," he says. "Kerry put down a marker: I'm a hero in Vietnam. We put down a marker: You're lying. You can't ignore that story." He was right. And *Unfit for Command* became a bestseller. Even if people didn't know the details of the allegations in the book or had heard about the authors' credibility issues or read the fact-check articles calling out its falsehoods, its mere existence was enough to muddy Kerry's credibility in a way he never recovered from. "If John Kerry loses the presidential election," declared *The New York Times* on October 10, "'Unfit for Command' . . . will go down as a chief reason."

Though the Swift Boat attacks received ample but mostly disconfirming coverage from mainstream outlets, that was not always the case at Fox News, where favorable reporting on the book alarmed some network veterans. It was a turning point for Fox, as the network's news division—not one of its opinion hosts—took up a cause against a major figure in the Democratic Party. The managing editor of the Washington bureau, Brit Hume, was exceedingly complimentary of Corsi's book on his show. Hume, the anchor of the 6 P.M. newscast, was widely known to lean to the right in his personal views, but was also considered by many of his peers and sources in Washington to be a top-notch journalist who had previously covered the White House for ABC News with distinction. But what few outside the network knew was that Hume had been a childhood classmate of Kerry's at the elite St. Albans School in Washington, and he was not shy about his distaste for the senator around the newsroom. On the air, Hume praised Corsi's book as "a remarkably well-done document." He insinuated that Kerry was a liar, and as the *Washington Post* noted at the time, pushed the Swift Boat story "day after day." To some inside Fox, this was when the network crossed the Rubicon. "When Brit started taking shots, it was open season," says Carl Cameron, the former Fox political correspondent whom Hume mentored. Cameron calls Hume's coverage of the first Bush and Clinton White Houses "stellar" and describes the turn Hume took with disappointment. "Management decided they were going to let him make that turn. It's an important part of what happened to Fox," Cameron says.

The Swift Boat story signaled that the lines were blurring. But until Beck, the network had never allowed one of its stars to become a major player in a political movement like the Tea Party. Roger Ailes would learn the same lesson as John McCain's campaign when it tried to bring similarly restive forces inside the tent and assumed it could control them. By the fall of 2009, Beck was more than just a TV star. He was a political brand of his own, and that was starting to overshadow his work at Fox News. He began holding his own Tea Party–like rallies. He founded his own organization he called the 9/12 Project, which he said was dedicated to restoring the spirit of unity that Americans had felt immediately after the September 11 attacks. Its manifesto read like the mission statement for a treatment program for recovering alcoholics, which Beck was. The "9 principles and 12 values" that he said guided the group included a mixture of spiritual and political pablum, like "America is good." He toured the country promoting his books with conservative stars like Newt Gingrich and Sarah Palin. On Saturday, August 28, 2010, exactly forty-seven years from the day that Martin Luther King, Jr., gave his "I Have a Dream" speech, Beck helped gather hundreds of thousands of people at the base of the Lincoln Memorial—the same site where King spoke—for an event he organized called "Restoring Honor." Civil rights leaders were appalled. Al Sharpton called it an attempt "to disgrace this day."

Around the country, candidates running for office were mimicking Beck's mantras and adopting his principles as their campaign platforms. He put up a page on his Fox website that included a pledge for lawmakers to sign in which they would vow to freeze spending and tighten immigration laws. Ailes was losing not only control over Beck but his patience as well. "He used to say," recalls Stirewalt, " 'the problem with predicting the end of the world every day is that sooner or later you have to deliver.' " In February 2010, Ailes participated in a discussion at Stanford University's Hoover Institution and was asked about a new *London Telegraph* ranking of the most influential American conservatives. His questioner pointed out that Ailes was No. 7, while Beck was a tick higher at No. 6. Ailes objected. "Glenn's actually not a conservative," he huffed. Ailes told colleagues that Beck had complained like a hypochondriac about various ailments he thought he had. At one point, Ailes said, Beck told him he was afraid he was going blind. "He's out of his fucking mind," Ailes told one of his on-air personalities.

Ailes's flash of irritation at the suggestion that he was less influential than Beck said a lot about that moment in Republican politics. Beck's celebrity and political influence were upending the balance of power at Fox and in the Republican Party. His impact on electoral politics was real. His 9/12 Project inspired a host of candidates who had never been particularly invested in politics before to run for Congress in 2010. One was Bobby Schilling, a pizza parlor owner from western Illinois whose lack of experience in campaigning was evident in his choice for campaign manager: his twenty-two-year-old son, Terry. Schilling recalls the realization that hit him about what was going on once he and his son started traveling the district. "We realized, wow, this is big. This is bigger than we thought." As for the people they encountered, Schilling says, "They were afraid, afraid of what was happening to America." There was also Joe Walsh, a banker from suburban Chicago. Walsh had a history of financial problems, including a bank foreclosure on a condo he owned, that made him a curious candidate for a time when fiscal responsibility was supposed to be a paramount concern for Republicans. Like Schilling, Walsh says he believed in the "citizen legislator" ideal that prominent conservatives like Beck were promoting. Walsh vowed he would sleep in his office and return to the district every weekend so the Washington swamp wouldn't corrupt him. And when he needed content for his campaign website, he pulled from the website of the Beck's 9/12 Project and other groups. He posted a list he called the "28 Founding Principles of the United States." No. 3: "The most promising method of securing a virtuous people is to elect virtuous leaders." No. 28: "The United States has a manifest destiny to eventually become a glorious example of God's law under a restored Constitution that will inspire the entire human race." Eventually he surprised everyone, including Republican officials in Washington who'd written him off, and won his primary.

Initially, a lot of this sounded refreshing to party leaders. Eric Cantor, one of the most senior Republicans in the House, was tempted to see these upstart candidates as motivated by the conservative ideals they often talked about. "We looked at the eruption of the Tea Party movement as a reflection of our ideological fight against big government," he says. But that was a mistake. "It was about anger," he adds. As a career legislator like Cantor saw it, "I thought you got elected to Congress to do stuff." It soon became clear, he says, that "what this seemed to be about was you got elected to Congress to *not* do stuff."

Or you could get elected to Congress and go on Fox News, which was one of the primary objectives of many of the candidates who would become part of the new freshman class.

Rarely have American voters punished a political party with such vengeance as they did the Democrats on November 2, 2010. Not even during some of the twentieth century's most dramatic upheavals had the party in power suffered so badly. Not Watergate. Not the Democratic landslides in 1964 that followed John F. Kennedy's assassination. Not the Republican Revolution of 1994. In fact, not since 1948, when President Harry Truman thrashed the "Do Nothing Congress" on his way to winning a first full term, had so many members of Congress from a single party been thrown out of office.

At the offices of the National Republican Congressional Committee on Capitol Hill, Guy Harrison, the group's executive director, needed some time before he could fully process the scale of the Republican victories that night. It seemed almost absurd how many seats they had been able to take away from Democrats. There were some races that they had no business winning, he told himself as he reviewed the list of roughly ninety races that the RNCC had targeted across the country. "Holy shit. We won that?" he exclaimed, only to be surprised again the farther down the list he scanned. "We won *that*?"

Harrison, a Texan with a burly build that had suited him in his youth as a football lineman, possessed the kind of brash self-confidence that had led him to make a wildly optimistic prediction a few days before the election about how the night would play out: Republicans, he said, would win sixty-four seats. They won sixty-three. As he was taking inventory that night, he saw a name that stopped him: Joe Walsh. The party hadn't given Walsh any money, figuring he was cooked because of his financial problems and news stories that his campaign was so poorly managed that staff quit en masse and sued him. "Do we have any way to get in touch with this guy?" Harrison asked his staff. No one did.

Walsh and the lawmakers who were part of what became known as the Tea Party Wave—eighty-seven Republican House freshmen who were not an ordinary class in any sense. They were people with no real political experience, no incentive to compromise on anything, and no desire to understand the horse-trading that made legislating work in Washington. To many of them, losing political battles against the right opponent—like the leaders of their own party—was winning. When the Congressional Research Service did its regular postelection review of their biographies, its staff noticed an unusual similarity among them. For the first time in recent memory, the most common occupation the incoming lawmakers of the 112th Congress listed was not law, but business. And compared with other Congresses, these newcomers had relatively little government experience. Thirty-two of them had never been elected to public office of any kind before.

They had careers in pest control, undertaking, auctioneering, roofing, and selling cars. There was a retired Northwest Airlines pilot; a former offensive tackle in the National Football League; an intensive care nurse; a dental surgeon; a youth minister; a thirty-nine-year-old district attorney better known for his role on MTV's *Real World*. Schilling, the Beck-inspired Illinois pizza parlor owner, won his race too. They often told themselves they were the very kind of patriot that the Founding Fathers envisioned when they created the House as the body whose power flowed from the people and whose door would be open to Americans "young or old, and without regard to poverty or wealth, or to any particular profession of religious faith," as *The Federalist* No. 52 described it.

Many of them left their families back home, packed their sleeping bags, and slept on cots or couches in their congressional offices. By some accounts, close to twenty Republican freshmen did this instead of renting or buying a place for themselves. They showered in the House gym. They filled filing cabinets with dishes and cutlery. They bought futons and pullout couches. The symbolism was not subtle. They would be frugal and practical, living within their means just as they said the government should. Some even vowed to return the money they would eventually collect from their congressional pensions. No one should mistake them for wanting to be a part of official Washington. They were only passing through, like a platoon of Marines on a mission to liberate an oppressed populace. And they might just burn the village down on their way out. Other Tea Party–adjacent players would adopt this not-of-Washington mindset too. *Breitbart News* ran its D.C. operations out of the Capitol Hill townhouse where Steve Bannon lived. Bannon took the helm of the website as executive chairman after Andrew Breitbart's unexpected death from heart failure in 2012, and he referred to the townhouse grandiosely as "the Embassy"—a sovereign territory in a foreign land.

Recruiting political novices to run in 2010 was always part of the plan from Washington, even if party consultants didn't always realize who they were getting. Harrison recalls being approached by state senators and legislators and county commissioners about running that year and, given the antiestablishment mood, discouraging them from doing so. There was a strategic upside here. Having no experience in office not only fit with that mood, it meant not having to defend a voting record.

In the Senate, Republicans were more skeptical of the Tea Party as a natural ally. McConnell, the Senate Republican leader, took a hands-off approach and dispatched aides out into the states with a mission, as one of them recalls it, to find out "who are these people and what do they want?" And he was correct to share his friend Ailes's skepticism. Clownish candidates cost McConnell seats that he otherwise may have picked up, like Christine O'Donnell in Delaware, who had to fend off accusations that she practiced witchcraft, and Sharron Angle in Nevada, who had apparent connections to Scientology and made false claims about Sharia law spreading in the United States. But McConnell also misread the anti-establishment anger that was motivating voters who supported candidates like these. He thought it would be helpful to appear in an ad for a Senate candidate in his home state of Kentucky who was facing a tough primary challenge from the right. The challenger, a libertarian ophthalmologist named Rand Paul, won the race with 59 percent of the vote.

The Republican path to the majority in the House included a candidate recruitment and support program called the "Young Guns." Harrison's committee conferred Young Gun status on candidates who could show that they had met a set of benchmarks demonstrating that they could be competitive in fundraising, organizing, and strategy. And in turn those candidates, ninety-two in all, would receive the official backing of the party committee and the money and infrastructure that accompanied it. But it was widely known at the time, though not acknowledged publicly, that "there were a lot of people who hadn't earned it," says Ken Spain, a deputy at the committee overseeing communications. The reality was sinking in that there were a lot of amateurs who weren't ready for prime time. Spain recalls how his bosses reacted when he expressed concern about some of the hard-right candidates: "Ken, you need to stop looking at this election by looking in the rearview mirror. This is going to be a totally different election. In some cases we're not going to get the candidates we want." He admits to being something of an idealist as he thought about what Republicans could do with their new majority. The Republican losses in 2008 in the suburbs and the party's poor performance with women concerned Spain, leading him to the conclusion that hard-line conservative candidates weren't the answer to winning those voters back.

But at the NRCC, Spain understood that the plan was not to win by preaching moderation. Part of his job included writing memos urging Republican candidates to take a hard line on refusing to raise the nation's debt ceiling, the total amount of money that the federal government is authorized to borrow to meet its existing obligations like Social Security, Medicare, and tax refunds. The consequences of using the nation's ability to borrow money as a means to a political end—a credit downgrade for the United States—weren't discussed.

And like most answers to questions about the Tea Party, the message from Republican Party leadership was not overly complicated: They would figure it out if and when they needed to. They believed the new class of lawmakers would be like the others preceding it: eager and willing to learn their role and deferential to leadership. But the issues that many of the professional Tea Party–aligned groups in Washington insisted their movement was fundamentally about were never really that interesting to many Republican voters. And the NRCC could see that in its own data. When it conducted focus groups in districts it wanted to flip, the opinions from voters that emerged told a more complicated story about government spending. They were unhappy about the bailouts—but not because the government had spent so much money. They said they didn't like the fact that the bailouts hadn't done much to help the economy or them personally. "They were fine with the government spending money," Harrison says. "They just thought it didn't do anything." The pollster for House Republicans, David Winston, analyzed the data from surveys of voters who participated in the midterms and reported in a postmortem that only 10 percent said that the national debt or spending was the top issue for them. By far, the economy and jobs were the most significant concern. A distant second was healthcare.

On election night, it didn't take long after the first polls started to close on the East Coast before Harrison and his staff could see that they were going to have a very good night. Some of them were gathered down the hall from Harrison's office in a conference room, getting race-by-race results by surfing cable and a new resource for up-to-the-minute information, Twitter. Just after 8:30, the results from the Ninth District in Virginia set the tone: a defeat for Rick Boucher, a fourteen-term Democrat who had built a loyal following delivering federal earmarks to build up the roads, sewer systems, and internet networks across his rural southwestern corner of the state. Taking Boucher's place would be a Tea Party–backed member of the state house of delegates, Morgan Griffith, the first Republican since 1983 to hold the seat.

That race was the first sign of a sharp backlash against Democrats across Appalachia, into the upper Midwest, and beyond, where the party's cultural connection to blue-collar, mostly white, union communities was fraying. Just to the north, in eastern Ohio, the coal country district held by Charlie Wilson was falling to Bill Johnson, a businessman who campaigned on lowering taxes and protecting the kind of coal jobs that he said Obama wanted to regulate out of existence. Across the border in western Pennsylvania, another casualty was Kathy Dahlkemper, a member of the coalition of centrist Democrats known as the Blue Dogs who opposed abortion and had voted against creating new environmental restrictions. Dahlkemper was replaced by an auto dealer and onetime Notre Dame football prodigy named Mike Kelly.

Republicans weren't just winning, they were rebalancing the country's entire political balance of power. Nearly half of the Blue Dog coalition of centrist Democrats was wiped out. Before the election, Democrats held both House seats in North and South Dakota, which are each represented by a single at-large member. But both incumbents lost. Six Democrats representing rural areas in Michigan, Wisconsin, and Indiana also lost. More fell in Arkansas, Louisiana, and Tennessee—where Democrats had managed to hold on in defiance of the generation-long Republican realignment across the rest of the South.

Republicans also captured more seats in state legislatures than at any point since the Roaring Twenties, guaranteeing them considerable leverage in the upcoming decennial redistricting process. In some states they would have unchecked power to make their newest House members all but impervious to defeat. This post-2010 period of Republican ascendancy at the state level was especially apparent in the South and the Midwest. Just twenty years earlier, the party had controlled not a single legislative chamber—upper or lower—in the South, according to the National Conference of State Legislatures. But by 2011, Republicans would enjoy full control of the legislature in six Southern states: Alabama, Florida, Georgia, North Carolina, South Carolina, and Tennessee. The 2010 wave was so powerful in washing away generations of cultural affinity for Democrats that in North Carolina and Alabama, Republicans reclaimed power at the state house for the first time since Reconstruction. Richard Nixon's political experiment with recruiting ancestral Democrats into his Republican Party seemed complete. Farther north, both the Assembly and the Senate flipped to Republicans in Wisconsin, which also elected a deeply conservative governor whom many Republicans saw as a possible presidential contender one day, Scott Walker.

This bumper crop of governors, congressmen, and senators was full of political prodigies. In the House there were people like Mick Mulvaney of South Carolina, a conservative state senator who took down one of the most powerful Democrats in Congress, the House Budget Committee chairman John Spratt, by painting Spratt as reckless and fiscally irresponsible. Waiting in the wings to take Spratt's chairmanship was a forty-year-old congressman, Paul Ryan of Wisconsin. Ryan, a protégé of the conservative reformer Jack Kemp, had impressed party leaders during his two decades in Congress—first as a staffer and then as a representative to a district outside Milwaukee—with an almost single-minded focus on budget and tax issues. Another member of the new class was Mike Pompeo of Kansas, a manufacturing executive and former Army officer with a Harvard Law degree who benefited from the political patronage of two libertarian-minded billionaires whose company was headquartered in his district, Charles and David Koch.

In Ohio, a former longtime congressman from the Columbus area and Fox News personality who filled in for Bill O'Reilly, John Kasich, had unseated the Democratic governor, Ted Strickland. Florida had a new senator: Marco Rubio, "our Cuban Barack Obama," as one of his campaign volunteers said on election night. Rubio, despite having engaged in politics and little else for his entire professional life, had earned his antiestablishment bona fides after forcing the state's moderate Republican governor, Charlie Crist, out of the Senate primary. *The New York Times Magazine* had put him on the cover in January 2010 next to the headline THE FIRST SENATOR FROM THE TEA PARTY? Conservative writers began calling him "the great right hope." Still, Rubio and his team recognized the double-edged nature of the Tea Party sword, and had harnessed its political power while keeping it at arm's length. At one political event in Orlando just before the election where Sarah Palin was the marquee attraction, Rubio's aides had him enter and exit in a way that ensured no photographers would snap a picture of him with her.

Then there was Joe Walsh. He had fully bought into the more reckless Tea Party campaign pledges, like voting against a debt ceiling increase. In an interview after his election, he vowed to stick with that despite the misgivings that party leaders like Cantor were expressing. "On principle and policy, the leadership is wrong," Walsh said, picking a fight before he'd even been sworn in. Once he got to Washington, he soon realized an easy way to turn those differences to his advantage back home. "I can take my act on Fox News," he says. "And Fox News loved it."

CHAPTER 5

The Executive

If you want a guy who is going rip somebody's
face off, Mitt is not going to be that guy.
—PETER FLAHERTY, aide to Mitt Romney

arah Palin's "One Nation" bus tour was rolling north through
New Jersey on Tuesday, May 31, 2011, when one of her aides,
Jason Recher, got the call he'd been expecting. Keith Schiller, Donald
Trump's head of security, wanted to talk through some of the logis-
tics of Palin's visit to Trump Tower in a few hours.

The former governor of Alaska was halfway through a jaunt up
the East Coast that week—a six-day, six-hundred-mile spectacle featuring selfie-seeking "Mama Grizzly" fans, caravans of journalists
from all over the world, and news helicopters chasing her chartered
bus from Washington to New Hampshire. The reason for the frenzy
was the widespread anticipation that she could announce she was
running for president at any moment. In reality, however, Palin was
harboring more serious reservations than were known publicly at
the time about having to spend so much time on the road away from
her family. And she was nervous about what the constant scrutiny of
another campaign would do to them. But the show had to go on—if
not for the staff on the payroll of her political action committee that
had raised nearly $1.7 million but also spent $1.5 million during the
first half of the year, then because without it she would likely lose

her relevance as a national political star. Keeping everyone guessing whether she would jump in was a huge story. If she decided to do it, she would upend the race for the Republican nomination, which was shaping up to be a rather dull contest between Mitt Romney, the former governor of Massachusetts, and a handful of other former Republican office holders who would try to peg Romney as stale and uninspiring. And about the only thing that could make the story of Palin's will she–won't she act bigger, and stranger, was Trump.

Recher's cell reception wasn't great, and he could catch only some of what Schiller was saying to him. Through the garbled line, he heard Schiller say something about "people" outside Trump Tower and "the press." Then the call dropped. Recher didn't think much of it, given the throngs of onlookers and media that had been trailing them for three days. Then Recher reconnected with Schiller, who told him the crowd outside was actually larger than what anyone was expecting: a few hundred people, along with a large contingent of reporters, photographers, and cameramen from New York City's notoriously aggressive press corps. Palin's trip had generated so much coverage so far that the media seemed to run out of things to say about her. They commented on her morning treadmill workouts. They compiled a list of her ten-year-old daughter Piper's antics. All the while, Palin seemed indifferent about the media's interest in her. Her staff seemed to be having more fun—but at the expense of the journalists who trailed her bus all week, feverishly trying to keep track of her while Palin's team gave them little to no information.

The Palins continued on toward Manhattan, making a quick stop at an electronics store so her father could buy a camera. When they got to Trump Tower, the family and the handful of aides who were traveling with them rode the elevator up to the penthouse, where Trump and his wife, Melania, were waiting. Counting Ivana Trump's visit to Anchorage in 1996, this would be the second of Trump's wives Palin met. Years after their encounter, she would say that Ivana Trump was the most famous person she'd met before she became governor. Now she had gotten out of Alaska, as she had talked about wanting to do that morning at the local JCPenney, and met plenty of famous people. Since 2008, she had been bombarded with invitations and calls from some of the GOP's most prominent figures, including Rudy Giuliani, the former mayor of New York; Ed Gillespie, the former RNC chairman; and Karl Rove, George W. Bush's political guru. Often she didn't bother to return their calls.

Some light snacks and bottles of water with the Trump logo had been set out. The Palins and the Trumps engaged in generic small talk as they took in the penthouse's expansive views of the city. Chuck Heath, Palin's father, asked Trump at one point where the Fresh Kills landfill was. Trump pointed south, in the direction of Staten Island. And Heath recounted how he and his wife had worked there on an important but unpleasant assignment for the Department of Agriculture when debris from the World Trade Center was hauled there after the 9/11 attacks: They had to trap and kill the rats and other pests that would rummage through the pile, which was strewn with human remains. Trump, usually never one to find himself at a loss for words, was speechless.

Palin's staff had wanted her to stop somewhere public to get a bite with Trump but requested that the restaurant be something downmarket. They didn't want the outing to seem too off-brand for her. The "Palin-Trump Pizza Summit," as some in the media breathlessly called it, took place at the Times Square location of Famous Famiglia, just a short ride away in Trump's limo. As the two of them were leaving Trump Tower under the glow of the warm late spring sun, reporters on the sidewalk jostled against one another. "Donald! Donald! Sarah! Over here!" they called out. "Do you think she should run?" asked one. Trump replied, "I'd love her to run." Later, he seemed to reconsider. Perhaps he had ceded too much of the spotlight to his guest. In an interview the next morning on *Fox & Friends,* he insisted that Palin had actually told him that *he* should run for president himself, a possibility he had also recently teased about in the media. But after several weeks in which he got considerable coverage—much of it for talking about Obama's birth certificate, his new obsession—he backed off. Still, he declared, "She'd love me to get back in the race."

Lately, he had put his head into Republican politics. He was watching Palin's moves closely. He could now see a clearer path by which an insurgent, Tea Party–style presidential candidate could do quite well by running against the party, even if he wasn't sure that would necessarily be Palin. He had remarked to friends that he thought she had tremendous political appeal, but that she also didn't seem to know what to do with it. Part of the reason he invited her in the first place was so he could size her up in person, people close to him would later recall. "Don't think Trump wasn't watching this," says Tony Fabrizio. "That's why he talked to her. He understood that there was a flash there." Trump didn't let the moment pass without taking the opportunity to weigh in on what he thought was the sorry state of the Republican Party, which as far as he was concerned had started to look more hopeless than ever with a policy platform that was full of bad ideas. In the Fox interview, he tore into party leaders like Representative Paul Ryan of Wisconsin for supporting policies he knew weren't popular with voters, like cutting Social Security and Medicare to reduce federal spending. "I am looking at the Republicans and I am seeing things that are like—they have a death wish," Trump complained.

Few professionals in the business were taking Trump's political advice seriously. But there were signs at the time that what was actually happening that afternoon in Manhattan was the beginning of the passing of the baton from Palin to Trump as the leader of the party's insurgent wing. The media appetite for her appearances and the crowds that followed her up I-95 that week pointed to a void in the GOP that Romney wasn't filling as the presumed presidential front-runner.

She was the woman who came the closest anyone ever had to leading the leaderless Tea Party movement. Working with speechwriters like Rebecca Mansour, who would later join *Breitbart* as a senior editor, and Peter Schweizer, a conservative investigative journalist who would co-found with Bannon a self-styled watchdog group called the Government Accountability Institute, Palin didn't pull punches when it came to criticizing people and institutions that were held in high esteem by traditional Republicans: corporate

America, political dynasties, military leaders, and Romney. Her public comments were taking on an even sharper populist edge. One major theme of her speeches was that American capitalism was thoroughly corrupted. "It's not the capitalism of free men and free markets, of innovation and hard work and ethics, of sacrifice and of risk," she would say at a speech in Iowa that summer. "No, this is the capitalism of connections and government bailouts and handouts." The words were Schweizer's, but Palin was speaking to the growing sentiment that both politics and the economy were rigged against ordinary Americans by the same corrupt interests. And "rigged" was also how Palin would later describe Romney's victory in the 2012 Republican primaries.

The experience of a proud, patriotic mother who sent her son off to war only to see him come back broken emotionally led Palin to reconsider the hawkishness she displayed as McCain's running mate. In a speech in the spring of 2011, Palin had expressed an attitude that sounded downright "America First" when she said there should be strict parameters for determining when the country sends troops overseas. "We should only commit our forces when clear and vital American interests are at stake. Period," she declared. Palin also talked about corruption in Washington as a scourge to be expunged like dirty water from a tub. The time had come, she would say in 2012, that "we drain the Jacuzzi, and throw the bums out with the bathwater." Palin had an irrepressible contempt for anyone she thought saw people like her as unworthy "Valley Trash." She punched down at them and accused them of fabricating their stories. "They just make stuff up!" she claimed. She belittled the Bush family as "blue bloods" who wanted to "pick and choose" the Republican nominee.

They were all the right words. But it seemed increasingly likely that she was the wrong vessel. Sometimes she appeared to lose her train of thought or sputtered while she spoke, raising questions about whether she could still captivate crowds as she did in 2008. She skipped the Conservative Political Action Conference altogether in 2011, a way station on the presidential campaign circuit that drew thousands of young conservative activists and party leaders.

She had also fallen out of favor at Fox News since Roger Ailes advised her not to respond to critics who had accused her of inciting the attempted killing of Gabrielle Giffords, a Democratic congresswoman who was shot in Tucson in January 2011. Palin lashed out anyway, saying it was "blood libel" to claim that her rhetoric had anything to do with the shooting. This infuriated many Jewish leaders who associated the phrase with anti-Semitism. She told people close to her that Ailes made her uncomfortable. She complained that he always commented on how he thought she was too skinny. "He's always telling me to eat more cheeseburgers," she would say, clearly annoyed. Once, after a private meeting in his office at Fox News headquarters in 2010, she came out looking white as a ghost. Ailes's assistant had asked that the aides and family traveling with her wait outside so the two of them could meet alone. And when she emerged, Palin said, "I'm never meeting with him alone again."

For all the difficulties Palin would likely encounter as a presidential candidate, Romney's team was not thrilled about the possibility of facing her in the primary. Many on his senior staff read the moment correctly: Their candidate, unfailingly polite and proper to the point that his idea of cursing was "H-E-double-hockey sticks," was temperamentally out of step with Republican voters. "We were concerned, initially, about Sarah Palin becoming a candidate," says Eric Fehrnstrom, a senior adviser. "We sensed there was some potency there." In a primary, she would be trouble. But in a general election, Democrats were salivating about the possibility of running against her. Obama's pollster, Joel Benenson, had put a question about Palin in one of his surveys in February and found that she had the worst standing of any of the possible Republican presidential candidates: 60 percent of Americans saw her unfavorably, with just 36 percent saying they had a favorable impression. Benenson's conclusion was that Palin was irrelevant. But those numbers obscured her popularity with the most motivated primary voters in the GOP, who were solidly conservative and would play a decisive role in picking the nominee. She was a powerhouse with the grassroots, especially when it came to fundraising. Even some in the Republican establishment warned that it would be a mistake to ignore her. Haley Barbour, the governor of Mississippi and former Republican National Committee chairman, acknowledged shortly after her bus tour that Palin was so popular in the party she "could raise enough money to burn a wet mule." Several polls of Republicans showed her leading or slightly trailing Romney. Among Republicans who didn't go to college and earned less than $90,000 a year, she was beating him.

These tremors of a backlash to Romney from the party's base intrigued a small group of conservative activists who had gotten to know Palin and believed she had the raw political talent to be, as one of them put it, "the bona fide rock star in a field of candidates who were really just cover bands." Right around the time of her bus tour, they persuaded Palin to meet with them to walk through what a campaign might look like. No one in this covert three-man presidential exploratory committee had ever managed an undertaking as complicated as a presidential campaign. But they all prepared detailed presentations to give to Palin and her husband, Todd, hoping to convey to them that they were deeply serious and that she had a clear shot at taking over the Republican Party.

They arrived at the Four Seasons in Scottsdale, Arizona, before dusk on a cloudless spring evening. The Palins had recently purchased a home in Scottsdale for $1.75 million, giving them a home base in the continental United States and adding to the speculation that she was thinking about a presidential campaign. All three men went into the meeting thinking Palin was their candidate. David Bossie, the veteran right-wing activist who ran Citizens United, presented first with a PowerPoint explaining how a Palin 2012 campaign would need to be structured in the early primary states: how many signatures she would need to qualify for the ballot; how much money she would have to raise. He did not sugarcoat how difficult it would be to beat Obama as the incumbent president. But he assured her that if she put in the work she could win the GOP nomination. There was a real hunger in the party to challenge the status quo, he said. And if people saw her do that, it would set her up as the undisputed leader of the party. "The one thing you must focus on is the race you're in. Don't look beyond it," Bossie said, echoing almost word for word what he had told Donald Trump about running when they met at Trump Tower the summer of 2010. Don't worry about Obama, he said. Worry about winning the primary first, and the rest will fall into place.

The other two to speak were Bannon, who was just finishing a laudatory documentary about Palin that he hoped would energize conservative activists ahead of her formal campaign announcement; and Schweizer, whose investigations into political corruption started from the premise that both political parties were too tolerant of corruption in their ranks. (Fabrizio, who knew Bossie well but not Bannon, was supposed to join them by speakerphone. But the Palins, who were extremely guarded, didn't like the idea of an open line with someone on the other end they didn't know.) Schweizer believed that the field of likely GOP candidates didn't talk enough about cronyism and Washington's swampy, self-dealing ways. He told Palin that economic uncertainty and anger was still a potent political issue, even with the recession in the rearview mirror, and that she could break through if she campaigned on a promise to hold Congress and corporate America accountable. He and Bannon both explained that Romney's background as the co-founder of his own private equity business and his status as the anointed establishment pick left a huge hole in the field. Run against power, they told her. Romney was Wall Street. She was Wasilla. Voters would see her as one of *us*.

Bannon in particular saw something primal about her appeal and believed she was uniquely suited to speak to the mood of angst in the Republican electorate and to topple the establishment even if she couldn't beat Obama. "You'll control the party apparatus," he told her. "We'll control the Tea Party." He occasionally appeared at the Palin fan clubs and festivals that sprung up after the 2008 election, telling crowds that she was the future of American politics. She attracted what he considered "the oddest lot of people I've ever met"— Christian women, families with children who have Down Syndrome, bikers, and the occasional lesbian. And they all saw themselves in her. "You know why they go after Governor Sarah Palin?" he said at a gathering of Palin fans at CPAC in 2012. "It's not because—just because she's Sarah Palin. They're going after you." Then he attempted to sketch out in incredibly evocative terms exactly what Palin's opponents saw in her that they deemed so worthy of their derision: "A fusion of Caribou Barbie and Bible Spice. She's a white trash tart who's too stupid and incompetent to do anything."

The Palins, who arrived at the Four Seasons dressed inconspicuously in leisure attire, were not especially enthusiastic as they listened. They asked questions occasionally that seemed like what a polite person would ask after a presentation they realized someone had gone to a lot of trouble to put together. They did not take notes. Bossie's comment that she would have to spend a lot of time on the road with donors whose wealth gave them an outsized sense of their political acumen seemed to stick with her. She turned toward Todd with a look of concern when Bossie said that being on the road for long stretches was unavoidable. A lot of her questions were about whether she would be able to split her time between being a mother and running for president. What if she had an obligation she couldn't miss at one of her kids' schools?

The sun went down, and the Palins thanked their hosts for their presentation and left. As Bossie, Bannon, and Schweizer collected their things and walked outside under the starlit desert sky, they were in agreement: *She doesn't want to do this.*

On the last day of Palin's bus tour, June 2, 2011, she was in Boston. That was also the same day that Romney planned to announce his presidential campaign in Stratham, New Hampshire, which was only about an hour away. The Romney team knew that a surprise visit by Palin in the same state, on the same day as their announcement, would suck the media's attention away from the event they'd been planning for weeks. When the two camps connected by phone, Palin's people pleaded ignorance. They said they had no idea about Romney's announcement. The two sides reached a détente. She would hold off crossing into New Hampshire until after Romney's speech, which was planned for the afternoon at a historic farm about twenty minutes inland from where Palin would be headed for a clambake.

In his speech, Romney conveyed the surety of someone who was well on his way to becoming the nominee, and pitched himself as the person who was best suited to replace Obama in the Oval Office. "Barack Obama has failed America," he said. "In the campaign to come, the American ideals of economic freedom and opportunity need a clear and unapologetic defense, and I intend to make it." *The New York Times* noted in its coverage that Romney, who had run for the nomination but lost in 2008, was benefiting from a long if not exactly inspiring GOP tradition: "It should be Mr. Romney's turn as the nominee. The party has a long history of picking a politician who has paid his dues on the campaign trail," the paper said. Some were downright cocky in their assertion that would-be disruptors like Palin didn't stand a chance. Fergus Cullen, the former chairman of the New Hampshire Republican Party, was asked to comment about Palin's road show as it rolled into his state. He insisted that she couldn't expect to thumb her nose at the GOP powers that be for much longer. Eventually, Cullen said, it would become clear who was really in charge. "At some point, the establishment has to be paid its due."

Before her clambake in the coastal town of Seabrook, Palin took a swipe at what had been one of Romney's proudest accomplishments as governor: signing a law that extended healthcare coverage to almost every Massachusetts resident. Later, she spoke about her vision for political leadership. "We have to get back to what made America great," she said.

The state's largest newspaper, the *New Hampshire Union Leader*, covered Palin's visit on its front page with a story and a large photo. Off to the right side of the page there was a smaller photo of Romney and a short caption informing readers that they could find news of his announcement inside.

"Is this over?" Romney sounded unsettled as he huddled with his advisers before his trip to New Hampshire. The cause for his alarm that his campaign might be dead before it ever got off the ground was not a possible rival like Palin. It was the editorial page of *The Wall Street Journal*. To Republicans like Romney, the *Journal* was the institutional voice that conferred respectability and legitimacy on politicians and their ideas. It also had the power to question that legitimacy in a way that could prove damaging. And Romney feared that might happen in light of a recent *Journal* editorial that compared his healthcare plan in Massachusetts to Obama's Affordable Care Act. The law, which Romney had once proudly pointed to as an example of the kind of bold, innovative leadership he was capable of, was now his scarlet letter. He had tried to distance himself from the now-toxic idea among Republicans that the government should have a hand in mandating and providing for universal coverage. A few weeks before he announced his campaign, he vowed that his first act as president would be to repeal the Affordable Care Act.

The fact that government-guaranteed health insurance had become such a political third rail since he signed the Massachusetts law in 2006 was an illustration of just how far to the right the Republican Party had shifted in the years since. It was just one of several ways he seemed poorly matched to an electorate he thought he could win over with attestations of his bona fides—like his claim at CPAC in February 2012 that he was "a severely conservative governor." It came off as awkward and insincere. Some critics said he made conservatism sound like a terminal medical condition, not a belief system. But it wasn't Romney who'd drifted away from the GOP. He had closely modeled his plan after a policy paper on covering the uninsured that came out of the Heritage Foundation, which was considered as much an institutional gatekeeper of American conservatism as the *Journal*. But given the rising influence of libertarian, free-market purists in the party like the Koch brothers, and Obama's unpopularity with Republican voters, any government intervention with Obama's name on it that created a mandate for health insurance was heresy on the right.

The distaste that conservatives had for social safety net programs had not always been so extreme. But it did become more doctrinaire in the party during the rise of Ronald Reagan–style conservatism in the 1980s, a philosophy he famously espoused in his first inaugural address in 1981: "Government is not the solution to our problem. Government *is* the problem." This led to a hands-off policy toward American business among Republicans. The entrepreneur was king.

And laws or regulations that prevented him from keeping as much of his profits and wealth as possible were seen as incompatible with the prevailing understanding among Republicans of freedom and liberty. This led to policies that allowed corporations and the super wealthy—like Romney himself—to pay relatively little in taxes as a share of their earnings. Here Romney was more in sync with the libertarian orthodoxy in the party. But the party was out of sync with its voters, who didn't see business tax breaks as very high on their list of concerns and were growing more skeptical about the GOP's deferential attitude toward corporate America. When Romney got in a shouting match at the Iowa State Fair in 2011 with hecklers who pressed him to commit to raising corporate taxes to preserve social welfare programs, he scoffed, "Corporations are people, my friend." The remark invited criticism that Romney was almost cartoonishly out of touch with middle America. "I'm not going to raise taxes," Romney went on. "And if you want someone who can raise taxes, you can vote for Barack Obama." But that couldn't have been more out-of-touch with how many in the emerging populist wing of the GOP saw it. Rebecca Mansour, who was working for Palin at the time of Romney's comment, heard it and thought to herself how revealing the moment was because, as she saw it, it showed how Republicans had "made corporations into sacred entities." And that was completely foreign to people like Palin. "'Corporations are people,'" says Mansour, "that's not something Palin would ever think." Mansour, who grew up outside Detroit in a large Lebanese-American extended family with relatives who worked in the city's automotive trade, knew Romney had handed his opponents a gift. She just wasn't sure many Republican Party leaders understood that.

It wasn't such ancient history when another of the GOP's leading candidates for president was a successful executive who took an expansive view of the government's role in promoting societal good, but who was also an ill-fitting leader for voters who shared a deep sense of cultural alienation and anger. He was George Romney,

Mitt's father, the governor of Michigan and former chief executive of the car manufacturer American Motors, who ran for president in 1968. As governor, he once declared that "Michigan's most urgent human rights problem is racial discrimination" and marched in a demonstration for racial equality in 1963. He supported increasing funding for Detroit's troubled public school system. He helped implement a state income tax for the first time. As head of American Motors, Romney bet on an environmentally conscious small car, the Rambler, and was mocked for it by his rivals at the Big Three automakers. But the Republican Party of 1968 would be Richard Nixon's, whose lukewarm feelings about civil rights and tough talk about bringing law-and-order to American cities were more in line with the sensibilities of white conservatives like Walter Headley, the police chief in Miami who admonished city residents in 1967, "When the looting starts, the shooting starts."

As similar as the Romneys were in their inability to be the culture warriors that voters wanted, they also embodied very different eras of American capitalism. And by 2012, the younger Romney represented the kind of wealth that many people weren't seeing as aspirational but as avaricious. While American Motors had undoubtedly made the older Romney very rich, it had also given thousands of employees a comfortable life that allowed them to purchase homes, cars, and second homes, and thrive as part of the great American middle class that grew out of the post–World War II era when such luxuries weren't limited to a relative few. Romney turned down bonuses and capped his own compensation. He said that no executive should make more than $225,000 a year, which would be almost $2 million today.

By the time his son ran for president for the first time in 2008, those ideas would have been called socialist by leaders of the Republican Party. With a fortune estimated at $350 million, the younger Romney would make considerably more money than his father ever saw, thanks to shifts in where the biggest profits in the economy were being generated and how that money was being distributed. Mitt's fortune came from a new profit center in finance: private equity, which allows relatively few individuals to make large amounts of money, often by investing in businesses where costs and jobs can be slashed to maximize profit. Companies like Mitt's Bain Capital took over businesses like American Motors and often laid people off, eliminating the kinds of jobs that helped lift people into the middle class.

Romney and his campaign aides mistakenly believed that enough voters would look up to him as proof that the American Dream was still alive and well, and see him as what they truly wanted in a president: a more competent chief executive than Obama had been for a country still struggling to pull through the Great Recession. "It was always, for us, an economic focus, not some sense of cultural focus," says Stuart Stevens, senior strategist for the 2012 Romney campaign. "We weren't fighting some great cultural war." Peter Flaherty, another campaign adviser, notes that Romney was never going to be the kind of warrior the Tea Party lionized. "If you want a guy who is going rip somebody's face off, Mitt is not going to be that guy," he says.

What voters wanted, in other words, was a president like the people Ailes was putting on Fox News. This included four of the Republicans who were often seen as possible rivals of Romney's in the primary. There was Palin, Newt Gingrich, Rick Santorum, and Mike Huckabee. By 2011, Ailes had created a system of political and financial dependency for Republicans with presidential aspirations that revolved entirely around him. Gingrich, the windy, self-important, and blunt-spoken former House speaker, was earning close to $1 million a year. Palin earned the same. Huckabee, a folksy Baptist pastor and former governor of Arkansas, earned about half that. And Santorum, the former Pennsylvania senator whose strict Catholic beliefs and Rust Belt appeal made him a hit with religious conservatives, was making about half what Huckabee did. Huckabee didn't end up running in 2012. But Gingrich and Santorum both had far more appeal with primary voters than Romney's aides hoped they would.

The Rasputin-like staying power of these presumably weak rivals was what some Romney strategists referred to as the "Not Mitt" phenomenon. And it kept Romney from locking in the nomination until April 10, 2012, when Santorum suspended his campaign. At any point in the race, enough voters would fall in love with one of Romney's angrier and more conservative opponents simply because that person was "not Mitt," as Russ Schriefer, Romney's top advertising consultant, put it. "It didn't matter who it was," Schriefer says. "They would pop up, then we'd take them out. Then another 'Not Mitt' candidate would rise in their place." There was Michele Bachmann, the Tea Party congresswoman; Rick Perry, the governor of Texas; Herman Cain, the pizza-chain mogul; Gingrich; and Santorum. Gingrich proved to be the most frustrating of the "Not Mitt" candidates for Romney and his team. Jolly and convivial one moment, sputtering and rageful the next, he brought the fight in a way Romney couldn't. He used the debates to brutalize the moderators, soaring past Romney in the polls and winning the South Carolina primary on January 21. He attacked and belittled his questioners. "I'm frankly not interested in your effort to get Republicans fighting each other," Gingrich snapped at John F. Harris of *Politico* in one debate. He told Fox's Chris Wallace at another, "I wish you would put aside the gotcha questions."

As Romney's advisers watched Gingrich perform on the stage, it dawned on them why voters were eating it up: He was giving them a preview of how aggressively he would confront Obama. The moderators were just props in his dress rehearsal. "People liked that the media was the stand-in for Obama," explains Schriefer. One exchange with Juan Williams of Fox News showed how effectively Gingrich could transport Obama onto the stage with him. At the debate on January 16 in Myrtle Beach, South Carolina, Gingrich let loose when Williams, who is Black, asked him whether he understood how offensive it was to have recently said that poor children could improve their work ethic by doing custodial work at school, and that Black Americans should demand jobs instead of being "satisfied with food stamps."

Gingrich shook his head dismissively. "No. I don't see that," he said, insisting that there was nothing wrong with some "light janitorial duty" for disadvantaged students to build character. The crowd hooted and applauded. And when Gingrich blamed Obama for high poverty rates—"The fact is that more people have been put on food stamps by Barack Obama than any president in American history," the former speaker said—the crowd roared.

Ailes did not think much of Romney. According to colleagues who were in regular meetings with him, he thought Romney was bad television. That also meant that Ailes thought he'd be a bad presidential candidate. "A stuffed shirt," he would scoff. According to a biography of the Fox News chief by the journalist Gabriel Sherman, he had once described Romney as "Chinese food." Twenty minutes after you eat it, Ailes said, "you can't remember what you had." One of the only things Ailes thought Romney had working in his favor on television was his resemblance to Cary Grant. The relationship between the two men was strained for several reasons, some having to do with Ailes's ego and others that stemmed from what he saw as Romney's deficiencies as a challenger to Obama.

Ailes thought Romney seemed weak and unenergetic in debates, which was particularly problematic because televised debates were playing a bigger and more decisive role in the Republican primary process than ever before. David Kochel, who was responsible for Romney's Iowa operation, recalls how much of the race moved to the airwaves that year. "It was the first time, to me, that it was really evident what you did in the state wasn't as important as what the national conversation was," Kochel says. "All the things a campaign is built to do—the ninety-nine-county tour, getting endorsements, earned media in the state—have a lessened impact." This was somewhat by Ailes's design, because he pushed for as many debates as the candidates would agree to do. Fox News hosted five of the twenty Republican debates held between the spring of 2011 and early 2012. People started calling the race for the nomination "the Fox primary." The Romney campaign aired its objections to Fox and other networks about having so many televised face-offs. But Ben Ginsberg, who was leading the Romney team's debate negotiations with the networks, recalls that Ailes thought he was helping. Fox News, Ailes said, was doing Romney a favor by "toughening him up."

The Fox debates reflected Ailes's vision of *American Gladiators*–style politics. Fox booked arena-type venues, brought in cameras that panned the audience high above like during professional sports games, and there was sometimes a fully stocked bar available to the audience before the show. Romney's team knew he was never going to be the kind of combatant that Ailes wanted to see, but they also knew they couldn't skip out on the debates once the primary season was in full swing. Romney worried that being too aggressive with his opponents could come off as hotheaded and intemperate. But his idea of aggression was Ailes's resting mode. Stevens recalls working with Ailes on the debate prep team for George H. W. Bush's 1992 campaign against Bill Clinton. Before one of the debates, Stevens remembers seeing Ailes with the president. "Roger is screaming at him, 'I want you to get in that fat fuck's face!' Right up there next to him, putting his finger in Bush's chest. And I remember thinking, 'Not how I would talk to the president of the United States, but okay.'" Ailes certainly did not see a fire in Romney. And as he watched the primary debates on television, he sometimes grew so frustrated that he shouted at the screen whenever he thought Romney missed an opportunity to land a punch—"What's the matter with this guy? He has no balls!" He once raised Romney's acquiescent demeanor with the campaign manager, Matt Rhoades. Ailes was in disbelief when he relayed Rhoades's explanation to Fox executives: "He doesn't want to seem like an angry guy." If Romney made it to the general election after all, Ailes grumbled, Fox News would have to drag him over the finish line.

Ailes not only believed voters would see Romney as weak, he thought they would find it difficult to identify with him. Ailes certainly couldn't—largely because of the enormous upstairs-downstairs cultural and social gap between them. Both grew up in the Midwest and had fathers who worked in the auto industry, but that's where the similarities ended. Ailes grew up about an hour east of Cleveland in the blue-collar manufacturing town of Warren, Ohio, where his father worked at a Packard Electric plant—a world apart from the prep school and country club life Romney had in the leafy Detroit suburb of Bloomfield Hills. Ailes didn't see those differences as superficial, explains Carl Cameron, who covered Romney's campaign. "Mitt Romney is an aristocrat who became the governor of Massachusetts—an educated man, a very successful businessman, and an elite," he says. "Roger Ailes was a bad boy from Ohio—blue-collar and disdainful of people who wear white-collar shirts and fancy ties." And since Romney was already wealthy, he didn't need Ailes to pay him a salary the way he did Palin, Gingrich, and the others.

But there was one wealthy man whom Ailes found to be unusually common in his touch with everyday Americans. When he was president of CNBC in the 1990s and gave himself his own talk show, Ailes invited Donald Trump on as one of his guests. In their 1995 interview on the program *Straight Forward,* which has since vanished into the void of canceled cable news programs, Ailes asked the forty-nine-year-old Trump about the seeming contradiction. "The guy on the street, the cabdrivers, the guys working on the road crews go, 'Hey, Donald! How's it going? Hey!' They—it's almost like they feel very comfortable with you, like you're one of them. And I've never quite figured out how you bridge that," Ailes said.

Trump responded that it probably had something to do with how he wore elite disdain as a badge of honor. "The people that don't like me are the rich people. It's a funny thing. They can't stand me . . . I sort of love it." Ailes asked whether Trump might run for president someday. Trump said that he was supporting Senator Bob Dole in the upcoming presidential election because Dole was the kind of politician who could actually get elected. Trump confessed that he was less sure that he could make it himself. "I'm not sure that somebody that really calls it like it is and says, 'This is what you have to do,' I'm not sure that kind of a guy gets elected," he said, insisting, nonetheless, "Everybody wants me to do it."

At Fox News, Ailes told executives that putting Trump on the network would draw in viewers who saw something aspirational in the successful real estate developer and his handsome family. He was "relatable rich," Ailes said. But there was another reason Trump would be a guaranteed ratings boon. By early 2011, Trump had become obsessed with spreading unfounded rumors about Obama's background. On March 28, Trump went on *Fox & Friends* and spent an entire segment talking about ways that Obama could be lying about being born in the United States. "It's turning out to be a very big deal because people now are calling me from all over saying, 'Please don't give up on this issue,' " he boasted.

Three days later, Fox News announced a new regular segment on *Fox & Friends,* "Mondays with Trump." A promo teased that it would be "Bold, brash and never bashful."

It had been less than a year since his involvement with the Ground Zero Mosque. But Trump had been busy during that time dipping his toe into other causes and conspiracies of the far right. Between the late summer of 2010, when he made national headlines for his offer to buy the downtown Manhattan building where a Muslim community center was to be built, and the spring of 2011, Trump found his voice with Republican voters. The line between the mosque controversy and the widely publicized disinformation campaign he waged about Obama's birth certificate is short and fairly direct, and much of it played out on the airwaves of Fox News. Building on the lessons he learned in 2010, he saw how many Americans had a deep and enduring fear of an enemy lurking within—and the popularity he could gain from feeding that fear. Whenever he mentioned the birth certificate to an audience, he got the ultimate reward. "They went wild," he said on *Fox & Friends* with no small amount of self-satisfaction.

Fox wasn't the only place where Trump was testing his new material. In February 2011, the month before his regular Fox segment was announced, Trump surfaced at the Conservative Political Action Conference in Washington. It was the CPAC crowd that gave him his first big opportunity to do a dry run for the birther conspiracy. He didn't discover CPAC on his own. The person who helped put him on the stage was Roger Stone, his on-again, off-again adviser and friend who suggested that Trump speak there as a way of raising his profile with conservatives. Trump had never heard of the event and didn't know the significant role it played in the Republican primary process. Stone explained this, telling Trump that if he went, "People would read it as an indicator that you're serious about running for president in 2012." Trump liked that. But he couldn't just show up and ask to be heard; he needed a sponsor before he could speak at the conference. Stone helped arrange for one of CPAC's newer and more controversial players to be that sponsor: GOProud, a group of pro-gay-rights conservatives that counted iconoclasts like Andrew Breitbart among its members. The group had already become a huge headache for CPAC's organizers after many Christian conservatives demanded that they be banned from the conference.

It wasn't the most flawless debut for Trump, but it didn't hurt him either. He promised he was pro-life despite his past support for abortion rights. He said he opposed gun control. He pledged to pursue foreign nations whose trade policies were hurting the American economy by collecting "hundreds of billions of dollars from other countries that are screwing us." These lines earned him a friendly reception. But what the crowd really loved was when he turned his focus to Obama's background. "Our current president came out of nowhere," Trump said. Sensing the crowd's receptiveness, he stayed on the subject, improvising as he ratcheted up his line of attack. "I'll go a step further," Trump continued. "The people who went to school with him, they don't even know, they never saw him. They don't know who he is. Crazy." The applause and cheers grew louder, and Trump still kept going. "Nobody knew who the hell he was!"

As he tried to make his way around the hotel where the conference was taking place, Trump couldn't move without being mobbed. Sam Nunberg, the consultant who first met Trump while he was working on a campaign to stop the mosque, recalls being at CPAC that day for a meeting with some officials for the Romney campaign. "That was when I saw he could get elected president. The cameras are all over him. I had never seen anything like that for a Republican," Nunberg says.

Trump didn't publicly mention the birth certificate issue for another few weeks. But those who spoke to him that winter say it was certainly on his mind. He began seeking out far-right lawmakers, operatives, and journalists who'd latched on to the subject. One of them was Corsi, who recalls receiving several phone calls at the time from Trump about his brand-new book, *Where's the Birth Certificate?* Corsi says that "Four times he called me up and asked me questions. And I tried to answer his questions as best I could. But you know, mostly with Donald Trump he was—he did a lot of the talking." Trump always had a specific question in mind—something that had been written recently about the issue—and it was clear to Corsi that Trump had been consuming a lot of material about the birth certificate beyond his book. "He was already on these subjects," Corsi says.

Soon, Trump was everywhere making wild claims in the media, finding a larger and larger audience for the false reality he was constructing. And he did so with the help of some of the biggest shows in television: NBC's *Today*, ABC's *Good Morning America* and *The View*, and of course *Fox & Friends*. He claimed to have hired a team of investigators and dispatched them to Hawaii. "They cannot believe what they're finding," he told NBC. But when asked to elaborate, he snapped, "That's none of your business right now. We're going to see what happens." He even tried to show how easily an original birth certificate could be obtained and sent his own to *Newsmax*. But when *Newsmax* published it, sharp-eyed readers noticed that it didn't have the markings that an official New York City document would have and started emailing Maggie Haberman, then with *Politico*, who reported that Trump had flubbed his own stunt. The "birthers," as devotees of the conspiracy theory were known, were now his people. And he was not shy in signaling his sympathies for them. "Hardworking, unbelievable, the salt-of-the-earth people," he said when he called in to Laura Ingraham's radio program, expressing dismay that these "great people" were being attacked for what they believed.

At Fox, he found *Fox & Friends* and *Hannity* to be the most accommodating. In April, Hannity asked Trump about a supposed connection between the birth certificate and Obama's religion, fusing one conspiracy to another and teeing Trump up perfectly. "Could it have to do with religion?" Hannity asked Trump. Trump didn't miss a beat: "Maybe it says he's a Muslim." There was no box, of course, for identifying a baby's religion on Hawaii's birth certificate. But this was a bridge too far for other Fox hosts, notably Bill O'Reilly, who was Trump's favorite host (and uncoincidentally the highest rated) and an occasional companion at Yankees games. "What, is he Baby Jesus?" O'Reilly once said dismissively to Trump on the air. "There was a sophisticated conspiracy to smuggle this baby back into the country?"

Off camera, Trump was burrowing down deeper into the rabbit hole of birtherism than many knew. One morning in April, a state legislator in Arizona named Carl Seel visited Trump's office along with two Tea Party activists, including Kelly Townsend, a future Arizona state senator who would take up Trump's fanciful cause that his 2020 loss in Arizona was the result of voter fraud. Seel was one of several far-right lawmakers across the country trying to codify birtherism into state law by proposing a bill that would require candidates to show proof they were born in the United States to get on the ballot. He had cold-called Trump Tower one night and left a message asking if Trump might be interested in coming to Arizona to help him promote his bill. Trump relayed a message back to Seel that he couldn't make it, but he invited him for a meeting at Trump Tower at 10 A.M. the following Thursday. With a crucial vote on his legislation approaching, Seel and his colleagues jumped on a plane and headed to New York. Trump greeted them warmly when they arrived at his office. "You're a really, really powerful man," he told Seel, who recalls, "He already had an excellent grasp of it, and I could tell he knew exactly what it was." When the subject of running for president came up, Trump was noncommittal. But he said he'd keep in touch. Seel recalls that Trump said if he indeed went through with it, he'd want the support of Republicans like them. "He'd want to come out to Arizona and talk to us more."

The day after Romney announced he was forming an exploratory committee for president in March 2011, Larry Kudlow of CNBC asked him about Trump's birth certificate claims. Romney was unamused. "I believe the president was born in the United States. There are real reasons to get this guy out of office," he replied. Trump badly wanted in on the action in the campaign. In December, he and Chris Ruddy at *Newsmax* cooked up a plan for Trump to host a presidential debate. Romney refused, which killed the idea because there could be no debate without the front-runner. With the primary contests approaching, he and his staff at the Trump Organization reached out multiple times to ask Romney if Trump could campaign for him. At first, Romney aides recall, Trump dispatched Michael Cohen to deliver a message to the campaign that he had "cleared his schedule" so he could join Romney on the trail and travel the country stumping for him. When that suggestion went nowhere, Trump called himself and offered to be of assistance however he could, assuring Stuart Stevens, "I'll get great numbers." Stevens politely explained that Romney did not have a problem with his name recognition, so good television ratings weren't imperative to his success. Trump even once told campaign staff that he would take media training so he could be as effective as possible making his case for Romney. Gail Gitcho, a senior aide on the campaign, didn't want to blow Trump off when she heard about his offer. But she was also skeptical, fearing that putting Trump on television to talk about her candidate would be a huge risk. She called Ari Fleischer, the former White House press secretary under George W. Bush, who ran his own consulting firm, to see if Fleischer might be open to giving Trump some training. Fleischer said yes, but only if Trump paid his executive rate of $25,000. Trump did not go through with the media training.

The Romney campaign noticed in its polling that while Palin wasn't there to organize the disaffected Republicans around one candidate, Trump started getting a lot of support once she was officially out of contention. "We concluded that this was not going to be a good thing to have Trump in the race against us," Fehrnstrom says. "Because he appealed to that same segment of the electorate that Sarah Palin was popular with." The solution, campaign strategists believed, was to try to "keep him sidelined," Fehrnstrom adds. After rebuffing his offer to help during the Florida primary, the senior staff agreed on a plan they hoped would minimize whatever damage he could do: Romney would accept Trump's endorsement before the Nevada caucuses. Voting was set for February 4, a Saturday. Romney was heavily favored to win already. And campaign aides knew that the weekend news cycle was one that most people wouldn't be paying much attention to.

Two young Romney communications aides, Ryan Williams and Andrea Saul, were dispatched to Las Vegas to meet Trump at his hotel just off the Las Vegas Strip on the morning of February 2 with instructions from headquarters to flatter him profusely and to brief him on a set of talking points. *This is the most important event Romney will do before the caucuses. We can't let anything distract us from that. The media will be looking for any attempt to drive a wedge between the two of you. There is such intense interest in your speech. Just look at how many reporters are already downstairs.* Trump's response was instant, Pavlovian. He made a beeline for the elevator and took it down to the lobby to begin the first of three press conferences he would give that day. Once word of Trump's impromptu media appearance hit Twitter, Williams started receiving angry messages from Romney headquarters in Boston.

When Romney arrived at the hotel with his wife, Ann, Romney could hardly conceal his disbelief at how he had ended up campaigning alongside the man he considered the court jester of American politics. "There are some things that you can't imagine happening in your life . . . and this is one of them," he said, standing where his staff had erected a wall of plain blue curtains to obscure the gaudy gilt and marble interior of Trump's hotel. The entire spectacle before the cameras was finished in less than seven minutes. The Romneys left as quickly as they could and took no questions from reporters. Few would have taken the scene for what it was—the ghosts of the Republican Party's soon-to-be past and its future standing uncomfortably together in a physical manifestation of the warring camps within. Romney, finding himself powerless to say no to Trump, discovered that no amount of scaffolding could prevent Trump from finding a way to steal the show.

—

Romney had a very different vision for what the future of the Republican Party was than Trump: Representative Paul Ryan of Wisconsin, his vice presidential pick. On substance and style, Ryan was as far as Republicans could get from Sarah Palin. He spoke in linear, clearly articulated paragraphs about issues that animated him—the federal budget, entitlement spending, taxes. Romney's selection process was mostly head and little heart, except for the genuine affection he developed for Ryan as someone he thought was brilliant and dazzling. Ryan checked the boxes with three attributes Romney told aides his running mate needed. He had conservative credentials and would therefore satisfy the conservative base, or so Romney's team believed. He was also competent and could be trusted to always represent a Romney administration well. A business partner of Romney's told campaign advisers that Ryan reminded him of the kind of person Romney would have hired in his private equity business because he was "client ready." And he would be an ideal partner to complement what Romney considered was a major deficiency of his: the knowledge and ability to manage Congress.

What Romney did not see as a deficiency was the fact that Ryan was the public face of a political philosophy that was so unpopular. It did not occur to him that voters would see Ryan as another entrepreneurial class Republican who didn't understand their anxieties or validate their grievances. Romney's team saw some of the potential downside, but mostly the upside. "We're the smart ticket, the responsible ticket," says Dan Senor, a campaign adviser and private equity executive who was close to Ryan. Seeing entitlement reform as an issue that could be a net negative for Romney, says Senor, "It just wasn't showing up in any of the polling, and it wasn't showing up in thought leadership circles on the right, and it certainly wasn't showing up in Congress." The campaign was hoping that Americans would look at Romney and want to "hire" him to fix the country. And if voters saw their choice as analogous to picking a manager to tackle a tough job, then the evident competency and intelligence of Romney and Ryan would be a decisive factor. Stevens had a phrase he liked to use—"This is not an eHarmony.com election. This is a Monster.com election"—to underscore that voters did not need to fall in love with Romney or Ryan. They just needed to like what was on their résumés.

Voters did not fall in love with Romney, nor did they hire him. This much was clear after Fox News called the state of Ohio and the race for Obama just before 11:30 P.M. on election night. Right before Fox was about to make the call, Ailes's head of news, Michael Clemente, called downstairs to a VIP reception area where Ailes had been watching the results with Rupert Murdoch and other executives. Clemente was hoping to give his boss a heads-up, but Ailes had already gone home for the night.

A few weeks after the election, Ailes and Clemente went to see Romney at the Essex House, a posh hotel on Central Park South owned by Romney's family friends, the Marriotts. The loss had not surprised Ailes, given his feelings about Romney's weaknesses. But it did sting to be beaten twice by Obama, a candidate he believed could have been taken out if only the Republican nominee had displayed the same aggressiveness as his network had. Republicans wanted a fighter, he groused to his staff, and instead they got someone with "no balls." But Ailes was in good spirits that day. He knocked on the door and announced himself with a humorous greeting: "Room service!" Romney was alone—no staff, no security, and none of the frenetic activity that had surrounded him at all hours during the campaign. He said that his loss hadn't hit him as hard as most people probably thought it would. He told Ailes he was at peace. "I think Ann was more upset than I was," he said. Ailes told Romney that the door at Fox was always open to him.

He did offer a few thoughts about why Obama had been re-elected. And anyone who knew Ailes knew it was the kind of paranoid thinking he had long urged his staff at Fox News to pursue as stories. The Democrats pulled a fast one, he said, just as they always do. "They make promises they can't keep. And they're dirty," Ailes said. "They cheat."

A few weeks later, on New Year's Day, Roger Stone called Trump to wish him well in the new year, which he did every January 1. Trump brought up the presidential election. "What's wrong with Mitt Romney? Why did I ever support this guy? What a loser." Then

Trump's thoughts turned to the election in four years. "You always said I could do this," Trump said. Trump claimed he was serious about running, though Stone had heard this before and was skeptical. Then he said something that made Stone think he might actually mean it.

"I trademarked 'Make America Great Again,'" Trump said. Stone knew this was a serious step for the notoriously tight-fisted Trump. A trademark costs money.

On November 19, thirteen days after the election, the United States Patent and Trademark Office recorded a filing for "Make America Great Again" under Donald J. Trump, 725 Fifth Avenue, New York, New York.

CHAPTER 6

The Autopsy

Cheer up. We'll win the next election, and we'll have a new face.

—MITCH DANIELS to Ari Fleischer in an interview
for the RNC "Autopsy"

T he second time felt different, and much worse. When Obama beat Republicans in 2008, there was a certain resignation in defeat. Even the most die-hard conservatives could see how it made sense, coming after eight years of a Republican president who left office with the lowest approval of anyone since Jimmy Carter, on top of two wars with no end in sight and one Great Recession. After the dust settled, they understood that it would have been kind of a miracle had McCain won. But 2012 was supposed to have been much easier. A languid economy and a new universal healthcare law that was confusing and unpopular contributed to a growing sense that the country was headed in the wrong direction. The unemployment rate remained stubbornly high at around 8 percent. Republicans convinced themselves that most Americans saw Obama the way they did: as a failed liberal ideologue who was ill-suited to lead a country that still hadn't rebounded from crisis. "The conventional Republican wisdom was we're a center-right country. And given a chance, the thinking went, the country would revert to center-right," explains Stuart Stevens, Romney's strategist. To borrow the metaphor Bill Clinton had used in 2008 to question Obama's preparedness, voters had rolled the dice once, but many Republican politicians and their consultants believed they wouldn't do so again. "There was always an element that saw Obama as an aberration," Stevens adds.

The idea that the majority of the country leans Republican no matter what the results at the ballot box say is fundamental to the way Republicans have long seen themselves as a party. In the 1960s, they were the people described by Senator Barry Goldwater, the godfather of modern conservatism, as "the forgotten American" whom he said comprised "the substantial majority of our people" but still had no voice in national politics. And when Goldwater suffered a crushing loss in forty-four states and the District of Columbia in 1964, his supporters consoled themselves with the illusion of massive popular support: 26,000,000 AMERICANS CAN'T BE WRONG! declared one bumper sticker distributed by the Conservative Society of America. (More than forty million people voted for Lyndon B. Johnson that year.) By the end of the decade, Republicans were identifying with the superlative that President Richard Nixon had given them in a speech in 1969: the "great silent majority"—Americans who were patriotic, God-fearing, and outraged by an anti–Vietnam War movement they saw as belligerent and amoral. In the Reagan years, many of these Americans heeded the call of the "Moral Majority," the national organization of religious conservatives led by Jerry Falwell that worked to elect Republicans who opposed abortion and homosexuality and said they refused to stand by and watch the devolution of American society into a socialist welfare state.

Heading into Election Day 2012, that same mentality muddled the Republican elite's ability to read the country. Smart Republicans, powerful Republicans, declared with certitude that they were getting their country back because that's what the people wanted. "Mitt Romney will win big tonight," predicted Steve Forbes, a two-time former candidate for the Republican nomination himself and scion of the famous publishing dynasty. Forbes was so sure that he put a number on the Romney blowout he could see coming: a win in the popular vote by a margin of 3 to 5 percentage points, plus victories in Florida, Ohio, Pennsylvania, Virginia, Colorado, and Wisconsin—

a sweep of big battleground states that no Republican had come close to achieving since George H. W. Bush in 1988. Many Republicans like Forbes argued that Democrats and the media were making bad, inflated predictions in their polls about Obama's turnout, echoing an idea that Romney's own staff had been promoting in the final weeks of the campaign as they looked at their internal numbers. There were others, such as Peggy Noonan of *The Wall Street Journal*, who grounded her prediction of a Romney victory not in polling but in intuition and three decades of experience in politics. "Something old is roaring back," Noonan wrote the day before the election, describing a "quiet, unreported" excitement among evangelicals, religious Catholics, and other churchgoers she said the polls weren't picking up. "While everyone is looking at the polls," Noonan claimed, "Romney's slipping into the presidency." But it wasn't just the excitement she could sense that colored Noonan's thinking. Romney, she said, just seemed to fit the part better than Obama. "He looked like a president," she wrote, describing how he appeared at a dinner where she had closely observed his body language and affect. "He looked like someone who'd just seen good internals," Noonan surmised.

It was an appealing thought—like being in on a joke that your opponents in the mainstream media and the Democratic Party were too smug to get. Romney's chief pollster, Neil Newhouse, would explain later that he had misread voter intensity. He assumed that many of the people who said they were voting for Obama but also weren't very enthusiastic about it weren't going to show up. And that didn't turn out to be the case. "I misinterpreted 'intensity' as having an impact on turnout," Newhouse says about why his polling showed Romney in a stronger position than he actually was. "Low intensity/low interest voters count just as much as high intensity ones," Newhouse says. The effect was similar to what Stevens had described when he predicted 2012 would be a "Monster.com election" in which voters didn't need to be madly in love with their candidate to vote for him. Only that sentiment turned out to be more important for Obama than Romney. These were honest mistakes—a misreading of a narrowly divided electorate.

But there were also illegitimate forces at work that were perpetuating false confidence in Romney's odds. Chief among them was Dean Chambers, a self-described "independent journalist" who ran a website called *UnSkewedPolls.com*. Chambers was at the leading edge of an insidious shift in the way conservative media was misrepresenting public opinion to its audience. He claimed to have a statistical secret sauce that unlocked the real numbers in the public polls. His "unskewing" happened by taking the raw data from available public surveys and manipulating it until Romney's totals were inflated to his satisfaction. Chambers wasn't doing anything sophisticated or proprietary with the math and modeling, as many of the people who followed his work believed. He was just basing his numbers on a hunch that Romney should be doing better in these polls than he was. Chambers's methods were criticized by pollsters of all partisan persuasions. One expert called his work the "creation science" of public opinion research. But the fact that it was junk didn't stop widely followed right-wing media from promoting it. *The Drudge Report* and Fox News both presented Chambers as an oracle. Sean Hannity parroted Chambers's slogan, telling his audience point-blank, "The polls are skewed." This kind of exposure allowed Chambers to bend reality and become something to Romney supporters that he wasn't: a bona fide authority who was speaking truths that powerful people in the media and the Democratic Party wanted to hide. When the election results proved he'd been wrong all along, Chambers did concede his mistakes and shut down *UnSkewedPolls.com*. Then he created a new website dedicated to propagating another fraud.

The reason Chambers now claimed he'd been wrong was that Obama had stolen the election. Chambers was far from the only one promoting this lie as a balm for shell-shocked conservatives who'd been assured victory. Stories about supposed instances of fraud circulated online and over talk radio at the time. Some seemed plausible at first glance, including one about a curious outcome in Philadelphia, where Obama received 100 percent of the vote in dozens of precincts. But when the Republican on the commission that oversees the city's elections interviewed voters as part of an investigation, he did not find a single person in those precincts who had voted for Romney. That was not how the story was told on Fox News, at *Breitbart,* and elsewhere in the right-wing media. The 100 percent totals for Obama were treated as evidence that fraud had in fact taken place—not as a logical outcome in precincts where the voters were overwhelmingly Black. Wild stories about voting machines that had somehow subtracted votes from Romney had already started circulating on social media on election night. One person who picked them up immediately was Donald Trump, who posted on Twitter about a nefarious-sounding plot to hack voting machines, foreshadowing his false claims about the 2020 election. "More reports of voting machines switching Romney votes to Obama. Pay close attention to the machines, don't let your vote be stolen." Then he called for people to take to the streets. "We can't let this happen. We should march on Washington and stop this travesty."

Whatever their reasons for assuming Obama should have lost, a lot of Republicans had believed their own hype. And now someone was going to have to explain to them what happened.

The granular data that answered that question was contained in a pair of reports that were sent to the Republican National Committee in the weeks after the election. One was an internal Romney campaign analysis of public exit polls and research conducted by the chief pollster, Newhouse. The other was a large survey of swing state voters commissioned by the RNC and conducted by a private research firm. The reports were the basis for what would become known as "The Autopsy," a blunt assessment of the GOP's deficiencies and blind spots. When the RNC released the findings in March 2013, they would shape the party establishment's consensus about how to win the White House back in 2016. Reince Priebus, the young and idealistic party chairman, considered it a priority to expand the GOP's appeal with voters who were younger and more diverse. On the day he presented the autopsy's conclusions to the media, which happened to be his forty-first birthday, Priebus described the ideal Republican candidate of the future. "Look at the youth in our party. Nikki Haley and Marco Rubio and Paul Ryan and Scott Walker," he said, beaming. "We have great Hispanic leaders in our party like Brian Sandoval [the governor of Nevada] and Ted Cruz [who had just been elected a senator from Texas]. . . . When it comes to youth, when it comes to diversity, we've made great strides."

From its inception, the autopsy was primarily tailored to and influenced by the thinking of Republicans like Priebus who believed that the party's insurgent wing was hurting it with the crucial swing demographics and fast-growing segments of the population. The autopsy's recommendations for how the party should soften its messaging were primarily written by Ari Fleischer, the former White House press secretary for George W. Bush, and informed by interviews Fleischer conducted with party donors, consultants, conservative media elites, and officeholders. Many told Fleischer a version of what another former Bush strategist, Mark McKinnon, thought was the problem: Republicans were too backward looking. "We're stuck in a time warp," McKinnon said, according to Fleischer's notes. There was plenty of hard data and anecdotal evidence collected during the autopsy confirming that many voters agreed. But they were playing an increasingly smaller role in how the Republican Party picked its presidential nominee, as the artificial equilibrium between party leaders and disillusioned rank-and-file voters was giving way. In their attempt to explain what went wrong, party leaders would badly misjudge yet again how to elect a Republican president, overlooking warning signs in their own data and ignoring advice from people who told them that voters were hungry for a populist candidate with celebrity appeal.

Priebus kept a chart in his office at RNC headquarters that depicted the pace of growth of the Hispanic population alongside the corresponding level of support a Republican candidate would need to win the presidency in the future. The line crept ever higher past 2012, 2016, and beyond. The conclusion seemed undeniable: There was no way the GOP could survive by winning a larger and larger share of the white vote in each election. And his belief was affirmed by the pair of post-election reports. Both rang the alarm about the GOP's overreliance on conservative voters and warned that the days were over when its poor performance with Black voters could be overcome with more white votes.

The Romney campaign's analysis confirmed that he had hit a ceiling with white voters. In Ohio, the Romney report noted, he won 58 percent of whites, compared to McCain's 52 percent four years earlier. But the analysis concluded that even with numbers like that, "the African American turnout was just too high to overcome." In Florida it was the same story, but Latino voters were the problem. Romney took 61 percent of the white vote to McCain's 56 percent. "The white vote moved as needed," the report said, "but missed getting it done with the expanding Hispanic voter community," which was now 17 percent of Florida's electorate, or 4 percentage points higher than in 2008. The campaign's analysis highlighted a significant miscalculation that complicated their ability to forecast the race: Romney didn't benefit as expected from his attempts to tie Obama to the recession. Far more people, in fact, blamed George W. Bush for the country's economic problems—a glaring sign that the party's economic policy was not connecting with voters. Romney and Ryan, the poster boy for free-market, "rising tide lifts all boats" conservative economic policy, had spent a lot of time telling Americans that Obama's policies were hurting the middle class. But voters didn't actually see it that way. And then the unemployment situation started improving, albeit slightly. "When the unemployment numbers came out and dropped below 8 percent, the degree to which you could argue that the economy was not improving fast enough was decreasing," acknowledges Stevens.

Voters overwhelmingly thought the policies of Romney and Ryan would help the rich over the middle class, the analysis said. "If there were ever a ticket that represented *The Wall Street Journal* editorial board view of the world, that was it," concludes Eric Cantor, who as the Republican's second-ranking leader in the House believed and championed many of those views. But what voters saw from Romney and Ryan, he adds, was a worldview that split Americans into two camps: "makers versus takers."

The second report was more detailed—and more damning. Based on a survey of three thousand voters in four swing states taken on November 7 and 8—Colorado, Florida, Ohio, and Virginia—the thirty-seven-page document told Priebus that the 2012 election was the inflection point he had feared. It highlighted the glaring incongruity between the way most voters saw the state of the country under Obama and the way that Republicans had been talking about it. Voters didn't want a "new steward of the national economy," it said, which was exactly how Romney pitched himself. It also said that people were quite optimistic about their own future financial situations even if they were struggling. This disconnect had hurt Romney with several different demographic groups, but especially with Latinos, whom the report concluded "simply do not view Romney or the GOP as having any personal connection to them." A major reason, it explained, was that many Latinos simply didn't share the Republican Party's overt hostility toward the federal government, which they felt should play an important role in people's lives. It demolished the idea that Obama was the candidate of the far left. More than 80 percent of Romney's coalition in the four swing states was white—and two-thirds of them called themselves conservatives, it said. By contrast, Obama's coalition spanned a much wider spectrum: "younger and more diverse, not only ethnically, but also ideologically as liberals make up less than half his votes," it said.

The report's biggest conclusion was spelled out in a section near the end titled "Developing a Long Lasting Winning Coalition." It said that Romney could have flipped Florida, Ohio, and Virginia if only he had done marginally better with demographic groups that his campaign neglected or alienated. There was a simulation of what Election Day would have looked like had Romney reached a certain threshold of support with groups he lost like Latinos, women, people making less than $50,000 a year, and moderates. If he had won 50 percent of women in all three states, which Bush had done in 2004, he could have beaten Obama there, the report said. Had he hit 40 percent with Latinos, he could have taken Florida.

The takeaway among many top Republicans when they saw

numbers like these was that they weren't missing the mark by all that much. Presidential elections were still being decided on a knife's edge, in just a small handful of states. Only 103,000 votes separated Obama and Romney in Ohio; 73,000 in Florida. That wasn't an insurmountable structural disadvantage that threatened to relegate Republicans to the wilderness for a generation. These were the Saturday afternoon crowds at a Big Ten college football game, in the words of one leading GOP pollster, Whit Ayres. Summing up the attitudes among many in the RNC, Henry Barbour, a member of the committee from Mississippi who would help Priebus pull together the autopsy, recalls, "We just missed this opportunity, and not by a whole lot of votes, to beat Obama. It was doable. We could have done it."

In other places, the report hinted at the appeal that a populist candidate could have. "Working women simply did not relate to Mitt Romney and felt he had no connection or understanding of their daily lives," it said. And to underscore the point, the Election Day simulation showed what would have happened had Romney won 45 percent of people making under $50,000 per year: Florida and Ohio would have been his. On the issue of immigration reform, the report struck a note of caution: Don't think it's a panacea for Latino voters. "It's not the top issue for them," it warned. "While talking about immigration in a way that does not turn off Hispanics is critical, they are not single-issue voters, and Republicans need to find a way to address their concerns on economic issues."

Upon returning to Washington, one of the first things the shell-shocked Paul Ryan did was to tell Republican colleagues on Capitol Hill and other prominent conservatives that Republicans needed to get behind immigration reform. Over the next year and a half he would spend countless hours reaching out to people in conservative policy and media circles who had strongly resisted any form of immigration leniency. He personally called radio hosts like Laura Ingraham and Rush Limbaugh. But Limbaugh cut him off immediately. "Paul, I know where you're coming from. But at the end of the day my listeners don't want to hear it," Limbaugh told him. Limbaugh was a conservative second and a broadcaster-businessman first. Unlike other right-wing radio personalities like Mark Levin, who had worked in the Reagan administration in several high-level positions, Limbaugh did not have a particularly strong ideological attachment to the Republican Party or conservatism. Nor did he see his job as serving a greater societal or political purpose. His description of his approach to radio in a 1990 interview with *Talkers* magazine remained as true in 2013 as it was then. Limbaugh said he thought too much of talk radio was "boring" and that listeners didn't want shows that went on about "local sewage problems" and other humdrum concerns. It was his primary objective, he said, to keep his listeners coming back to him for more. "I'm here to have people listen to my show more than they listen to any other show," he declared. When he spoke to leaders of the Heritage Foundation, Ryan insisted the immigration issue would open doors that had been slammed shut in Republicans' faces. "We don't have an entry point to Hispanics. We can't talk to them unless we do immigration reform," he said. But Heritage staff knew from their internal surveys of the group's national membership where their rank and file were and where the group's official policy positions were out of sync. They could see, for instance, that on the issue of trade, Heritage's free-market philosophy wasn't popular. But with immigration, there was little daylight between Heritage's generally more restrictive views and what the Republican base wanted.

Ryan, like Priebus, was a Generation X Republican from Wisconsin whose conservative views were forged in an era when he knew almost nothing but Republican presidents. They saw Ronald Reagan elected twice by such overwhelming margins that the idea of the GOP as the "big tent" party was not a pie-in-the-sky abstraction but a reality. They watched Reagan deliver on his promises: bringing the Soviet Union to heel, cutting taxes—and signing into law an immigration reform bill that critics from the right attacked as "amnesty." They hoped to inspire the next generation of Republicans the way Reagan had inspired them. And immigration reform was a pillar of their brand of aspirational conservatism. It was an easy issue for business interests like the Chamber of Commerce and wealthy donors to get behind, many of whom ran companies that would benefit from provisions making it easier for foreign workers to obtain visas. Devotees of laissez-faire economics thought it made sense philosophically because fewer impediments on where labor could move was a key ingredient of a free market.

It also addressed a concern that party leaders like Priebus believed needed to be dealt with: the shrill, off-putting tone that Republicans sometimes used when talking about historically marginalized groups. This included not only immigrants but gays, women, and people of color. "There is a common denominator that no one could argue with," Priebus says. "Do you believe people ought to be treated with dignity? Yes or no. Then let's change the way we communicate." He often spoke about the need to lower the temperature in the culture wars—encouraging the very kind of civility that many Tea Party Republicans rejected as timid and ineffective. Priebus believed, as he often told people at the time, that unless "we get our mouth straight," the GOP would have "no way to grow the room."

When Priebus tapped Fleischer as the lead writer of the autopsy, he was putting in charge one of the Republican Party's more skilled spin doctors and a loyal ally to Bush. That said a lot about what Priebus believed had gone wrong and how he thought the party needed to fix it. The party, he believed, fundamentally had a messaging problem and would need to stamp out the no-apologies culture of rage and grievance that was amplified by the insurgent right. With Romney's loss, he was already on thin ice. And a report that would be seen as critical of the party's activist and social conservative wings could help galvanize more internal opposition to him. He couldn't put his name on it, so he picked Fleischer and a committee of four other trusted allies to help take off some of the heat. "Reince realized that if the party was going to move in a different direction, it would be good to have a committee recommend that—to armor himself," Fleischer says. First Priebus turned to Barbour, the Mississippi RNC member and a friend who had organized the coup that ousted Michael Steele in 2011. Another senior member of the autopsy team was Sally Bradshaw, one of Jeb Bush's most trusted advisers who had worked with him before and during his time as governor of Florida. To ensure that minority viewpoints were well represented, Priebus turned to Glenn McCall, member of the committee from South Carolina, who was Black, and Zori Fonalledas, another committee member from Puerto Rico.

"Our group of five," concedes Fleischer, "was more 'establishment' than 'outsider.'"

So were many of the people whose advice he relied on. He filled notepad after notepad with critiques and insights from people who had held some of the highest elected offices, worked for prestigious media outlets, and ran successful businesses. He asked Peggy Noonan, the *Journal* columnist, to set up a small dinner party for him. Noonan invited a group of people Fleischer didn't know well but whose names he recognized as movers and shakers in the party—donors, fundraisers, and operatives who'd worked with the RNC over the years. The guest list, he recalls, "could not have been more establishment Republican." They met at a Tribeca apartment that belonged to one of Noonan's friends. Fleischer took notes as the guests at the table shared with him the problems they believed precipitated Romney's loss. One said that Republicans weren't accepting of "people with hyphens"—a reference to African Americans, Hispanic Americans, and other minority and immigrant groups. They hired "too many suits" as their messengers and were hopelessly out of step with pop culture. Democrats offered a menu of "candy and alcohol" to their voters, one dinner guest complained, while Republicans were serving "broccoli and vegetable juice." Being the pro-life party was fine, but Republicans should also talk about supporting reasonable exceptions for when abortion should be legal, urged another.

It was similar to what Fleischer would hear in many of the focus-group-like sessions he attended as he conducted his research—over dinners, in office visits, and on phone calls.

"Cheer up. We'll win the next election, and we'll have a new face," said Mitch Daniels, the former governor of Indiana. Dick Armey, the former majority leader in the House, described the way Republicans had treated Latino voters as "criminal negligence," telling Fleischer, "You can't call someone ugly and expect them to come to the prom with you."

Governor Scott Walker of Wisconsin, who had just beat back a Democratic effort to recall him from office only to see Romney lose his state by almost 7 percentage points, said that Republicans weren't explaining why conservative policies are better than liberal ones. Walker agreed with the assessment that Republicans needed to do a better job of watching their tone, and he warned Fleischer to be wary of the corrosive influence that talk radio was having on voters and politicians.

Jeb Bush's son, Jeb Jr., organized a meeting of about thirty Hispanic entrepreneurs and community leaders in Miami that Priebus attended in January. The message they delivered was unsparing. The party is too white, too conservative, and too narrowly focused on talking to those who already agree with it. "The brand of the Republican Party in the Hispanic community has disappeared when compared to the days of George W. Bush," one said. Another criticized the party for spending "way too much time selling to the base, and too little time selling ourselves to others who are on the fence." Another called the network of conservative groups that often supported Tea Party candidates and right-wing causes "a huge business with people protecting their piece of the pie."

One area of interest to Fleischer and the autopsy committee was the group of voters who once felt an affinity for the party but now no longer identified as Republicans. To study these "lapsed Republicans," the RNC sent Ayres, the highly regarded Republican pollster, to conduct a set of focus groups in Des Moines and Columbus, Ohio. In his report summarizing his findings, Ayres described a striking area of agreement between those who were more moderate and those who were conservative. These lapsed Republicans, he said, saw their former party as

> out-of-touch with the middle class, nominating candidates who are unable to connect with them in any meaningful way. They think too many party leaders have no real understanding of the challenges facing middle-class families. These people feel under

enormous economic pressure with a lagging economy and rising taxes, and they believe no one really gets their situation or understands their plight. That image was sharply exacerbated by Mitt Romney, whom many of these people believe was a good man who had no clue about the life they were living. . . . They want someone to speak for the middle class, and they believe neither party does so today.

Ayres described how difficult it would be to stitch together a winning center-right Republican coalition because of all the internal fissures. Many conservatives had given up on Republicans, he said, because they "view DC elites with contempt, and believe that those elites want to run Tea Party people and religious conservatives out of the Party."

The party's problem reaching middle-class Americans came up in other interviews as well. Rich Lowry, the editor of the *National Review,* told Fleischer that Republicans spent too much time stressing vague concepts that didn't mean anything to voters, like freedom and liberty, when they should be focusing on economic mobility. Tom Ridge, the former governor of Pennsylvania and Homeland Security secretary under Bush, claimed the party had a compassion deficit with voters. "They don't care what you know until they know you care," he said.

On January 14, one of Fleischer's interviewees was different from the Republican insiders he was used to talking to. Amy Kremer, the sharp-elbowed Tea Party activist who had cycled through various high-level positions at different right-wing political groups, told Fleischer that the party wasn't reaching enough people. Much of their conversation didn't shed new light on the Tea Party–establishment divide for Fleischer. She said that Republicans seemed clueless about how to effectively mobilize the voters that the movement had empowered. She offered up a cliché about the need to "get government out of the way."

But then she gave an example of a political figure who was connecting with new audiences: Donald Trump. This surprised Fleischer.

He listened as Kremer said that Trump understood the culture and how to use his celebrity to reach people who were otherwise disengaged from politics. She said the GOP needed more leaders like that. Fleischer was intrigued enough by the suggestion that he jotted down "Donald Trump" in his notes with a line about his pop culture savvy. He drew a star next to Trump's name. Then he filed his notes away and forgot about it.

On the morning of March 18, 2013, Priebus delivered the findings of the autopsy to an audience at the National Press Club in downtown Washington. Rebranded as the "Growth & Opportunity Project"—a more optimistic title that bore no relationship to a corpse—the report was striking in its bluntness. It cautioned that the party would be unable to win presidential elections in the future unless it committed to making major changes in the way it spoke to voters, organized its primary process, raised money, and recruited candidates. "Our message was weak. Our ground game was insufficient," Priebus said. "We weren't inclusive."

It hit hard on the theme that the party had become captive to its far-right flank, often in language that implicitly criticized the no-compromise ethos of Tea Party activists and social conservatives. It called on the party to "embrace and champion" comprehensive immigration legislation, which Congress had not been able to do since 1986.

> The Republican Party needs to stop talking to itself. We have become expert in how to provide ideological reinforcement to like-minded people, but devastatingly we have lost the ability to be persuasive with, or welcoming to, those who do not agree with us on every issue. Instead of driving around in circles on an ideological cul-de-sac, we need a Party whose brand of conservatism invites and inspires new people to visit us. . . . Our standard should not be universal purity; it should be a more welcoming conservatism.

In the end, what Priebus was essentially recommending was to nominate in 2016 a candidate who wasn't fundamentally different from Romney in policy and ideology, just in different packaging. Rubio, Ryan, Walker, and Haley all believed in the same small, deregulated approach to government that helped the makers, not the takers. What was left entirely unsaid in the autopsy was whether any of those candidates could get through the next Republican primary.

The phrases "middle class," "working people," and "working families" appeared only a handful of times in the autopsy's ninety-eight pages. The report did acknowledge the difficulty Republicans had convincing ordinary Americans they care and chided politicians for talking about economic policy "like bookkeepers." But the disconnect is framed as a messaging problem, not a policy one. There are one hundred mentions of Hispanics or Latinos, making it clear where the report's authors felt the biggest opportunity for new votes was. The concept of winning votes among the fast-growing, non-white parts of the population was not new, of course. It had been self-evident and uncontroversial to many Republican leaders for a generation and was embraced by social conservatives and business leaders alike. Ralph Reed, the protégé of Pat Robertson and leader of the Christian Coalition, declared a few weeks before the 2000 election, "This is a very different party from the party that sits down on Labor Day and cedes the black vote and cedes the Hispanic vote, and tries to drive its percentage of the white vote over seventy percent to win."

Fleischer recalls that adding the passages about embracing comprehensive immigration reform—which Republicans had blocked during Bush's second term after a revolt from the right—was met with "some resistance" as he and the other members of the team worked through several drafts. Some, like Bradshaw, believed that without recommending any concrete proposals, the report would seem hollow. "There was a big discussion about whether what had to change was tone or substance. I was in the tone *and* substance camp. Particularly on immigration . . . I didn't think all you could say was we had to be more welcoming," she says. But with Republican leaders on Capitol Hill nervous about being held to a list of new legislative demands, especially one that would anger conservatives, the report stopped short of making more than a generic recommendation for a comprehensive reform bill. The authors steered clear of abortion in the end, despite hearing from many of the people they interviewed that the party was too rigidly pro-life and unwelcoming of those who felt differently. One line in an early draft that was cut would have reinforced the idea that ideological purity tests on issues like abortion and gay marriage were hurting the party. The final version included a gentler critique: "When it comes to social issues, the party must in fact and deed be a big tent." The authors decided it would be too explosive to go beyond that.

So glaring was the omission of any discussion about how the party's economic policies might be repelling voters that a group of conservatives produced their own postmortem attacking the RNC's report. One Republican pollster who worked to put together the retort from the right, Kellyanne Conway, read the autopsy and thought it seemed illogically dismissive of the voters who had just propelled Republicans to huge victories in 2010.

The conclusion was, " 'Mitt Romney lost but he wasn't supposed to lose.' Says who?" Conway says. "I think they were trying to find what's wrong with the voter, not what's wrong with the party. And that's a problem." The party that Priebus thought he could save with the autopsy, she says, was already dead. "This is not a fresh cadaver."

The American Principles Project, which along with the Susan B. Anthony List had first surfaced in Tea Party circles during the throwdown over New York's Twenty-third Congressional District, brought Conway in to help with the research for the postmortem, which they nicknamed the "Autopsy of the Autopsy." It accused Republicans of running away from issues like abortion and gay marriage that had considerable motivating power for the conservative base. "The Left punches on social issues, the Republican and conservative elites retreat and change the subject," the report said. The group hired a research firm to analyze the television ads run by the top four

Republican entities that were on the air before the election: the Romney campaign, the RNC, and two super PACs, American Crossroads and Restore Our Future. It reviewed 120 ads. The report noted that there were scant references to "workers, wages, and the middle class compared to mentions of 'business,' 'small-business' or the neologism 'job creator.' " It said that unless Republicans learned to address the "empathy gap" between its voters and its elected officials, the party was doomed. "We have built our economic message around business owners and bosses, not workers and their wages."

On the Friday before the autopsy came out, Donald Trump flew to Washington to make his second appearance at CPAC. He warned about the political fallout for Republicans if undocumented immigrants living in the United States ever became citizens. "Every one of those eleven million people will be voting Democratic," Trump said. He talked to reporters from conservative-friendly websites like *Breitbart* and *The Daily Caller*.

After Trump cooled on the idea of running against Romney in 2011, Sam Nunberg wrote a strategy memo that outlined the dissatisfaction in the party with the presumptive nominee, basing his argument in part on the racist conspiracy theories about Obama's background. The memo—like a premortem analysis—discussed Romney's weaknesses, including his record on issues important to conservatives like abortion and the distaste that many right-wing media personalities like Limbaugh expressed for him. "Mitt Romney is naturally a flawed candidate and his coronation will leave both the Tea Party and Social Conservative base despondent," said the memo, dated June 23, 2011. It went on to describe how many voters would desire a third-party candidate:

> The Social Conservative will be left with the Mormon Mitt Romney or the alternative of Barrack Obama [*sic*], a Muslim who converted to the doctrine of Black Liberation Theology in his twenties. The Tea Party will be left with a Socialist and a Big

Government Republican. The Independent will be left without a clear alternative. The gap for the TRUMP HOSTILE TAKE-OVER OF 2012 will be feasible for a path to the Presidency.

The day after Priebus presented the report, Trump was in the middle of a Twitter fusillade against Mark Cuban, the tech entrepreneur and owner of the Dallas Mavericks. "@mcuban swings like a little girl with no power or talent," Trump fired off at 7:07 A.M. Nunberg, who followed conservative media closely, had been watching as the right ripped apart the autopsy. On the radio, Limbaugh rejected the entire premise that the party needed to embrace inclusion and moderation. "So we gotta be more tolerant," he said dismissively. "That means cash in our chips on our core principles." Mark Levin called for Priebus and the rest of the leadership of the party to be shown the door. "Damn it, if it's not changed, if these people aren't thrown out, we're going to lose." Nunberg brought it up with Trump, who agreed that he should register his disapproval too. The response Nunberg crafted for Trump posted to Twitter at 2:47 P.M.: "@RNC report was written by the ruling class of consultants who blew the election. Short on ideas. Just giving excuses to donors." And at 3:19 P.M. he weighed in again, tweeting that the recommendations on immigration in particular would be devastating for the party: "Amnesty is suicide for Republicans."

Then he went back to attacking Cuban.

CHAPTER 7

★ ★ ★

America First, Second, and Third

We had nothing to lose.
—Patrick J. Buchanan

What Scott Brown really needed from Jeff Sessions was money. But Sessions would send Stephen Miller first.

On the day in late October 2014 when Miller turned up in Manchester, New Hampshire, the staff at Brown's campaign headquarters wasn't quite sure what to do with him. He looked out of place in a slim-fitting gray suit with a pressed white dress shirt and a skinny tie—an edgy look among his button-down colleagues on Capitol Hill, and most definitely too formal for the flannel-and-fleece look that New Englanders are partial to in the fall. After one of Miller's younger colleagues on the Brown campaign told him it was fine if he came into work wearing something a little more casual, Miller loosened up a little. He showed up the next day in the suit but no tie.

Miller was the communications director for Sessions, the junior senator from Alabama. Most Republicans outside of a hard-core circle of activist media and far-right politicians tended not to pay Miller or his anti-immigration advocacy much attention. But those who did had a large following with Republican voters, and they included Laura Ingraham, the staff of *Breitbart*, and Matt Drudge. As a Senate staffer, Miller was known for his long, digressive rants about what he thought was wrong with the bipartisan consensus on immigration reform in the United States Senate. He sent memos to his colleagues that they hadn't asked for and could run to more than twenty pages. He complained that too many Republicans were blindly supportive of theoretical policies that "weren't supported by actual flesh and blood people in the Republican Party," as he liked to say. He was formal and solicitous, sometimes to the point of striking co-workers as stiff. He signed emails "Most Sincerely, Stephen." He didn't just say thanks when someone heard him out, he was "deeply appreciative of your time."

Working for Sessions was a good fit for the twenty-nine-year-old. Even for a conservative Republican from the South, Sessions stood out for his hard-nosed opposition to efforts in Congress to offer any form of legal status or the promise of citizenship to people who were not documented. He also didn't care much for legal immigration. Often, he was at odds with the well-financed and high-powered interests in his own party. Karl Rove, who had been friends with Sessions since their days together in student Republicans clubs in the South, tried debating the issue with Sessions in 2007 when Rove was rounding up Republican votes on Capitol Hill for an immigration overhaul that George W. Bush had hoped would be a major piece of his domestic legacy.

"Jeff, we have Nobel laureates who are immigrants, entrepreneurs, small businesspeople," Rove would argue. "You're looking at these people as all a negative when in reality they're adding wealth to our country and spirit to our national environment."

But it was a nonstarter with Sessions. "I don't care. All they're doing is depressing labor and wages," Sessions replied. He attacked the bill, calling it "No illegal alien left behind," after Bush's signature education initiative, "No Child Left Behind."

When the measure failed to attract enough Republican support and died in the Senate, Sessions did a victory lap and noted the help of a powerful force in killing it: talk radio. His fellow senators had scrambled to pass it, Sessions said, "before Rush Limbaugh could tell the American people what was in it." Six years later, when the battle over immigration heated up again in Washington, most of talk radio's biggest voices were opposed to a bipartisan reform bill that was taking shape in the Senate. But this time, Republicans who supported it like Senator Marco Rubio did considerable work persuading conservative media stars to hold their fire, or to at least give them the airtime to argue their case. Limbaugh had Rubio on. Roger Ailes, whose inner pro-establishment sympathies had kicked back in after 2012, invited Rubio to New York to brief Fox News executives on what was in the bill. When Rubio arrived in Ailes's second-floor conference room at the Fox headquarters, Ailes offered the senator his chair as a gesture of good faith. And for a time, at Rubio's insistence, Fox cut back on running footage of migrants scaling border fences. Even Sean Hannity seemed amenable and announced that his position on immigration had "evolved" since Republicans' losses in 2012. "We've got to get rid of the immigration issue altogether," he told his audience.

For a communications strategist like Miller whose job was to kill the bill, not having the biggest megaphone in cable news on his side was a serious disadvantage. His workaround was *Breitbart,* where editors and writers felt no such pressure to dial back the nativism. When the Senate began debating the bill in the summer of 2013— doing exactly what the RNC autopsy recommended—Miller started employing a strategy he described as "negative reinforcement." Working with friendly media, he aimed to draw fire from conservatives on lawmakers who supported measures like making more visas available to foreign workers. This involved placing a damaging if not entirely accurate story about provisions in the bill in a publication like *Breitbart* or *The Daily Caller,* and then getting Drudge to post a link to the story, which would in turn drive coverage on talk radio. And Miller would sit back and watch with delight as a senator like Rubio was inundated with angry phone calls over a faux controversy like the "Marco-phones," free cellphones that the senator supposedly wanted to give to migrants along the southern border. The statements Miller churned out for Sessions were full of overheated language and superlatives. "Immigration Bill Would Be Biggest Setback for Poor and Middle-Class Americans in Decades," said one that was typical of the hyperbole Miller employed. "Special Interest, Extremist Groups Wrote Immigration Bill," said another.

The New Hampshire Senate race the next year was Miller's dry run for the anti-immigrant campaign he would help Donald Trump run in 2016. At first glance, it seemed like an odd place to wage a battle over immigration. The state shares an international border with Canada. Illegal immigration is not a major law enforcement concern. The state's immigrant population was one of the smallest in the country, with roughly 5 percent of its more than 1.3 million residents counted as foreign-born in 2014; 3 percent of the population was Hispanic. But Brown's message didn't require the presence of actual immigrants to connect with voters. His message also wasn't diluted when it became clear that Brown wasn't really talking about immigration in the context of how it affected New Hampshire. His ads used scenes of the rocky, arid landscape of the U.S.–Mexico border in the Southwest, not the U.S.–Canada border in the Northeast. Brown, a telegenically good-looking and approachable former state legislator, is better known for the Senate race he actually won in 2010 in Massachusetts as one of the first breakout stars of the Tea Party. But his New Hampshire race often goes unappreciated for its significance as a hinge point in the Republican Party's evolution on immigration policy. Ryan Williams, who worked as a communications strategist for the Brown campaign, had never heard of Miller before and asked the *Breitbart* writer Matthew Boyle who he was. Boyle, who had also relocated from Washington to New Hampshire for the sole purpose of being on the Brown race full-time, told Williams, "'Oh, man. This guy is the sharpest guy in politics.'" Miller's work there foretold the renewed role that anti-immigrant sentiment would have in Republican campaigns across the country in the next election cycle thanks to a new cadre of hard-right restrictionists who rejected the premise that a softer tone on immigration was key to growing the party. "The Brown campaign in '14 was like the test run for these guys," says Williams.

Scott Brown understood the intensity around immigration on the right and was willing to use it in a way that many Republicans at the time were not. Even as a member of the Massachusetts state legislature, Brown had argued that America needed to be more selective about the kinds of people it admitted from other countries. In

2006, when he was a member of the Massachusetts state Senate, Brown proposed legislation that would have enacted a host of restrictive new laws, including requiring that judges ask for a defendant's immigration status; precluding people in the country illegally from being eligible for public housing; and forcing employers to verify that their workers have proper documentation. He still maintained his sheen among Tea Party supporters nationally for the breakout role he played in one of the movement's first big races. After Senator Edward M. Kennedy of Massachusetts died in 2009, Brown won the special election to replace him—becoming the first Republican to represent the state in the Senate since 1979. (He lost reelection two years later to a populist candidate on the left, a Harvard law professor named Elizabeth Warren.)

After Brown decided to decamp to New Hampshire and run against the Democratic incumbent, Senator Jeanne Shaheen, he and his team believed the conservative angst over Obamacare would be their winning issue, as it had been for many Republican candidates since 2010. But they quickly saw that the issue wasn't enough on its own to counter the perception that Brown was a carpetbagger from the liberal bastion next door. His record on guns was problematic. Being pro-choice didn't help either. "We were coming in from Massachusetts, we knew that we needed more," explains Eric Fehrnstrom, a senior adviser. "Healthcare alone was not enough to win against a popular incumbent," adds Fehrnstrom. Tea Party themes of excessive spending and massive budget deficits weren't doing the trick. For Brown, there simply wasn't any other issue with the same power as immigration.

Against the advice of Republican leadership in Washington, Brown decided to run on the issue. He would explicitly disregard the advice of the RNC autopsy, which was barely a year old, cutting against the conventional wisdom then about the risks of using an anti-immigration message in a purple state where moderate voters were key. Peter Flaherty, another senior aide to Brown, recalls that the campaign was going out on a limb. "We were the first ones in the country up with an immigration ad. And the national experts were like, 'You're not going to run an immigration ad,'" Flaherty says.

"Yeah, we are." In his ad, Brown accused the Obama administration of not doing enough to vet who was coming across the border, claiming that the government had its priorities backward. It required more rigorous screening of people getting on a domestic flight, Brown said, than those entering from Mexico on foot. "It was more of a 'lawlessness versus respect for the rule of law' type of argument that was woven into public safety and public health," Flaherty explains.

There was another thread that made the Brown campaign see immigration differently. Several of the top strategists, including Flaherty and Fehrnstrom, were veterans of Mitt Romney's first campaign for president in 2008. And they saw how immigration kept coming up when they least expected it. "It was always a live issue. We recognized that early on, as Mitt was traveling in 2006, 2007," says Fehrnstrom, who recalls how resonant it was in Iowa. "And what was surprising to us, as Easterners, was that here we are in a Midwestern state, and all they want to talk about is immigration." Romney was also thrown off at first, especially when he encountered questions on subjects he had never heard of that sounded like quackery—including an alleged government plan to build a massive transcontinental highway connecting Mexico, the United States, and Canada. In fact, the so-called NAFTA superhighway was a conspiracy theory fanned by far-right media activists like Jerome Corsi.

Since the autopsy came out in March 2013, the political calculus on immigration had changed. Business and faith leaders supported the Senate bill, and it passed that summer with fourteen Republicans voting yes. But the Republican-controlled House was a dead end, despite Paul Ryan's pleas for support. Then, with the midterm elections just a few months away, a humanitarian crisis at the southern border exploded as tens of thousands of Central American children arrived, most unaccompanied by their parents. Many were fleeing violent and impoverished homelands with human traffickers their families had sometimes paid the equivalent of thousands of dollars. Some were just toddlers. It was on a scale unlike anything the United States had experienced since the Mariel Boatlift in 1980, when Fidel Castro told Cubans they were free to leave the country, and 125,000 of them boarded boats for the United States. Brown saw this as an opportunity, not only because of the political salience of the issue but because, given his service in the National Guard, he could frame the problems at the border as a national security threat that he was uniquely suited to address.

And then there was the shock of Eric Cantor's defeat. In June, the Republican House majority leader lost his primary by eleven points to a conservative economics professor who made illegal immigration a central element of his campaign. The explanation for precisely why Dave Brat beat Cantor in their suburban Richmond district is more complicated than either candidate's position on immigration alone. Cantor was fighting a perception among voters that the demands of his leadership position had made him inattentive to the district. Brat's supporters framed his run as a referendum on Republicans they accused of doing more to help undocumented immigrants than struggling workers at home. Often lost in the post-election analysis was that Democrats crossed party lines to vote against Cantor in the Republican primary, which is allowed in Virginia. But the immigration narrative stuck, in part because hard-liners would not be denied their pound of flesh. And that's the story they told. For weeks before the race, *Breitbart* and Ingraham and other radio hosts like Mark Levin had been talking up the Cantor–Brat primary as their opportunity to send a message to Republicans who were backing immigration reform. A few days before the election, Ingraham headlined a fundraiser for Brat at a country club near Cantor's home in the Richmond suburb of Glen Allen. It drew so many people that the overflow parking lined Cantor's street and almost reached his driveway. "Don't discount intensity. And when you marry intensity with this media opportunity that we didn't have ten years ago, it's powerful," Patrick M. McSweeney, a Republican activist in the state who supported Brat, told *The New York Times*.

Though it was not widely known at the time, Stephen Miller was an unseen hand in the race, working as an informal adviser and occasional ghostwriter for Brat. He told Brat to hit Cantor on an issue that only the hardest-core conservatives were latching on to at the time: opposing any form of leniency for the so-called Dreamers, the undocumented immigrants who had been brought to the United States when they were young children. Cantor had supported granting them citizenship, as did most Americans who believed it was unfair to punish someone for a crime their parents had committed. But Miller urged Brat to oppose all relief for people in the country illegally, no matter whether they arrived on their own as able-bodied adults or in the arms of their parents when they were babies. Brat didn't need much encouragement. He relished attacking Cantor on the issue and settled naturally into his role as the newest voice of the opposition to the GOP establishment. "Eric Cantor doesn't represent you," Brat insisted at a rally of anti-immigration demonstrators shortly before the election. "Eric Cantor represents large corporations who want a never-ending supply of cheap, low-wage foreign labor."

The involvement of Miller, Ingraham, and *Breitbart* in the Brat race was a partnership they would replicate in New Hampshire. And it was not just about picking a fight over immigration but inflaming a culture war that Miller had been an eager combatant in since he was a teenager. His entry in his high school yearbook included a quote from Theodore Roosevelt, "There is room here for only 100 percent Americanism, only for those who are Americans and nothing else." While in college at Duke University, he used his column at the student paper, *The Chronicle,* to establish himself as the campus Bill O'Reilly. He asked in one piece why there was no Christmas tree in the quad. (Miller is Jewish.) He complained that Hollywood made plenty of gay-themed television shows and movies, but not ones "about the evils of the Islamic holy war." Occasionally he put politics aside to gripe about the quality of student life, which he once suggested could be vastly improved with the construction of a "resort-style outdoor swimming pool."

His time on campus coincided with one of the most racially contentious episodes of the mid-2000s. A Black woman hired to dance at a house party accused a group of white lacrosse players of raping her, setting off a raging national debate over racism and classism at one of the country's most elite universities. But once evidence emerged that the woman had fabricated her version of events, many conservatives saw the story as an example of the overeager media rushing to convict three innocent men on the basis that they were white and privileged. Miller used his column to excoriate his classmates, school administrators, local prosecutors, and the accuser. America, he wrote, was "a nation paralyzed by racial paranoia." He tried to draw attention to a crime in which the roles were reversed—a white Duke student told police that she was raped at a Black fraternity—and wondered where all the outrage was. The left, he wrote, "is quite right about one thing—there is racial disharmony in our society. And if they want to know the cause, they need look no further than the mirror."

In 1991, a few days before Christmas, Pat Buchanan made a trip to the North Country of New Hampshire and saw what he would later describe as the catalyst for his first presidential campaign. He visited a paper mill where many workers had just been informed they were losing their jobs. An aide who was traveling with Buchanan that day, Greg Mueller, recalls how tense the scene was. No one seemed to have the patience for small talk with a politician. They politely took Buchanan's hand when he offered it to them, then most quickly looked away. "These are really rough, tough-looking guys," says Mueller, who remembers thinking, *This is not going well.* Then a stocky, shorter bearded man reached out and looked Buchanan in the eye as he shook his hand. "Save our jobs," he said. For Buchanan, the exchange was especially poignant because the man seemed about his age. Then he returned to Manchester and picked up the local newspaper. Inside there was a story about the Export-Import Bank, the federal entity that helps businesses fund projects overseas, financing a paper mill in Mexico. Buchanan was incensed. "I said, 'What the hell are we doing?' We're shutting down our own companies here and we're sending aid abroad to companies in Mexico doing the same thing," he says. "For what? Chinese goods down at the mall? This junk?" His thoughts settled on one question: "Who is the economy for?"

Buchanan would tell that story many times over the years as he explained the seeds of his 1992 campaign for president—a no-apologies, nationalistic insurgency that was a watershed moment in Republican politics. But just as critical to informing his decision to challenge George H. W. Bush, the sitting president of his own party, was an issue that has been overlooked in the analysis of Buchanan as a figure who was ahead of his time in the GOP. Racial preferences in employment was a deeply contentious issue in the early 1990s. Bush was under pressure from left and right over legislation in Congress that aimed to broaden protections for women and minorities who faced discrimination at work. Conservatives claimed that such laws would force employers to hire specific quotas of women and minorities to avoid lawsuits. Bush had already vetoed one bill, the Civil Rights Act of 1990, claiming that it would "introduce the destructive force of quotas into our national employment system." But he signed a second, less sweeping measure the following year, infuriating conservatives like Buchanan.

In an unpublished manuscript that Buchanan wrote about the 1992 campaign, he says the bill signing was the break point that forced him into the primary. "I was beside myself," Buchanan wrote. He fumed to his co-host on CNN's *Crossfire*: "I can understand why people are voting for Harris Wofford and David Duke." Wofford, the less recognizable name of the two, was a civil rights attorney and a driving force behind the creation of the Peace Corps who'd just beaten the former Republican attorney general of the United States, Dick Thornburgh, in a race for Senate in Pennsylvania. Thornburgh, Buchanan notes dismissively in the manuscript, had run "as a George Bush Republican" and claimed to be at home in the "corridors of power." Duke, a former Klansman who tried to take his white supremacist views mainstream with a 1988 campaign for president, had just posted a surprisingly strong showing in the governor's race in Louisiana but ultimately lost.

Buchanan understood that many white Americans would blame Bush for effectively making it legal to discriminate against them. He was one of them. And he felt betrayed. "Again, the President seemed to have gone out of his way to make fools of us," he wrote. "I thought that if I, a friend who had been George Bush's most visible surrogate on the TV talk shows in 1988, was so angry, how must they feel in Middle America?" He continued,

> In the press analysis, Duke's vote showed how racist Louisiana was; and Wofford's triumph showed Pennsylvania wanted national health insurance. The press read its own biases into the returns. But one need not have been a graduate of The Richard Nixon School of Politics to know what was up. Voters had just given the political establishments of both parties early wake-up calls; We have had it with the lot of you, voters were saying; there is a populist revolt brewing; it is broad and deep, and it is headed your way. . . . If Duke with his Klan baggage could poll 39 percent (he had gotten 44 percent in a U.S. Senate race a year earlier), and Wofford could effect a 50-point turnaround, perhaps I could make history in New Hampshire where I knew, from that visit a year earlier, times were as tough as they were in Louisiana.

Buchanan, who would eventually run for president three times, gave many white voters something that Reagan or George H. W. Bush couldn't: an intellectual framework that explained why it wasn't wrong if they felt, as he often put it, "This isn't the country we grew up in." If you were a person who'd lost your job, who believed that a minority applicant had taken your kid's spot at a competitive college, who hated being asked to press 1 for English, Buchanan probably made sense to you. He had been a speechwriter for Nixon, who claims he told the president to destroy evidence during Watergate—"Burn the tapes," Buchanan says he advised. His wordsmanship helped Nixon arouse the passions of the "silent majority" during the period of noisy civil unrest over Vietnam. It was Buchanan who urged Nixon to go to war with elite elements of American society like the Washington press corps, advising the president in a memo that he should attack them as "a tiny and closed fraternity of privileged men, elected by no one." Nixon and his vice president, Spiro Agnew, did just that, reading from the script Buchanan wrote for them. And the "silent majority" cheered them for it.

Buchanan, who had been a devotee of Reagan-style, supply-side conservatism, announced his conversion to a more nationalist, nativist worldview in a 1990 essay in *The National Interest* he called "America First—and Second, and Third" that questioned the nation's commitments and entanglements overseas. It would become a foundational document of Buchanan's campaign for president in 1992. It escaped few of Buchanan's critics that the phrase "America First" had for decades been associated with the anti-Semites who joined the movement of the same name that tried to keep Americans out of World War II. To this day, he keeps a piece of framed stained glass on a coffee table in his suburban Virginia home that says "American First."

By 1990, Buchanan had given up the public sector and was a successful syndicated columnist and cable news personality reportedly earning more than $500,000 a year as co-host of the CNN shoutfest *Crossfire* and a regular panelist on *The McLaughlin Group*. Some considered him "the most visible and maybe the most important conservative in America," as the conservative writer Fred Barnes described him then. He criticized the Bush administration for becoming too consumed with ambitions abroad while the economy at home collapsed. And his punches landed. The Persian Gulf War in 1991, a high-water mark for the Bush presidency, ended as a victory for the country and pushed the president's approval ratings to 90 percent. But when a severe recession hit, the patriotic euphoria faded. It was clear to Buchanan that Bush's embrace of open international trade and labor markets was leaving millions of Americans wondering who was looking out for them at home.

Buchanan's views about free trade were out of sync with the conservatives in his party, who had been taught that fewer barriers and restrictions on both were the proper manifestation of the unique style of freedom that had allowed the United States to triumph over the Soviet Union. Markets yearned to be free, just like people, they thought. And once the shackles of government mandates, tariffs, and rigid border controls were broken, prosperity would flow, freeing societies and their people everywhere. "That's the way we'd been raised. Almost a religious belief," he says, noting how he had supported the 1965 act that liberalized the country's immigration laws. But with the end of the Cold War, Buchanan started to doubt the relevance of these conservative axioms. Mueller, his communications strategist on the 1992 campaign, could see at the time how the end of the Cold War left conservatives without as strong a case to make for free markets as catechism. "When you look at it that way—we're going up against the empire of the Soviet Union—we were all free market capitalists. That became a very important social and economic viewpoint cast wide in the Republican Party." But in Buchanan's mind, that old binary world order of communism-versus-capitalism could no longer justify the party's fealty to a hands-off, business-knows-best economic agenda. "You structure the economy for the good of the people. You don't structure the economy according to some nineteenth-century abstract idea," Buchanan says he concluded.

One day in the spring of 1992, his first presidential campaign running on fumes, Buchanan stood looking out on a stretch of the border known as Smuggler's Gulch, a sun-baked canyon between Tijuana and San Diego that Mexican migrants used to enter the United States illegally. He was on a tour with federal agents, who pointed out the spots where people slipped through undetected rather easily. Up to five thousand were coming across every weekend, they said, and they couldn't keep up. He told them he had the solution: "Build the damn fence," Buchanan said.

He meant "the Buchanan fence." The nickname vastly understated the scope and ambition of the large-scale public works project the architect had in mind: a concrete-buttressed structure with extra-fine metal meshing, to make climbing it all but impossible, that would run along hundreds of miles of the border. In the spots where a fence alone seemed unlikely to do the job, Buchanan proposed digging ditches. And inside would be more fencing, according to his ten-point border security plan. Then legions of newly hired patrol agents and the military would help make the border impenetrable.

With just a few weeks before the California primary on June 2,

Buchanan had almost no money and no support from official Republican channels, which were unified behind Bush. And he had not been able to replicate the jolt he delivered to Bush and the party establishment in the New Hampshire primary in February when he won 40 percent of the vote. The Buchanan operation had always been small and scrappy, consisting of a close-knit circle of loyalists from its earliest days: his campaign manager and younger sister, Bay Buchanan; a press secretary, Mueller, who was almost always at his side; a researcher in Washington; and two pollsters in their early thirties who were just breaking into Republican presidential politics, Tony Fabrizio and Frank Luntz. But by the time California rolled around most of them were gone. And Buchanan says, "Basically our campaign was being run by the Secret Service."

That day at the border Buchanan had little to lose. He had been polling only from 10 to 15 percent of the vote against Bush in the most recent contests. As migrants selling drinks at a makeshift refreshment stand looked on, he delivered a fiery speech. He called the flow of Central Americans into the United States an "invasion that involves at least a million aliens a year." He said Bush's failure to deal with it was "a national disgrace" that was contributing to "social problems and economic problems and drug problems." And he insisted that large numbers of immigrants were criminals currently sitting in California jails.

Though his evidence on this last point was shaky, the claim had originated with someone Buchanan considered the most reputable of sources: William P. Barr, the attorney general of the United States. In April, riots had broken out in Los Angeles following the acquittal of four police officers who were filmed savagely beating a Black man named Rodney King. In his assessment of the damage, Barr had provided an estimate that one-third of the six thousand people arrested were in the country illegally. Federal immigration officials disputed the number, saying it was actually much lower. Still, Buchanan found the image of thousands of criminal immigrants ransacking the nation's second-largest city irresistible, mentioning it several times at campaign stops across Southern California that week. Standing outside a jail in Los Angeles where some of the arrested rioters were being held, he declared, "Foreigners are coming into this country illegally and helping to burn down one of the greatest cities in America."

During his visit, Buchanan also met with the mother of a teenage boy killed by a drunk driver who was an undocumented immigrant, an encounter that he would talk about in speeches for years. An aide in the Bush White House at the time, Pete Wehner, notes the starkness of Buchanan's "America First" talk. "That was American carnage," he observes, adding how Buchanan was using these exaggerated stories to justify a sharp departure from decades of established policy on trade and foreign affairs. "It was isolationism, protectionism, and nativism," Wehner says.

Nativism had always been present in the Republican Party, but it was largely a niche concern confined to the far right. The mainstream of the GOP had long held a Cold War mentality that immigration was part of what confirmed America's goodness as a free society. Reagan, who hired Buchanan as his communications director, spoke fondly of what immigrants contributed to the country. "We all came from different lands but we share the same values, the same dream," he said in a speech during his 1980 campaign overlooking of the Statue of Liberty. "Let us pledge to each other with this great lady looking on that we can, and so help us God we will, make America great again." Gallup in fact would not record instances of Americans mentioning immigration as a top concern in surveys until 1993. Even in California, where illegal crossings were on the rise, the issue was still only at a simmer. The boiling point would arrive in 1994 with Proposition 187, a ballot initiative approved by 59 percent of California voters that would have barred undocumented immigrants from public services like schools and nonemergency healthcare had the courts not struck it down.

But Buchanan's results on primary day in California were a sign that something was afoot. Since there was no mathematical chance that he could deny Bush the nomination at that point, casting a ballot for Buchanan was, politically speaking, like voting for a dead guy. The dead guy did surprisingly well, winning 26.4 percent of the vote. He looked closely at the numbers as they came in that evening and immediately saw a pattern. In places where concerns over illegal immigration were most acute—the big urban counties closest to the Mexican border: Los Angeles, San Bernardino, San Diego—he performed the best, winning 30 percent of the vote.

The California results emboldened him. He demanded a bigger voice for conservatives at the Republican National Convention later that summer. He asked for revisions to the party platform's position on immigration, which before 1992 amounted to a single paragraph. Writing in the memoir he never published, Buchanan described his frustrations as he pushed for more recognition of what his campaign and its supporters had accomplished:

> We had won three million votes; we had tens of thousands of loyal troops; we brought something to the table. I wanted to be with the President and party in November; but we weren't going to crawl back into the Big Tent. Nor were we going to permit our people to be treated like undocumented aliens who just waded across the Rio Grande.
>
> We belonged to the party. Indeed, we felt we had been more loyal to its principles than those who defeated us.
>
> Moreover, we had nothing to lose.

The Bush campaign acquiesced, reasoning that it was better to have Buchanan and his people placated and on the inside rather than firing at them from the outside. It agreed to add new language to the platform that warned of the threat from illegal immigration and called for securing the border. Bush also agreed to Buchanan's demand that he be given a prime-time speaking slot during the convention. And that's where he fired inside the tent. The vanquished candidate delivered one of the most memorable convention addresses in modern times—known as the "Culture War Speech." It left moderate Republicans and liberals horrified by his attacks on the agenda of "radical feminism," "homosexual rights," and "abortion on demand" that he said would be implemented by the joint presidency of "Clinton and Clinton." But the most famous line was a description of the epic battle he said was underway: "A cultural war, as critical to the kind of nation we shall one day be as was the Cold War itself," he declared. He wrote in the memoir that he gave the full text of his speech to the Bush campaign thirty hours before delivering it and that "no one asked me to change a word," other than to ask that he mention Bush's efforts to help oppressed peoples win their freedom.

Media coverage of the convention portrayed the event as hijacked by the "Buchanan Brigades," the quasi-military nickname Buchanan gave his followers. And in the aftermath of Bush's loss in November to Clinton, the speech would become central to the story line about an aloof president who lost his grip on his party. When Buchanan read these dispatches, he was delighted. One piece in particular caught his eye: an essay in *The New York Times* written by the Nixon biographer Garry Wills. GEORGE BUSH: PRISONER OF THE CRAZIES, the headline said. "The fringe has taken over," Wills wrote. Buchanan took it as a compliment. The bristling response from his critics, he wrote, was "the surest measure" of his campaign's success.

By the time Stephen Miller arrived in New Hampshire—twenty-three years after Buchanan's visit to the North Country paper mill—he had started making a pitch in memos to his Republican colleagues in the Senate that their party "must run as the party of the American worker." Miller was determined to recast the immigration debate. As he saw it, Republicans were better served if they avoided the humanitarian questions about what the "huddled masses yearning to breathe free" added to society and focused instead on what he thought immigrants were taking away from American citizens: their jobs. He asked the staff at the National Republican Senatorial Committee for time to brief senators and their aides on how they could be more persuasive by talking about immigration not as a matter of law and order and national security but as something that affected the bottom line. He describes the simple formulation he used: "My opponent, John Smith, is prioritizing making life better for people who are here illegally. If you elect me, you're sending me to Washington to fight for you." He urged Republicans to present the question as a simple us-versus-them issue: "Are you there to represent American citizens or are you there to represent illegal aliens?"

Shortly after he got to New Hampshire, he asked for a meeting with some of Brown's staff to talk to them about a suggestion he had for sharpening the candidate's immigration message. Brown didn't need to be told how to hammer the issue. At times, it seemed immigration was all he wanted to talk about—even if the voters didn't. He once convened a town hall specifically for the purpose of addressing the matter. But the local paper, the *Union Leader,* noted that only two questions from the audience had anything to do with immigration. And other Republicans, mindful of the party leadership's advice to soften their image with Latino voters, criticized Brown for making it so central to his campaign. "I'm sure the polling is on his side: Who is against having a secure border?" Fergus Cullen, a former chairman of the New Hampshire Republican Party, told a reporter at the time. "But it's a cynical play, and I'm disappointed in Brown for using this issue this way. Immigration is a complex issue with a lot of nuance, and border security is just one part of it. He knows that."

But the race tightened, alarming Democrats. A group with ties to the pro-immigration organization Fwd.us, which was funded by Facebook's founder, Mark Zuckerberg, swooped in to bolster Shaheen by spending at least $1 million on ads that praised her for helping veterans but conspicuously left out any mention of immigration. Donald Trump had been periodically checking in on the race. And as he saw the polling improve for Brown, he tweeted out his support for the Republican. Brown had until that point mostly focused on how illegal immigration and lax border control threatened national security. He saw it as the most effective way to raise the issue, since it tied into his military background and two of the biggest stories of the day: an Ebola epidemic in Africa and an emboldened Islamic State. "It was more of a lawlessness vs. respect for the rule of law type of argument," Flaherty explains of the campaign's strategy.

Policy was outside Miller's purview as a temp communications staffer. He didn't even have a desk or a phone at Brown headquarters. But that didn't stop him from making his pitch to Brown's aides that the candidate should also tie immigration to job insecurity and the economy, as Buchanan had done, and to disregard any advice that warned Republicans to watch their tone. Before he went up to New Hampshire, he had written an early version of a memo that he would later revise and expand into one of the most widely cited pieces of his work two years later when journalists were attempting to explain the belief system of this formerly obscure junior Senate staffer who was suddenly a senior policy adviser at the White House. He called his nineteen-hundred-word manifesto "Winning the Immigration Debate—and the Election." Released under Sessions's name, the memo was an indictment of the traditional GOP campaign playbook and the political establishments of both parties:

> Immigration policy directly affects voters in ways that Washington "experts" do not see or understand. It impacts their jobs, wages, hospitals, schools, communities and security. The failure of politicians to understand these real and deep concerns has produced an increasingly large gap between what politicians say about immigration and what voters actually think. (Imagine for a moment immigration policy from the perspective of an American worker who has lost his job to lower-paid labor from abroad.)

Recognizing that most candidates were not as focused on immigration as he thought they should be, Miller argued that the issue was paramount. "At this moment in time, there is likely no issue that—done properly and with authenticity—can do more to motivate voters for or against a candidate than immigration," he wrote, suggesting Republicans play rough—because that's what voters cared more about than sounding inclusive. "Hard-hit working people need to see the Republican candidate step into the ring and throw some real punches on their behalf. They want to see the Republican look the camera in the eye and say: 'I am going to fight for you. I am going to fight for your jobs.'" Miller ended the memo on a dramatic flourish with a subtext that wasn't difficult to interpret: America First. "This is our chance to stand up and fight for the good and decent people of this country who pay their taxes, fight our wars, follow the rules, love their country, and expect only in return that their country will put their needs first."

He forwarded his memo to Brown's staff, along with some polling data that backed up his claims, which he had also leaked to *Breitbart*. Williams recalls how much it foreshadowed what was to come. "Stephen's whole perspective was what you saw in the Trump campaign: This issue can be used to reach out to blue-collar voters, people who ordinarily wouldn't think of voting Republican," he says. Brown wasn't as sympathetic as Miller had hoped. At a debate with Shaheen in Concord on the same day his staff met to hear Miller out, Brown pivoted briefly to the economic impact of the immigration legislation Shaheen had voted for, calling it "an opportunity for the president to authorize upwards of 11 million people to get jobs." *Breitbart* noted Brown's shift approvingly in an article by Matthew Boyle that was headlined SCOTT BROWN NAILS SHAHEEN ON IMMIGRATION: 'I WANT TO FIGHT FOR JOBS FOR NEW HAMPSHIRE' OVER JOBS FOR ILLEGAL ALIENS. But mostly he kept talking about immigration as a law-and-order matter.

Miller's impact on the race was more direct in the way he helped steer the conservative media's most vocal immigration hawks to cover Brown. He was in constant contact with staff from *Breitbart*, which was now under the direction of Steve Bannon and had dispatched Boyle, its most aggressive Washington reporter, to New Hampshire because editors wanted someone exclusively assigned to a race they believed would have major implications for the national debate over immigration. Miller also kept in close contact with Julia Hahn, a radio producer for Laura Ingraham. "He was on the phone with Laura Ingraham every day giving them updates," Williams recalls.

Ingraham had been an early booster of Brown's 2010 campaign. Flaherty recalls that she "propelled Scott into the national conversation" at the time. In the summer of 2014, Ingraham was one of talk radio's most vocal immigration hawks. She repeatedly invoked Cantor's loss on her show as a lesson of what would happen to Republicans who caved on "amnesty," the preferred term the right applied to any proposal to extend legal status to people in the country illegally. Her ideal candidate for president in the next election, she told her listeners, was Jeff Sessions, even though Sessions had no plans to run. She loved quoting Pat Buchanan. "The Buchananite core," she liked to say, "has always been the heart of the GOP." She praised Brown for not listening to the Republicans who were telling him to stop talking about immigration. "I need you to go to ScottBrown .com and support him," she implored her audience, most of whom weren't in New Hampshire and couldn't actually vote for him. And she explained why it was so important that the Republican Party had more people in office like Brown: "He's standing up for you, your wages, and your ability to get a decent job. He's standing against the GOP establishment who's telling him, 'Shhhh. Be careful how you talk about these issues.' "

Brown lost by fewer than sixteen thousand votes, or 3 percentage points. After the election, Boyle bragged to colleagues that his work with Miller had paid off, saying, "We made it way closer than it should have been." Miller insisted to colleagues that Brown could have won if he'd been more explicit about the economic harm of illegal immigration. A few weeks after the election, Dave Bossie, president of the conservative group Citizens United, was one of the few to put on the record what he believed had happened in New Hampshire. Bossie declared that immigration was the issue that all Republicans would be focused on by 2016—not healthcare, not debt or deficits. "This is going to become the Obamacare for the 2016 cycle," he said. "You're going to see a constant drumbeat, a constant march. It will be no one thing. . . . When you call down the thunder, sometimes it's not pretty."

Miller went back to Washington, where he thought his work in the Senate had largely run its course. And he started thinking about his next steps and whether there would be a presidential candidate who was more open to his immigration messaging.

CHAPTER 8

★ ★ ★

"That's Hitler!"

I love him because YOU hate him!
—A friend, to Sarah Palin

On the second Saturday in April 2014, Donald Trump boarded his helicopter and flew from New York to Manchester, where he was set to speak at the New Hampshire Freedom Summit. The organizers, who included his old friend Dave Bossie and Americans for Prosperity, the Koch-funded political group, intended for the event to be an early convening of the Republican Party's likely presidential candidates in 2016. That was not the reason for inviting Trump. He was their way of generating media attention and selling tickets, and little more. Though Trump had gotten more serious about running compared with 2011 and had a long list of invitations to speak at other political events in the coming months, he was not entirely sure that a presidential campaign would be a risk worth taking. He'd become increasingly concerned after listening to the advice of his daughter Ivanka that it could be a very hard race to win. He knew that Hillary Clinton would be the Democratic nominee and a formidable opponent. And he thought of her as a friend, which would complicate running against her. She and Bill had attended his third wedding, he liked to point out. During one recent trip to Iowa, Trump had wondered aloud about his chances. "It's going to be very

hard to beat the first woman candidate," he said to the group traveling with him, surprising them with this sudden slump in confidence.

After Romney's loss in 2012, Trump began regularly calling on a
small team of formal and informal political advisers to help him feel
out the Republican landscape. They included his on-again, off-again
friend of three decades, Roger Stone; Sam Nunberg, the young operative whom Stone introduced to Trump when Nunberg was working on a campaign opposing the construction of an Islamic center
near Ground Zero; Michael Cohen, Trump's lawyer; Bossie, who
was a veteran conservative activist; and Kellyanne Conway, who ran
a small polling company and had met Trump after moving into one
of his condo towers in Manhattan in 2001. Lately, Trump had been
trying to act like a serious presidential hopeful and was making occasional trips to Iowa and New Hampshire. But very few people
were taking him seriously. The local press covered him as a celebrity,
not a candidate. And conservative political activists largely considered him a novelty act.

After Trump landed in Manchester, liberal protesters heckled
him as he made his way into the venue. They seemed to be some of
the only people there who were genuinely interested in seeing him.
His advisers had been so focused on getting better coverage that
they had compiled a list of all the journalists who were attending
and made notes for Trump about how friendly they were. But most
of the ones who expressed interest weren't with outlets whose coverage would confer on Trump the mainstream respectability he craved.

When it came time for his speech, Trump started out slow. The
audience looked bored and seemed to applaud only out of a sense of
obligation, as it did when Trump criticized Obama as a failed president who had "no respect" from other world leaders. The room was
far from full, with more than a few empty chairs. Some in the crowd
actually rolled their eyes as he boasted of his uncommon intelligence
and superlative credentials. "I went to the Wharton School of Finance. I was really good at this stuff," he declared.

But then Trump mentioned immigration, and the crowd grew
more engaged. "You either have a country or you don't have a coun-

try," he said, earning a round of applause. Trump allowed that, yes, there were decent, hardworking immigrants. But there were a lot of bad ones too, illegal ones. He said he had a plan for them: "We have to get them the hell out." The crowd whooped and applauded some more. And he kept going.

"You know I heard Jeb Bush the other day," Trump said. Before he could finish his sentence, a few people started groaning. "He was talking about people that come into this country illegally, they do it for love," he went on. The audience booed. "That's one I've never heard of before," Trump said dismissively. They laughed and applauded some more as he built up to his climax. "You know, I'm a builder. I build great buildings," he said, drawing a breath.

"Building a border—they talk about, 'Oh, I don't know. How could we possibly build a fence that nobody can climb over?'" Trump asked in a sarcastic tone.

"I would build a border like you've never seen before," he declared. "Nobody's climbing over. Nobody."

As clumsily as he had delivered the line—how exactly would someone "build" a border?—it killed. The room rumbled with cheers. And the seeds of what would become Trump's most famous anti-immigration battle cry were planted. One of the political consultants traveling with him that day was Nunberg, who had prepped Trump for the speech. As was his custom, Nunberg had written an outline of what Trump should say containing a list of bullet points, most no more than two to three sentences long. Trump was prone to long digressions and preferred outlines to fully written speeches, which he couldn't and wouldn't stick to. "I don't like to be told what to say," he would tell staff. "Look at Romney. I'll end up like that."

About midway down Nunberg's outline, between the talking points on China and national security, was a suggestion about how Trump should raise the issue of immigration: "Here is a great opportunity to criticize Jeb Bush." He urged Trump to emphasize border security and to contrast his strict, zero-tolerance positions on illegal immigration with other Republicans. There was no mention of building anything—not a fence or any other kind of barrier at the border. And when Nunberg heard Trump deliver the line about it that morning, he couldn't recall Trump ever mentioning a fence before in one of his speeches.

In that very moment, the defining image of a presidential campaign that was still fourteen months from getting off the ground started to take shape. True to form, Trump's border wall began as an extemporaneous riff that sprang as much from his sensibilities as a developer as it did from his intuition about what his audience wanted to hear. And while the mainstream media coverage of the Freedom Summit gave other Republicans like Ted Cruz and Rand Paul top billing, it did so through the frame that Trump had constructed on a whim. Jeb Bush hadn't even attended the event, yet he was the headline. JEB BUSH WAS PUBLIC ENEMY NO. I AT ONE OF THE YEAR'S BIGGEST CONSERVATIVE GATHERINGS said *Business Insider*. *The Washington Post*: DONALD TRUMP MENTIONS JEB BUSH AT TEA PARTY EVENT, GETS BOOS FROM THE AUDIENCE. Trump flew back to New York that afternoon in a good mood.

As well as Trump was received by the crowd in Manchester, the prevailing belief among conservative activists for most of the next year would be that whatever Trump was doing with this ostensibly campaign-like road show, it had very little to do with actually getting Trump elected president. He had publicly flirted with running numerous times, making the biggest spectacle of his apparent interest in the White House before the elections of 1988, 2000, and 2012. His 1988 stunt had also included a trip up to New Hampshire on his helicopter. And he hated that the media kept treating his previous dalliances as disqualifying, especially the New Hampshire one nearly thirty years ago. When it came up, he admitted to his advisers that he hadn't ever intended for it to be taken seriously. "It was bullshit. That shouldn't count," he said, explaining that it was entirely self-promotional and designed to generate headlines ahead of the release of his book *The Art of the Deal*.

Apart from his past dalliances, there were other reasons to doubt he would go through with it this time. The long list of likely Republican candidates was so full of top-flight political talent and brain power that Trump looked like a lightweight by comparison. They included current and former governors, senators, a Fortune 500 chief executive, and a pediatric neurosurgeon. The media would cover them over him, his aides warned in a December 2014 memo titled "The 'Serious? Question," a reference to the widely held perception that Trump was anything but. Conway, whose firm did opinion research for conservative groups like Bossie's Citizens United and Marjorie Dannenfelser's Susan B. Anthony List, had conducted a poll a year earlier to test Trump's political viability. The results doused his aspirations with a bucket of cold water. In his home state of New York, only 12 percent said that he should run for president. And just 27 percent said they'd want Trump to run for governor. And more than anything else, Conway noted, people said they didn't want him to run for either.

Even with his regular trips to early primary states, Trump had a hard time translating his public appearances into any kind of quantifiable political credibility. Bossie kept inviting him to candidate cattle calls. Tea Party groups and other conservative organizations also regularly invited him to their events because he was guaranteed to draw a crowd. But if pollsters were including him in their surveys at all—and many did not—Trump rarely got more than 5 percent. As journalists chronicled his exploits on the campaign trail, they often depicted him for what he was: an insult comic whose attacks on would-be rivals—Bush ("a total fool"); Rubio ("a horror show"); Romney ("a choker")—kept audiences laughing.

But few in the media or elsewhere seemed to consider that all that laughter was pointing to a deep dissatisfaction among Republican voters with the more conventional choices in front of them.* In December 2014, a column in the New York *Daily News* said that the developer's new hotel in the nation's capital was "as close as Donald Trump will get to the White House." In January 2015, Chuck

---

* Full disclosure: This reporter attended the Bossie-Koch event in Manchester in April 2014 and was offered the opportunity to stick around for Bannon's show and listen to Trump's interview. I haughtily declined.

Todd said on NBC, "Nobody is going to mistake Donald Trump for a presidential candidate, I don't think, other than Donald Trump these days." In February 2015, the *Los Angeles Times,* when describing the outer fringe of the party, lumped Trump in with Phil Robertson of *Duck Dynasty* fame.

But Trump was starting to step into the lane in the Republican Party that most people assumed another outsider politician like Ted Cruz, Rand Paul, or Scott Walker would fill. The decline of the Tea Party as the vehicle for conservative discontent during the Obama years left the insurgent wing with even less cohesion than before. And the diminishment of Sarah Palin as a credible opposition figure meant there was no one on the stage with the crossover appeal as a politician and a celebrity that she had, for better or for worse. She claimed to be considering a run for president again in 2016, but few were taking her seriously. Her public remarks were becoming more disjointed, sometimes to the point of incoherence. She delivered an especially bizarre speech at one of Bossie's Freedom Summits in Iowa in January 2015, rambling on about the perils of "the man," sounding straight out of the 1960s. "The man can only ride ya when your back is bent. So strengthen it. Then the man can't ride ya," Palin said.

Trump, who spoke at the same event, kept doing well with the crowds. They cheered him now when he said he was considering running. Bossie noticed the difference in how Trump was being received by early 2015, and Palin's slide by contrast. He just couldn't be entirely sure how much of that was a reaction to Trump's celebrity and how much of it might suggest that Trump was forging a deeper bond with conservative voters. "It's almost like a baton being passed," Bossie recalls of Trump's rise and Palin's slide. "And she didn't want to pass it at all."

Once, several years before Trump formally entered politics, one of his guests at Mar-a-Lago asked him how he had created a brand with such enduring mass-market appeal. "The audience tells you where to go," Trump responded, offering as an example how he liked to test out lines when he was giving a speech. That way, he explained, he could avoid saying something they didn't like. "If it doesn't work and the audience doesn't applaud, I'll never use it again," Trump said.

One of the things that Trump unwittingly connected between his presidential campaign and the American tradition of populism was its use of immigrants as effective scapegoats. Like most of his decisions about the campaign, Trump didn't come to believe that immigration would work with Republican primary voters because he had commissioned a thorough examination of popular opinion. Friends often laughed at how he didn't seem to know the difference between an unscientific poll that any reader of *The Drudge Report* could click on and a professional, statistically weighted survey of likely voters. But that is not to say he lacked a grasp of recent history. Trump like to talk about Ross Perot's 1992 third-party campaign against George H. W. Bush and Bill Clinton. Perot had famously likened the impact of NAFTA on American jobs to a "giant sucking sound." Trump admired the simplicity of Perot's appeal as a businessman with no patience for the inefficiencies of government. He borrowed from Perot in his speeches, insisting that he would be the president who could "get things done." Trump also loved the aspirational themes of Reagan's 1980 campaign against Jimmy Carter, which is why he borrowed the slogan "Make America Great Again," which Reagan had used.

But often, Trump just improvised. And when something worked and the audience responded well, he kept doing it. "In his mind, he doesn't know how the people are going to react," says Bossie. "So he's saying these things and he's testing." At Bossie's Iowa Freedom Summit in January, Trump was more detailed in how he articulated his plan for border security. "We have to build a fence," he said. The audience loved it. And Trump kept the line in his speech from then on. "When he gets positive feedback, it stays in his speech and morphs into what it ends up being: a big, beautiful wall," explains Bossie.

But as well as that line had gone over with the audience, Trump once again found his appearance largely eclipsed by Republicans who were thought to be more serious. And it infuriated him. The fair-haired boy to emerge from Bossie's Iowa event was Governor Walker of Wisconsin, who dominated the news after giving what the media and the Republican political establishment hailed as a goalpost-setting speech. Walker talked about being a fighter and beating the Goliath-like labor unions that had tried to recall him from office. He presented himself as a man of modest means like most Americans and described what it was like to use coupons to buy a shirt at Kohl's department store. Afterward, Walker shot to the top of the polls. Trump stayed in single digits. Trump, who had no idea who Walker was, couldn't believe it. "Who the fuck is Scott Walker?" he growled as he saw Walker's performance praised in the media.

One thing Trump did know after seeing cable news coverage of Walker's speech was that Walker didn't have "the look." Trump had always been image-conscious. His frame of reference for how something or someone should look was the movies. As a young man, he had dreams of making it big in Hollywood. He initially wanted to attend the University of Southern California, not Penn, and enroll in film school. "They said that was like the Wharton School of cinema," Trump said in 2014 to David Rubenstein, the private equity manager and philanthropist, recalling how his life might have taken a different turn. Trump would ultimately pursue real estate under the tutelage of his domineering father. It would have been a nonstarter for the son of Fred Trump—a developer of houses and apartment buildings in Brooklyn and Queens whose concept of masculinity was fixed in the 1940s—to chase his passion in the arts and forgo a role in the successful family business. But the image Trump had of himself was of someone suited for a more glamorous life. After he branched out on his own in Manhattan real estate, he liked to tell people that he approached the business with the movies in mind. "I brought Hollywood to the real estate business," he would say.

When it came to politics, Trump saw things the same way. He was the director, screenwriter, cinematographer, and leading man of the television production he considered the 2016 election to be. His preternatural fixation about how he looked on screen meant he constantly micromanaged his on-camera appearances. "This shot sucks," he would fume if something didn't look right. One reason he preferred calling into shows for interviews was he didn't have to worry about being at the mercy of a news director or a cameraman he didn't trust. He once walked out of a live interview with *CBS This Morning* while he was on the road campaigning after seeing the hotel room where the camera had been set up and deeming it too dumpy-looking. Television news producers who had worked with him over the years recall how he demanded where the camera should be pointed at him because he was always conscious of which angles he thought were his best. "He walks right over to the Steadicam guy," one veteran news producer recalls about shooting an interview with Trump, referring to the stabilizing camera mount that television shows use to create smoother images. "He's directing the shot—'No, there!' He's pointing, ordering the guy around." And the producer concedes that the shot did look better once Trump had finished arranging it. "Damned if he wasn't right."

Trump's judgments about his potential rivals for the Republican nomination were skewed heavily by their appearances. Conway recalls his take on Rand Paul, the slightly built, curly-haired senator from Kentucky: "Doesn't have the look." Conway had firsthand experience watching Trump operate well before his interest in politics started to bloom. In 2006, she took a seat on the board of the Trump World Tower, the condo building near the United Nations where she and her husband, George, lived on the eightieth floor. Trump offered George the seat after he had supported Trump in a dispute with a group of owners. George asked Kellyanne if she wanted to take it instead. She did. And at her first meeting, she was surprised to find Trump sitting at the table. People who went to work for Trump were often surprised by how involved he was in the smallest details of his companies. He personally signed checks to vendors and seemed to know the details of the work they had—or hadn't—finished. When Steve Bannon joined the Trump campaign full-time in 2016, he was struck that Trump seemed to know the status of certain construction projects, right down to the work being done in a particular hotel room. "I wonder how big this company actually is?" he asked himself.

While there were some details of his business and his on-camera aesthetic that were never too small to involve himself in, he was not so engaged when it came to intra-party Republican politics. The fault lines inside the party were never of much interest to Trump. "We didn't talk about party politics," Conway says. "He's a personality guy. 'What do you think about this one? What do you think about that one?'" Once in a speech to Republicans in Florida, Trump sized up Romney and offered just one positive observation. "Romney had one thing going for him," Trump scoffed. "He's good-looking. Other than that, there's nothing, okay? Even when he walked around the stage, he walked like a penguin."

His impulse was to be drawn to whatever divided Republicans. Then he picked a side and hammered whoever wasn't on his. He noticed that he was often rewarded doubly when he went after Republicans who were tied to the Bush-Romney-establishment wing of the party. So he started picking more fights, settling on targets like Karl Rove because they generated the most attention. "When Trump saw that it caught on, he just kept going," Nunberg recalls. He stepped up his attacks on Twitter, which by 2015 was a weapon he wielded more prolifically and proficiently than any of his rivals. "Why do people give @KarlRove contributions when they know he is a loser who has no idea how to win?" Trump posted in January 2015. It was also not lost on Trump that Rove was not well liked by the party's hard right, which considered him the most prominent example of the kind of consultant who agreed with the conclusions of the 2013 autopsy.

Trump's use of Twitter to antagonize his enemies was another example of how he was benefiting because of—not in spite of—rejecting the deliberative, cautious planning that usually went into a presidential campaign. Only a fraction of Republican voters were regularly checking Twitter in 2015. Tony Fabrizio, whom Trump would later hire as his 2016 campaign pollster, conducted a survey in 2017 to measure Twitter use among Republicans and found that even then, two years after Trump kicked off his campaign, still only

17 percent of Republicans nationwide said they checked the social media platform daily. And 59 percent said they didn't look at Twitter at all. But Trump knew who was checking Twitter compulsively: the journalists covering the race. "He just knew that when he said something outrageous the media would carry it. He would post it on Twitter, and there it would be on TV," Fabrizio says. Trump would start calling himself "The Ernest Hemingway of 140 characters," referring to the limit Twitter placed on the length of posts until 2017. "It would change the news cycle," says Bannon, who describes watching a giddy Trump do this in real time. Trump would be in a room full of people with CNN on the television, the network he discovered was the most responsive to his tweets. "Hey, watch this," he would say. Then he'd tap out a tweet from his phone. "Boom. It would come right up on the chyron. I mean, literally, it's two seconds," Bannon recalls. And Trump would point at the screen, satisfied with his accomplishment.

As he pressed ahead with plans for a formal announcement of his candidacy in the late spring of 2015, he was involved in the smallest visual details of the event, which he wanted to take place at Trump Tower on or as close to Flag Day as possible, which is also his birthday. He peppered his staff for their input right up until showtime. "Do you think I should wear the black suit?" he asked aides. One said yes because it was the look people would recognize from *The Apprentice*. "No. You're wrong," Trump said. He preferred the dark blue suit and red tie, he explained, because he liked the way it matched the row of American flags lined up onstage behind him—another detail Trump had personally overseen during the planning. Trump started his speech that morning in the food court area of the Trump Tower atrium with an attestation to his own greatness. "Thousands," he said of the crowd size. "There's been no crowd like this." At most, there were hundreds. And some were paid to be there. A complaint later filed with the Federal Election Commission alleged that a company assisting the Trump campaign with organizing the event hired actors at fifty dollars apiece to "wear T-shirts and carry signs and help cheer [Trump] in support of his announcement."

Trump then started mocking his rivals for having amateurish-looking announcements compared with his. They looked sweaty, he said, and spoke to small crowds, which he equated with the inability to be an effective commander in chief. "Some of the candidates they went in, they didn't know the air conditioner didn't work. They sweated like dogs." Ergo, "How are they going to beat ISIS?" Trump wondered.

The opening line in the prepared text was one of the few he would deliver verbatim from the script that morning. The speech had been written by Nunberg and Corey Lewandowski, the first of three campaign managers Trump would cycle through over the course of the next eighteen months: "Our country is in serious trouble," the script said. And then Trump largely improvised for the next forty-five minutes. As written, the remarks should have taken about seven and a half minutes to get through. The text was heavy on the themes that his advisers hoped would make Trump stand out as someone who repudiated traditional Republican politics: He wouldn't touch Social Security or Medicare and he would never make a mistake like the war in Iraq. There were only a handful of references to Mexico in the final version. There was a line about the barrier on the border he planned to build, which was no longer a mere fence but now a "massive wall." He started to veer sharply off script about two minutes in, when he jumped ahead and pulled a line out from the middle of the speech that would come to dominate the news coverage of his announcement and the entire presidential campaign for weeks.

"The U.S. has become a dumping ground for everybody else's problems," he said, sparking some scattered cheers. Taking that as a cue that he was on a roll, he started improvising. "Thank you. It's true," he said. "And these aren't the best and the finest. When Mexico sends its people, they're not sending their best. They're not sending you. They're not sending you," he continued, pointing to supporters who were hanging over the balcony railing above. "They're sending people that have lots of problems, and they're bringing those problems with us. They're bringing drugs. They're bringing crime.

They're rapists. And some, I assume, are good people. But I speak to border guards, and they tell us what they're getting."

That day, even as he took the step that so few expected him to and declared his candidacy, many believed it was all just another publicity stunt. Television networks and major newspapers sent junior members of their political staffs or feature reporters to cover him. At Fox News, Roger Ailes was skeptical. "Don't you understand?" Ailes dismissively told colleagues before Trump formally declared his candidacy. "This guy is negotiating a new deal with NBC. And as soon as he gets it, he's done." A Fox News poll that came out the week before Trump's announcement had him at just 4 percent. Bush and Walker were tied for first place with 12 percent each. And when Trump sat down for an interview with Bill O'Reilly after his announcement speech, O'Reilly treated Trump's signature campaign promise as a joke. "I actually laughed when you said you're going to build this giant wall from San Diego to Brownsville and the Mexicans are going to pay for it," O'Reilly scoffed. "The Mexicans aren't going to pay for the wall."

There was a notable exception to the skepticism: *Breitbart*. Bannon sent a team of two writers to New York, including Matthew Boyle. Trump had promised Boyle a sit-down interview after his speech, which would become one of numerous items *Breitbart* published that day about the 2016 presidential contest's newest entry. Its coverage was exhaustive, to the point of overkill, right down to the published transcript of Ivanka Trump's introductory remarks.

That morning, Bannon watched Trump's announcement live from the $2.35 million townhouse in Washington where he lived that doubled as *Breitbart* headquarters. Bannon thought about all that had transpired in the five years since Bossie had first asked him to talk to Trump about running for president, and how he had laughed—"Of what country?" On the night before the announcement, Bannon spoke to Trump on the phone and wished him luck. And when he saw Trump make his entrance that morning, he thought he knew exactly what he was seeing.

That's Hitler!, Bannon thought, as the opening scene of Leni

Riefenstahl's seminal work of Nazi propaganda, *Triumph of the Will,* flashed through his mind. He meant it as a compliment. As a documentarian himself who had studied and admired Riefenstahl's work, Bannon saw some of her visual techniques in Trump's production. To create the illusion that Hitler towered over everyone around him as a figure of superhuman proportions, Riefenstahl would keep him tight in her frame, often placing him on a higher plane than his adoring subjects. *Triumph* opens with a shot of Hitler's aircraft high above Nuremberg as it begins descending through the clouds. When it touches down in a field, the massive crowd that has assembled to greet their leader rejoices. Hitler smiles as he drinks in the adulation. Bannon thought that Trump's entrance looked strikingly similar, and that he was witnessing someone with an uncanny sense for manipulating public perception. At 11:05 A.M., Trump appeared in the atrium and stepped onto an escalator. One idea that had been discussed by Trump's advisers was to have him emerge from the elevator, which was how he often made his grand entrance on *The Apprentice.* But by choosing the escalator, the cameras would have to follow him in one largely continuous shot as he descended past cheering fans until he reached the bottom. Another person watching Trump's speech was Stephen Miller, who immediately got in touch with Bannon and asked to be connected to Lewandowski so he could pitch himself for a job on the campaign.

The Mexico remarks cost Trump lucrative business relationships. The Spanish-language network Univision broke the dam on June 25 with an announcement that it was canceling its telecast of Trump's Miss USA pageant, which was just a few weeks away. Next was NBC, which aired *The Apprentice* and its spinoff *The Celebrity Apprentice.* The network said on June 29 that it was severing all business ties with Trump. On July 1, Macy's said it was phasing out Trump's line of suits, shirts, and ties, calling his comments about Mexican immigrants "inconsistent with Macy's values." Then José Andrés, the Spanish-born celebrity chef who had planned to open a restaurant in Trump's new hotel in downtown Washington, backed out of their deal. And ESPN ditched its plans to hold a celebrity golf tournament in California at a Trump course.

The conventional wisdom in Republican consulting circles at the time was that Trump had essentially ended his campaign the day he announced. Many of his rivals believed so. Advisers to Rand Paul were in a meeting at their Washington headquarters when word of Trump's Mexico remarks started circulating. The prevailing opinion in the room was that Trump had gone too far. Fabrizio, who was working as Paul's pollster at the time, disagreed. "Have you met Republican primary voters?" he asked sarcastically. "They are going to eat this up." As much as Trump's business ventures were hurting, his poll numbers were not. For the first time, he climbed out of the lower rung of Republican candidates. When Fox News went into the field with a poll at the end of June, it showed Trump in second place behind Bush. Ailes leaked word early to Trump, who was so excited he announced the news to his team at Trump Tower. "We're number two. Can you believe it?" he said, sounding almost in disbelief.

Trump started giving the audience more and defied predictions of his imminent demise. Far from backing off his Mexico remarks, he called for a boycott of Macy's and filed a $500 million lawsuit against Univision. When Jorge Ramos, Univision's top anchor, tried to ask Trump a question at a press conference, Trump snapped at him in what sounded like a nativist attack on the Mexican-American journalist. "Go back to Univision," he barked. And Ramos was escorted out of the room. He made his corporate foes punchlines in his speeches to crowds that were growing larger by the day. "The silent majority is back, and we're going to take our country back," Trump declared in Phoenix at a rally that drew several thousand people.

In August, the campaign released a paper outlining for the first time the actual policy principles that would govern Trump's approach to immigration. Though some reports cited Ann Coulter as the author, Coulter had only contributed a few suggestions over email to Lewandowski and didn't read the document before it went up online. (After seeing it, she tweeted that it was the "greatest political document since the Magna Carta.") The author was actually Stephen Miller, who thought that Trump should not apologize for anything he'd said and double down. In the paper, Miller repeated Trump's contention that he would make Mexico pay for the wall, but also explained how—threatening to "impound" wages earned by undocumented Mexican immigrants and increase the fees that Mexican executives and diplomats pay for temporary visas, among other punitive steps. "Mexico's leaders have been taking advantage of the United States by using illegal immigration to export the crime and poverty in their own country," it said, echoing the most controversial lines from Trump's announcement speech. As the uproar from Trump's critics grew louder and pundits predicted with certainty his imminent collapse, Miller noticed that the intensity of the support from the people at Trump's rallies seemed to multiply. They weren't upset about the xenophobia. They didn't care that he was coarse and juvenile. As he followed news reports of the rallies, he heard Trump's supporters effectively turning the situation upside down. They were mad that Trump's critics could get so outraged over his words but at the same time be relatively unsympathetic to the economic and social problems Trump was calling out, however crudely. "If you're a steelworker in Pennsylvania who's had his hours cut, how mad could you be bothered to get by Donald Trump's tone on immigration? Where's that on your list of concerns?" Miller says.

And many saw themselves in Trump. To pull this off required an extraordinary suspension of disbelief. Here was a man who bragged compulsively about being rich and powerful but who was complaining, in effect, that he was a victim. He flew into their communities on his private jet to tell them how poorly treated he was, and it didn't come off the least bit insincere. Swaddled in privilege and given to gaudy displays of material excess, Trump didn't live anything like most Americans. He certainly had never known what it was like to smell like fish all summer like Palin had. Devoid of empathy, incapable of humility, and unfamiliar with what it means to suffer consequences, he behaved and spoke in ways most would never dare. And yet Trump's habit of seeing persecutors everywhere he looked did not come off as paranoid or self-obsessed to his fans. It seemed perfectly reasonable because while they may not have used the vulgarities and hyperbole that he did, they agreed with what he was saying and pictured how they'd be persecuted too if they dared to agree with him out loud in the wrong company. And the fact that he was wealthy and powerful seemed to bolster their fears as even more plausible: *If they can do this to someone who has this much, what would happen to me?*

Few understood this better than Palin. Now that she had little hope of becoming president herself, she started to pull close to Trump. After Trump's announcement, a friend emailed her with some insight into his popular appeal that she found so interesting she put it in a column she wrote for *Breitbart* in July. "Tell those smart alecks bashing Trump on TV, 'I love him because YOU hate him!'" her friend wrote. Political elites, Palin said in the piece, were "clutching their pearls and whimpering for smelling salts," while the voters were cheering him on. She urged Trump to keep going. "More power to you, Donald. Here's to 'Making America Great Again!'"

Palin's piece was just one element of the Trump-Bannon-*Breitbart* partnership that was heading in a more audacious direction, obliterating boundaries that had kept even the most partisan news organizations like Fox from engaging in overt assistance to a political campaign. As aides at Trump Tower were preparing their candidate for upcoming debates on Fox News and CNN, Bannon consulted with Nunberg on a memo that outlined for Trump the foreign policy and defense issues that were likely to come up. Bannon also helped the Trump campaign organize a trip to the southern border that summer that would cement a vital new political allyship for the candidate. *Breitbart* had opened a Texas bureau in 2014 as part of an expansion that Bannon hoped would position the site to more aggressively cover the emerging fronts in what he described as a "cultural and political war" that was escalating around the globe. (*Breitbart* opened a second office in London, where discontent over Britain's ties to the European Union was growing and E.U. opponents were organizing a campaign to exit the alliance.) In Texas, *Breitbart* writers had cultivated ties with agents working for the U.S. Border Patrol, who leaked to the website stories of shelters being overrun by child migrants in 2014. With Bannon acting as a conduit, the Trump campaign connected with Border Patrol agents in

Laredo, Texas, where Trump planned a speech in late July. A group of agents in plainclothes showed up to cheer him on. One, Luis Villegas, twenty-eight, told *The Washington Post* that Trump's stance on immigration motivated him to get involved in politics for the first time. "I believe in what he's throwing out there," Villegas said.

Sometimes *Breitbart* staff even encouraged Trump to make statements he wouldn't have made on his own. In September, when Jeb Bush questioned Trump's conservatism and tried to underscore his point by repeating it in Spanish—*"El hombre no es conservador"*—Boyle sensed an opening that Trump did not: Bush's bilingual crack would rile up the anti-immigration, English-only wing of the GOP base. Boyle asked for an interview. And when Trump got on the phone, Boyle kept nudging Trump but didn't get anywhere at first. "Don't you think that by speaking Spanish, Jeb Bush is going to upset the base?" Boyle asked, rephrasing the question several times before Trump finally caught on. "Okay, I see what you're trying to do," Trump said. The lead quote from Trump in the story that appeared on *Breitbart* later that day blew up: "I like Jeb. He's a nice man. But he should really set the example by speaking English while in the United States." News outlets everywhere, from *People* magazine to Iowa Public Radio, picked up the story.

By the summer of 2015, the Republican National Committee had all the evidence it needed proving how off its autopsy had been. Gary Coby, the RNC's digital advertising director, first noticed this in the surprising feedback he was getting from voters after Trump's announcement. As a way of gathering the contact information it needed to raise money, the RNC had been running digital ads on Facebook and other websites that invited people to take a straw poll. If they clicked "yes," they would be directed to a separate page that listed the Republican candidates and asked them to pick a favorite. Then, to submit their results, they had to enter their email. It was a three-step, somewhat cumbersome process by design, and many people considered it too invasive to complete. But it weeded out lukewarm partisans, helping the RNC build an email list of the kinds of voters who were most engaged and likely to donate. Coby could see that the people who were actually finishing the survey were overwhelmingly Trump supporters. Trump was crushing the straw poll by a ratio of about 2 to 1. "The excitement for him versus everyone else was just off the charts," Coby would later explain in an interview for a political science textbook. Coby, who had honed his skills in previous jobs in digital political marketing, thought it was remarkable that so many more Trump fans were coming to the RNC compared with the other candidates. It seemed to him as if they wanted to send the RNC a message: We love him, and we're watching you to make sure you don't screw him. Coby also monitored a separate trove of voter feedback that the RNC had: emails that were coming in from across the country from people offering effusive praise for Trump. Many were expressing the belief that the RNC was trying to fix the nomination for one of the more conventional candidates. "Some people weren't always trusting that the RNC was going to be fair with him," Coby says.

Trump understood there was a deep undercurrent of mistrust to mine among people who were skeptical about the official Republican Party apparatus. And as he traveled the country that summer, one of his favorite themes was to complain about not being treated "fairly" by the party. Reince Priebus, the party chairman, worried that Trump's talk about fairness was actually a way of giving himself an exit ramp to a third-party candidacy, which would have split the conservative vote and doomed Republicans in the general election. So he insisted that Trump sign a pledge to support the eventual Republican nominee, whoever it happened to be. This took some finesse on Priebus's part. "I'll get everyone else to sign it first. You'll be the last one," he promised Trump. Priebus took the pledge up to Trump in Trump Tower in person and got him to sign it on September 3. And with that, the party leadership had momentarily wrested some control of their nomination process back from Trump.

—

But there were clear signs that the party was not as in command as its leaders thought. In August, the United States Chamber of Commerce held a retreat for its senior staff on Maryland's Eastern Shore. In preparation for the gathering, Scott Reed, the Chamber's chief political strategist and party veteran who had run Bob Dole's 1996 presidential campaign, asked his research team to compile an analysis of the media coverage of each Republican candidate. The results he presented were "the canary in the coal mine," Reed recalls. Seventy percent of the coverage was about Trump—print, online, broadcast, social media. The rest of the sixteen candidates divided up what was left over, a few percentage points each at the most. This kind of glaring incongruity between Trump and his rivals was not solely a media phenomenon. The new GOP chairwoman in Michigan, Ronna Romney McDaniel, Mitt Romney's niece and granddaughter of George Romney, decided to drop in on a Trump rally in early August in the town of Birch Run, about ninety miles northwest of Detroit. When she got there, two thousand people were waiting for him to arrive. *I've never seen a crowd like that for a primary candidate in my life,* she thought.

McDaniel was the very profile of the voter that conventional political wisdom said Trump should repel: a college-educated mother of two in her forties who lived in an upscale suburb in a battleground state. She was a relentless networker who had used her famous name and disarming lack of pretentiousness to get elected as state party chair. And when she met Trump in the summer of 2015, he was only one of the seventeen candidates she intended to introduce herself to. She told herself she would look every one of her party's presidential candidates in the eye and try to convince them that the right Republican could win Michigan—something last accomplished by George H. W. Bush in 1988. This kind of salesmanship was a regular part of the job. But what she saw that evening at the Birch Run Expo Center made her realize that Trump might be the one. It wasn't just the large crowd or the way they erupted when Trump reframed his message on trade to appeal to an audience in the cradle of the American auto industry. "They're taking our factories and building these massive plants in Mexico," he declared. "Why don't we just let the illegals drive the cars and trucks across the border into our country?"

Ronna McDaniel sensed that there were more traditionally Democratic union voters there than would be at a typical Republican event. Her suspicions were soon affirmed. A group of activist conservatives that included the DeVos family, one of the biggest financial backers of the Michigan GOP, had sent organizers to the rally to gather signatures for a petition. It aimed to repeal a Michigan law that required private contractors to pay union-scale wages and benefits on construction projects funded by the state, which guaranteed higher wages for the blue-collar workers who paved roads and built schools. But it was the kind of labor-friendly policy that free-market, economic libertarians like the Koch brothers or the DeVoses hated, and these kind of pro-business interests had long been at war with Michigan's labor unions. (A prominent member of the DeVos family, Betsy, held Ronna McDaniel's job as state party chair in the late 1990s and early 2000s.) Afterward, McDaniel checked out of curiosity how many people had signed the petitions. Almost no one had.

This is not our crowd, she thought.

CHAPTER 9

A Death in Texas

It is sad to see a judicial confirmation process needs to resemble a
political campaign. But that is where we are.

—LEONARD LEO, September 2006

Trump's offenses against the antiabortion movement were so le-
gion and stretched back so many decades that it seemed there
would be no vanishing them down the memory hole.

He had tried explaining them away with a poll-tested personal
anecdote about the epiphany he said made him realize he was pro-
life. This was an old trick that his friend Kellyanne Conway urged
her male clients to do. As a way of making their opposition to abortion sound less judgmental and uncompassionate, Conway coun-
seled them to talk about a personal experience—for instance, seeing
the ultrasound of their unborn child for the first time. For years,
Trump had been telling the story of "a friend" whose wife he said
had become unexpectedly pregnant. The couple was leaning toward
an abortion but then changed their minds and ended up with a
beautiful, talented child, Trump would say. But when social conservative activists heard Trump tell this story, more than a few of them
thought he was talking about himself and one of the three wives
with whom he had children. It wasn't exactly reassuring.

Trump's support for abortion rights in the past was one of the
biggest political liabilities his team had flagged as it tried to head off

a backlash to his candidacy from the religious right. Part of the problem was that there was an actual paper trail of his support for abortion rights, and it was long. Trump's political team had flagged for him his past financial support for groups like NARAL, the abortion advocacy organization, and to Democratic politicians who were major supporters of the pro-choice movement like Senator Chuck Schumer of New York and Terry McAuliffe, the governor of Virginia. Trump was also on tape saying things like "I am pro-choice in every respect." That quote, from a 1999 interview he gave to *Meet the Press,* had started appearing in an attack ad produced by a super PAC supporting Ted Cruz. The PAC's president was Conway, who had gone to work for the group in 2015 and not for Trump, whom she doubted would ever conduct polling. But one didn't need to know Trump personally to realize that his public record on abortion or any number of issues important to social conservatives was voluminous, its contradictions manifold and well-documented. There was also the matter of his sister, Maryanne Trump Barry, a federal judge who had written an opinion in 2000 that was critical of a law that would have banned a procedure opponents called "partial-birth abortion." It wasn't merely that she was his sister, or that perhaps her views could be interpreted as a window into his real beliefs about *Roe v. Wade.* It was worse, as far as many social conservatives were concerned. He'd said he might consider putting her on the Supreme Court.

Trump's consultants had urged him to tread lightly on the issue whenever it came up. Compounding his difficulties with the religious right, Trump didn't know how to speak their language. When he addressed more socially conservative audiences, aides often took extra care reminding him to be on his best behavior. "No cursing. . . . The local press will not cover cursing favorably," they warned him in briefing materials before he spoke to the Southern Republican Leadership Conference in New Orleans. They tried to get him to work mentions of God into his remarks, which he almost never did in a serious way. Finally, he came up with a way to do it that satisfied him. "I will be the greatest jobs president that God ever created," he would say—a line he would use for years to come even though it made him sound like someone who thought he'd have a divine mandate to run the country. Trump sometimes talked more about the exceptions he supported to an abortion ban than a ban itself, which was problematic because the most serious antiabortion activists don't favor any exceptions under any circumstances. But it was best, they told him, that he emphasize how rare these exceptions were if he did talk about them and to focus on the ways he would make it harder for women to get an abortion with a ban after the fifth month of pregnancy and, ultimately, by seeing *Roe* overturned. For someone who boasted of his singular ability to read an audience, he sometimes fell flat with large crowds of religious conservatives. Once, during a speech to the student body of Liberty University in 2012, the evangelical institution co-founded by Jerry Falwell, Sr., Trump mentioned in an aside how he always insisted on making his future wives sign prenuptial agreements, and that it was something the students should keep in mind for themselves. "I always say always have a prenuptial agreement," he told the students. They had little reaction.

In theory, Trump's lack of a firm position on abortion could have helped Republicans rebuild trust with the women the RNC autopsy said had been turned off by their rigid position on the issue. But that kind of thinking did not anticipate the sense of siege and urgency and betrayal that the pro-life movement would be feeling as the 2016 election approached. Trump was a man whose insults and denigrations of women would seem to disqualify him from ever being elected in a country where 51 percent of the population is female. Still, the possibility that Trump could become the Republican nominee was especially alarming to many of these activists. And as Trump's 4 percent in the polls became 14 percent, and then 24 percent as the end of 2015 closed in, they started to panic. The work of activists like Marjorie Dannenfelser had put women at the forefront of the movement. No longer were the leading antiabortion organizations so dominated by men, with women relegated to the background and back offices. Having observed the success of women like Louise Slaughter and Nancy Pelosi, who helped lead the pro-choice caucus in Congress the 1990s, Dannenfelser became determined to replicate that model in the pro-life world. And by 2016, she and a growing number of women like Conway had taken on prominent roles with national social conservative organizations.

The phrase "Never Trump" was still months away from becoming the ubiquitous Twitter hashtag and slogan for the movement of conservatives looking to stop Trump's nomination at the Republican National Convention. In fact, it does not appear to have been used at all in the media as a reference to the opposition to him before the February 1 Iowa caucuses. But the sentiment of "Never Trump" was the heart of a scalding denunciation of him in a group letter that Dannenfelser spearheaded in January 2016. It was a campaign cri de coeur for the ages. She recruited thirteen other women leaders of socially conservative groups from across the country to draft the letter to Iowans, urging them to "support anyone but Donald Trump." The candidate-agnostic approach reflected both the desire by the women not to endorse any of Trump's rivals and create tension within the memberships of their respective organizations. But it also pointed to the widely shared belief among religious conservatives that literally *anyone* on the ballot who was a Republican would be a better nominee than Trump.

"On the issue of defending unborn children and protecting women from the violence of abortion, Mr. Trump cannot be trusted," the letter began. They intentionally tried to appeal to voters beyond those who would be swayed by the issue of abortion alone and depicted Trump as a menacing and boorish lout of a man.

> Moreover, as women, we are disgusted by Mr. Trump's treatment of individuals, women, in particular. He has impugned the dignity of women, most notably Megyn Kelly, he mocked and bullied Carly Fiorina, and has through the years made disparaging public comments to and about many women. Further, Mr. Trump has profited from the exploitation of women in his Atlantic City casino hotel which boasted of the first strip club casino in the country.

America will only be a great nation when we have leaders of strong character who will defend both unborn children and the dignity of women. We cannot trust Donald Trump to do either.

But the biggest unknown of a Trump presidency, as the women spelled out, was that the next president could be responsible for picking as many as four justices to the Supreme Court. And this was not a job they said Trump should be trusted with either. Their suspicions were not misplaced. While Trump floated a wide range of possible Supreme Court nominees throughout the campaign, in public and in private, often they were not lawyers or judges he admired for their legal philosophies or interpretations of the Constitution. They were people he knew from television such as Jeanine Pirro, the host of a weekend show on Fox News that Trump regularly watched and occasionally planned his flight schedule around, directing his personal pilot to adjust the route accordingly so the satellite signal wouldn't fade. Trump told friends that he thought Pirro would make a fine justice. He also talked about the possibility of nominating Andrew Napolitano, a Fox News legal analyst and former New Jersey Superior Court judge who would have been doubly unacceptable to many on the religious right. Not only was he friendly with Maryanne Trump Barry, he is also gay. Napolitano liked to tell friends a story about the time Trump told him how much he'd absorbed about the law from Napolitano's television appearances. "Everything I know about the Constitution I learned from you on *Fox & Friends,*" Napolitano recalled. After he was elected, Trump invited Napolitano to Trump Tower during the transition, suggesting he was indeed serious about giving the judge some kind of position in the government. During their meeting, for part of which Mike Pence was present, Trump ribbed Pence for his anti–gay rights views. Addressing Napolitano, Trump gestured toward the archconservative vice-president-elect and said, "You'd better be careful because this guy thinks it's a crime to be gay. Right, Mike?" When Pence didn't answer, Trump repeated himself, "Right, Mike?" Pence remained silent.

That was Donald Trump when it came to the issues social conservatives cared so deeply about: flippant, disengaged, and disinclined to care. Dannenfelser and the women of the antiabortion movement had articulated the dismay that many other activists on the right had been feeling for months as they watched Trump rise in the polls. At that point, many of them still believed that the voters would stop him—or that he would stop himself and self-destruct.

All the proof Tony Perkins needed that Trump was not cut out for a future in the Republican Party came on the morning of July 18, 2015, as Perkins waited backstage in an auditorium on the campus of Iowa State University. He was next up to speak to the Iowa Family Leadership Summit, an important stop on the Republican presidential campaign circuit where evangelical activists and candidates come together to talk religion, politics, and the future of the country. By coincidence, Perkins happened to be the speaker slotted right after Trump. Before Trump's arrival, Nunberg advised him in a memo that the crowd was not automatically going to be eating out of the palm of his hand. "The audience is CHRISTIAN SOCIAL CONSERVATIVES. They are open to your candidacy but NEED TO KNOW that their issues are IMPORTANT TO YOU." Trump would completely disregard the advice. But in a pattern that would repeat itself throughout the campaign—surprising his own advisers and most leading evangelical conservatives—it didn't matter. And he only became more popular with the evangelical rank and file.

As Perkins watched Trump's performance that day, it struck him as unlikely that many people in the room or the broader conservative movement would like what they were seeing. Politicians who are trying to win the favor of conservative evangelical Christians tend not to belittle rituals of the faith like Communion. They tend not to curse or insult people by questioning their intelligence. They tend to be respectful and gracious toward those who have suffered. Once he took the stage, Trump sat hunched in an armchair opposite the man who would be conducting a question-and-answer session with him, the pollster Frank Luntz. It went downhill from there. Trump swore when Luntz asked about Common Core education initiatives. "People in Washington, frankly I don't even think they give a damn about education." Taken aback, Luntz asked Trump if that was really the kind of language he wanted to be using.

It was. "We're so politically correct that we can't move anymore," Trump said. The audience didn't balk. It applauded.

"Don't you feel you went too far in what you called Mexicans?" Luntz followed up.

"Oh no. Not at all," Trump said, earning more applause and cheers.

But what about other insults like calling John McCain, a war hero who spent five and a half years as a prisoner of war in Vietnam, "a dummy," Luntz pressed him.

"Not a war hero," interjected Trump, who received a diagnosis of bone spurs that allowed him to avoid military service. He explained that he preferred war heroes who had not been captured by the enemy. Though there was some discomfort in the overwhelmingly evangelical audience at this remark, evident from a few audible groans, far more people were either laughing or applauding. And that only encouraged Trump to keep going. "See, you're not supposed to say that somebody graduated last or second to last in their class because you're supposed to be like Frank says—very nice," Trump said dismissively, referring to McCain's record as an admittedly lackluster student at the United States Naval Academy.

Luntz had never intended to bring up McCain in his questioning but found Trump so obstinate that he thought he should try harder to extract at least a modest acknowledgment of humility or contrition. He tried to steer the conversation toward the topic he knew many in the audience wanted to hear Trump talk about: God and faith.

"Have you ever asked God for forgiveness?" Luntz asked. This drew some chuckles from the crowd.

Trump dodged the question with a joke about going to church, getting bored, and sometimes secretly thinking about leaving "a little early." But who among them didn't? Trump asked. They laughed some more.

Luntz tried a second time: "But have you ever asked God for forgiveness?"

"I'm not sure I have," Trump finally admitted. It was possible, he said, that he did when he took communion at church, a rite he then described and pantomimed for the audience. "When I drink my little wine," he said, daintily raising his hand to his mouth to mimic taking a sip, "and have my little cracker, I guess that's a form of asking for forgiveness."

He boasted of his business success, "I've made some of the great deals. I own some of the great properties in the world." And he cursed some more. "We need somebody that can take our jobs back, Frank, because we're going to hell. Our country is going to hell. And Frank doesn't like the word 'hell,'" he said, addressing the audience directly. "But we're going to hell."

Perkins had been listening to Trump and was sure he'd just heard the front-runner sink his own candidacy. He was waiting in the wings for his cue to walk out as Trump exited the stage. *He's toast,* Perkins said to himself. *This guy doesn't know what he's doing.* They passed each other without saying a word. It was difficult to imagine two men who were more different. Perkins ran the Family Research Council, a politically influential policy group that pushed Republicans to take hard-right positions on issues like marriage, LGBTQ rights, abortion, and school prayer. Its major donors included conservative families who were known for their association with the Bush wing of the Republican Party. Edgar and Elsa Prince and Richard and Helen DeVos, both wealthy couples from Michigan, were major patrons of the Family Research Council and had helped fund the construction of the group's headquarters in downtown Washington. A plaque on the wall in the lobby pays homage to them for making the building possible, "with the prayer that God will use it for His glory." (The two families were joined by marriage; the Princes' daughter, Betsy, married one of the DeVoses' sons, Dick.) Perkins had been devoting much of his attention to what he believed would be the defining schism on the religious right in 2016: the decision of whether to support Marco Rubio or Ted Cruz. Perkins was partial to Cruz, whose fire-and-brimstone style was closer to his own fundamentalist sensibilities.

Perkins had been studying the Bible since he was five. He helped convert his parents, who initially brought him up in Oklahoma in what he describes as "an unchurched home." At fifteen, he began preaching in nursing homes. He entered politics in 1995 after winning a seat in the Louisiana state house, where he became known for pursuing two causes with uncommon conviction. One was to restrict legal gambling, an effort that was not terribly well received in a state synonymous with riverboat casinos. The other was to try to make it harder for couples to get divorced. As Perkins listened to Trump, a man who owned casinos and had been divorced twice, he was hardly alone in thinking that evangelical Christians would recoil at what had just happened. That was the overwhelming consensus of the country's political establishment.

Luntz agreed too. And to mark the occasion he saved a copy of the next day's *New York Post,* which had on its cover an illustration of Trump lost at sea as a shark circled his raft. The headline said: TRUMP IS TOAST.

Luntz and Perkins, while from very different factions of the GOP, were representative of the elite, high-level thinking in their party about Trump. Luntz was from the Republican Party's coastal, win-through-moderation wing. He, like Perkins, had just witnessed the way the audience responded with clapping and whooping. Yet they both made the same assumption: The crowd was reacting to Trump the vaudevillian performer, Trump the WWE barbarian. Surely this was not a man whom evangelical Christians would trust to pick as many as four Supreme Court justices.

Antonin Scalia turned in for the night at around 9 P.M. on Friday, February 12, 2016. "It's been a long day and a long week; I want to get some sleep," the Supreme Court justice said as he excused himself from dinner and walked back to his suite, one of the most spacious at the exclusive Cibolo Creek Ranch, a thirty-thousand-acre retreat in the remote Chinati Mountains of West Texas. For what would end up being his last meal, Scalia was seated near the resort's owner, a Houston businessman named John Poindexter, and Poindexter's girlfriend. Their conversation focused on subjects close to Scalia's heart: Italy and Catholicism. Poindexter recalls how they compared notes about visiting Vatican City early in the morning before the mist had been burned off by the sun. Scalia reminisced about how he found the experience moving and spiritual.

Scalia's day had begun with a Southwest Airlines flight from Washington's Ronald Reagan National Airport to Houston. As a member of the Supreme Court he was entitled to an escort by the United States Marshals Service and requested one for the first leg of his trip. But he decided to let the marshals go in Houston, where he caught a connecting charter flight that would take him directly to the ranch, which has its own mile-long airstrip to accommodate its well-heeled clientele. He arrived around noon local time. He and some of the other guests, who like Scalia were hunters, piled into a Humvee for a bird expedition later that afternoon. "He charmed everyone on the truck," Poindexter says. Scalia stepped out of the vehicle and walked around a bit but never picked up a gun that day, Poindexter recalls.

Poindexter had met Scalia through a mutual friend and invited them both to accompany him and members of his hunting fraternity, the International Order of St. Hubertus, whose roughly seven hundred members call themselves Ordensbrothers and honor traditions that date back to the late 1600s. When Scalia didn't emerge from his room early the next morning, Poindexter figured the justice was either sleeping or working. He noticed the curtains in his suite were still drawn. A little after 11 A.M., when Scalia still hadn't appeared, the owner began to think something was seriously wrong. He summoned a close friend of Scalia's who had accompanied the justice on the trip and together they knocked on the door, called his name, but heard nothing. Poindexter used a key to open the door and the two of them entered the suite. When he saw Scalia in the bed, he appeared in "a state of repose," Poindexter recalls. "I felt for a pulse, I put my face in front of his to see if he was breathing." He detected neither. Understanding that the justice could not be resuscitated and that this would be a news story of incredible magnitude, Poindexter began thinking about how to keep word from leaking before Scalia's family could be notified. He sent his guests off to a lunch in a far-off part of the ranch without mentioning anything. Then he started calling the authorities, including different regional offices of the Marshals Service—Houston, El Paso, San Antonio. He described in the vaguest terms that he had a serious problem on his hands that they would want to know about. It took several calls before he finally reached someone he felt comfortable telling what had really happened.

Poindexter helped arrange for a Catholic priest to administer last rites. The marshals worked in round-the-clock shifts, staying with the justice's body at all hours. They collected all his personal items from the suite, logged them for inventory, and sent them off for safekeeping in a vault inside their closest outpost, which was about an hour away. To carry Scalia back home to Washington, they arranged for a plane and secured an American flag to be placed over his coffin. Officials looped in on the planning were ordered to exercise extreme discretion. "Please keep this information confidential. We want this to be handled as discreetly as possible," one wrote in an email.

At 11:05 P.M. on Sunday, the plane carrying Scalia's body touched down at Dulles International Airport. The Washington he returned to for the last time was already a much different place, descending deep into a partisan war over the future of the court.

Mitch McConnell, the Republican Senate majority leader, didn't have to think long about what he would do. Only about an hour passed between the time he learned of Scalia's death during a Valentine's Day weekend getaway with his wife in St. Thomas and when his press office issued a 118-word statement that would tee up the conservative transformation of the Supreme Court that the right had been planning for a generation. He didn't even wait to inform the Republican chairman of the Judiciary Committee, Chuck Grassley of Iowa. "The American people should have a voice in the selection of their next Supreme Court Justice. Therefore, this vacancy should not be filled until we have a new President," McConnell said.

Trump had other things on his mind than a looming Senate confirmation fight and the conservative majority on the court. In an interview on Monday with the radio host Michael Savage, the two discussed whether Scalia might have been murdered. "I'm hearing it's a big topic," Trump said. "They say they found a pillow on his face, which is a pretty unusual place to find a pillow."

The political history of the United States in the post–World War II era is a story, in large part, of how one political party exercised a remarkable amount of influence over two of the three branches of government. From the boom times of the 1950s through the recovery and expansion of the 2010s that followed the Great Recession, this party occupied the White House the majority of the time. Two of its presidents won victories so overwhelming that they set records for votes received in the Electoral College that stand to this day. During this period, twenty-six vacancies opened on the Supreme Court. A president of this party would fill eighteen of them— including all four chief justices. No president from the opposing party had the opportunity to name a single justice for the quarter century from 1967 through 1992.

This is the story of the post–World War II Republican Party, a political enterprise so dominant that it sometimes seemed liberalism in America was dead. But one of the more peculiar features of American conservatism is that despite decades of Republican rule, many true believers grew embittered and resentful of their party. They thought it was run by weak-willed leaders who compromised and sold out once they got in power. They could trace their betrayal back to Eisenhower, who failed to roll back the New Deal as the right had hoped. Instead, he expanded Social Security, raised the minimum wage, and made the federal bureaucracy even larger. His greatest offense in the eyes of many on the right was making the moderate former governor of California, Earl Warren, the chief justice. The Warren Court implemented some of the most liberal reforms of the twentieth century. It desegregated the nation's schools, took state-mandated prayer out of classrooms, gave all criminal defendants the right to a lawyer, and required fairer proportional representation when states draw legislative districts. (It all seemed too much even for Eisenhower, who would later describe Warren and Justice William Brennan, another Eisenhower pick who would emerge as one of the court's critical defenders of abortion rights, as two of the biggest mistakes of his presidency.)

The next Republican president, Richard Nixon, was no better for conservative purists. In a later edition of her seminal book, *A Choice Not an Echo,* the conservative activist Phyllis Schlafly summed up the right's disapproval in an entire chapter on the Nixon administration that she titled "Betrayal at the Top." She charged that his capitulation to what she called "the Eastern Establishment" was "early and total." Nixon did indeed give the right a lot to dislike about his presidency. He oversaw a vast expansion of the powers of the federal government that included signing legislation to protect the nation's air and waterways through a new government overseer, the Environmental Protection Agency. He supported a guaranteed national income to help alleviate poverty—$1,600 a year for a family of four, or roughly $11,000 in today's dollars. And in foreign policy, he infuriated the hawkish right when he attempted to cultivate a closer relationship with Communist China.

While Ronald Reagan's eight years in office remain a high-water mark for the American right, his legacy on the Supreme Court is mixed. Though he nominated Scalia and filled the lower courts with young conservatives, Reagan was also responsible for picking Justices Sandra Day O'Connor and Anthony Kennedy. Both gradually revealed themselves to be more socially liberal than expected. Ultimately, O'Connor and Kennedy would be responsible for some of the most consequential Supreme Court decisions on social issues of the last generation—ruling that affirmative action, abortion rights, and gay rights were all protected under the Constitution. Conservatives tended not to hold O'Connor and Kennedy against Reagan as a betrayal, per se, but rather as the symptom of a larger problem: Even in victory, conservatives still somehow managed to lose.

Few understood and lived this resentment better than Schlafly. After Scalia's death, she reminded readers of her newsletter that electing a Republican president was no guarantee the seat would be filled by a conservative. "President Reagan had three vacancies on the Supreme Court, yet placed only one conservative there, Justice Scalia," she wrote. Schlafly, a mother of six with a law degree and a master's in political science, eschewed the feminism that many women of her era embraced. She first made a national name for herself in the 1960s by railing against the scourge she called the "secret kingmakers" of the GOP's coastal elite. She was among the most prominent conservatives who gave voice to the large contingent on the right that believed their political defeats were part of a wider conspiracy. These kingmakers, she insisted, were seeking to keep people like her shut out of positions of power by rigging the party machinery in favor of Republican candidates who were too timid and moderate. She warned of an alleged Communist infiltration in the government and railed against the Roosevelt legacy of big government and its "America Last" policies, as she put it. Too often, she said, Republican politicians appeased the moderates in their ranks or capitulated to them entirely.

A Choice Not an Echo captured the essence of the fights between the activist right and the party leaders that would split the party for decades to come: Republicans too often nominated candidates who were "Democrat-lite," offering voters no real choice between the two parties. The book contains episodic stories that Schlafly used to illustrate the various ways she believed the Republican leadership cheated its voters. She gave her chapters names like "The Big Steal." And she identified a variety of co-conspirators working alongside the kingmakers. Next to the big banks and East Coast liberals, Schlafly was probably most disdainful of the media and its polling, which she wrote was as "phony" as the oracles of ancient Greece and used as "a weapon" to suppress the conservative vote. She devoted a chapter to the media she called "The Pollsters and the Hoaxers," in which she describes the Gallup Poll as loaded with "trick questions." In 1967, when she ran for president of the National Federation of Republican Women and lost, she refused to accept the results. As Geoffrey Kabaservice described her reaction in *Rule and Ruin,* his history of the modern GOP, Schlafly "claimed ever after that she had been robbed."

Schlafly, who turned ninety-one in 2015, liked Donald Trump. "They don't know what to do with him," she would say, recalls Ed Martin, who co-authored her monthly newsletter, the *Phyllis Schlafly Report,* and worked alongside her during the 2016 election. Schlafly was delighted by the way Trump tormented his Republican rivals and antagonists in the media. By Thanksgiving, she was telling people she thought Trump could be the nominee. "She says, 'I think he's the guy,'" Martin says. "And John (her son) and I were both like, *really?* We like the guy, sure. But we don't know." Her affinity for Trump—someone who had shown very little devotion to the conservative causes that were Schlafly's livelihood and passion—made more sense than it might have appeared. One of her favorite senators, Martin says, was the immigration hardliner Jeff Sessions. And as Trump's campaign started developing deeper connections in the conservative movement, the aide dispatched to Schalfly's orbit was Stephen Miller, who was working full-time for Trump by the time Scalia died. Miller kept in regular touch about the possibility of an endorsement. "Miller we knew really well," Martin says.

Trump struck Schlafly as the purest antiestablishment Republican candidate in the field, and that went a long way with her, given how little regard she had for legacy candidates like Jeb Bush. Illegal immigration had become a core issue for Schlafly later in life, so Trump's history of offensive and divisive comments hardly troubled her. In fact, it was part of the appeal. She spoke disparagingly of immigrants from Latin America, whom she blamed for eroding traditional American family values. "They try to tell you they're very pro-family, but they have a tremendously high illegitimacy rate," she told a right-wing outlet in 2014. She warned that any immigration reform bill that granted citizenship to people in the country illegally would be "suicide for the conservative movement and the Republican Party."

Around Christmas, Martin arranged for Trump and Schlafly to

speak. Trump was attempting to line up a string of major endorsements ahead of the Iowa caucuses from brand-name conservative figures to help quash questions about whether he was a closet liberal. "I'm not going to endorse you," Schlafly told him when they spoke. At one point their conversation turned to the issue of the Supreme Court and what kind of justices Trump would name, which was still a topic he had not figured out how to address in a way that satisfied the right. "Why don't you tell people you'll put Ted Cruz on the court?" she advised him. He said it was an interesting idea, and that he'd consider it.

Donald F. McGahn II had one qualification that Trump valued in a campaign lawyer above all else: his years of service with the Federal Election Commission, the body charged with enforcing the laws that regulate how campaigns can raise and spend money. Trump was worried he would end up owing money to the government if he ran afoul of any regulations. "I don't want fines," he would say to his staff. So he asked for the best lawyer who could help him get out of it if he did end up getting fined.

McGahn was also a vital link to a Republican social and professional circle that was unknown to Trump but crucial in his effort to be taken seriously by conservatives. For all his disregard for the party's institutional legacies and leaders, Trump learned after Scalia's death that there was one elite entity that would be extremely useful to him: the Federalist Society. Since law school, McGahn had been a member of the group, which cultivated conservative legal talent through a network that spanned academia, the nation's top law firms, the Justice Department, and the federal courts. The idea was to start a national fraternity of like-minded law students who could network and debate and share ideas that weren't popular on their liberal-dominated campuses. They started small in the early 1980s, with members from elite schools, including Yale, Harvard, and the University of Chicago, who would get together for the occasional pizza lunch and seminar. David McIntosh, one of the founders, recalls that his contribution was to enlist one of his professors at the University of Chicago who had developed a national reputation in conservative legal circles for his incisive thinking on the limits the Constitution placed on federal power: Antonin Scalia.

Fortuitously, the graduation of the Society's first members coincided with the beginning of a golden age for the American right. The Reagan administration, which was led by committed conservatives such as Attorney General Ed Meese, was looking to appoint people who would execute its vision to reorient the federal bureaucracy and the courts further to the right. "This quickly turned out to be a very good networking opportunity," says Jeremy Rabkin, who was one of the early speakers at Federalist Society events and became a mentor to many conservative undergraduates he taught at Cornell University, such as Ann Coulter, the future pundit-provocateur, and Leonard Leo, a Long Island native raised in a deeply religious Catholic family. Both would go on to found Federalist Society chapters in law school, Coulter at the University of Michigan and Leo at Cornell. Members helped one another land clerkships with prominent judges and jobs at top law firms—the entry points into the highest and most elite echelons of American law. "People say, 'Oh, well that's a good way to get a clerkship.' And then after the clerkship they go on to work in the Justice Department and the White House," Rabkin explains of those first years.

Also key to the Federalist Society's success was how it made the relatively small conservative legal world even smaller. Its members mostly knew one another, by reputation if not directly. The society was how Leo met a Yale Law School student his age named Brett Kavanaugh. It was also how he became acquainted with a judge on the United States Circuit Court of Appeals for the District of Columbia Circuit, Clarence Thomas. And after Bush nominated Thomas to the Supreme Court in 1991 and one of Thomas's former employees, Anita Hill, accused him of sexual harassment, Leo, then in his mid-twenties, worked with a team of researchers assisting the judge. As part of his work, Leo searched for evidence that he and Thomas's allies hoped would undermine Hill's credibility. He combed through years of the judge's old carbon-copied phone messages, scanning them for evidence that Hill had tried to contact him at odd times and with a frequency that would suggest she had developed an inappropriate attachment to her former boss.

After Scalia's death, McGahn arranged to have Trump meet Leo, who was now the Federalist Society's executive vice president. During the George W. Bush years, Leo was part of a network of well-connected lawyers who had helped the administration reassure its activist allies that the president's Supreme Court nominees, John Roberts and Samuel Alito, both federal appeals court judges and religious Catholics, were sufficiently conservative. Leo, who was also co-chair of the Republican National Committee's Catholic outreach program, argued that treating Supreme Court confirmations as anything less than a full-blown political operation was malpractice. "It is sad to see that a judicial confirmation process needs to resemble a political campaign," he said at a Federalist Society lecture to University of Virginia law students in 2006. "But that is where we are." If Leo was saddened about the state of judicial confirmations, he certainly wasn't sentimental about it. He told the Virginia students how the effort to confirm Alito, which he helped coordinate, cost close to $15 million and involved a slick public relations campaign that used polling and advertising to sway public opinion.

Leo has a large family, reminiscent of the days when Catholics often had a half dozen children or more. He and his wife, Sally, had seven. Their daughter Margaret, who had spina bifida, died in 2007. Leo has said that he promised her before she passed away that he would attend Mass daily, and that he kept his word. When he goes on the road for work, his staff knows to find him the closest Catholic church so he won't miss a service. He saved the titanium rods that were surgically inserted in Margaret's spine and keeps them on his desk, he once explained, "as a reminder of what a bad day really is." Like many parents of children with disabilities, he is deeply anti-abortion. A conservative lawyer and blogger who is well known in legal circles on the right, Edward Whelan, said of Leo in 2016, "No one has been more dedicated to the enterprise of building a Supreme

Court that will overturn *Roe v. Wade* than the Federalist Society's Leonard Leo." Leo was also a close friend of Scalia's and read from the Old Testament at his funeral.

When McGahn brought Trump to meet Leo, Trump floated an idea that Leo had not heard from him or any other presidential candidate before about filling Supreme Court vacancies.

"What about a list?" Trump asked. "Look, nobody knows me in this area. And I want people to understand what I stand for." Leo recalls realizing that as a campaign tactic, a list could be Trump's way of saying to conservatives, "I want people to know my brand, and this is going to be it." Leo was used to presidential candidates who spoke in platitudes about the type of justices they would pick. They were vague—intentionally so, because their words would be scrutinized by liberals and conservatives alike. They didn't give out a list of names. "Look at what Romney said and both Bushes, particularly George W. Bush," Leo says of other Republican nominees who were far more circumspect and said little beyond how they would name judges in the mold of Scalia or Clarence Thomas. On a basic level, Leo could see Trump knew enough to understand that conservatives felt they had been burned by Republican presidents when it came to the court, whatever his limitations might have been in grasping the details. "He got it," Leo says. Still, he adds, "That is not to say that he is steeped in originalism and textualism."

Trump had become convinced that the court was a pivotal issue in his campaign, so he put the word out wherever he could that conservatives didn't need to worry. Around the same time as Trump met Leo, he also sought out the Heritage Foundation, Washington's leading right-wing think tank. At a meeting with its leader, Jim DeMint, Trump asked DeMint for suggestions for names for his list. This request served a dual purpose. First, the Trump campaign would get recommendations that were blessed by a leading conservative group. And in seeking their guidance, he would be paying homage not just to Heritage but to DeMint, the former senator from South Carolina who was a favorite of the Republican Party's hard-right activist wing.

But the Heritage staff, many of whom remained wary of Trump, immediately flagged a potential legal complication. They could not furnish a presidential campaign with anything of value without running afoul of campaign finance laws. So they devised a workaround. A lawyer with the group, John Malcolm, penned an opinion piece that he would publish on a Heritage website. That way it was accessible to all even if its target audience was just one person: Trump. "This was as available to Bernie Sanders as it was to Donald Trump," Malcolm says. He published his list of eight candidates on March 30.

Trump released his list on May 19, which included eleven potential nominees to fill the Scalia seat. Six of Malcolm's eight names were on it. It read like a wish list for the right, with names of judges who were unknown to most people outside activist conservative circles and who were in some cases so conservative they probably stood little chance of being confirmed in the Senate. Several had questioned the constitutional right to an abortion. Eight were men, and all were white.

To understand why something as simple as a list of judges' names was so important to conservative voters is to understand how the psychology of the modern Republican has evolved. The decision by George H. W. Bush to renege on his vow not to raise taxes did more than just doom his reelection in 1992. It made betrayal into an organizing principle for the right. Bush had memorably promised, "Read my lips: No new taxes" in his acceptance speech at the 1988 Republican National Convention. The idea originated with two advisers known for their respective talents for stirring an audience's passions: Peggy Noonan and Roger Ailes. But it was not a universally popular idea inside Bush's campaign. As Bob Woodward described in his retelling of how the pledge was conceived, Bush did not want to bind himself to any such promise. One senior Bush adviser who had expertise in budget and fiscal matters, Richard Darman, had actually struck the infamous phrase from Noonan's draft when he first read it, saying it was "stupid and irresponsible." Ailes and Noonan objected. Ailes loved the Hollywood drama of it and how it recalled Clint Eastwood's tough-guy routine from his Dirty

Harry movies. It was sure to grab the media's attention, he argued. Noonan restored the line in her revisions. Darman deleted it again. Ailes and Noonan eventually won the argument and got their indelible TV moment. But it ultimately came at a huge cost for Bush. As president, he signed a tax increase as part of a 1990 budget deal with Democrats. And he would never live down those three memorable words.

Conservative activists had been using pledges to hold Republican politicians to policies they favored with mixed success before Bush's tax reversal. The most famous was Grover Norquist's tax pledge, which he introduced in 1986. "We don't have the structures that the left has: organized labor, trial lawyers, big city political machines," says Norquist. "So people sort of tip their hat at you. 'Yeah, government needs to be limited. I agree.' But you need a guardrail." Norquist's innovation was to make politicians put their signature on his "Taxpayer Protection Pledge." It committed politicians—in writing—to oppose "any and all" tax increases for as long as they served in office. He made candidates sign it in the presence of a photographer. He took the standard letter-sized version of the pledge and turned it into a 3-by-4-foot poster that he rolled up in a cardboard tube and mailed to politicians who'd signed it. To this day, Republican politicians still proudly display their signed pledge posters in their offices.

The potency of the concept was immediately clear to Republicans. But it didn't have real political force until Bush lost in 1992. "Had he been reelected," Norquist explains, "it would have destroyed the pledge, made it largely symbolic." The party was never the same once the idea caught on. In 1994, a Republican member of Congress from Georgia, Newt Gingrich, enlisted the help of Luntz, the pollster, and Luntz's twentysomething protégée, Kellyanne Fitzpatrick (later Conway). They devised the "Contract with America"— a written checklist of various reforms and legislation the Republicans promised to bring to a vote if Americans elected them to the majority. It included cutting welfare, strengthening the military, term limits for committee chairs, and of course tax cuts. They published the contract in a place where as many Americans as possible could see its ten points. "The big argument that summer was do you put it in *Reader's Digest* or *TV Guide*," recalls Conway. The party ended up going with *TV Guide* because the magazine guaranteed them a perforated page so people could tear it out and could "check off whether the Republicans had done it," Conway says. On the page were the words "If we break this contract, throw us out. We mean it."

A new bar in Republican politics was set. If voters were going to buy in, they wanted a receipt. And Trump had given them one. "This way," said a reassured Dannenfelser, "we know he's not going to appoint his sister."

CHAPTER 10

No More Bushes

We weren't going to be able to make him mad, and we weren't
going to be able to give him an all-white family.

—TIM MILLER, strategist to Jeb Bush

Mike Murphy was in his office in the Mid-Wilshire neighborhood of Los Angeles watching Donald Trump descend the escalator on television. He had seen this act before. It was in August 1999 at the Hilton Coliseum in Ames, Iowa, on the day of the presidential straw poll. And that was a better performance as far as he was concerned. Murphy, a Republican strategist, had been working on Lamar Alexander's presidential campaign. He could still feel how the arena pulsed with excitement—"like the roof is creaking," he says—as Pat Buchanan took the stage. Buchanan was getting worked up about China and imagined for the audience what his first conversation as president would be with the country's premier, Zhu Rongji. "He'd say the name of the Chinese leader, enunciating the *ping, ping* sounds," Murphy recalls. Buchanan then promised to deliver an ultimatum:

"Sir, you're going to stop persecuting Christians," Buchanan thundered. "You're going to stop bullying our friends on Taiwan. You're going to stop pointing missiles at us—or you're going to have sold your last pair of chopsticks in any mall in the United States of America!"

The crowd leaped to its feet, erupting in the signature staccato chant of Buchanan's campaign, "Go, Pat, go!" Another line that really brought the house down, Murphy recalls, was what Buchanan said toward the end of his speech about President Bill Clinton. "If I'm the chief law enforcement officer of the United States, I guess the first thing I'd have to do is turn to Bill Clinton and say, 'Sir, you have a right to remain silent.'" The crowd was on its feet again. Air horns blared.

But Murphy, the chief strategist for the exceedingly well-funded super PAC supporting Jeb Bush, was less sure that Trump had as much to offer Republican voters as Buchanan did. He believed it was an insult to the nation's collective intelligence to suggest that there were enough Americans to make Trump president. "He'll never be president of the United States. Ever," Murphy would say later in an interview, once Trump's campaign was fully underway, believing as Bush did that Trump had a record of duplicity and buffoonery that was too well-established for voters to trust him with the presidency. Bush was the kind of politician who prized honesty to such a degree that it sometimes complicated the jobs of his hired operatives, whose craft has always involved the occasional white lie and stretching of the truth. He kept tabs on the media fact-checkers and took note when one of his rivals had recently been given a "false" rating. When one of his own statements was rated "true," it went up on the wall at his campaign headquarters in Miami. "They would frame it every time Glenn Kessler or *PolitiFact* gave Jeb a 'true' rating," says Matt Gorman, a campaign aide. Bush couldn't stand to watch Fox News, which he said made him want to change the channel to ESPN after a few minutes. He said Trump's announcement speech was divisive and wrong, and brushed it off as irrelevant bluster from an attention-seeking novice. "He's doing this to inflame and incite and to draw attention, which seems to be the organizing principle of his campaign," Bush said. It was also out of step with the voters, Bush thought. "To make these extraordinarily ugly kind of comments is not reflective of the Republican Party."

But it was. And the potential reward for displaying that kind of ugliness had only grown in the seven years since Bush's older brother struggled to pronounce the last name of the young iconoclastic governor who would become the face of the GOP's conservative wing. Bush's inability to see that the GOP was now the party of Buchanan, Palin, and Trump reflected the fact that candidates like him—like his father, his brother—had almost always eventually won their battles with Republican insurgents and then went on to win their general elections. They could be brutally efficient. Murphy's frequent collaborator, Larry McCarthy, had helped elect the eldest Bush with the infamous commercial from 1988 that introduced the name Willie Horton to the nation. Horton, a Black convict who had committed first-degree murder, was issued a weekend pass from prison and while on leave raped a woman and assaulted her boyfriend. In McCarthy's ad, a narrator recounted Horton's crimes with a cool matter-of-factness—"stabbing a man, and repeatedly raping his girlfriend"—as a mugshot of Horton with a large scraggly beard and an Afro appears in the center of the screen.

Murphy was eager to turn the skills he and McCarthy had perfected over two decades of campaigning against Trump. Only now, for all their success in mining the country's divisions and anxieties to get Republicans elected, their skill set would prove woefully inadequate against a candidate like Trump, who knew no boundaries. Loquacious and good-humored, Murphy possessed a psychoanalyst's grasp of the flaws in the human condition and a comedian's wit. He learned about comedic timing and joke telling from his friend Dennis Miller, who taught Murphy tricks of the trade like how words beginning with a hard-C sound usually sound funnier. Murphy often liked to describe the 2016 Republican primary with a metaphor fitting for an Angeleno: a traffic-choked highway. The candidates were like cars, and winning the nomination was all about finding the right lane. There are lanes for mad-as-hell Tea Party outsiders, compromise-inclined political pros, evangelical Christians, and military heroes. Some ride the dotted line between lanes, knocking from one to the other to find the path of least resistance. Others find it's best just to pick one and stay there.

Murphy had been through enough presidential races to know that eventually they usually culminated in a battle between one candidate in the outsider lane and another in the establishment lane, or the "sane lane," as he called it. He had beaten the outsiders before, starting with the godfather of them all, Buchanan. Murphy helped produce George H. W. Bush's media in that race and was part of a team that came up with a devastating ad revealing that the self-described "America First" candidate drove a foreign-made Mercedes-Benz. The establishment candidates almost always won—Bush, Dole, McCain, Romney—because they were known quantities with deep relationships to major donors and could lock down important endorsements relatively early on.

And that is what Murphy was helping Jeb Bush do in 2015. He was running a massive political machine called Right to Rise, whose airy name evoked a certain nostalgia among Republicans who were convinced their party had drifted from the "compassionate conservatism" of George W. Bush. Murphy's theory of how Bush would win the nomination in 2016 was simple and linear and supported by plenty of recent historical precedent. Jeb would "dominate the establishment lane," he explained to prospective donors. Historically, about 65 percent of the voters in the Republican presidential primary were in the establishment lane. The remaining 35 percent voted for the outsider, and that was just not enough to stop Bush, he believed. Plenty of other people believed it too. And the fundraising numbers told the story: This son and brother of presidents was owning it. By the end of June 2015, Bush was drawing more money and support than any other Republican candidate. An NBC News/*Wall Street Journal* poll had him at 22 percent, with his nearest competitor, Scott Walker, trailing by 5 points.

Murphy convinced donors to fatten Right to Rise with $118 million in 2015. Between that and what the Bush campaign was raising directly, Bush's apparatus was taking in more than $640,000 a day during the first six months of the year, *Politico* noted at the time. Bush's closest competitor, Ted Cruz, had less than half that. So overwhelming was their fundraising advantage that Bush allies borrowed a phrase to describe it popularized during the George W. years: "shock and awe," which is what Bush's brother had called the massive bombing campaign he undertook in Iraq in 2003. To these

Republicans, the idea that Bush was a four-letter word was almost inconceivable. They needed all that money because they had to clear out a considerable pileup in the sane lane first. Two governors, Chris Christie of New Jersey and John Kasich of Ohio, were a threat, as was Bush's protégé from Florida, Senator Marco Rubio. Grind them down, Murphy believed, and that would leave Bush in a one-on-one with Ted Cruz, the outsider conservative he believed was eminently beatable and most likely to survive the longest. "And that was the model we all believed worked," Murphy says.

Jeb Bush and his wife, Columba, who was born Columba Garnica de Gallo in the central Mexican city of León, had raised a modern, multiethnic American family with three children who spoke Spanish and English. Bush himself was fluent in Spanish, a fact he liked to demonstrate by switching back and forth between the two in speeches and interviews. Like his brother, he wanted to work on a solution to legalize the twelve million immigrants in the country illegally but struggled to find an approach that didn't put him at odds with his party's hard-line conservatives. Less than two weeks before he formally announced his presidential campaign, Bush teased his entry into the race by tweeting "Coming soon . . ." which he then followed up in Spanish a few minutes later: *"Próximamente 6.15.15."* His announcement, which he delivered inside the gym of a community college in Miami, was not the standard lily-white Republican affair. A Cuban family serenaded the crowd in Spanish; a Black minister offered a prayer; the Colombian-born mother of a child with a developmental disability praised Bush's leadership as governor. People waved signs in Spanish: TODOS POR JEB!—Everyone for Jeb. Bush broke into Spanish when he delivered his speech: *"Ayúdanos a emprender una campaña que les da la bienvenida." Help us lead a campaign that welcomes you.* At one point, pro-immigration activists interrupted him, shouting that his support for legal recognition but not citizenship for undocumented immigrants wasn't good enough. Afterward, he told his staff that he was glad it had happened, because it gave him an opportunity to talk about the need to pass immigration reform, which wasn't in his prepared remarks but was a subject he cared deeply about and had co-written a book on.

The entire event was the personification of Bush's 2014 comment that he wanted to be the candidate who was willing to "lose the primary to win the general." The only thing more out of step with the Republican base than the comment itself—a criticism of the outsized influence that the party's right wing plays in presidential primaries—was where Bush made it: at the *Wall Street Journal* CEO Council annual meeting in 2014. But he didn't think he was saying anything remarkable. It was the same phrase, word for word, that he and his old friend Murphy would use with each other all the time. Other old comments would prove just as problematic. "Way too many people believe Republicans are anti-immigrant, anti-woman, anti-science, anti-gay, anti-worker, and the list goes on and on and on," he said at CPAC in 2013, uttering the same sentiments that one of Bush's top aides, Sally Bradshaw, was delighted to see when she read them a few days earlier in a draft of the GOP autopsy that she had been helping put together. "It was risky, but Jeb loved that speech," says Bradshaw, who had worked with him on his first but unsuccessful campaign for governor in 1994. "He felt he needed to encourage the party to shift with the changing demographics and do what was right." As Bush and his team tested the waters for 2016 and looked at how the CPAC speech was received aside from the excoriations in conservative media, they were heartened to see that the mainstream press was treating it as a bold move. It was a validation of Bush's premise and as sure a sign as any that he was indeed losing the primary.

Compassion and competence wouldn't win the primary in 2016. And there were striking parallels between the problems Bush was having connecting with the Republican electorate and Romney's inability to be the brawling culture warrior that voters preferred. "He was 'too serious.' He talks about policy. He reads books," says David Kochel, who became a senior strategist to Bush, listing what had by then become disqualifying attributes for a GOP presidential nominee. "He wasn't angry enough," Kochel adds. Bush wanted to run an earnest campaign. He had the staff structured so the substantive issues a president deals with received top priority. The largest department initially was the one dedicated to policy, with three dozen people churning out papers about his positions on military defense, foreign relations, and other heavy topics. "That was by design," says Bradshaw. Bush, she recalls, was intent on not being the kind of candidate "who would go down to the border for a photo op and say the border should be closed." A big part of her job was looking for ways to present Bush as an honest public servant so they could make a contrast with Hillary Clinton, who was struggling to answer questions about why she had concealed emails on a private server while she was secretary of state. So Bradshaw hired a team to comb through hundreds of thousands of emails from Bush's time as governor and compiled them in an ebook, *Reply All: A Governor's Story 1999–2007*, that showcased his meticulous attention to the smallest details of the job. "Somebody emails about a pothole, and Jeb responds," Bradshaw says.

Bush was also averse to negative campaigning. His race was supposed to be as positive and upbeat as the exclamation point that adorned his yard signs and buttons. (Using "Jeb!" as a logo dated back to his early Florida campaigns when he and his consultants needed a way to differentiate him from his famous family.) He said he didn't want to go after Trump initially on the grounds that he wouldn't stoop to Trump's level and saw little to gain from being drawn into a fight with a man who displayed no sense of boundaries. "The attitude was, for a while, don't get in the mud with a pig," explains Tim Miller, a Bush aide. Bush told aides: "I'm not a grievance candidate. I won't run a grievance campaign." His instincts told him to keep his responses to Trump as substantive and policy-driven as possible. In response to the uproar over Trump's remarks about immigration and Mexico, Bush suggested that his rival read his book on the issue, which at 304 pages was longer than anything Trump had read since college—and possibly ever. (Trump offered a snide response when asked about it: "That would be exciting.") Even Bush's own mother was saying he could stand to turn up the heat. "He's almost too polite," Barbara Bush, the former First Lady, said. "I don't advise him, but if I gave him advice, I would say, 'Why don't you interrupt like other people do?'"

After starting the summer in first place, Bush dropped to third by August. At a debate that month, Megyn Kelly of Fox News asked Bush about his criticism of Trump's language as divisive. He called for unity and inclusion. "We're going to win when we unite people with a hopeful, optimistic message. I have that message," Bush responded. Trump responded by dismissing the notion that anyone should be worried about politeness when the country was on the brink. "We don't have time for tone. We have to go out and get the job done," Trump said to a round of applause.

The lack of apparent fire in the belly opened the door to Trump's most effective line of attack against Bush—that he was "a very low-energy kind of guy." Bush crammed dawn-to-dusk campaign events into his schedule; Trump rarely if ever spent a night away from Trump Tower, flying home at the end of a day that sometimes included just one rally. The critique proved more damaging than the Bush campaign understood at first. It was demonstrably false and yet still affected how many primary voters saw him because they had an entirely different understanding of what it meant to be an energetic leader. "Voters didn't think he was low-energy in the literal sense," Miller says. "What they didn't like about him was that he didn't have energy for the things that they wanted: insulting people and tearing the faces off of liberals and the media." That summer, as Bush's poll numbers continued to slide, the campaign's pollster added a question into one of their surveys they had never asked before: *What do you like the least about Jeb Bush?* The top two responses were about being a Bush and his demeanor. He wasn't passionate or angry enough, people said. The third was his stance on immigration.

It was a campaign Bush and the people working for him were proud of. But it also cut him off from the biggest lane on the GOP's highway.

—

Seeing the Republican Party as they wanted it to be—not what it actually was—led Bush strategists inside and outside the campaign to focus their resources and energy in the wrong places. No one on Bush's team expected Christie would get very far. But they thought his endorsement could mean something, and they encouraged Bush to keep the line of communication open with him, which Bush did so they would be on good terms when he inevitably dropped out. A Christie endorsement—one governor to another—would help Bush against Rubio, a protégé he had developed a father-son relationship with when Rubio was getting his start in the Florida legislature in the 2000s. But the rival Murphy worried most about emerging as a threat after the New Hampshire primary was John Kasich, who as governor of Ohio and longtime member of Congress had one of the best résumés as well as visibility with the conservative base from a cable news career. Kasich came off as familiar and folksy and had a bit of a populist edge, which he parlayed into his own weekend Fox News show, *Heartland with John Kasich*. He also did an occasional stint as a fill-in for Bill O'Reilly.

Right to Rise spent a considerable amount of time and resources digging into their "sane" competition. Its scouring of Kasich's past was so thorough that at one point Murphy dispatched a small team of gofers to Westerville, Ohio, where Kasich had archived papers from his nine terms in the House with the local library. Kasich had sent so many items—schedules, travel records, press releases, his old desk—that Murphy needed three people to scan in material from the dozens of boxes. All that digging turned up an occasional gem that he and McCarthy could feed as red meat to Republican primary voters, like a letter from Bill Clinton thanking Kasich for voting to ban assault weapons in 1994. Kasich also concerned strategists inside Bush's campaign, who discussed and ultimately executed stunts like planting people in the audience at his town halls to say things like, "I have a hard time deciding between you and Hillary and Bernie."

It was all misspent time and energy. McCarthy and Murphy threw whatever they could at Trump. They tested everything with real voters in focus groups. Nothing they put on the air was a poor performer in the tests. But none of it moved the numbers enough for Bush. For one ad, they hired an ice sculptor to create a miniature Trump and then let it melt as their cameras rolled. The narrator read a list of Trump's baggage, including his supposed support for "partial-birth abortion," his four bankruptcies, and his real estate training scheme, Trump University. The narrator concluded: "If Trump wins, conservatives lose." As well as the ad had tested, the more telling information to come out of Right to Rise's focus groups was what voters were saying about Bush. People were repeating strange counterfactuals. They said Bush was too much of a creature of Washington, when he had only worked in state government in Tallahassee. So strong was the association that people made between Jeb and Washington that some focus group participants were convinced he had grown up in the White House.

Perhaps so many people on Bush's team saw the party they wanted to rather than the party that actually existed because they were living one of the most open secrets in Republican politics. The people who tended to run the campaigns often weren't all that conservative themselves. Murphy was socially liberal and favored immigration reform. Like several consultants who worked for the Bushes, including Ken Mehlman and Mark McKinnon, Murphy signed a 2013 amicus brief urging the Supreme Court to legalize gay marriage. Miller, who is gay, was no social conservative either, a fact that had become the subject of some criticism from activists who suspected that the liberal politics of some of Bush's top advisers were a reflection of his own views. Sally Bradshaw didn't think twice about her support for gay rights and had encouraged her Presbyterian pastor not to be discouraged after his endorsement of same-sex marriage led some to quit his church. Kochel, who spent much of his time in Iowa, had been public about his feelings that the GOP needed to rethink its position on social issues, saying in a 2013 interview, "The culture wars are kind of over, and Republicans largely lost."

McCarthy, who worked for clients all over the Republican ideological spectrum, was not exactly a hard-liner himself and considered Susan Collins, the moderate, pro-choice Republican senator from Maine, one of his favorite clients.

Though it didn't do him much good in the end, Bush was probably the most conservative of them all. When he ran Florida from 1999 to 2007, Bush waded into some of the country's most polarizing political and cultural battles. He effectively eliminated race-based affirmative action in higher education and government contracting. He took an expansive view of the Second Amendment and often boasted that he had signed the "Stand Your Ground" self-defense statute, which later became a national flashpoint after the killer of an unarmed Black teen, Trayvon Martin, used the law to win acquittal. And before most Americans ever heard the name Terri Schiavo, a Florida woman in a vegetative state whose case opened a wrenching national debate over end-of-life decisions, Bush had already gone to extraordinary lengths to keep her alive against her husband's wishes. Watching Bush branded as a moderate, said one political analyst who covered his administration, was absurd. "The notion puzzles Floridians who watched him govern for eight years," he wrote.

The campaign tried to armor itself against the anticipated criticism from the right. Aides compiled a 251-page document that served as a how-to guide on the dozens of conceivable ways an opponent or a reporter or a voter at a town hall could try to trap Bush with a question about whether he was really a conservative. It was a testament to the Bush campaign's preparedness and professionalism, but also a glaring reminder of his vulnerabilities. Many of the questions dealt with something he or a member of his family had said or done over the course of the generations the Bushes had been in public service.

—*Your father broke with conservative orthodoxy on taxes and judges. Your brother broke with conservative orthodoxy on entitlements and spending. Which orthodoxy are you going to break?*

—*Would the country have been better off if your father won and Ronald Reagan lost?*
—*Why did you once present Hillary Clinton with an award for her public service?*
—*What did you mean when you said in 2012, "I used to be a conservative"?*
—*Why did you say you could only watch Fox News for a few minutes before changing the channel?*

Bush's staff also tried to keep track of all the answers he had given when these questions came up, and that made the list even longer because often they weren't the same. Then there were the questions his own mother raised. Nothing quite cut to the heart of Bush's challenges as what she had told Matt Lauer of NBC News in 2013 during an interview at the dedication of the presidential library for her eldest son, George W. By then Jeb was rumored to be interested in 2016, and Lauer asked whether she thought he should run. The famously blunt former First Lady barely waited for Lauer to finish with his question, showing that she had indeed given the matter a lot of thought and wasn't thrilled. "He's by far the best qualified man. But no, I really don't," she said. She went on to explain that in such a great country with so many great families, the Bushes had no monopoly on the gene pool of presidential attributes. It was time to let someone else try. "We've had enough Bushes," she said.

Whether voters heard his mother's comments and found in them a new way to express what they already believed, or they weren't aware and just didn't like the idea of another Bush, the sentiment was pervasive and damaging. After the Lauer interview aired, McCarthy and Murphy kept hearing words to that effect. "No more Bushes" was the most repeated phrase they heard in the focus groups that Right to Rise conducted. "We were not going to be able to change his name, and we weren't going to be able to make him mad, and we weren't going to be able to give him an all-white family," Miller says.

—

By the end of the summer, Bush was in the single digits in national polls. In August, Alex Castellanos, a Republican strategist who had worked with Murphy and other consultants in the Bush orbit, wrote Bush an email and recommended a course of action he said could pull Bush out of his slump. But as much as Castellanos wanted to help his longtime friend, his advice was to be someone Bush never could be.

> We are afraid we are losing our country and you are seen as talking philosophy . . . voters don't think your ideas are relevant and don't pay any attention to them because you have yet to demonstrate that you are strong enough to fight for us and ensure our survival.
>
> . . . you need to be feared, hated, and attacked.
>
> go to the naacp and tell 'em black lives matter when black people take them, too. and 93% of black homicides are intraracial not inter racial. you can get attacked for that.
>
> go to the naacp and tell 'em they are being screwed by the teacher's unions. barack obama sends his kids to the school of their choice, why can't they? tell 'em they are selling their children out for political acceptance. you'll get attacked for that.
>
> go to the news media and tell em they are pussies. they create false crises about political correctness to generate eyeballs and make money. it's moral profiteering. no wonder no one respects them. tell them they are failing to meet their responsibilities to the country. tell them they have become the "more of the same" media. you'll get attacked for that.
>
> . . . your strategy now seems to be last man standing. that is a loser's strategy . . . you need to do something better than waiting for others to lose, my friend.

Bush came in sixth place in the Iowa caucuses and fourth in the New Hampshire primary. Eleven days later in the South Carolina primary, Trump won handily, beating his closest challenger, Rubio, by 10 points. Bush came in fourth with about 8 percent of the vote. He announced he was suspending his campaign that evening. Introducing him before his concession speech was Bush's friend and supporter, Senator Lindsey Graham. Bush did not utter Trump's name. But there could be little doubt whom he had in mind when he said it was imperative that the next president be someone who understands they are "a servant, not the master" and will commit to governing with "honor and decency."

CHAPTER 11

Meet Me in St. Louis

How do you pay them back? You go right to
Bill Clinton, and you take it to the debate.

—David N. Bossie

Aaron Klein was on the subway in Manhattan heading down-town from a meeting at Trump Tower on the afternoon of September 24, 2016, when his phone lit up with an alert from *The Drudge Report*. Donald Trump had just pulled the pin on another hand grenade in the presidential race, teasing that he might invite a special guest to the upcoming presidential debate. It was Gennifer Flowers, the former television reporter and amateur country singer whose claims about a twelve-year affair with Bill Clinton almost destroyed his presidential campaign in 1992.

Klein, the senior investigative reporter for *Breitbart,* knew Flowers and her stories about the Clintons well. He had been cultivating her as a source for months. Most of the mainstream media and Clinton's allies dismissed the idea that her husband's sins from decades ago could somehow be a political liability for her. But Klein and his editors thought there was much to be dredged up, for several reasons. Resurfacing the former president's extramarital escapades served the purpose of reintroducing into the public consciousness the generally unpleasant memories of the "enough already" variety that seemed part and parcel of having one of the Clintons back in national office. They also believed they could tarnish one of the most appealing aspects of her political brand—her image as a glass ceiling–shattering champion of women—by presenting Hillary as an active and eager participant in a coordinated campaign to shame and disparage her husband's accusers.

Klein had connected with Flowers in 2015 after sending her a message through a website she used to promote her singing career. He was surprised to learn that once he told her who he worked for and what he wanted to do with her story, she was willing to cooperate. He called her periodically to check in. Then one day a package arrived: old cassette tapes of the phone conversations Flowers recorded with Clinton, which she had first played at a press conference in 1992 right before the New Hampshire primary. Flowers offered Klein more details she said supported her claim that she had carried on a long-term relationship with Clinton. (He had admitted to a brief sexual encounter, but nothing more than that.) But one thing Klein had never discussed with Flowers was the possibility of appearing as Trump's guest at one of the debates. Once he was back aboveground, he called his former boss, Bannon, who had just taken a leave from *Breitbart* to become the chief executive of Trump's campaign as part of a last-ditch reshuffling of the senior management that brought in veteran Clinton tormentors Kellyanne Conway and David Bossie. Klein told Bannon that Trump's idea wouldn't fly.

"This is not the way it is supposed to work," he said.

Bannon, despite being only a few weeks into the job, knew that career survival with Trump meant improvising around the whims of a capricious boss who often didn't distinguish between what was actually true and what he wanted to be true. "Dude, see if she'll come to the debate."

Klein reached Flowers by phone later that day. But she was adamant that she had no interest in attending. "Absolutely not," she said, offering a litany of excuses. Reemerging publicly to be turned into a piñata all over again by the Clintons was not appealing in the least. This was not, however, the message she relayed to the public on social media, where she gamely played along and hinted that she might show up at the debate after all. After she posted the tweet, Klein called her back to ask if she was really reconsidering. She was not.

Klein had one of the most vital roles in Republican politics at the time, though few knew about it. "I'm not looking for people that want to win Pulitzers. I want people who want to *be* Pulitzer," Bannon was fond of saying. "There's a huge difference. Pulitzer understood that [journalism] was an advocacy platform. It wasn't about 'fair' and 'balanced.' If you want to be fair and balanced, you're in the wrong place." Bannon's cool dismissal of the slogan Roger Ailes used to dress up Fox News in a veil of nonpartisan purity hinted at how fundamentally conservative media was transforming itself in the Trump era. This was different from degrading the level of the discourse, legitimizing a conspiracy theory, or winking and nodding at racists. It was the moment when right-wing media started to become indistinguishable from a Trump political operation. And once again, *Breitbart* was the vanguard. Even Ailes, the man largely responsible for introducing Trump to the Republican base as a political figure, had limits with the man. By the time Trump was the presumptive nominee, Ailes was already complaining about the monster he'd helped empower. "I hate it when he calls me," the Fox chief told colleagues. "He talks to me like I talk to you. He cuts me off. He doesn't let me finish my sentences. He constantly interrupts me." Thanks in part to a *Breitbart* smear campaign against Megyn Kelly in 2015 after she asked Trump tough questions about disparaging women at one of the debates, many of his supporters were already skeptical of Fox News and saw it as another tentacle of the Republican establishment determined to stop him. By design, Fox News had a news division with bureaus across the globe that employed professional journalists. That allowed Ailes and his public relations staff to point to its newsroom and have some plausible deniability against charges that it was state television for the GOP. But the network's independence also meant it could rough up the home team and occasionally produce great moments of television and get big ratings, which is what Ailes ultimately wanted. The Kelly-versus-Trump spat served this purpose, as did the work of

Fox's decision desk, which was known for its aggressive but accurate early calls on election night that had occasionally left Republicans despondent when they were on the losing end.

But Bannon's first priority wasn't creating must-see moments, unless they were in service of the ultimate goal of helping boost Trump and the uprising he was leading against the Republican establishment. The relationship between Klein, who once worked for the same website that gave Jerome Corsi's conspiracies a wider audience, and the Trump team was far more than a friendly media-campaign alignment of political interests. It was a full-blown strategic partnership. Klein's close collaboration with the Trump campaign in the weeks before Election Day would eventually culminate in his execution of a sabotage operation against the Clintons under the direction of Bannon and other senior Trump advisers, who allowed campaign staff to assist Klein with pulling off something altogether new and norm-shattering in American politics. Bannon could have cited a different model from Joseph Pulitzer's to describe *Breitbart*'s campaign to bring down the Clintons in 2016. It was closer to a hybrid of *60 Minutes* and *Cheaters,* the show that features men and women who've been cheating on their partners as they're surveilled by a clandestine camera crew and then confronted with the evidence. Gennifer Flowers's bombshell accusation in the 1992 campaign wouldn't be the last time that a dirty bomb detonated over the presidential race, leaving many Americans with a sinking feeling that the process by which the world's greatest democracy elects its chief executive was veering into dark and undignified territory.

Klein, then only thirty-six, wasn't yet a teenager when Flowers came forward. But just a few years later he would be wreaking havoc through the media himself. When he was in college at Yeshiva University in the late 1990s, he took over as co-editor of the twice-monthly student paper, *The Commentator.* After determining that the publication was decidedly underwhelming in journalistic ambition—"a glorified synagogue newsletter," Klein called it—he tried to up the paper's metabolism by publishing a series of articles that were highly critical of school administrators. Soon he started noticing that copies of the paper were going missing from the racks on campus where students usually picked them up. Suspecting that the university was behind the thefts, Klein published an article that claimed so and then demanded that the administration reimburse him and his staff for the cost of roughly eighteen hundred papers. The thefts caught the attention of *The New York Times,* which inquired with Yeshiva's dean of students. Soon after, Klein received a letter from the dean with a check for $1,850 inside.

Klein, the product of an Orthodox Jewish home with ten children, was conservative politically and believed that Democrats were fair-weather friends to Israel. From his earliest days as a professional writer, his worldview and his dislike of Obama put him in the company of some of the most notorious modern-day pamphleteers on the far right, including the editors of *WorldNetDaily,* the platform that launched Corsi's birther conspiracy. The website hired Klein when he was in his twenties, which helped introduce his writing to the broader conservative media world. He played a role in most of the flashpoints in the Republican insurgency in the decade after Obama's rise to national prominence. He started writing books, including *The Manchurian President: Barack Obama's Ties to Communists, Socialists and Other Anti-American Extremists.* He became an occasional guest on Fox News and talk radio, and he eventually hosted his own weekly show for the conservative Salem Radio Network.

One of Klein's favorite tricks was to coax known associates of terrorist groups into saying sympathetic things about American liberals, creating a guilt-by-association taint on someone like Obama even though there was no actual association. In 2008, for instance, Klein made national news for an interview he conducted with Ahmed Yousef, a top adviser to Hamas leadership in Gaza, who told Klein that the militant group was keen on Barack Obama. "We like Mr. Obama," Yousef said, comparing the young senator to John F. Kennedy and saying he admired his "vision to change America." If you were looking to provoke conservatives in 2008, there were few better ways to do it than this. The interview exploded. John McCain seized on it and questioned his rival's commitment to keeping Americans safe. It hardly mattered that Obama condemned

Hamas. Yousef's "endorsement" of Obama, as it was being covered by outlets on the right, was the talk of the campaign trail for weeks. Then, two years later, while the raging debate over the proposed Islamic community center near Ground Zero divided the nation, Klein interviewed a Hamas co-founder who said that construction ought to move forward. His comments predictably created another public relations headache for the development and its supporters, which now had to contend with the story line that a group classified by the United States government as a terrorist organization supported its project.

Work like this caught the eye of editors at *Breitbart,* who hired Klein in 2015 as an investigative reporter who would split his time between the United States and Jerusalem. *Breitbart*'s interest in a Middle East operation seemed far afield of its core mission but was actually similar to what it was doing in the United States: stoking cultural divisions by promoting the conservative Netanyahu agenda and other right-wing, anti-Palestinian causes. And Klein, who would later go on to work for Prime Minister Benjamin Netanyahu, was just the person to help stir the pot. In 2016, with Democrats almost certain to nominate Clinton, Klein started developing relationships not only with Flowers but several other women who said they felt forced or coerced into having sexual contact with Clinton. This included Paula Jones, whose lawsuit against the president for sexual harassment eventually led to the revelation of his sexual relationship with Monica Lewinsky and triggered his impeachment. There was also Juanita Broaddrick, who said that Clinton raped her in 1978. Klein had been in touch with a third Clinton accuser, Kathleen Willey, who said that he had kissed and groped her against her will during his first term as president.

Before Flowers's tweet, Bannon and Klein had casually discussed the possibility of pulling an outrageous stunt at one of the debates: What if they could persuade some of the women who said Clinton had forced himself on them to get together and speak to the press about their stories? Bannon mentioned the idea to Trump. But Trump jumped the gun after seeing news that Hillary Clinton was considering inviting his nemesis Mark Cuban to the debate. Throwing out Flowers's name had been a mistake on his part. The story of a possible appearance by the former president's alleged paramour at the debate lit up the slow news cycle that weekend. But inside the Trump campaign, response to the idea of organizing a press conference with these women at the debate was tepid with almost everyone but Bannon. There was certainly no love lost between Republicans and the Clintons. In the past, Republicans saw little that was out of bounds about the Clintons' personal life. But there was something that even many of Trump's closest allies found beyond the pale about reintroducing these women to the public after so long. Bill Clinton wasn't on the ballot. The incidents allegedly took place decades ago and were already widely known. And some Trump aides worried that their candidate was in no position to be dredging up allegations of another man's infidelity. Asked about Flowers on *Fox News Sunday* on September 25, Mike Pence insisted it wasn't the kind of below-the-belt politics that Trump would be stooping to. "Donald Trump is not about that," Pence said, and he explained that his running mate wanted the debates to be focused on issues and policy. Pence chided the Clinton campaign for trying to turn the debate into a reality show, which he suggested was undignified and beneath Trump. "Hillary Clinton thinks this is an episode of *Shark Tank*," he said, referring to the ABC reality show Cuban appeared on. "But this is serious business," Pence added, evincing no awareness of his hypocrisy as the running mate of a man who woke up every morning thinking about how to be at the center of the media's attention.

In the weeks ahead, there would be a story of sexual misconduct to convulse the campaign. But it would not be about Bill Clinton. And the Gennifer Flowers idea wouldn't stay dead for very long.

Partisan media has long played an important but peripheral role in Republican presidential campaigns. And often its purpose was to sow doubt about Democrats through misinformation. "There is this strain of specific political types of conspiracies that run through conservative media," says Nicole Hemmer, a media scholar at Columbia University who points to a watershed moment in 1964. That year, supporters of Barry Goldwater distributed a book called *A Texan Looks at Lyndon,* which advanced a series of wild claims against Lyndon Johnson, including that he was involved in the assassination of John F. Kennedy and other crimes that advanced his political ambitions. The Goldwater campaign largely kept its distance. Republican Party leaders denounced the book as a cheap smear. But the book was wildly successful. More than seven million copies eventually went into print, and according to some accounts it was second only to the Bible as the best-selling book in Texas. Getting it into the bloodstream of American conservatism was the work of outside right-wing groups like the John Birch Society, which bought the book in bulk and sold it to bookstores at the cut rate of twenty cents a copy. *The Texas Observer* recognized its appeal among the hard right, reporting in a September 1964 piece that the book was one of "the major underground factors in the campaign against Lyndon Johnson."

By 1996, the far right was still imagining its Democratic opponents as depraved criminals. Now it was the Clintons, whom Republicans went to great lengths to discredit as corrupt and ruthlessly ambitious through a barrage of media smears and quasi-investigations. Bill Clinton's long-rumored philandering was the issue that first made the minds of his conservative antagonists run wild. And writers like David Brock gave them ammunition with his reporting for *The American Spectator* that told of sordid adventures from the governor's mansion in Arkansas, where Clinton allegedly had state troopers arrange sexual escapades for him while he was in office. The tales of Clinton as an insatiable, incorrigible Lothario completed the right-wing caricature of him as a contemptible baby boomer: draft-dodging, morally bereft and self-indulgent but too craven and ambitious to admit he had inhaled marijuana. Some of the propagators of the most outrageous myths about the Clintons were powerful players in the Republican Party, including members of Congress who used their investigatory powers to further disproven claims that the couple was involved in the death of one of their former associates from Arkansas, the deputy White House counsel Vincent W. Foster, Jr., who shot himself in a park. That was what Hillary Clinton was referring to when in 1998 she famously described the forces out to destroy her husband as a "vast right-wing conspiracy." Vast or not, it was certainly well funded and executed with the help of the leadership of the Republican Party. The wealthy Republican benefactor Richard Mellon Scaife bankrolled various efforts by two conservative publications, *The American Spectator* and the *Pittsburgh Tribune-Review,* to attempt to prove the Clintons' guilt in a number of schemes related to the real estate development known as Whitewater. This included everything from Clinton's misuse of his influence as governor to Paula Jones to Foster's "murder." One of the reporters working for Scaife at the *Tribune-Review* was Christopher Ruddy, formerly of the *New York Post,* who would go on to write a book about the subject, *The Strange Death of Vincent Foster: An Investigation,* and start the website and magazine *Newsmax,* which he ran out of an office in West Palm Beach.

No matter how far-fetched it may have seemed to most Americans that the president of the United States and his wife had ordered a hit on their friend and covered it up, the lie lived on. In Congress, the most outrageous Clinton rumors were fed by the Republican chairman of the House Committee on Government Reform and Oversight, Dan Burton of Indiana. Burton's chief investigator from 1996 to 1998 was none other than Bossie. But Bossie's overly zealous pursuit of damaging information on the Clintons eventually got him let go after he oversaw the public release of deceptively edited transcripts of an interview with a former Clinton associate serving time in prison for tax evasion and mail fraud, Webster L. Hubbell.

Republicans displayed little shame about using the official trappings of their political power to pursue the Clintons. But they did occasionally exhibit moments of self-awareness and regret. The Speaker of the House, Newt Gingrich, had pushed for Bossie's ouster after the Hubbell tapes were revealed to have excluded possibly exculpatory quotes. Bob Dole, the Republican presidential nominee in 1996, wanted nothing to do with the Foster story or other wild Clinton conspiracy theories. Scott Reed, Dole's campaign manager, thought it would debase the candidate. "It was beyond the pale, it wasn't presidential, and that wasn't the kind of campaign Dole wanted to run." But in those days, Reed says, "you had an actual smell test" about what kind of attacks against the opposition were legitimate and what weren't. When Dole did broach the subject of Clinton's infidelity, he did it in an elliptical way, referring to it in conservative code as part of a "moral crisis" threatening the country. "That doesn't mean that meetings weren't going on elsewhere around town," Reed concedes, referring to discussions among Republicans about how to spread the stories from Brock's reporting on the state troopers. "But we'd never bring it into the presidential campaign."

Trump brought it into his campaign the moment he hired Bannon, Bossie, and Conway. Conway's husband, George, had been one of Paula Jones's lawyers in her lawsuit against the former president. (The couple were introduced by Ann Coulter, who as a young Washington lawyer and onetime Senate staffer helped publicize the Jones case.) And then there was Trump himself, a candidate who showed little awareness of or regard for the unwritten rules governing the conduct between rival campaigns, but who also was inclined to believe in the wildest conspiracy theories as long as they fit with his prejudices. In what could be seen as the ultimate pot-kettle-black kind of deflection, Trump loved to talk about Bill Clinton's exploits. One story in particular he enjoyed telling on the golf course was about a time he played with Clinton and supposedly watched as the former president ogled women in the pro shop. (Trump's golfing companions were left to wonder what his contribution to the dialogue was.)

At *Breitbart*, Klein's plans were coming together by October. He managed to get three of Clinton's accusers—Jones, Broaddrick, and Willey—to agree to a sit-down on-camera interview. The date was set for Friday the seventh. *Breitbart* spared no expense. They rented one of the presidential suites at the Watergate Hotel, a twenty-four-hundred-square-foot space with a kitchen, living room, dining room, and library. They turned one of the rooms into a hair and makeup studio and ordered a buffet. For the interview, the three women sat on a couch, with Klein across from them in a chair. He nudged them to unload on Hillary, and the floodgates opened. "What do you say to the millennial voters," Klein asked, "who believe that Hillary stands for women?" Willey called Hillary a "fake feminist." Jones was clearly still seething twenty years after her ordeal, having been called a "bimbo" by Clinton defenders and dismissed by James Carville with the cruel but memorable one-liner, "If you drag a hundred-dollar bill through a trailer park, you never know what you'll find." Jones looked at the other two women and asked them indignantly whether Hillary had ever shown any contrition for how they were treated. "Has she ever tried to talk to any of y'all to apologize?"

But October 7 would be remembered as the day another taped interview jolted the campaign. While Klein, Jones, Willey, and Broaddrick were deep in conversation at the Watergate that afternoon, *The Washington Post* reported one of the most explosive stories in the modern history of presidential politics. The paper had obtained a video recording of Trump from 2005 in which he boasted to Billy Bush, the tabloid news host and first cousin of Jeb and George W. Bush, that his celebrity status entitled him to force himself on women. The *Post* published the video of the old *Access Hollywood* interview, in which Trump could clearly be heard saying off camera that he was so famous that women didn't care if he tried to "grab 'em by the pussy." But none of the women nor Klein knew any of this because they hadn't looked at their phones since they sat down to start the interview. Nor would they express toward Trump any of the disgust they reserved for Bill and Hillary Clinton.

Trump and his senior team were at Trump Tower doing debate prep when an email from the *Post* landed in the inbox of Trump's senior communications aide, Hope Hicks. Hicks handed a printout of the email to Bannon. "It's not that bad," Bannon said, scanning the printout too quickly to realize the scale of the catastrophe that was about to hit them.

"Would you read this?" Hope Hicks, Trump's typically unflappable spokesperson and de-escalator of crises shouted at him, incredulous that he could just gloss over the "grab 'em" line.

There was little question that Trump would have to respond by doing something he never did—apologize. But how his team of advisers could craft an apology in a way that Trump would actually agree to proved difficult. Eventually, they settled on a euphemism to downplay Trump's comment that he mostly approved: "locker room banter." Trump hated the word "banter." "Not banter. Talk. Locker room talk," he insisted. But Trump didn't want his statement to end there.

In a truly audacious move, he demanded that they throw in a line attacking the Clintons, whom he blamed for the leak of the tape. He was seething with anger. The media was having a field day all at his expense, he complained, yet they would continue to give the Clintons a pass like they always did. "I've said some foolish things, but there's a big difference between the words and actions of other people," he would say in a short video apology he recorded at Trump Tower, looking directly into a camera with a digital backdrop of the nighttime Manhattan skyline behind him. "Bill Clinton has actually abused women, and Hillary has bullied, attacked, shamed, and intimidated his victims. We will discuss this more in the coming days."

Breitbart rushed to publish its story, with Klein's interviews, that evening, but it did little to cut through the maelstrom of the *Access Hollywood* tape revelation. Neither did another late-breaking story that day, when WikiLeaks released thousands of emails that were hacked from the personal Gmail account of Hillary Clinton's campaign chairman, John Podesta. Trump perseverated on the Clintons all evening, galled at what he saw as the unfair double standard he was being held to by the media. After a restless night, at 8 A.M. on Sunday, Trump sent out a tweet with an excerpt from Klein's interview. In it, Broaddrick sobbed and trembled as she described being raped twice by Clinton. None of it was taking any pressure off Trump. "It's not enough. It's not enough," Trump grumbled to his aides. They all knew they needed something much bigger.

Trump's final words in the statement he made on Friday night were the last thing Americans would hear publicly from him for more than twenty-four hours: "See you at the debate on Sunday."

—

Late on Saturday afternoon, Klein's phone rang. "You're on," Bannon said. "But no one can know. We have to keep this extremely confidential."

Not even Trump knew what Bannon, Bossie, and a very small circle of Trump's senior staff were planning, because they were afraid he might get cold feet and call it off. They would wait to tell him until the last possible second what was about to go down once they were in St. Louis. The plan was that Klein would arrange to bring Jones and the other women to St. Louis on Sunday evening. Then they would all meet with Trump, hold a press conference, and watch the debate from inside the hall where Bill and Chelsea Clinton would also be. It would be a surreal scene, with the former president and his family just feet away from women who'd accused him of sexual assault—all while the man who boasted of committing similar acts of sexual assault laughed it up backstage. "We have to pay them back," insisted Bossie, who shared Trump's baseless suspicion that the Clinton campaign was responsible for the *Access Hollywood* leak. "And how do you pay them back? You go right to Bill Clinton, and you take it to the debate."

But Klein had no idea where the women were. They had all scattered since he taped the interview with them the day before. Now he had barely twenty-four hours to track them all down, get them to agree, and make sure they were all on planes to St. Louis. Jones was the only one of the three who was still in Washington. The Trump campaign booked plane tickets for Jones and her husband, who was traveling with her. Klein was supposed to escort them along the way. But he could foresee too many potential complications. If this was supposed to be a secret, how would he be able to ferry Jones—who was still instantly recognizable to Americans over the age of thirty who had lived through the Clinton impeachment—through two airports that would be crawling with political professionals and journalists on their way to the debate?

Then there were the problems he didn't see coming. When Klein and Jones reached the American Airlines counter at Reagan National Airport early Sunday morning, the agent told them she had no record of Jones's reservation. The only Paula Jones booked to go to St. Louis was on a flight that didn't leave until later in the week. "Idiots!" Klein fumed. The campaign had booked the ticket for the wrong day. To make matters worse, Klein noticed that Chris Matthews, the MSNBC host, was in line with them. A political savant who had covered the Clinton impeachment, Matthews would no doubt recognize Jones if he saw her, even in the baseball cap she had on. Klein tried to position himself in front of Jones to obstruct Matthews's view. It apparently worked. Yet Jones still didn't have a ticket on their flight, so Klein called campaign headquarters to get Jones rebooked on the only flight that still had availability that day. But it wasn't scheduled to arrive in St. Louis until forty-five minutes before the press conference, leaving almost no room for error. Klein got on his flight, American 4512, and told Jones he would meet her at the airport in St. Louis as soon as she landed that evening. He boarded just before 10 A.M., nerves shot.

Luckily, Jones's flight landed on time. Klein met her at baggage claim. But when he tried to wave her into the chauffeured SUV the Trump campaign had arranged for them, she refused. "I'm not going anywhere until I get my bag," she said. It had her makeup and the dress she planned to change in to. She said there was no way she could do a press conference on national television without it. The baseball cap and heather-gray zip-up hoodie she was wearing would not suffice. Klein pleaded with her. *Please, Paula. We have no time for this. You look fine as you are.* But Jones wouldn't budge. When the baggage carousel finally started to spin, by some miracle her bag was the first one off. Klein snatched it, and they dashed off to the car.

As they sped toward the hotel, it dawned on Jones that they were so short on time, there probably wasn't going to be an opportunity for her to change and get into makeup. "Just put your makeup on here in the car," Klein told her. So Jones started applying lipstick and eye shadow as the SUV sped around corners at high speed and wove through traffic—not exactly ideal conditions for a task that requires a steady hand. When they pulled in to the Four Seasons, Jones decided her makeup wasn't good enough. She told Klein she needed to fix it.

"Paula," Klein pleaded, "you have time for one or the other—fix your makeup or change into the dress. You can't do both." Fine, she conceded, she would forget the dress and fix her makeup. When she was finished, Klein escorted Jones through the Four Seasons, stashing her in alcoves and behind doors every time he thought he saw a reporter. The hotel was swarming with them because the Trump campaign had sent out an alert summoning the media there under the ruse that they would be permitted to see Trump's "debate preparations."

Trump had been upstairs in a suite much of the afternoon preparing. Finally, Bannon and Bossie and Jared Kushner, among the only people who knew of the plan, decided they had to break the news to him as the media assembled a few floors down. Trump closed his eyes as he listened to them walk through the particulars. He opened his eyes when they were done. "I love it," he said. Priebus, who was there helping with debate prep, had not been read in on the situation. Bossie threw him off the scent by saying he was taking Trump downstairs for a minute. "Reince, we have some donors downstairs and we told them we'd take Mr. Trump to go see them," Bossie explained. Then they got into the elevator.

Trump took a seat at the center of a long table in one of the hotel's reception rooms. Broaddrick was to his immediate right, and Willey was to the right of Broaddrick. A third woman, Kathy Shelton, was also there to tell her story of how Hillary Clinton had defended the man who raped her as a child. (Clinton, twenty-seven years old at the time, was running an Arkansas legal aid clinic and took the case only after being appointed by the court.) Jones, in flawless makeup but informal attire, took her seat at the very last second. Her casual appearance—the cap, the hoodie—stood out next to the other women. With everyone in place and the campaign's Facebook Live stream up and running to document the event, Trump staff ushered the media into the room for the big reveal.

Trump introduced them as "four very courageous women" and let each of them speak. When reporters tried to ask him about the tape and whether he thought it was really acceptable to grab women the way he described to Billy Bush, Jones defended him with the energy and indignation that none of his closest female aides like Conway or his daughter Ivanka could muster. "Why don't y'all go ask Bill Clinton that? Ask Hillary as well," Jones snapped. Back in the presidential suite, Priebus knew what had happened only from seeing it on television. "Thank you for not telling me," he told Bossie once they were all back upstairs, seeming to acknowledge the stunt for what it was.

The press conference was not carried live by the cable networks, so the only people who knew about it either saw it on the social media feeds of the journalists there or watched it on Trump's Facebook Live stream. However, the campaign had given the women its tickets in the VIP box, where they would have been seated next to Bill and Chelsea Clinton and in Hillary's line of sight from her position on the stage. When the leaders of the independent body that hosts the debates found out, they threatened to have the women removed. The prospect of a confrontation between the former president and his accusers on live television—which is exactly what the Trump campaign wanted—was not a spectacle the debate commission wanted to risk. The Trump campaign relented and agreed to seat the women elsewhere in the hall. By coincidence, Trump had a decades-long beef with one of the debate commission co-chairs, Frank Fahrenkopf, the former chief executive of the American Gaming Association. Fahrenkopf had accused Trump of failing to pay his dues to the association. And Trump, whose properties once included casinos in Atlantic City, complained that Fahrenkopf had it out for him because he was, in Trump's judgment, "a Vegas guy."

As tens of millions of people were tuning in from around the world, they saw as the networks broadcast footage of the women walking into the hall, looking for their seats as other members of the audience gawked at them. Stunned newscasters struggled to explain it all—who the women were, what they had all alleged against Clinton, and how awkward it was that they were all now in the same room together. Part of the assumed flaw in the strategy to reintroduce the Clintons' history with these women into the national conversation was that the news would remain sequestered in the right-wing echo chamber, where it would be an obsession for the *Breitbarts* of the world but few others. The mainstream media had long ago moved on and probably wouldn't cover their stories—unless they had to.

That's exactly what *Breitbart* and the Trump campaign did: They forced the rest of the media to cover the spectacle they created. It was an updated version of the playbook Jerome Corsi had used in 2004 to get the mainstream media onto the Swift Boat story. Just as Corsi knew the media would have to cover the controversy, the Trump campaign understood that once the women were in the debate hall within shouting distance of the Clinton family, this would no longer be just a *Breitbart* story. News outlets published some of what the women had said at the press conference in the hours and days that followed. So when Broaddrick said that night, "Mr. Trump may have said some bad words, but Bill Clinton raped me and Hillary Clinton threatened me," she was reaching a much larger audience than usual. *The Washington Post,* CBS, CNN, and others reported her words, and millions of Americans heard them—many for the first time because while Jones's allegations were well known, Broaddrick's and Shelton's had not been widely covered.

In the history of modern presidential campaigns, no candidate had pulled off such a ruthless act of vengeance in public. It ultimately may not have changed any votes. But it changed the game, proving to Trump and his allies that there was nothing off-limits anymore, no lines they couldn't cross if the goal in the end was to vanquish a political opponent. Even if the stunt didn't cost Clinton a single supporter, what mattered was that Trump and his campaign would come to believe that it had. And they would see that as a reason to justify an ever more vindictive brand of politics once they got to the White House.

Months later, Kushner ran into Klein at a reception in Washington and told him how helpful he had been in Trump's unexpected victory. "My father-in-law wouldn't be president without you," Kushner said.

—

Opponents of Bill and Hillary Clinton have long possessed a remarkable capacity to imagine them guilty of the most sensational crimes. But there had been nothing like what happened three weeks after St. Louis, with the birth of the most mendacious Clinton conspiracy theory yet—one that was so bizarre and implausible that it eclipsed anything from the fever swamps of the 1990s. The release by WikiLeaks of the first batch of hacked emails from Clinton's campaign manager—two thousand messages dropped only thirty minutes after the *Post* published its *Access Hollywood* scoop online—set off a frenzy in the media and among political consultants in both parties to search for anything revelatory. At various times the *Associated Press* had as many as thirty journalists combing through them. The creation of maximum chaos right before the election was the work of WikiLeaks's founder, Julian Assange, who had hinted at having dirt on Clinton back in June and then released twenty thousand hacked emails from the servers of the Democratic National Committee in July. On October 4, Assange announced a sequel of sorts: He would be making public a million documents related to the presidential campaign. These diversions had a rapt but impatient audience at Trump campaign headquarters—and with Trump himself, who was eagerly anticipating the leak and had told associates over the summer that he believed more was coming from Assange. Campaign officials went so far as to prepare a press strategy and messaging for the eventual data drop.

But they weren't the only ones paying close attention to the emails. After the Podesta release, users of pro-Trump message boards in the online communities 4Chan and Reddit began poring over the tens of thousands of pages and claimed to have deciphered a code they said Podesta used to communicate covertly about child sex trafficking. The explanations given by the true believers of this conspiracy theory—which would soon become known as #PizzaGate—strained credulity. They claimed that benign mentions of pizza and cheese and other foods in the emails were actually hidden references for different pedophilic acts. The words "cheese pizza," for instance, were supposed to be code for "child pornography" because the phrases shared the initial letters *c* and *p*. Message board users also claimed that emails to Podesta from the owner of a kid-friendly pizza parlor in northwest Washington, Comet Ping Pong, pointed to the restaurant as the hub where children were trafficked. And because of the owner's social relationships with other prominent Democrats from the Clintons' orbit, the conspiracy theory widened to include the involvement of much of the Democratic establishment.

Like all conspiracy theories, the reasons why Pizzagate seemed plausible to those who were inclined to believe it were the small kernels of truth at its core that got misrepresented. 4Chan users had in fact used the term "cheese pizza" as code for "child pornography" in messages. But Podesta hadn't done anything of the sort. There were references to cheese plates and macaroni and cheese and pizza pies in the context of work dinners, social functions, and other meals that almost any American could probably find buried somewhere in their emails. It was typical email mundanity. But through the eyes of someone who had absorbed two decades of dehumanizing, defamatory stories that made the Clintons seem capable of almost anything, it was a smoking gun. There was also truth to the claim that Comet Ping Pong's owner, James Alefantis, was friends with powerful Democrats. But this was Washington—a company town, and not a very large one at that, with professional and social circles that often overlap. Alefantis is gay, another fact that conspiracy theorists seized on to smear him as a child molester. He had also once been in a relationship with David Brock, the Clintons' onetime bête noire who had since apologized for his attacks on them in the 1990s and was now overseeing an independent pro-Clinton super PAC. But they had been broken up for five years.

On the Saturday night before the election, Alefantis got a voicemail from a reporter at the *Washington City Paper* who closely followed right-wing conspiracy theories, Will Sommer. "Do you know about this online conspiracy theory that you're running a child slavery ring out of Comet with Hillary Clinton?" Sommer asked him. He hadn't heard anything about it. He shrugged it off, finding it somewhat amusing that his emails had been among those included in the Podesta WikiLeaks trove. When Alefantis started noticing strange comments being left on Comet's social media accounts as well as on his own personal accounts, he shrugged that off too and put his settings on private so only his friends could leave messages. But as the baseless stories about Comet and the Clintons kept spreading, the restaurant became more of a target. Online, people were comparing the restaurant's logo to a symbol the FBI had identified as one used by pedophiles. They were similar only in that the head of a ping-pong paddle—which Comet incorporated in its logo design because of all the ping-pong tables at the back of the restaurant—is shaped somewhat like the wings of the butterfly in the logo cited by the FBI. People started calling the restaurant and threatening the staff. Prominent pro-Trump conspiracy theorists like Alex Jones of *InfoWars* started talking about the child trafficking as if it were real. "Pizzagate is real," he told the listeners of his online show. "Something's going on. Something's being covered up. It needs to be investigated."

Edgar Maddison Welch, a twenty-eight-year-old from Salisbury, North Carolina, had been learning about Comet and Pizzagate online. He listened to Alex Jones and enjoyed *Wild at Heart,* a book popular with evangelical Christian men that emphasizes the importance of fierce, warrior-like masculinity. He told his girlfriend that what he had seen about Pizzagate online was making him "sick." On the morning of December 4, a Sunday, Welch got into his Toyota Prius and left home before his girlfriend woke up. He brought an AR-15, a .38 caliber revolver, and a shotgun. He filmed a video of himself making the trip from North Carolina to Washington and explained his plans. "We have a duty to protect people who can't protect themselves, to do for people that can't do for themselves," Welch said. Earlier he had tried to recruit two friends to join him, telling one of them in a text message that he was set on "raiding a pedo ring, possibly sacrificing the lives of a few for the lives of many." But in the end, he went alone.

At around 3 P.M., Welch walked in through the front door of Comet Ping Pong with the loaded AR-15 slung across his chest and the .38 pistol in a holster on his hip. When the restaurant staff noticed him, they immediately called the police. He walked to the back of the restaurant but didn't see anything that looked to him like a door or a passageway to a secret room or a tunnel where he imagined sex traffickers would stash the children they abducted. He tried to pry apart the stage. He flipped over ping-pong tables. When he found a door that was locked, he tried jimmying it open with a butter knife. When that didn't work, he used his rifle to shoot through the lock. When the door finally opened, there was nothing inside but personal belongings of the restaurant staff. After about twenty minutes inside, Welch left through the front door and found police waiting for him. He put his hands in the air and walked backward toward them. And as the officers handcuffed him, one of them asked what he was doing there. "Making sure there was nothing there," he said. The officer didn't understand, so Welch clarified. "Pedophile ring." Another officer who seemed to know what Welch meant said, "Pizzagate. He's talking about Pizzagate."

CHAPTER 12

"Give Them What They Want . . ."

So they keep coming back.

—PRESIDENT DONALD J. TRUMP,
referring to Christian conservatives

When news of the *Access Hollywood* tape broke, Ralph Reed
was at the movies in suburban Atlanta. He had taken advantage of what had been, until that moment, a fairly slow Friday afternoon and sneaked out of the office to see *Sully*, the Clint Eastwood
film with Tom Hanks starring as the hero pilot Chesley "Sully" Sullenberger. As Sullenberger was executing his white-knuckle landing
of US Airways flight 1549 in the Hudson River, Reed's cellphone
started buzzing. He ignored it. Then it buzzed again, and again. Unable to concentrate on the movie, Reed fished his phone out of his
jacket pocket and saw all the missed calls, text messages, and emails,
many from reporters seeking his comment about something Trump
had said.

Reed had no idea what they were talking about. So he pulled up
the *Post* article they were all referring to, scrolled down to the video,
and held his phone to his ear so he could hear what Trump had said.
He was a bit startled by Trump's cavalier description of how he
could use his celebrity to violate women. But Reed also thought about
many of the ways the tape wasn't so incriminating. For starters, the
tape was a decade old. He thought Billy Bush was kind of egging

Trump on. And Reed thought Trump was probably just making it up—boastful talk about sexual conquests from one man to another. There was another bit of evidence Reed found exonerating and ze-roed in on. At one point, Trump leans in to hug a woman who comes over to greet him. Catching himself—and clearly aware of the fact that he was now in front of a rolling camera, which he had not been when he made the "grab 'em" comment—he says that his wife Me-lania would have approved of the embrace. It was just an innocent hug. Reed interpreted this as a signal—*I'm taken*—though he had no way of knowing this was what Trump had intended. "Every mar-ried man knows that," Reed said to himself. As far as he was con-cerned, case closed. As for what he would tell the reporters who had been asking him whether Trump had just killed his chances with evangelical Christians, the voters Reed knew best, Reed didn't need to give it much thought. From his seat in the dark theater, he tapped out a two-sentence statement dismissing the idea that religious con-servatives would weigh the tape as a major factor in their vote, given all that was at stake in the election. "I think a ten-year-old tape of a private conversation with a TV talk show host ranks pretty low on their hierarchy of their concerns," he wrote. Then he put his phone away and focused his attention back on *Sully*.

Reed, a father to two daughters, was taking one of his girls with him on a business trip the following week to Liberty University in Virginia so she could take a campus tour. As head of one of the country's largest evangelical political groups, the Faith and Freedom Coalition, Reed was set to address the Liberty student body at one of its weekly convocations, the campuswide gatherings held in the school's ten-thousand-seat arena where attendance is mandatory and the guest speakers often include ambitious politicians looking to burnish their image with the evangelical community. When he touched on the subject of Trump's remarks, Reed told the students that he was offended as a father. He did not dwell on what those words actually were, instead referring opaquely to "eleven-year-old comments."

The message he delivered was, in essence, that if the students had any hang-ups about Trump after hearing this tape, they should get over it. There were far larger matters that should be weighing on the conscience, he said. "On issue after issue involving grave and intrinsic moral evils and essential moral rights, there are major differences between the two leading candidates," Reed declared. "And to ignore them is an abrogation of our responsibility as followers of Christ and as moral actors in a dark and fallen world."

For social conservatives who weren't as transactional as people like Reed and Jerry Falwell, Jr., the head of Liberty University and the son of its famous founder—or who weren't actually invited on Trump's plane to spend time with him—moments like the exchange with Billy Bush made it harder to envision a Trump presidency as something that was ultimately good. Reed, despite his own belief that the tape was much ado about nothing, knew that many of the voters Trump needed to turn out would have to engage in a bit of magical thinking to see him as the defender of conservative Christian values they hoped he would be. So Reed urged the Liberty students to get creative. They should use their "moral imagination," he said.

Reed didn't intend it, but his comment would foreshadow the conflicts, doubts, denial, and rationalizations that Trump's most religious Christian supporters would experience during the four years of his presidency. "As Christians, we have to use our moral imagination to fully grasp both the limits and the possibilities of politics," Reed said. He acknowledged the possibility that some might find this exercise unpleasant. But in the end he said they had no choice: "Refusing to muddy our boots with the mud and mire of politics is simply not an option for a follower of Christ." Liberty's president and Reed's host that day, Falwell, Jr., was blunter and more eager to go straight for the mud. "Five years from now, when we're sitting here and we see the Constitution being ripped apart," Falwell said, describing what he expected if Clinton got to name Justice Scalia's successor and possibly more to the Supreme Court, "nobody is going to remember what horrible things Donald Trump said over a decade ago."

Their thinking reflected a consensus that had hardened fast among prominent religious conservatives in the hours after the *Post* published its story. They displayed very little of the doubt and despair that racked party officials and Trump's own running mate, Mike Pence. Pence entirely disappeared from public view for the weekend, leaving many to wonder whether he would quit the race or attempt to execute a secret plan that was under discussion at the highest levels of the party: the formation of a new ticket with him and Condoleezza Rice. Pence told advisers and friends, "This is Trump's mess, and he should be the one to clean it up." Pence wouldn't participate in any of the campaign's efforts to defend Trump. In fact, Pence had been so shaken after hearing the tape that he wrote a letter to Trump and had it hand delivered to the penthouse in Trump Tower the morning after the news broke. In it, Pence shared his sadness and disappointment, encouraged Trump to seek God's guidance, and said he would be praying for his running mate. Trump didn't mull very long over the misgivings Pence had expressed. He wasn't happy about the contents of what he would later obliquely describe as "the somewhat negative letter." But he also seemed ready to move on. Trump would brush off the letter, saying, "I've had a lot worse." Pence, though an evangelical, was more aligned in his sensibilities with the party's status quo politics, saw the tape the same way GOP leadership and the mainstream media did. He assumed it was fatal. Attendant in this analysis was the assumption that the churchgoing, socially conservative voters like Pence who made up the cornerstone of the Republican base would never abide such indecency.

But that missed the mark entirely. Evangelical leaders circled the wagons. For decades, religious conservatives thought they should back candidates who fit a mold that looked a lot like how they saw themselves: churchgoing, humble, devoted to their families, and committed to a high standard of moral conduct. From Gary Bauer to Rick Santorum, from Mike Huckabee to Mike Pence, the political model was consistent. But once Trump convinced conservatives that he was fighting their battles in the culture wars and winning, many of them took that to mean that the attributes and values they'd long wanted in their politicians weren't relevant anymore. Trump's model worked. And they were starting to prefer it. Reed, Tony Perkins,

Jerry Falwell, Jr., Franklin Graham, and other male evangelicals immediately quashed any second-guessing of Trump or talk that Christians should cast a write-in ballot, or not vote at all. Some, like the author and radio preacher Eric Metaxas, laughed it off. "BREAKING: Trump caught using foul language, combing his hair oddly. Could this be the end of his campaign?" Metaxas said in a tweet he later deleted. Graham, son of the "pastor to presidents," Billy Graham, claimed that Clinton was no saint herself and blamed the media for hyping the story. "My prayer is that Christians will not be deceived by the liberal media about what is at stake for future generations," he wrote in a Facebook post.

To hear what was on the tape and conclude that it was irrelevant was the essence of what it meant to be a religious conservative and a Trump supporter in 2016. Most Americans who voted for Trump understood they were making a bargain. They accepted the crassness, the cruelty, the "locker room talk," because he was their last resort. Many of them had preferred other Republicans. But they weren't an option any longer. And Trump was the only one they thought might be able to give them their country back before it was too late. To Christians who believed that an increasingly secular American society was pushing them to the margins and demonizing and stigmatizing their beliefs, Trump's nostalgic promise to "make America great again" was powerful. Trump didn't intend on speaking to the anxieties of religious conservatives when he said things like "Our country is going to hell." But he was.

It helped that Trump had literally put his promises to Christian conservatives in writing in a way that was even more explicit than his list of Supreme Court nominees. With Election Day approaching, he agreed to sign a pledge from the Susan B. Anthony List that bound him to commitments that no other Republican presidential nominee had made before. Trump hadn't planned to until it fell in his lap. Conway told him about it in the car on their way to Phyllis Schlafly's funeral on September 10 in St. Louis, where he had been asked to speak. The letter he signed included an explicit vow to nominate only "pro-life justices to the Supreme Court"—ones that would overturn *Roe v. Wade,* an outcome with such seismic public health and political consequences that other Republican presidential nominees would only tiptoe around it—and an assurance that he would sign a law that would ban abortion in almost all cases starting at twenty weeks after fertilization. By agreeing to follow through with this extremely narrow set of demands, he was effectively ceding his autonomy to exercise one of the most important powers of the presidency. And that bought him incalculable goodwill with conservatives. If anyone questioned how he got religious conservatives to see the *Access Hollywood* tape as mere "locker room talk," this was it.

Falwell Jr. shared a concern about the *Access Hollywood* tape that had gained popularity among Trump's defenders: He said the release was planned. "I think it might have even been a conspiracy among establishment Republicans who have known about it for weeks and who tried to time it to do the maximum damage," he claimed in a radio interview the weekend the story broke. Other evangelical leaders justified their continued support for Trump by equating it with a burden they had no choice but to shoulder. They were refusing to take the easy way out—as God would have wanted. "It's a lot easier to opt out and take the Pontius Pilate option and say, 'I'm going to wash my hands of this,'" says Richard Land, president of Southern Evangelical Seminary. "My eighteenth choice out of seventeen candidates," he says, explaining how he arrived on Trump as his choice. "Once again I was faced with, in a fallen sinful world, a binary choice of Mrs. Clinton and Donald Trump. And my moral compass told me that Mrs. Clinton was by far the greater evil. And unless she's running against Lucifer, that would be my assessment."

The calculation: Donald Trump, at least he's not Satan.

Many justifications like these about voting for Trump came from evangelical men. But the women of the religious right would also offer explanations of their own that were important in giving conservatives a permission slip to vote for him. And they settled on the conclusion that it was morally indefensible to abandon Trump. Penny Young Nance, president of Concerned Women for America, worried after hearing the tape that it would hurt Trump with the evangelical women she knew. Nance was like many women in the conservative movement who bought into Trump late. She had been one of the signers of the letter in Iowa that implored voters to support anyone else. She always had a nagging concern that a revelation from Trump's past would resurface and jeopardize his candidacy—some hot mic moment from his interviews with Howard Stern or a disclosure of a previously unknown former mistress. The revelations in the tape were "just awful," Nance says. But she found a way to compartmentalize it.

She decided that it was guy talk and nothing more. "He was blustering to Billy Bush—a playboy from New York," Nance says. Like many of her peers, she thought about the possibility of a Clinton presidency and then did a kind of risk assessment. "You had two deeply flawed people. I'll take my deeply flawed one," Nance explains. Sarah Palin weighed in almost immediately with a similar explanation, saying that as a former sports reporter, "I've heard much worse in locker rooms."

On one level, the yawn that the tape elicited from many social conservatives recalled the similar response from the right over the revelation in 2008 that Palin's teenage daughter Bristol was pregnant. Though many in the media and the political establishment assumed that conservatives would greet the news with disapproval, they largely shrugged and instead saw it as another sign that Palin was as regular as they come. Cissie Graham Lynch, a granddaughter of Billy Graham, urged people to "set all emotions aside" and focus on the bigger picture in the election: the Supreme Court. "This could affect an entire generation. This will affect my children and their children's children," she said.

Marjorie Dannenfelser was devastated at first when she heard the tape. She took the weekend to process it. "Like Mike Pence," she told friends. She fought bitterly with her twenty-one-year-old daughter, who couldn't comprehend how her mother could still be considering voting for Trump. She went back and forth about what to do, knowing that members of her own family might not speak to her for a long time if she sided with Trump. "It was one of the harder things I've ever done," she says, adding that she realized the "clarity of the choice" after thinking of what a Clinton presidency would mean to her ultimate goal of overturning *Roe v. Wade*. After the election, her daughter cut off communications with her for several weeks.

In the four and a half weeks between *Access Hollywood* and Election Day, Trump's popularity with Christian conservatives only grew stronger. A poll that the Public Religion Research Institute conducted in the first week in October found that 65 percent of white evangelicals supported him, which was lower than what Romney received in the final vote in 2012. But Trump would go on to win 81 percent of the white evangelical vote.

On Election Day, the offices where the campaign worked on the sixth and fourteenth floors of Trump Tower were empty for much of the morning and early afternoon. It seemed like a foreboding sign. Priebus arrived at campaign headquarters that day wheeling a suitcase as if he expected to be returning on the Acela to Washington that evening. Conway, the campaign manager, was nowhere to be seen. If Trump did indeed lose, no one could be sure he would concede, given how coy he had been when asked if he would accept the results no matter what. The Clinton campaign had sent word to Trump's team that they weren't going to wait very long to find out. He had fifteen minutes, they said, from the time the *Associated Press* made its call in the race to start speaking, or she was going out there.

Trump was rarely spotted on the fourteenth floor. Mostly he spent the days in his office on twenty-six or in his penthouse, which occupied the top three levels of the building. He and Pence and their wives spent a good portion of that evening cloistered away in the Trump residence, awaiting word on their fate. The media's exit polls looked terrible for Trump when they came out around 5 P.M. Nearly two-thirds of the country saw him unfavorably, the numbers said. Only 37 percent said he was qualified to be president. Marc Short, Pence's top adviser, was sent the exit poll data by email from a reporter. It looked so dismal that he sent Pence a text message with the highlights, hoping to soften the blow from the defeat that he assumed was imminent. But after 8 P.M., with Florida reporting strong numbers for Trump around Tampa Bay and in rural areas, Trump decided to head down to the campaign's war room on the fourteenth floor and watch the returns there. At 10:50 P.M., the AP called Florida for Trump. At 11:11 P.M., it called the next big battleground for him, North Carolina. Aides took that as another encouraging sign, as the state had appeared to be heading in the wrong direction in the final days of the race. Trump needed some time and a quieter space in which to process it all, so he and Pence and their wives headed back up to the penthouse. Members of the senior staff soon followed, crowding into a service kitchen where they watched for more updates on a small television.

Stephen Miller and Bannon were working in the dining room on a draft of a victory speech for Trump to give. Ivanka Trump walked in and asked to see what they had come up with. "This is interesting," she said as she read, sounding neither critical nor especially enthusiastic. She offered some suggestions about making the speech more conciliatory, something perhaps about bringing the country together, she said. "Okay, you guys play with it," she said, and then left the room. About fifteen minutes later, Trump walked into the dining room. "You guys working on the speech?" he asked. He had some small questions and suggestions. He seemed tired and said that he wanted the remarks kept short. Then he offered his thoughts on tone. "Maybe we should talk about bringing the country together," Trump said, graciousness and reconciliation not exactly being defining features of his campaign. Bannon looked at Trump dumbfounded and thought, *Who has taken over his body?*

Priebus and Chris Christie, who had also been giving Trump advice all night about what to say, agreed that even if Trump wasn't elected as a uniter, he should act like one that night. In miniature, this was the same fight that had been going on inside the Republican Party for years. The populist, no-compromise renegades were at odds with the party insiders who wanted a softer, more inclusive approach.

Just after 2:45 A.M., Trump walked onto the stage at the Hilton Midtown and delivered one of his shortest speeches to date. He spoke for only about six minutes on actual substance and then rambled through a long list of people he wanted to thank. He talked about his desire to "bind the wounds of division" and of coming together "as one united people." He acknowledged the country's diversity and promised his government would serve people "from all races, religions, backgrounds, and beliefs." And he made a new kind of pledge: "I will be president for all Americans."

The speech immediately raised questions about what kind of president Trump would be. Now that he had won, would he veer to the center as many Republican presidents ultimately had? Was he just pandering to the conservative base all along so he could win? It was encouraging to think so for Americans who were squinting and trying to imagine that his presidency might not be what they had feared. But it would not take long for Trump to show the country that he had no intention of being the president for "all Americans."

Ordinarily, most of the planning for the enormous task of vetting and hiring the thousands of people needed to run the vast federal bureaucracy—including the four thousand appointed by the president himself—would take place in the months between the party conventions in the summer and the inauguration the following January. The process is a formality, but an important and statutorily required one because it helps ensure that the government won't be critically disrupted as the country transitions from one president to the next. And the nominees, Republican and Democrat alike, have typically approached it seriously. In May, Trump had given the job of overseeing this effort to Chris Christie. But it was soon clear to Christie and everyone else inside the Trump campaign that this was at best a nominal responsibility. The same kind of superstitiousness that made Trump opposed to writing a victory speech in advance was also applied to his feelings about the transition. He complained that planning extensively for one would jinx him. He also believed that the people working for him should be focused first and foremost on winning the election. They could worry about human resources issues later.

"That's why Romney lost—because he spent all his time picking his cabinet," Trump said on more than one occasion when questions about the transition came up. Trump was full of theories on why Romney had lost.

After Bannon got back to Trump Tower around 3:30 A.M., he asked his staff to put him in touch with the person who had been overseeing much of the day-to-day transition business, a private equity manager from Tennessee named Bill Hagerty. But they reported back to Bannon that Hagerty was on vacation in the Bahamas. People had not exactly been lining up to fill key jobs inside Trump's transition operation. In fact, it was an open secret in Republican circles that the people who joined in the final weeks before Election Day were tokens meant to quiet the grumbling from conservatives who didn't trust Christie. These hires included elders in the conservative movement with ties to the Reagan administration and the Heritage Foundation like Ed Feulner, the longtime president of the conservative think tank, and Ed Meese, Reagan's attorney general. Feulner was in his seventies; Meese in his eighties. And even with the clout they brought, they couldn't change the fact that they were not empowered to do much of anything, given Trump's aversion to their work. "It was a fake transition," recalls one friend of Feulner's.

This left a huge void to fill on the morning of November 9. Bannon sat in his office and flipped through the binders that Christie had compiled with his recommendations for job candidates. He had never looked at them before. As a former naval officer, Bannon had an interest in playing a role on Trump's foreign policy team and asked someone on his staff to find out how many appointments Trump would have to make to top national security positions. When the answer came back that it was ninety people, Bannon was in disbelief. "Ninety? We don't know ninety people!" he said.

But Mike Pence knew ninety people. Jeff Sessions knew ninety people. Two days later, Christie was out. Trump put Pence in charge and gave senior advisory positions with the transition team to Sessions and other allies who were known to and trusted by conservatives in Washington. There were few decisions that Trump and his team made in the days following their victory that would prove as meaningful as the overhaul of the transition and placing Pence in such an influential role. "It bought loyalty with movement conservatives who maybe weren't always so comfortable with what they saw on the campaign trail," says Andy Surabian, an aide who worked on the campaign and briefly in the White House.

Winning created a paradox for the Trump campaign. As a candidate, he had spent more than a year feeding off the mistrust that many Americans felt toward political officeholders. He had denigrated the Republican Party's political professionals as incompetent and corrupt. He couldn't turn to them now and ask for help running his administration. Not that many of them would have anyway. Fifty of the most senior national security officials in the party, for instance, had signed a letter in August warning that Trump "would be the most reckless president in American history." This dynamic opened up the highest levels of the American government to an entirely new class of people—disruptors and agitators and the occasional misfit whose résumés never would have been given more than a glance in other transitions. But with Pence empowered to hire almost anyone he wanted, the new administration would begin filling up with other conservatives. These were evangelical Christians, anti-abortion activists, and pro-corporate economic libertarians whom Pence had gotten to know through his work with the Koch political operation.

"In that vacuum, there wasn't a power structure," says Short, who would eventually become Pence's chief of staff in the new administration. In planning meetings, the hiring process was informal. It was, Short explains, "What should we do for this position? How about so-and-so? Anyone object? Okay!" Often, Trump discussed several different positions with the people who came in to interview with him. Ryan Zinke, a congressman from Montana and former Navy SEAL who often criticized the government for being too heavy-handed in its management of federal land in the West, had talked about more than one possible job with Trump. When Trump decided to nominate him to run the Interior Department, Pence called with his congratulations. "Congratulations, Mr. Secretary," Pence said. Zinke replied, "Of what agency?" Other candidates seemed hopelessly mismatched for the jobs they would eventually get. Mick Mulvaney, a fiscal hawk, Tea Party–style member of Congress from South Carolina, was under consideration for the job of running the Office of Management and Budget. When someone on the transition team told him that Trump, who had expressed little interest in dealing with the federal deficit, wanted him, Mulvaney responded, "He does know who I am, right?" While many conservatives understood that Trump was not exactly an ideological kindred spirit who pored over policy papers from the Heritage Foundation in his spare time, they soon discovered how real the disconnect with their new president was. In one of their early conversations after the election, Trump and Paul Ryan discussed priorities for what would be the first government under unified Republican control since George W. Bush's second term. Ryan brought up the subject of reducing the cost of Social Security and Medicare by cutting benefits, an issue that he believed in passionately even though it was widely unpopular and easily skewered by Democrats. In 2012, when Ryan was Mitt Romney's running mate, one progressive group had produced an ad that showed a dark-haired man vaguely resembling Ryan pushing an elderly woman in a wheelchair toward a cliff and dumping her over the edge. Trump had campaigned against reducing benefits for the elderly—and was having none of Ryan's suggestion. "You just tried that four years ago. How did that work out?" he said, adding curtly, "No, thank you."

The recommendations of the vice-president-elect, who up until that point had not been particularly influential in the Trump orbit, helped elevate people whose names most Americans would be hearing for the first time but who were well known to conservatives as true believers. There was Mike Pompeo, a congressman from Kansas and evangelical Christian whose district was home to the business conglomerate run by the Koch brothers. Their political operation had in fact steered more money to Pompeo than to any other federal politician. Pompeo had a history of making inflammatory comments about Muslims and Barack Obama, once accusing the former president of siding with "the Islamic East" over "the Christian West." He would become the nation's new intelligence director. Many of Trump's appointees seemed to have been picked because of their professed disdain for the government functions they would now oversee, like Mulvaney at OMB. As a member of Congress, Mulvaney was known for his advocacy for slashing spending and shrinking deficits. Now he would run the government agency responsible for developing and implementing the federal budget. Betsy DeVos was the former chair of the Michigan Republican Party who used her family fortune to fund school voucher initiatives, a favorite cause for conservatives who believed that state and federal mandates and teachers unions were saddling public schools with bad instructors and ineffective curriculum. Her work in Michigan had aimed to divert tax dollars away from public schools. Now she was in line to run the Department of Education. "Betsy DeVos is not the type of person who would have a job in any other cabinet," notes the veteran conservative activist Frank Cannon. Tom Price was a Georgia congressman and orthopedic surgeon who was fiercely opposed to the Affordable Care Act and had spent years studying how to dismantle the law. Trump put him in charge of the Department of Health and Human Services. Eight cabinet secretaries were evangelical Christians, including Pompeo, Price, and DeVos. After being confirmed by the Senate, Price proposed forming a Bible study group for them all to join. The pastor picked to lead it, Ralph Drollinger, described how thrilled he was that Trump and Pence had brought in so many religious Christians to lead the new administration. "These guys are really on fire for Christ," Drollinger said. In some cases, Drollinger noted that the Trump administration was "actually plucking members" of the House and Senate Bible study group for top jobs.

It was looking to be a very good four years for religious conservatives. And Trump intended it that way. After the election, he had spoken to Short about how he thought he could maintain his bond with the evangelical Christian community. He realized how essential they were to his victory and that he couldn't win a second term without them. Trump told Short, an evangelical himself, that his strategy was quite simple: "I'm going to give them what they want, so they keep coming back."

—

Around Christmas, with Inauguration Day fast approaching, Trump retreated to his Palm Beach estate, Mar-a-Lago, and hosted Rush Limbaugh for a visit. "Rush said something to me—it was very interesting," Trump recalls about the encounter, which is one of the few that he found formative enough during his presidency to describe when asked about the people who had an impact on his thinking. Republican presidents always cut bad deals with Democrats, Limbaugh told him, and it never worked out well. Liberal policy became law, conservatives felt marginalized, and Democrats never gave the Republicans any credit for it.

"'Bush did it, both Bushes did, and others: They always try and appease the left,'" Limbaugh said. "'And no matter how much you try, no matter what you do, they'll always hate you. And they'll always screw you.'"

Trump thought it was good advice. He replied, "I agree."

There would be no mushy middle for President Trump, not in the kinds of policies he would pursue or in the style of leadership he would adopt. At every juncture when he had the opportunity to moderate a position or dial down the temperature, as he had done on the night of his election, he would decline. His inaugural address on January 20 was a grim vision of a country in decline, its citizenry engaged in an us-versus-them struggle for survival against cunning adversaries abroad and self-serving politicians at home. In the sixteen-minute speech, delivered in a cold rain, Trump excoriated politicians "who are all talk and no action, constantly complaining but never doing anything about it." He spoke of the "reasonable demands of righteous people" to live in a country where families weren't "trapped in poverty in our inner cities" and where "rusted-out factories" weren't "scattered like tombstones across the landscape." Drugs and crime "have stolen too many lives," he said, vowing to end these scourges. "This American carnage stops right here, and stops right now," he declared. "I will fight for you with every breath in my body. And I will never ever let you down."

It is possible to see almost every decision Trump made as president through the promise from his speech: Would it let his voters down? Seven days into his presidency, Trump delighted his supporters and enraged his opponents when he announced that the United States was closing its borders to foreign nationals from seven predominantly Muslim countries, suspending the entry of Syrian refugees and prohibiting refugees from any other country from entering for 120 days. The so-called travel ban was a reworked version of the "Muslim ban," which Trump had proposed as a candidate in late 2015 when he called for a "total and complete shutdown of Muslims entering the United States" after a terrorist mass shooting in San Bernardino, California, claimed fourteen lives. Trump's critics denounced the policy as hateful and unconstitutional, and it was quickly blocked in federal courts. But Trump refused to concede the issue. His administration got to work revising the ban so it exempted people who had American visas and removed Iraq from the list of excluded nations. On March 6, Trump signed the new order. He was dismissive of those who questioned his motives. When Senator Chuck Schumer of New York delivered a tearful denunciation of the policy as un-American at a press conference in January, Trump accused him of hiring an acting coach and questioned his manhood.

Trump kept pushing on the travel ban for one simple reason: "The people liked it," he says. Polling showed that the ban was not exactly unpopular. Americans overall were split relatively evenly on the issue, and public opinion for and against generally tracked with the split in the popular vote in 2016. But those polls didn't show the full picture of how powerful an issue it had become for Trump's base. In early 2016, when Trump appeared well on his way to becoming the Republican nominee, a scholar who studies voting trends in the GOP, Henry Olsen, traced Trump's surge to the top of the pack to December 7, 2015—the day he announced that if elected he would ban Muslims from entering the United States. "His appeal skyrocketed," Olsen wrote in an article describing his observations. "One must not underestimate how important the proposed ban is to Trump's voters and to his appeal," he added, noting that while exit polls showed that roughly two-thirds to three-quarters of Republican primary voters supported the ban, those numbers understated how crucial the issue was to his voters. "Between 80 and 90 percent of his voters back the ban," Olsen said, "meaning that it unites his backers more than any other concern."

Four days after Trump ordered the first travel ban, he announced his selection of a nominee to succeed the late Justice Antonin Scalia on the Supreme Court. He had added Neil M. Gorsuch, a forty-nine-year-old federal appeals court judge from Colorado, to his revised list of candidates in September. Gorsuch was considered a slam dunk among conservatives, known for being deeply wary of the gradual expansion of the government's administrative and regulatory powers and for expressing opposition to euthanasia. Social conservatives were heartened, taking that as a sign he would be just as disapproving of abortion even though he had not ruled on the issue himself as an appellate judge. Gorsuch had been thoroughly vetted by Don McGahn and Leonard Leo of the Federalist Society. On the sixty-eight-page Senate questionnaire that Gorsuch had to fill out as part of the confirmation process, his answer about how he first came to Trump's attention was "I was contacted by Leonard Leo."

Gorsuch's confirmation on April 7 would signal the beginning in earnest of a much larger effort by conservatives to reshape the ideological composition of more than a quarter of the appeals courts during Trump's term, a matter of profound impact considering that appeals judges often get the last word in cases that the Supreme Court never hears. The public campaign to defend Gorsuch's nomination in the Senate—involving three dozen of the best-financed, most battle-hardened activist groups in the conservative movement—was extremely well organized. The Judicial Crisis Network, a group with ties to Leo and other Federalist Society types, said that its campaign for Gorsuch alone would cost $10 million. Working off Trump's list, the group had even purchased URLs with the names of several different candidates. The website, ConfirmGorsuch.com, went live at 8:05 P.M. on the night that Trump announced his decision. "Millions of voters said this was the single most important issue to them when they voted for me for president," Trump told a group of supporters in the East Room of the White House. "I am a man of my word. I will do as I say." In the audience were Leo, Perkins, Reed, Dannenfelser, and a dozen other conservative activists invited by Trump.

James Robison, a televangelist the Trump campaign courted, liked to tell a story about how he called Trump's cellphone at one point after the election just to see if he would still answer. Like other Christian conservatives, Robison was used to being doted on by the Republican nominee's campaign before the election but then quickly being forgotten about. But Trump, he said, actually picked up. Conway, whom Trump rewarded with the title of White House counselor, understood that conservatives saw the new administration as "a rescue mission years in the making." Trump didn't just pay attention to them and take their calls, he solicited their advice and invited them to small private dinners in the Blue Room. "It's not just about policy but respect. And they just haven't felt respected," she explained. Conway's new role was the ultimate representation of the ascendancy of the conservative outsider in Trump's Washington. Her new spacious West Wing office was the same one that Hillary Clinton had occupied when her husband was president. (Given how close it was to the Oval Office, Conway couldn't resist repeating a crude joke to friends about Monica Lewinsky. Referring to Hillary, Conway would say, "I don't know why she wasn't down there more often checking in on him.")

Perkins recalls how the George W. Bush administration kept him and other activists at a distance. "Bush is a nice guy. But his view was, 'I know. I'm an evangelical. I'm a Christian. I'm a conservative. You guys don't need to tell me what to do,'" Perkins says. But Trump put up no such resistance. He was busy granting so many policy wish list items to social conservatives that it seemed as if activists like Perkins were at the White House every other week for an executive order signing. "I've been to the White House I don't know how many more times in the first six months this year than I was during the entire Bush administration," Perkins said seven months into the new administration. Trump rolled back accommodations for transgender students in public schools. He reinstated a ban on giving funding to health providers abroad that discussed abortion as a part of family planning. He signed legislation that aimed to cut off money for Planned Parenthood. He invited Republican activists to small formal dinners in the Blue Room and policy discussions in the Roosevelt Room.

He inquired constantly about his standing with them. "Do the Christians know all I'm doing for them?" he asked at one dinner in the Blue Room of the White House with conservative activists. "Do the pro-lifers like me?" he asked a golfing companion. Indeed they did. "He's comfortable with us because we have a deal that works," Dannenfelser said that summer, having put the dispute with her daughter after the *Access Hollywood* tape behind her. "This is who he is, and how he wants to do politics." It bought him incalculable goodwill. On Friday, January 19, 2018, Trump became the first president to speak live via satellite to the annual March for Life in Washington, an event other Republican presidents had gone to awkward lengths to keep their distance from since it started in 1974, speaking to the crowd by phone or delegating someone else to speak in their place. It had been a busy week at the White House on the policy-making front. Trump had expanded religious freedom protections for healthcare providers opposed to abortion or transgender patient care; created a new Conscience and Religious Freedom Division within HHS; and signed a proclamation declaring January 22 National Sanctity of Human Life Day.

But another Trump scandal had broken that week, seemingly threatening the president's alliance with his most socially conservative followers. An adult film star who went by the stage name of Stormy Daniels alleged that Trump had slept with her and then paid her through his longtime lawyer and fixer Michael Cohen $130,000 to keep quiet. Penny Young Nance of Concerned Women for America, a fastidious planner who constantly solicited opinions from her members, had taken to compiling a list of all the steps Trump had taken that conservatives could be proud of. This was in part because it gave her something tangible she could send out in fundraising solicitations and tout the conservative movement's success. But it was also a way of heading off complaints about Trump's personal conduct, which had slowed considerably since the election but still came up every now and then. Other conservative groups, like the Susan B. Anthony List, the Faith & Freedom Coalition, and the Family Research Council, all had lists of their own and used them for similar purposes.

Nance's list at that point one year in—it would grow considerably over the next three years—contained nine detailed bullet points, ranging from Trump's attempt to strengthen the United States' relationship with Israel to protecting people who believed their religious freedom was under attack. When she heard the news about Stormy Daniels, Nance had flashbacks to *Access Hollywood*. And she expected to hear from dismayed women all across the country. But her phone barely rang. Then one day an older donor called to register her concern about the allegations.

Nance knew just the way to calm her down. She turned to an assistant in her office and said, "Send her the list."

CHAPTER 13

Holy War

If they can destroy Roy Moore, they can destroy you.

—STEVE BANNON

On November 8, 2017, exactly one year to the day after Trump's election, a typed, single-spaced letter from two *Washington Post* reporters arrived at Roy Moore's campaign headquarters. At a little over a page in length, it spelled out in discomfiting detail how several women had accused Moore, the former chief justice of Alabama and the Republican candidate for an open U.S. Senate seat, of fondling, kissing, and harassing them when they were teenagers. One of the women who agreed to be identified by the *Post* said that she was only fourteen when Moore, then an assistant district attorney in his early thirties, saw her in court, asked her for her number, and tried to date her despite being aware of her age. There seemed no question from the details provided by the *Post* reporters in their letter that they had nailed their story. They went on to describe three more on-the-record interviews with other women who claimed that Moore had pursued them as sixteen-, seventeen-, and eighteen-year-olds, given some of them alcohol, and kissed them in some cases. The reporters said they had corroborated the accounts of all four women through interviews with more than thirty people and by checking court records where they could. "We would welcome the chance to speak with Mr. Moore about the accounts these women have provided," they wrote, asking that the campaign respond "within 24 hours."

Moore did not make himself available to the *Post*. But his campaign did immediately flip a copy of the letter to *Breitbart,* whose reporters and editors had been working closely with the candidate and his staff ever since his upset victory in the Republican primary in September. Until the election on December 12, *Breitbart* would become the de facto crisis communications shop for the Moore campaign, spreading doubt about the credibility of the women and casting the allegations in a light that would make Trump and many of his supporters doubtful of them. It was a reboot of their strategy to recover from *Access Hollywood* by staging a spectacle with Bill Clinton's accusers at the debate: Take a serious accusation backed up by credible evidence, and so thoroughly muddy the waters around it that many people would start to see it as part of a plot to destroy an innocent man and disenfranchise his voters.

What the Republican Party had become under Trump was on full display in Alabama that fall. It was hostage to paranoid politicians and their supporters who blamed a rigged system for every setback. Its leaders defended the indefensible because they feared that doing otherwise would cost them their purchase on power. Its friendly media helped craft a world they and their audience wanted to see, not the world that actually existed. The support for Moore from the White House and the acquiescence of Republicans who decided that they could tolerate him simply because he wasn't a Democrat raised a question with profound implications for the party: If Republicans wouldn't draw the line here, what else would they be willing to excuse or deny in their pursuit to hang on?

With the *Post*'s letter in hand, *Breitbart* rushed to sabotage the *Post* by leaking news of the newspaper's scoop before it planned to publish. AFTER ENDORSING DEMOCRAT IN ALABAMA, BEZOS'S WASHINGTON POST PLANS TO HIT ROY MOORE WITH ALLEGATIONS OF INAPPROPRIATE RELATIONS WITH TEENAGERS; JUDGE CLAIMS SMEAR CAMPAIGN, the headline screamed. But it had little impact on how the story was received in Washington and by Republicans in Alabama who always thought Moore was a crank and a clown. Within a few days, more than a dozen Republican senators—mortified by the possibility that their newest colleague could be a man who'd been accused of fondling a fourteen-year-old girl—called on Moore to quit the race. This included Senator Mitch McConnell of Kentucky, the Republican leader. The Republican National Committee pulled its field staff out of Alabama. The official Senate Republican campaign committee cut ties with Moore. Its chairman, Senator Cory Gardner, went even further and said that Moore should be expelled immediately from office if he won. It seemed like the breaking point that had been a long time coming: At last, the party establishment was reasserting its power over the rogue president and his followers.

But Moore and *Breitbart* and Trump were only getting started in pushing the GOP's political and cultural reality further away from the mainstream. Moore's response to the women was unequivocal: "This garbage is the very definition of fake news and intentional defamation." The story line was set. A fake news conspiracy was afoot in Alabama, spread by the corporate media interests of a liberal billionaire from Seattle with a long history of feuding with Trump. In the four and a half weeks between the *Post* story and the election, *Breitbart* would become functionally indistinguishable from the Moore campaign. Aaron Klein was the opposition researcher. Slightly hobbled with a toe he had broken as he hurried to finish a story, he spent his days and nights digging through court filings and knocking on strangers' doors in pursuit of anything damaging he could find about his latest target: the four women who spoke to the *Post*. Bannon was the senior strategist and sometimes acted as if he was on the ballot himself, holding rallies for Moore and drawing large crowds as a warm-up act for the candidate.

Matthew Boyle, whose combative personality and girth earned him the nickname of Mini Me to Bannon, was like the campaign flack. He berated other media, including Sean Hannity, for being too credulous while telling anyone who would listen that Moore was all but guaranteed to beat the charges and win. In conversations, Boyle often spoke as if he were on Moore's staff, using "we" interchangeably when talking about the campaign and their work at *Breitbart*.

At some Moore events, *Breitbart* seemed to have as many people working as the campaign itself, and Boyle moved freely in and out from the press section to the backstage area where the Moore staff was camped out. Boyle immediately gelled with the environment. He drove around Alabama in his rental car blasting country music with the windows down as he chased leads about Moore's accusers, many of which were never publishable. He badgered strangers everywhere he went—inside bars, outside restaurants where he was taking one of his many smoke breaks, at valet stands, or in an Uber—with questions about whether they believed the accusations. He was delighted to discover that a surprisingly high percentage of them said no.

Breitbart started streaming Moore's campaign events live. Moore became a regular guest on *Breitbart*-affiliated radio programs. Having built a following by telling conservatives they could not trust the mainstream media because it colluded with the left, Bannon and his staff were now colluding themselves.

Very little of *Breitbart*'s work in Alabama was even acknowledged by the mainstream media this time, but that didn't matter to them because this was a different kind of operation than they had executed before. It was enough to plant the seeds of doubt among those who wanted—or needed—to believe that Moore's denials might be true. It gave religious conservative leaders a reason to justify keeping their expansive grassroots networks engaged on the ground even if they found it distasteful to be associated with Moore. Ralph Reed's Faith and Freedom Coalition, for instance, went ahead with plans to reach more than three hundred thousand Alabama voters through phone calls and direct mail. It persuaded powerful opinion leaders like Hannity to come back into the fold after they had started to doubt Moore. It clarified for voters who the real enemy was: the conspirators in the national media who had tried to take out Trump the same way by dredging up old accusations.

Klein and his brother, with help from a part-time document gofer, combed through Alabama courts for records that said anything about the women. He was more of a fish out of water than Boyle. Before arriving in Alabama, he'd never set foot in a Walmart.

With his broken toe, he hobbled from door to door hunting down a tip provided by the Moore campaign that one of the restaurants where Moore had allegedly assaulted a woman never existed. He asked neighbors if they remembered it being there. He looked through old newspapers to see if it had ever been advertised. The lead proved to be false, as were many that the campaign gave him. Sometimes the tips came from Moore himself, other times from his wife, Kayla, who never wavered publicly in her defense of her husband. Klein, growing frustrated that nothing was panning out, offered strategic advice to the campaign. He said the judge should take a lie detector test to disprove the allegations. Moore declined. But like other conservatives, he put aside his misgivings in service of the larger goal of keeping Republicans in control of the Senate—a devil's bargain, he understood.

Meanwhile, Bannon, who had been broomed out of the White House in August after barely seven months in the job as chief strategist to the president, fed the bottomless pit that was Trump's sense of victimhood. He told the president that there were striking parallels between what was happening to Moore and his own situation with the *Access Hollywood* tape. "This is Billy Bush weekend all over again," he said. Moore was under attack—just as Trump had been. Trump agreed and said he saw the similarities. It wasn't a coincidence that the *Post* story had dropped when it did so close to the election, he thought. "If you look at what is really going on, he totally denies it," Trump said when he spoke publicly about Moore in late November for the first time. "He says it didn't happen and, you know, you have to listen to him also."

The dam was beginning to crack.

When Karl Rove was a middle-aged Republican operative working on state judicial races in the 1990s, he had a rule of thumb for his candidates in Alabama. "You never need to travel more than fifteen miles from I-65," recalls Matthew McDonald, a lawyer in Mobile who used to work with Rove. The interstate is Alabama's spine, running from north to south past the major population centers of

Huntsville, Birmingham, and Montgomery. Then after Montgomery, the interstate takes a slight jog toward Mobile, where it ends just a few miles from the bay. All told, roughly half the state's population lives in those four metropolitan areas. Rove didn't exactly say that the rural Alabamians who lived beyond his target didn't matter. But that's how many of them thought Republicans like Rove felt—and why many of them voted to elect a contrarian like Roy Moore to statewide office in 2000 when he ran to become chief justice of the Alabama Supreme Court. He won by beating the candidate that Rove was helping in the Republican primary.

Moore soon became nationally known for reasons that many Alabama Republicans were ashamed of, thinking it made them look backward and hung up on lost causes. But when Moore commissioned a 5,280-pound stone slab inscribed with the Ten Commandments and had it installed in the state judicial building in Montgomery, many religious conservatives saw it as the fulfillment of Moore's pledge to restore Christianity to its rightful place in Alabama law. Liberal groups like the American Civil Liberties Union sued, arguing that it was a flagrant violation of the constitutional imperative to keep church and state separate. After a seven-day trial in 2002, a federal judge ruled that the monument's presence in a state facility was a violation of the Constitution and ordered Moore to remove it within thirty days. He refused.

His defiance made him a hero to many conservatives even as it drew unflattering comparisons to another Alabama politician who developed a national following after he ignored the federal courts: Governor George Wallace, the unapologetic segregationist who stood in the doorway of an auditorium on the University of Alabama's Tuscaloosa campus in 1963 to protest a court order to admit two Black students. (The comparison to Moore was enough of an embarrassment for Wallace's daughter, Peggy, that she once felt compelled to go on the record in a local paper and denounce the judge's conduct as "grandstanding" that was "dangerous" and nothing like what her father had done.) A bipartisan state panel ruled in November 2003 that Moore had "placed himself above the law," and it expelled him from office. But Moore correctly predicted then that

his fight was only just beginning that day. "The battle to acknowledge God is about to rage across the country," he told a crowd that
gathered outside the court awaiting word of his fate. He had become
a martyr in the eyes of many Alabamians. "Roy Moore for Senate!
Roy Moore for president!" they chanted as he left the hearing.

The Senate campaign would have to wait until after Moore was
removed as Alabama's chief justice a second time, in 2016. He had
run again for the job in 2012, and won. On election night, as voters
across the country sent the nation's first Black president back to the
White House for a second term, Moore seemed more interested in
looking backward. "I have no doubt this is a vindication," he said.
The audience at his victory party showered him with shouts of
"Amen." Decorating a snack table nearby was a small replica of the
Ten Commandments installation. Moore did not try to move the
titanic monument back this time. But he found a new reason for
defying the federal courts in June 2015 when the United States Supreme Court recognized a constitutional right to same-sex marriage,
legalizing it in all fifty states. Moore had condemned homosexuality
as an "inherent evil" and said he could not abide children being
raised by same-sex parents. He ordered Alabama's probate judges to
disregard the ruling and not to issue any marriage licenses to gay
and lesbian couples. The same state judicial body that had suspended
him in 2003 moved quickly to do so again. And by September 2016,
Moore was taken off the bench for good—unemployed right around
the time that Alabama would be needing a new senator.

Moore, whose supporters still addressed him as "Judge" long
after he was removed from the court, had said and done things that
would have disqualified almost any other politician from seeking
public office again. He denied evolution. He questioned Barack
Obama's citizenship. He campaigned in a cowboy outfit and bran-
dished a pistol onstage to prove his devotion to the Second Amendment. He once said that slavery wasn't entirely irredeemable as an
institution because it kept Black families close and intact. When the
first Muslim was elected to Congress, Keith Ellison of Minnesota,
Moore denounced him for planning to take his oath of office on the
Koran and compared it to being sworn in on a copy of Hitler's *Mein*

Kampf. Moore once implied that George Soros, the billionaire funder of liberal causes who was born into a Jewish family, was going to hell. And when Moore's wife later tried to stand up for him, her tone-deafness about what exactly constituted anti-Semitism showed. "Fake news would tell you that we don't care for Jews," Kayla said. But that couldn't be, because, as she explained, "One of our attorneys is a *Jee-yew*."

The fact that Moore had all this baggage, and that his followers loved him not in spite of it but because of it, made him a perfect figure for the moment of reckoning the GOP had been trying to avoid since Trump's election. Trump had carried Alabama with 62 percent of the vote, beating Clinton by 28 points. But as popular as he was there and in the rest of the Deep South, the question of how much influence he ultimately had over the national party and its representatives in Washington was still an open one.

Only nine months into his term, Trump remained somewhat of a detached leader. His bonds with other elected Republicans were weak for the most part. Rich Lowry, the editor of *National Review*, was among the most astute in diagnosing the dilemma that Trump was facing as a president who won after running against his own party. Trump had no bloc of allies in Congress he could count on to deliver legislative victories. "There's this disjunction," Lowry said. "He doesn't have a congressional party. He doesn't even really have a wing of a congressional party." Republicans were discovering that without Obama, who gave them a persona and a set of policies to unite against, they couldn't agree on much. The issue that had united them in a near single-minded focus during Obama's presidency— repealing the Affordable Care Act—left Republicans hopelessly divided now that they controlled the House, Senate, and White House, and repeal was no longer a hypothetical protest vote. To put in perspective the zeal with which they tried to undo the law once they took control of the House in 2011, House Republicans had voted on a repeal measure on thirty-seven separate occasions by the spring of 2013, accounting for no less than 15 percent of the time they spent on the floor conducting legislative business.

But when faced with taking action that would have actual social and economic consequences that included leaving twenty-four million Americans uninsured, their professed will to get rid of the law crumbled. When Trump worked with Speaker Paul Ryan and Republican leaders to pass a bill that he hoped would get to his desk for his signature, internal disagreement about the scope of the repeal forced him to pull the bill before it could go down in defeat. Trump responded by attacking the most conservative members of his party in the House Freedom Caucus for not going along with it. They demanded the bill do more to roll back regulations on insurers and remained largely in lockstep against the president. *Politico* noted how the conservatives' defiance was a slap in the face to Trump. "The Freedom Caucus stared down its own commander in chief and won—delivering a black eye to his early presidency and potentially damaging the rest of his agenda."

The clash between burn-it-to-the-ground insurgents who favored a culture warrior like Moore for Senate and mainstream, establishment Republicans who wanted a more conventional candidate was becoming a huge distraction for Trump. And he was racked with doubt about how much he wanted to be involved ahead of the September 27 primary vote. Moore was the clear choice of voters who also loved Trump. But at the urging of leaders on Capitol Hill like Mitch McConnell, Trump had already endorsed the establishment-friendly incumbent who had been appointed to the seat, Senator Luther Strange, who won the president's support after voting yes on the healthcare repeal.

Trump's uncertainty about where he stood with his party—and his insecurity about taking sides in a Republican primary—can seem like an episode misremembered from another presidency, one in which the commander in chief was someone more capable of self-awareness and self-doubt, and members of Congress were bolder in exercising their independence from the leader of their party. Still new to the Washington game and eager to score the kind of big political victory that had eluded him on Capitol Hill, Trump was often reliant on Republicans who did not share his zero-sum approach to politics. Their advice to him usually reflected a sense that a president's decisions should further the goal of preserving and expanding power in Congress. In August, Senator Bob Corker, the Tennessee Republican who had publicly questioned Trump's mental stability and competence before the 2016 election, met with the president and warned him that Strange's campaign was in trouble.

"We have a real problem in Alabama," Corker told the president, who was unaware of the situation. The senator said the only way to prevent Moore from beating Strange was if Trump went down to Alabama and campaigned for Strange himself. Trump, ever the finger-in-the-wind decision maker, was reluctant to dig in for a candidate who could lose. Senate Republicans and their allies knew this, so they hatched a plan. The United States Chamber of Commerce, which was backing Strange, commissioned a poll that showed Alabamians would respond well to a personal visit from the president. The Chamber sent the poll to the White House. Eventually, Trump relented and agreed to go to Alabama.

A few days before the election, on September 22, the president headlined an event in Huntsville at an arena downtown that holds about ten thousand people. Most of the seats were full. Strange, who introduced Trump that evening, spent most of his speech making a curious argument for why Republicans should turn out for him. A vote for Strange wasn't really a vote for Strange, he insisted. It was a message to the Republican establishment "that Alabama stands by its president," declared Strange, a beneficiary of deep connections to the party establishment. Trump swanned out onto the stage to the familiar strains of "Sweet Home Alabama," flashed his Cheshire Cat grin, and clapped his hands. It wasn't an intuitive pairing. Strange was a former lobbyist who was close to Republican power brokers in Alabama like the state's senior statesman, Senator Richard Shelby. Strange had been the state attorney general when Governor Robert Bentley picked him to fill the seat that Jeff Sessions held before Trump made him attorney general. But the process had the stench of the very kind of "swamp" quid pro quo that Trump railed against because Strange was investigating Bentley for misusing his office and reportedly attempting to conceal evidence of an extramarital affair, giving the appointment the appearance of impropriety.

Trump let almost thirty seconds pass as he soaked up the adoration from the crowd before he finally walked over to the lectern to start speaking. He had gotten to know Strange over the previous nine months and genuinely liked him. But whatever affection he had for the senator was not as powerful as the anxiety he had that Strange could lose the primary to Moore.

"I'll be honest. I might have made a mistake," Trump told the crowd. Then, from the stage, he held a dialogue with himself about how he would be blamed if Strange lost. "If Luther doesn't win they're not going to say we picked up twenty-five points in a very short period of time. They're gonna say, 'Donald Trump, the president of the United States, was unable to pull his candidate across the line. It is a terrible, terrible moment for Trump. This is total embarrassment.'" Sure, Strange was a good man, the president continued, but so was Moore. And if Moore were to prevail in the primary, "I'm going to be here campaigning like hell for him," Trump promised. He sounded not only indifferent about the intra-party fight he had just inserted himself in the middle of, he seemed bored with the whole thing. "The last thing I want to do is be involved in a primary. Okay? I could be sitting home right now," he said, before mustering the faintest, most perfunctory praise of Strange. "Gotta vote for him."

Strange's allies were dumbfounded. Scott Reed, the chief political strategist for the United States Chamber of Commerce, was watching on television. He thought to himself that the president sounded like "a guy who was on his way to go see his shrink, and just laid out everything that was bothering him that day." Reed texted Shelby, who was in the audience. The Chamber had bought out every digital billboard in the state it could find to remind Alabamians that Strange was the only candidate Trump had endorsed. And here was Trump torpedoing their whole plan. "It looks terrible," Reed texted Shelby, who replied that he agreed. But as bad as it seemed on television, Shelby assured Reed that it was actually much, much worse in person.

Alabama Republicans appeared to share Trump's lack of enthusiasm for Strange when they voted on September 27. Moore won by 9 points, sweeping the state's rural areas and even the more populous pockets of the state around Mobile and Montgomery. He lost only four counties. Three of them were along the vote-rich I-65 corridor that had been a bulwark for establishment Republicans in the past. "We're dealing with a political environment that I've never had any experience with," a weary-sounding Strange said in his concession speech. "The political seas, the political winds in this country right now are very hard to navigate. They're very hard to understand." Within hours of the race being called, Trump was already trying to wipe his record clean and started deleting supportive tweets he had posted about Strange. The people wanted Moore, so Moore would be Trump's guy.

Steve Bannon believed that Trump's endorsement of Strange was like another healthcare repeal or the new Republican plan to enact a massive tax cut that would overwhelmingly benefit the wealthy: a bland, bad idea that people who didn't understand Trump were insisting on. (Another person who saw that the tensions playing out in Alabama were part of a larger struggle over the Trump presidency was Sarah Palin, who traveled to Montgomery to campaign for Moore. "Guys, the swamp, it's trying to hijack this presidency," Palin said at a rally for Moore before the September vote. "The swamp is trying to steal the victory that we worked so long and hard for.")

Bannon's argument to Trump all along had been to reject any kind of consensus approach when dealing with establishment Republicans or Democrats. He reasoned that accommodations or moderation wouldn't buy Trump any goodwill—echoing what Limbaugh had told Trump at Mar-a-Lago during the transition. "It's never going to be enough. They hate you. They hate the very mention of your name. And they're trying to destroy you," Bannon said to the president before leaving the White House in August. Whether the issue was being more lenient with children of undocumented immigrants or apologizing after claiming that "very fine people" had marched alongside the white supremacists and neo-Nazis who caused a riot that summer in Charlottesville, Virginia, Bannon told Trump that he had nothing to gain politically by showing the slightest hint of contrition or willingness to compromise. Others, said Bannon, might try to convince Trump that "there's a political constituency for that." But he disagreed. "I just say there's not. You've got the base, and you grow the base."

Roy Moore had not been Bannon's first choice, or the preference of most other Trump Republicans. Mo Brooks, an anti-immigration hard-liner who represented the very northern part of Alabama, was their candidate. But Trump refused to endorse him because Brooks had criticized him during the 2016 presidential primaries, calling him a "serial adulterer" who would never fulfill his promises if elected. On August 10, during what would be Bannon's last week on the job as White House chief strategist, he told a reporter he thought Trump had confused his base by supporting an establishment Republican like Luther Strange. "People are going, 'I don't get this,' " he said. Bannon had stayed behind in Washington while most of the senior staff traveled with the president up to his golf retreat in Bedminster, New Jersey. Sitting in a makeshift office in the Old Executive Office Building because the West Wing was undergoing repairs, Bannon said that Trump had not only hurt himself but wouldn't be able to help Strange win. "The establishment has fucked him, and we're either going to play by their rules or they're going to play by our rules," he said, offering a prediction about the primary: "Moore is going to win. I'm telling you, it's going to be a holy war down there."

After Moore won, it wasn't enough for Bannon to sit back and assign stories to *Breitbart* writers that propped up Moore. Bannon flew to Alabama and campaigned alongside Moore. As he framed it, this race was a contest between the good, decent people of Alabama and the corrupt Republican establishment in Washington, who Bannon said regarded Moore supporters as "a pack of morons." Speaking to a crowd in the city of Fairhope just outside Mobile, Bannon said, "They think you're nothing but rubes. They have no interest at all in what you have to say, what you have to think or what you want to do." And he pledged that their "day of reckoning is coming."

Boyle continued trying to prevent conservatives from jumping ship once the allegations in the *Post* surfaced. Hannity had been one of Moore's biggest boosters in conservative media aside from *Breitbart*. He tried to help Moore salvage his reputation by inviting him on his radio show in November. But the explanations Moore gave during the interview were so bizarre and contradictory that Hannity started to have doubts. "If we did go out on dates, then we did. But I do not remember that," Moore told Hannity. And, worse, when Hannity asked him if it was his practice to date teenagers, he responded, "Not generally, no. If I did, you know, I'm not going to dispute anything. But I don't remember anything like that." This strained even Hannity's remarkable capacity to gloss over the flaws of the political figures he promoted. Dating teenagers, it seemed, was Hannity's red line. He gave the judge a twenty-four-hour public ultimatum to provide a satisfactory explanation of his innocence or get out of the race.

This triggered a crisis inside the Moore campaign—which meant a crisis for *Breitbart*. The campaign set to work drafting a letter to Hannity attempting to clarify the judge's remarks and lay out a plausible line of defense. Boyle got to work on Hannity.

"Not happy with you bro" began a text exchange between Boyle and Hannity the night the Fox News host made his demand.

"He can't deny knowing her. He wrote notes to her," Hannity wrote back.

"Yes he can."

"He wrote that note to her. Read it, Matt," Hannity responded, referring to a woman who had come forward with what she said was a note from Moore that he had written in her high school yearbook. "He KNEW her."

"Gloria Allred wrote it," Boyle scoffed. "You were the last thing holding Fox together. Guess not anymore."

"Matt, stop the nasty comments. I explained to you—"

"Enjoy the ratings crash. You're done to *Breitbart,*" Boyle fumed.

Hannity's resolve buckled fast. The following night, he capitulated on the air. "The people of Alabama deserve to have a fair choice," he said. "I'm very confident that when everything comes out, they will make the best decision for their state. It shouldn't be decided by me, by people on television, by Mitch McConnell."

Bannon, *Breitbart,* and the Moore campaign were making a different kind of argument to Alabamians. There were two likely explanations for why someone would vote to send Moore to the Senate knowing what they knew about his political past and his alleged involvement with teenage girls. First, they shared a similar worldview to his and wanted their elected leaders to govern in a way that reflected fundamentalist Christian values. Or, if they were not especially religious, they might see Moore not as an ideal candidate but as a way to express their disgust for the establishment politicians who looked down on them, called them "deplorables," and would think nothing of destroying their well-being and way of life if it allowed them to hold on to power. In either case, it became much easier to ignore a story about sexual abuse, or to believe that it was simply the fabrication of enemy forces looking to rig the election in their favor. And Moore eagerly perpetuated the idea that politics wasn't a war of ideas and policies as much as it was a battle that would determine whether Christian civilization would survive.

Bannon was not subtle in his appeal to these insecurities when he campaigned again for Moore in December a few days before the general election. An attack on Moore is an attack on you, just like an attack on Trump was an attack on them, he said. "They want to destroy Judge Moore," he thundered from the stage in a banquet hall made to look like a rustic barn outside Mobile. "And you know why? They want to take away your voice." He added, "If they can destroy Roy Moore, they can destroy you." Many voters seemed to agree, much as they had that *Access Hollywood* was nothing. "I believe in innocent until proven guilty, but even if he's guilty, I'll back him all the way," a Baptist deacon named Kenneth Frost told the *Los Angeles Times*. "I still feel he's a Christian man—and nobody's perfect."

Republican leaders in Washington were suddenly facing the growing likelihood that Moore might actually win. They muted their criticisms of him. They stopped threatening to expel him. White House officials publicly said they were concerned about a rush to judgment. "It would be a very dangerous precedent for any of us, for any person in this country to just be cast aside as guilty because of press reports," said Kellyanne Conway. Then, a week before the election, the Republican National Committee, at Trump's direction, reversed itself and agreed to fund get-out-the-vote efforts for Moore. And Trump issued a full-throated endorsement of Moore on Twitter.

Trump was bending the party to his will. Those who did dare speak out against their party fit what would become a familiar pattern for Trump detractors. Most no longer worked in electoral politics. Many were alumni of the Bush, Romney, or McCain campaigns. Peter Wehner, a former speechwriter and adviser to George W. Bush and an evangelical Christian himself, was emblematic. The Moore episode made him begin questioning whether he wanted to be associated with the church anymore. "Assume you were a person of the left and an atheist, and you decided to create a couple of people in a laboratory to discredit the Republican Party and white evangelical Christianity. You could hardly choose two more perfect men than Donald Trump and Roy Moore," he said. "Where exactly is the bottom?"

On the night of the election on December 12, Bannon walked into the VIP room at the community center in downtown Montgomery where the Moore campaign had set up to await the results. He was giddy about the prospect of rubbing Moore's victory in McConnell's face and started riffing about what his victory speech might say. "Judge Moore is a good man, a righteous man and an honorable man. And if you were an honorable man . . ." Bannon said, his voice trailing off as he contemplated what to say next. Boyle told Bannon he needed to pick out a song to walk out to and suggested "Street Fighting Man" by the Rolling Stones.

While the first returns to come in looked good for Moore, the optimism in the VIP room started to deflate as the night wore on. A little before 9 P.M., Bannon took an elevator down to the lower level and slipped out a back door, where his SUV was waiting to take him back to his hotel. At 9:24 P.M. local time, Fox officially called the race for Moore's opponent, Doug Jones, the first Democrat Alabama had sent to the Senate in a quarter century. It was an aggressive and early call by the network's decision desk, coming before other news outlets had declared a winner. But after the exit polls in 2016 proved initially misleading, overstating Hillary Clinton's strength, Rupert Murdoch decided Fox News would pull out of its agreement with the other news organizations that helped pay for exit polls and go its own way.

Moore had just barely lost. Only about twenty-one thousand votes, or 1.5 percentage points, separated him and Jones when all the ballots were counted. Before Moore went out to address his supporters, he stood backstage in a holding area with a group of about fifteen of his core supporters, family members, and staff. "Where's Steve?" Moore asked, unaware that Bannon had ducked out. A young woman called out, "Judge, we want to be up there with you—as women." They all bowed their heads and said a prayer.

Then Moore walked through a large set of double doors and shuffled toward the stage, alone. "It's not over," he told the crowd. He wasn't conceding the race.

Roy Moore was just the kind of embarrassment that Republicans in Washington always feared Trump might unleash on them. Now the party owned Trump's failure. The president understood the magnitude of the loss and how it had badly damaged his reputation—even among the Christian right, the bedrock of his support. He immediately started making amends. As a face-saving measure, he announced his intention to move the American embassy in Israel to Jerusalem, a demand that conservative Christians and Jewish groups had made for decades but that no president had been willing to do because of the potential for such a move to further destabilize the region. It was a token that mattered to conservative Jewish donors like Sheldon Adelson and evangelical leaders, who both held the belief in Israel as the Judeo-Christian holy land. But Trump would need something much bigger to repair the damage.

And his problems were piling up. In January, the Stormy Daniels allegations broke. On another legal front, the special counsel investigation into the Trump campaign's dealings with Russia was proceeding. His former national security adviser, Michael Flynn, had just pleaded guilty to lying to federal agents and agreed to cooperate. With the midterm elections on the horizon, the prospects for Republicans looked grim. They would likely lose control of the House. Frank Cannon and Marjorie Dannenfelser were not alone among conservative activists who wondered what shoe was about to drop next. Cannon thought of how women's groups and abortion rights activists didn't turn on Bill Clinton during the Monica Lewinksy scandal and the impeachment. "They set up a dynamic in which it was more important to judge him by what he did on policy," Cannon argued to friends who questioned whether they should distance themselves from Trump. Dannenfelser agreed. "I don't want to be that person who defends Bill Clinton no matter what," she explained. "But I don't spend a whole lot of time trying to figure it out because of the list." She meant the list of conservative policy achievements that groups like Conservative Women for America and SBA List kept updating. By early 2018, the one that Dannenfelser and her staff had compiled was long enough that it had to be condensed into ten of the biggest items, including Trump's appointment of numerous abortion opponents to high-level administration jobs and the confirmation of Justice Neil Gorsuch. Hypothetically, Cannon suggested an idea about the one development that could virtually ensure that Trump had a free pass from conservatives in perpetuity. If Justice Anthony Kennedy were to retire, Cannon said, "It quickly becomes, 'Stormy who?'"

On June 27, 2018, Justice Kennedy announced his retirement from the Supreme Court, giving Trump the chance to name a second justice in as many years in office. Kennedy's seat represented something Scalia's didn't: an opportunity to tilt the ideological balance of the court in a more conservative direction. Kennedy, like Scalia, had been appointed by Reagan. But unlike Scalia, he was a swing justice whose liberal opinions on same-sex marriage and abortion rights had infuriated conservatives. It would be a war with Senate Democrats to replace him. Now that Republicans were down to fifty-one seats since Moore's loss, there was very little room for error.

Trump's nominee to replace Kennedy, Judge Brett M. Kavanaugh of the U.S. Circuit Court of Appeals for the District of Columbia, had exercised the kind of caution on the bench that had become typical of someone who wanted to be a Supreme Court justice in the modern era. His paper trail, though long, was largely lacking in opinions on contentious social issues that could torpedo his advancement. What ended up almost undoing him was not any of his legal writing but rather an allegation of sexual assault from a high school acquaintance that would almost negate all his judicial caution and calculation. The accusations were chilling. According to an account his accuser, Christine Blasey Ford, gave to *The Washington Post* recalling the incident from the early 1980s, "Kavanaugh pinned her to a bed on her back and groped her over her clothes, grinding his body against hers and clumsily attempting to pull off her one-piece bathing suit and the clothing she wore over it. When she tried to scream, she said, he put his hand over her mouth."

Brett Kavanaugh was no Roy Moore. And the accusations against him were not as well documented or suggestive of a pattern of sexual misconduct. But the clash over his confirmation played out on the same cultural battlefield, with Republicans claiming to be the victims of an elaborate sabotage operation perpetrated by liberal Trump opponents with the help of a complicit mainstream media. The key difference was Kavanaugh, an avatar of prep school privilege and Brooks Brothers Republicanism in whom many white conservatives saw themselves. Through Kavanaugh, Trump would redeem himself in the eyes of many Republicans who hadn't been as willing to join him in his other culture war crusades against the left, many of whom harbored serious misgivings about his stewardship of their party.

The confirmation battle brought the establishment wing of the party into the fold for the remainder of his term in office, flooded the Republican National Committee coffers with campaign contributions from donors who'd all but given up on the party, and energized conservative activists going into the midterm elections.

On the day Kavanaugh testified in front of the Senate Judiciary Committee and defended himself against Ms. Ford's charges, he erupted in a Trumpian torrent of resentment and rage. He accused Democrats of coming after him to exact "revenge on behalf of the Clintons," a reference to the role he played as a young lawyer working on the investigation by Ken Starr, the independent counsel. He said he was being smeared after leading an exemplary life—number one in his high school class, captain of the football team, admitted to Yale Law School.

Kavanaugh's supporters, who included people far outside the Beltway angered by what they saw as an injustice, called the entire thing a farce meant to hurt the president.

"This is about Donald Trump getting in one of his guys," a sixty-year-old retired pipe fitter, Tony Gardner, from Robbinsdale, Minnesota, told *The New York Times*. Senator Lindsey Graham spoke to the way Kavanaugh was a stand-in for white men everywhere who were bothered by the way society seemed to have devalued them. "I know I am a single white male from South Carolina. And I am told I should shut up," Graham said, calling the episode "the most despicable thing I have seen in my time in politics." Trump told aides that he felt Democrats were "destroying this man and his family." Mike Davis, an activist who worked with conservative groups to rally support behind the embattled nominee, understood that many Americans would see reason to fear for their own families: "If they can take out Brett Kavanaugh, they can take any of you out, any of your kids." Republicans who'd sworn off politics because of Trump started picking up their phones to give. One wealthy donor to Karl

Rove's political group, American Crossroads, hadn't given anything until the Kavanaugh hearings. Then he called Rove one day and said, "We've got to keep the Senate. This is crazy. I'm sending you two million dollars." Ronna McDaniel, formerly Ronna Romney McDaniel until Trump picked her to lead the RNC and asked her to ditch her maiden name, told people that Kavanaugh opened the floodgates. "Without a doubt," she said, "it was the easiest time we had raising money."

Kavanaugh was confirmed by a vote of 50–48 on Saturday, October 6.

CHAPTER 14

The Party

The Republican establishment today bends the knee to Caesar.

—Patrick J. Buchanan, March 2, 2017

Denver Riggleman hadn't been a member of Congress for a full year yet, but he was a quick study when it came to learning the rhythms of his colleagues in the House Republican conference. One of the first observations the career intelligence analyst had was that anytime there was a function catered with Chick-fil-A sandwiches, it would get crowded fast. One day in 2019, Riggleman, whose district runs through the middle of Virginia from the Washington exurbs to the North Carolina border, recalls walking into the room in the Capitol basement where House Republicans usually gathered for their all-member meetings. When he saw the huge line, he assumed, "Must be the Chick-fil-A."

But it wasn't. Riggleman looked up toward the front of the room and was stunned to see the president's daughter holding court with a group of enthralled-looking congressmen. "What is Ivanka Trump doing here?" he wondered. Irreverent and unfiltered, Riggleman couldn't help but roll his eyes at what he thought was a "big gaggle of sycophants" elbowing their way past one another to get a word in with their esteemed visitor. From time to time, Ivanka was known to meet with groups of Republicans on Capitol Hill to promote the initiatives she worked on as a White House adviser, such as paid leave for workers who needed time off to care for their families. But for many Republicans in Congress, more front-of-mind than any pet policy of the eldest Trump daughter was the opportunity for face time with a member of the Trump family. Riggleman grabbed a fried chicken sandwich and stood off to the side with another freshman, Anthony Gonzalez, a young, similarly independent-minded member from Ohio. Then Kevin McCarthy, the Republican leader, spotted them and motioned to them to join him at the front of the room, clearly intending for them to meet Ivanka. "I don't want to go up there," Riggleman said, turning to Gonzalez, who didn't see much point in it either. But they obliged their leader, ditching their chicken sandwiches and making their way over for a few minutes of polite small talk. For Riggleman, the episode was a kind of eureka moment in his understanding of the major changes redefining his party. "I'm an elected member of the U.S. Congress. Why am I sitting here wasting an hour of my day listening to Ivanka Trump?" he says. Yet when he told other colleagues that he was less than impressed with the idea of sitting through a presentation by the First Daughter, he said they couldn't believe how he could be so dismissive. "You should have seen their faces," he says. "It was a conga line to try to get to her. And I think they thought Ivanka was like their meal ticket to get into the inner circle. She would come in like royalty. And she was treated like an elected official. I just thought that was wrong."

Riggleman was hardly the first Republican to observe what he believed was a troubling trend toward groupthink about Trump and his family. The most important credential to have as a Republican was no longer a commitment to vote for a set of right-wing policies or a signed pledge to wave around as proof of one's conservative authenticity. It was professed devotion to the president. As the Alabama Senate race and Kavanaugh confirmation demonstrated, the belief that Trump and the people he represented were under constant siege created a culture in the party where to question Trump was to side with the people who wanted to destroy you. And no matter how conservative or pro-Trump someone had been, they could render that record largely irrelevant if they dared speak up.

Joe Walsh, the former Tea Party congressman from suburban

Chicago who became a talk radio host after losing reelection, was not exactly a portrait of moderation. Walsh had attacked Black Lives Matter activists as "punks" and questioned whether Muslims could be trusted. Before the 2016 election, he vowed that if Clinton won, "I'm grabbing my musket," while imploring his followers, "You in?" Despite all this, the conservative media conglomerate Salem Media Network announced it was giving him a nationally syndicated show in February 2017. But Walsh says he quickly got the message from management that there was no room on the air for commentary that was critical of Trump. A few months into Trump's term, Walsh started to sour on Trump and Republicans in Congress after they failed to agree on a plan to repeal the Affordable Care Act. And as a former congressman who had run on the issue himself, he was furious because Republicans controlled the House, Senate, and White House. But Salem management, Walsh says, told him to stay away from the issue. "I got a call saying, 'If you disagree with Trump about anything, you have to ignore that topic,'" he recalls, describing the dictum from on high at the company: "Sign on to Team Trump and speak well of him. That's where our audience is." On occasion, Walsh would still defy this unwritten rule and criticize the president, as he did when Trump signed a budget that increased spending well beyond what Republicans had been telling their voters was sustainable. His bosses were not pleased. "I got read the riot act," he says. Then he went back to defending Trump in the interest of keeping his job. "It's about manipulating your audience. Who listens to us? Middle-aged white people. You want to feed their grievances, feed their resentments. 'Everyone wants to silence you!'" Yet he was the one being silenced.

Across the conservative movement, activists were discovering that the way to survive was to enlist themselves in the president's battles. Tea Party Patriots, one of the biggest groups to emerge out of the national movement, was raising $20 million a year in 2011 and 2012 and employed thirty people. In 2017, the first year of the Trump White House, the group collected only $4.8 million and had a staff of fifteen. As it tried to adapt, its causes became whatever Trump wanted to talk about: the special counsel investigation into his campaign's ties to Russia; the "tyranny" of Big Tech; liberal judges.

Anti-Trump voices were disappearing from the conservative media landscape all across the country. Bill Kristol's *Weekly Standard* was shuttered by its owner at the end of 2018. Charlie Sykes, whose two-decade career as a radio host in Wisconsin helped make him one of the state's most influential conservative voices, refused to get on board with Trump and left his show after the election. At Salem, the popular host Hugh Hewitt transformed his persona from that of a Trump skeptic to a strident defender, choosing the path of least resistance with his network bosses and the audience. Hewitt had once memorably stumped Trump during a debate by asking him about the nuclear triad of defense by aircraft, submarine, and land-based missiles. Trump seemed to have no idea what Hewitt was talking about. But like most right-wing media hosts who kept their jobs, post-2016 Hewitt rejected most criticism of the president as the hysterical rantings of Democrats and Never Trumpers who continued to deny his legitimacy. Glenn Beck, who had insisted that it was "moral" and "ethical" to oppose Trump in the 2016 general election, completely reversed himself. Beck even reprised some of his apocalyptic predictions from the Obama years, warning that Trump's loss in 2020 would spell "the end of the country as we know it." Outlets that were trusted for their political independence, like *RealClearPolitics,* started to skew pro-Trump. In late 2017, the bulk of the website's straight-news reporting staff was suddenly laid off. As an affiliated foundation took hundreds of thousands of dollars from wealthy Trump supporters, it published pieces labeled "RealClearInvestigations" that amplified Trump's claims he was being targeted by "Deep State" conspirators.

Trump, probably more than anyone else, appreciated how swift and punishing the judgment of the audience could be. He noted with no small amount of self-satisfaction how conservative media outlets suffered for giving voice to a point of view that contradicted or questioned him. "A lot of people don't want that," he says. "They don't want to hear negativity toward me." Indeed, the data showed that many Republicans were migrating toward media where that negativity would not intrude. In 2016, the Pew Research Center found that 40 percent of Trump's supporters cited Fox News as their main source of news. No other outlet was even close to having such a hold on the attention of his voters. CNN, which was the second-most-popular source, was the choice of only 8 percent of Trump supporters, while 7 percent said Facebook. When Pew asked Americans where they were getting their political news three years later, it found that the homogeneity on the right was even greater. Sixty percent of Republicans or people who leaned Republican said they had gone to Fox within the last week. It was this environment that led one anonymous member of Congress to describe to *BuzzFeed News* the lengths to which Republicans had to go to display fealty to Trump. "Trump has said he could stand in the middle of Fifth Avenue and shoot someone dead and not lose any supporters," the member said. "Well, if that happens, I'd better be photographed stuffing a body into the trunk of a car, or my constituents will demand to know why I'm not supporting the president." Among those to agree with that premise was Pat Buchanan, who wrote an essay titled "It's Trump's Party Now." Buchanan seemed quite satisfied with the turn of events. "The Republican establishment today bends the knee to Caesar," he wrote.

The myth of infallibility and invulnerability enveloping Trump was similar to previous campaigns by right-wing conspiracy theorists and Trump himself to distort reality in a way that made the other side seem more monstrous and evil. The reality television star who tried to prevent Muslims from building a community center near Ground Zero and spread a conspiracy theory that Obama wasn't really an American was now, as president, an authority for the large segment of people who shared the same fears and believed the same falsehoods. The Tea Party supporters Trump claimed as his own in 2010—"the Tea Party loves me"—shared not only a deep dislike for Obama but a troubling tendency to believe things that were demonstrably untrue. Two national surveys of the electorate in 2012 found that voters who identified as Tea Party Republicans were far more likely than other Republicans to believe various fallacies: Obama was born in a different country (51 percent of Tea Partiers said yes compared with 37 percent of other Republicans); Obama was a Muslim (52 percent vs. 40 percent); Iraq possessed weapons of mass destruction when the United States invaded in 2003 and the Affordable Care Act implemented "death panels" (64 percent of Tea Partiers said yes to both). Noting this trend at the time, two political scientists observed that Tea Party adherents "appear to exist in their own distinct cognitive world."

Where did they learn to accept these fallacies as fact? Apart from Fox News and websites like *Breitbart,* Rush Limbaugh was perhaps the most influential force reshaping the right's current belief system. Trump and Limbaugh, who became golfing buddies after the election, shared a showman's intuition for giving the audiences what they wanted—and understood to stay away from what it didn't want. "Rush understood it better than anybody," Trump says. Together they helped build the foundations of a philosophy for their followers that was rooted in a sense of victimization, exclusion, and systemic unfairness. For years, Limbaugh made a case for why his listeners should mistrust the institutions that Americans interacted with in their daily lives. He coined a name for them: "the Four Corners of Deceit"—government, media, academia, and science. Their job was to "lie to students and the American people," he said. He claimed that the ultimate goal of the leaders of these cabals was a form of mind control that presented lies as irrefutable facts. This framework gave him a way to explain away societal ills. Pervasive racism? It was a myth that made Americans hate their country. Global warming? "Everybody knows it's a hoax," Limbaugh insisted. Many of his fans believed they were experiencing something akin to enlightenment as Limbaugh lectured to them. "I feel like I'm back in school . . . I'm getting so much good information from you," said a caller named Mary, from Castroville, Texas, when she spoke to Limbaugh on the air in 2017. Mary sounded especially annoyed at the suggestion that racism was still a major cause for concern in the United States. "Maybe I've been asleep for a long time, but when did we become such a racist society?" she asked. Limbaugh told her she was right. "We just elected the first Black president, the richest TV personality in America is a Black woman," he said, "and yet at the same time they want to tell us what racists we all are?"

The absence of much of an objective standard of truth in this media bubble meant that by the time someone like Trump came along, his reality could become theirs—and the Republican Party's. He changed the kinds of policies Republicans had to embrace, the way they had to conduct themselves as officeholders and candidates, and even their acceptance of which foreign countries Americans should consider their true adversaries. He could challenge bedrock American values by embracing authoritarians and they wouldn't criticize him for it.

During Trump's first year in office, the Republican pollster Whit Ayres put together a deck of slides for his clients that showed the numerous ways Republicans had shifted their views on bedrock principles, an exercise that he found both depressing and eye-opening as a way of getting Republicans to understand the strength of the new president's grip on voters. The deck showed that support for free trade had dropped sharply from 2015, when 56 percent of Republicans said they thought it was sound policy, to just 36 percent who said so. Trump was also helping turn them against entire institutions of American society. Ayres noted a steep drop in the percentage of Republicans who said that colleges and universities had a positive effect on the country: 54 percent in 2015, compared with 36 percent two years later. Ayres also showed how the share of Republican voters who were accepting of bad conduct from their political leaders had grown. The percentage who said they believed that a politician could be a good public servant even if he or she behaved immorally in private had more than doubled from 2011 to 2016, from 36 percent to 70 percent. Then there was a slide on the approval rating of Vladimir Putin of Russia. One-third of Republicans had a favorable impression of him—triple the share who said they did in 2015. A considerable faction of the party of Ronald Reagan had evidently forgotten or now disregarded Reagan's exhortations about the "Evil Empire" that was the Soviet Union. They scoffed at the notion that Trump was betraying American values when he befriended and spoke admiringly of the murderous dictator of North Korea, Kim Jong-un. "Why shouldn't I like him?" Trump once told Sean Hannity during an interview. When Obama's administration engaged Iran in an attempt to prevent the country from developing nuclear weapons, Republicans said he was treasonous. When Trump did the same with an actual nuclear power that had threatened to strike the United States, he was Winston Churchill.

Trump's ability to alter the way his followers saw major policy debates even seemed to apply to immigration, the issue that he had taken a zero-tolerance approach with during his campaign. The Heritage Foundation, which conducts regular online opinion surveys of its members, asked a question after Trump's election about whether it would make a difference to their own views if Trump suddenly reversed himself and said he would support being more lenient with the millions of undocumented immigrants living in the shadows by offering them a form of legal status. Much to the astonishment of Heritage staff who were privy to the survey results, a majority of those who responded said they would be fine with it as long as Trump was.

One of the simplest and most effective ways of signaling one's solidarity with the president was to act like him and talk like him. Todd Harris, a Republican strategist who had worked for a mix of insurgent and establishment candidates for over two decades, was by no means a Trump Republican. He had worked on John McCain's 2000 presidential campaign as a junior staffer and for Arnold Schwarzenegger's gubernatorial campaign in California. In 2016, he advised and made ads for Marco Rubio while Trump decimated Rubio's hopes of becoming president with schoolyard taunts about "Little Marco" and his flop sweat. In 2018, one of Harris's clients was Brian Kemp, the secretary of state in Georgia who was fighting an uphill battle for the Republican nomination for governor. Kemp would need to beat the party establishment's favored candidate and heir apparent, the lieutenant governor, Casey Cagle. To do that, he would use the old strategy of getting to the right of the front-runner on touchstone culture war issues like guns and religion. But Harris knew that it wasn't enough just to get to the right of an opponent anymore. Kemp would have to outdo his rival in a contest that was more performative than philosophical.

Harris had started pitching clients with a new vision for how the Republican Party had evolved in the days since Reagan. No longer was the GOP like a stool with three legs, each representing a segment that cared most about a single issue: social conservatism, economic conservatism, and national defense. Harris said there was now a fourth leg to the proverbial stool that was all about attitude. He called it "stylistic conservatism," reasoning that voters cared just as much, if not more, about the way a candidate talked as they did about what specific issues the candidate supported. The more aggressive, unfiltered, and politically incorrect, the better.

Harris got his first taste of how successful this formula could be before Trump was a factor in Republican politics, in the 2014 Iowa Senate race. His candidate, a little-known state senator named Joni Ernst, shot to the front of the pack of Republican candidates after Harris produced an ad in which Ernst talks about applying a skill she acquired growing up on a farm—how to remove a hog's testicles— to Washington. "I'm Joni Ernst. I grew up castrating hogs on an Iowa farm," she says, smiling, with a twinkle in her eye. The ad, with its catchy tagline "let's make 'em squeal," became one of the most memorable spots produced by any Senate campaign in the television era, and it helped Ernst win the primary and the general election. Harris, a native Californian, got the idea after talking to Ernst one day about what it was like growing up in Iowa. "Wait, you did what?" he exclaimed.

Harris reasoned that with Kemp, leaning into political incorrectness like Trump did was the way to break out. One of Harris's ads featured Kemp vowing to "round up criminal illegals and take 'em home myself." In another, Kemp tried to burnish his Second Amendment credentials by polishing a shotgun while sitting next to a young man he said hoped to date one of his daughters. But the ad that Harris made right before the election was the one that most effectively channeled Trump's style and arguably won him the Republican nomination. Harris wasn't exactly a head-banging conservative, so Trump's style didn't come naturally to him. But he discovered it wasn't very difficult to emulate. In search of ideas, Harris had typed "politically incorrect" into a Google image search and found a sign that said "God, family and country." And that gave him the idea for an ad that showed Kemp standing next to his pickup truck delivering a monologue that could have come straight from Trump's mouth. "I'm Brian Kemp, and I believe in God, family, and country—in that order," he said. "I say Merry Christmas, and God bless you. I strongly support President Trump, our troops, and ironclad borders. I stand for our national anthem. If any of this offends you, then I'm not your guy." (In an earlier draft of the script, Kemp expressed his unapologetic political incorrectness with a bit more sarcasm, saying that if anyone was offended, "You should probably vote for my opponent. He supported Jeb Bush. So, you know.") After the ad ran, Trump endorsed Kemp, who in November was elected Georgia's new governor. The other standout ad Harris's firm produced that election cycle was one for the Republican congressman who would become Florida's next governor, Ron DeSantis. The spot shows DeSantis reading a copy of Trump's *The Art of the Deal* to his infant son and instructing his toddler how to build a wall with toy cardboard blocks.

As well as the Trump-facsimile approach worked to excite conservative voters, Republicans also had ample evidence in 2018 that becoming the Party of Trump was creating an energy of equal power that motivated voters against their candidates. Ayres, the GOP pollster, observed the dichotomy in focus groups often. He would find voters like a man who lived near Scranton, Pennsylvania, who declared that Trump was "the best president in my lifetime, and one of the best presidents in history." Then other voters would describe such strong aversions to Trump that they wanted to take it out on the entire Republican Party by voting against their candidates regardless of whether those candidates were allies of the president. Swing voters—especially those who were more moderate, higher income, educated, and female—were abandoning the party. And they were in a punishing mood. So powerful was this backlash against the president that top party strategists were bracing for a wipeout in the House of Representatives—even if Trump was in denial. By February, the Koch political operation had concluded that there was at least a 60 percent chance they would lose the House. Frank Luntz, the Republican strategist who advised Kevin McCarthy, gave a presentation to McCarthy's House colleagues that predicted Republicans would lose forty seats. Luntz urged a different approach than strategists like Harris and warned Republicans that they needed to do more than just regurgitate Trump-style one-liners and borrow from the parts of his message in 2016 that many found optimistic and unifying. "It is impossible to get Republicans to realize why Trump is so successful," Luntz complained at the time. "What they have picked up from Trump is the aggressive tactics. What they did not pick up is the sentiment that we are on the same side, we are fighting this battle together."

If there was very little that seemed positive about Republicans' messaging, that was likely because Trump himself was focused on revenge, having become obsessed with the Democrats, the special counsel, and Republicans he accused of disloyalty. His political instincts were often self-destructive. He endorsed Republicans who took his side against those who didn't, even when that meant his party was nominating a candidate for the general election that stood to lose to a Democrat. In South Carolina, he endorsed the Republican opponent of Representative Mark Sanford, a frequent Trump critic. Sanford lost. And on the night of the primary, the winning candidate, Katie Arrington, took to the stage at her victory party and declared, "We are the party of Donald J. Trump!" Trump was so proud of his apparent ability to dictate the fates of his detractors in the party that he boasted about it in a way that other Republicans took as a subtle threat: *Cross me and this could be you.*

He sometimes did so when his interference seemed almost certain to cost Republicans a House seat. Barbara Comstock was a Republican congresswoman from Northern Virginia whose district was filled with the kinds of well-educated, upscale voters who recoiled from Trump. She had managed to get through her primary without waking up one morning to find that Trump had endorsed her opponent on Twitter, which seemed more than a remote possibility to her given that she had criticized him on more than one occasion. Most recently, she had opposed Trump's threat to shut down the federal government over a dispute with Democrats about funding for his border wall. Comstock's district included large numbers of federal workers who would have been left without pay. She thought the idea was insane, not to mention something the nation's chief executive would be utterly irresponsible for endorsing.

By coincidence, Comstock was scheduled to visit the White House and meet with Trump and a small group that included other Republican lawmakers shortly after Sanford was defeated in his primary in June. Trump told Comstock that he was the reason the congressman had lost, which she took as a menacing, unspoken message: She should realize how lucky she was that he decided not to come after her. "I just put out a tweet, and he's gone," Trump said to her. "It was not subtle," Comstock recalls. But then Trump insisted he could help Comstock in her race, rewriting the history of his performance there in 2016 as he looked her in the eye. "I almost won Virginia," Trump said. In fact, he lost by more than 5 percentage points. Later on, with the general election just a short time away, Trump recorded a robocall urging voters to reelect Comstock—an attempt to insert himself in her race in a way that defied polling and logic. She had never asked for it. He was toxic in her district, she thought. And she was stunned when the head of the National Republican Congressional Committee, Steve Stivers, called her and said that Trump asked her to use it. She refused. "If he asks, say you called me and I didn't call you back," she told Stivers.

Comstock was blown out in November, losing to her Democratic opponent by more than 12 points. In Pennsylvania, Republicans lost races for Senate and governor by wide margins, and four of its incumbent members of Congress were defeated. In South Carolina, the Democratic candidate narrowly prevailed over Arrington. By the time all the ballots were counted, Republicans would lose forty seats, and with them their majority in the House. The possibility that Democrats would deploy their newly acquired investigatory power to uncover information they could use to impeach him was suddenly no longer abstract. And Trump's allies were already working to discredit and delegitimize any impeachment before it ever got off the ground.

A few days after Thanksgiving, David Bossie was the guest of honor at a party at a Midtown Manhattan steak house to celebrate the release of a book he co-authored with the former Trump campaign manager Corey Lewandowski. The subject of the book, and Bossie's remarks, hinted at what was to come. *Trump's Enemies* purported to pull back the curtain on what the authors described as a "Deep State" plot to undermine the president. And as Bossie stood in the middle of a private dining room to thank his guests, he warned of the "vast left-wing conspiracy" that was afoot in Washington—a mischievous appropriation of the phrase Hillary Clinton had used to describe the work of Bossie and others against her husband two decades earlier, the last time the country had gone through an impeachment crisis.

When Limbaugh told Trump after the 2016 election that the left would always hate him and never credit his achievements, the host was channeling the strain of grievance that he had cultivated for years on his show. The idea that critics of the president were consumed with and motivated by hatred was a new twist on an old sentiment that had been ingrained in American conservatism for decades. But in ways Limbaugh probably could not have known, he was giving Trump and his supporters a powerful and persuasive way to explain away Trump's worst transgressions. "We are watching pure, raw hatred," Limbaugh said in a comment typical of the president's praetorian guard in the right-wing media. "They hate the man, and they hate the people who elected him." Any outrage directed at Trump, no matter how justified, became a shield for him and his media allies. Sean Hannity described the people who wanted the president impeached as the "hate-Trump media mob." Kellyanne Conway claimed that these bitter, sad sacks "still can't get over the election results." Some of Trump's defenders were talking about his political opposition in militaristic terms as Democrats in Congress and an independent counsel continued moving forward with separate investigations into whether Trump had known about Russian efforts to help his campaign. Evangelical leaders were especially loud and histrionic on this point. "I believe we are in a coup d'état," said Franklin Graham, adding that Trump's enemies wanted "to destroy the president and take over the government by force."

On December 18, 2019, Trump became only the third American president to be impeached. The House of Representatives voted—with no Republican support—to approve two charges of high crimes and misdemeanors against him, stemming from a botched attempt to pressure the Ukranian government to investigate the family of former vice president Joseph Biden, the man Trump worried could be a serious impediment to his reelection. Few worked harder to legitimize for his audience new authority figures to help insulate Trump from political damage than Hannity, with his self-righteous claims of being on a mission to deliver "truth, every single night, every single week." Throughout Trump's term, but especially in its last two years, Hannity presented unsourced, unsubstantiated rumors from his guests as "investigative reporting that nobody else does," all in the name of "setting the record straight," as he liked to say.

This was the model he had used for years, cloaking the information he gave his audience with words that people traditionally associated with credible, nonpartisan journalism. "I describe what I do as the whole newspaper," Hannity explains. "Reporting, opinion, sports, gossip." He outrageously claims to produce more investigative reporting "than any other show in the country," attempting not just to put himself in the same league as an investigative powerhouse like *60 Minutes*, but above them. By appropriating the language of mainstream news gathering, as Jerome Corsi did, Hannity could establish himself as something more than just a talk show host. He was an authoritative source and a substitute for the objective news outlets he denigrated.

Two *Hannity* regulars who became all-stars in the lineup of Trump-friendly journalists were the writers John Solomon and Sara

Carter—"great, objective journalists," Hannity called them when he introduced them to his audience. He hosted the two on his show or prominently featured their work close to two hundred times in four years. Fox hired them both as contributors. The duo, who both cycled through a number of publications during Trump's presidency and sometimes self-published, helped spread the alternate narrative that Trump's dealings with Russia, Ukraine, and his subsequent impeachment weren't the real story. The actual wrongdoing, they claimed, was the cover-up of various abuses of power supposedly committed by Obama, Clinton, and Biden. Among other unfounded assertions they spread, Solomon and Carter's stories helped support Trump's seemingly out-of-left-field assertion that officials in the Obama administration had been "tapping my phones," as he claimed in a notorious 2017 Twitter post.

To Hannity, it was the biggest political story since Watergate. And a typical segment of his on the subject, which he covered repeatedly, sounded like a high school math teacher walking his students through a complex equation. This, from March 2017, was typical: "We're going to uncover two shocking pieces of evidence that may show the unmasked members of the Trump team may have been surveilled by officials inside of the Obama administration. . . . I want you to remember very crucial words, four words: surveillance, unmasking, intelligence leaking. Now, first, pay close attention."

Critics noted that the intentional use of repetition was a tactic of skilled propagandists because repetition leads to familiarity, which leads to acceptance. Hannity and other conservative media stars placed Solomon and Carter on a pedestal alongside the great journalists of the mainstream media, bolstering their authority and misrepresenting the veracity of their work. Mark Levin, Hannity's Fox colleague and a fellow top-rated radio host, once declared they were "like the Woodward and Bernsteins of our time." Hannity complained that their stories "deserve far more credit and coverage than you've been getting." Trump, who promoted their work from his Twitter feed, once asked why Solomon and his other media boosters hadn't been awarded the Pulitzer Prize. At a rally in October 2019, the audience howled as Trump called out his favorite media personalities by name, conferring icon status on them among his people: "Sean Hannity and Rush Limbaugh, Laura Ingraham and Tucker Carlson, Judge Jeanine. And Watters. My Watters," he said, referring to the buffoonish host of Fox's 5 P.M. show, Jesse Watters, who had once starred in a cringeworthy segment for Bill O'Reilly's show in which he approached Asian people in New York's Chinatown with racist questions like "Am I supposed to bow?" and "Do you know karate?" When Trump named Solomon, he asked, "Why aren't these people getting the real Pulitzer Prize? Because they were right. They called it right." People in the crowd nodded along. "Thank God we have them on our side," Trump said.

In reality, Solomon's work was so problematic that one of his employers, *The Hill,* started labeling his reports as opinion in 2018 and conducted an internal review of his articles after colleagues complained about his reliance on sources who had an interest in protecting Trump. Colleagues also suspected that Solomon was being protected by the publication's owner, Jimmy Finkelstein, a New York publishing executive who had been friends with Trump and his personal attorney Rudolph Giuliani for decades. Giuliani revealed in 2019 that when no one else would pay attention to dirt he claimed to have on the Biden family's business dealings, he handed it over to Solomon. "I really turned my stuff over to John Solomon," Giuliani said. "I had no other choice."

Trump later admitted in an interview with Hannity, of all people, which didn't draw much attention at the time, that his statement about having his wires "tapped" by Obama—the underpinning of one of the central story lines in right-wing media and the catalyst for the writing that made Solomon and Carter's work the right's gold standard for what it considered journalism—was something he basically fabricated. He admitted that he'd actually made the allegation based "on a little bit of a hunch." And he pointed out that he had put the phrase in quotes. "You can sort of say whatever you want," he explained. Hannity didn't bother to ask Trump for any clarification.

In February 2020, *The Hill* announced that it had completed a review of Solomon's articles and appended editor's notes to his work on Ukraine, saying it lacked important context and disclosure in many cases. By then, Solomon had left to start his own website, *Just the News*. He also published on his personal website, where his slogan was "Reporting Truth."

A nearly impenetrable protective space now enveloped Trump. Inside was an artificial reality where the baseline belief was that his failures were never the result of his own poor judgment, but rather were the fulfillment of the revenge fantasy that a rage-blinded mob had cooked up since the day he won. And by the beginning of the fourth year of Trump's presidency, with the impeachment proceedings winding down, an entire network of conservative journalists, radio hosts, cable news pundits, and activists was at work reinforcing a see-no-evil mentality when it came to the president's behavior. In service to him and the voters and viewers who wouldn't hear it any other way, they deployed an arsenal of half-truths, obfuscation, wishful thinking, and outright disinformation unlike any other modern political media campaign. In the year before Election Day 2020—a period during which he was impeached for abusing the power of his office; minimized a once-in-a-century global health crisis that would claim more than seven hundred thousand American lives; treated a national awakening on racial injustice as a personal attack; and ultimately lost his bid for a second term—Trump's approval rating among Republicans only dipped below 90 percent a handful of times, according to Gallup. And even the lowest point wasn't low at all. Eighty-five percent of Republicans still said he was doing a good job.

To experience 2020 inside this world was to see some of the most damning evidence ever to emerge about a president's abuse of the office as triflingly insignificant. It was to believe that the real bad actors were conspirators inside the government like career foreign service professionals and intelligence analysts. Later, those malign elements would include infectious disease experts, people wearing masks to protect themselves from a deadly airborne disease, a journalist who dared to ask of the president "What do you say to Americans who are scared?," and ordinary Americans who saw something meaningful in an incontestable three-word declaration of equality: Black Lives Matter. That is to say nothing about what the people living inside this bubble would believe if, for instance, the president poisoned their faith in the integrity of the country's electoral system with false stories about ballot rigging, and then told them that he had actually won when he hadn't. It wouldn't be true. But it was definitely what the audience wanted to hear.

As the end of his impeachment trial in the Republican-controlled Senate neared in early February 2020, Trump also pondered what to do about what could be his final State of the Union address. He told only a handful of aides about his plans. Trump had decided to invite Limbaugh as his guest and present him with the Presidential Medal of Freedom, the highest honor a civilian can receive. The invitation also caught Limbaugh entirely by surprise, who was with his wife preparing to head to the hospital for the first of several procedures to try to slow the Stage IV lung cancer spreading inside him.

"I need you down here tonight," the president told the radio host when he reached him on his cellphone. Trump, who relished using the presidential pulpit to antagonize his rivals and reward friends, loved the thought of Pelosi having to sit and listen as he lavished praise on a man liberals regarded as a Neanderthal. Limbaugh's cancer diagnosis added a split-screen dynamic that injected more drama into the scene that the president found delightful. He figured, correctly, that while Republicans would leap to their feet and cheer Limbaugh, Democrats would sit in stony silence. And then the right-wing media apparatus where Limbaugh was king would pounce on those "hate-filled" politicians, criticizing them for being unable to bring themselves to graciously applaud a dying man.

Later that week, after he received the cancer treatment that Trump's invitation had forced him to postpone, Limbaugh returned to the air and excitedly told his audience the details of his trip to

Washington. He spoke for so long he had to take four commercial breaks before he finished the entire story. Based on what he had seen of the president, Limbaugh told his audience that he was more certain than ever that Trump was on his way to a second term.

"He's unbeatable, folks. He's indomitable," Limbaugh declared.

★ ★ ★

CHAPTER 15

Dishonor and Defeat

We were getting ready to win this election.
—President Donald Trump, November 4, 2020

Two hundred and fifty Republicans sat in judgment of Donald Trump as Congress weighed whether to impeach him, remove him, and disqualify him from holding federal office again. Only one voted yes. Mitt Romney, the junior senator from Utah for a little more than a year, worked long, late nights during Trump's Senate trial in January and February. He gathered his staff at the end of the day's testimony to rehash what had happened. But nothing he heard ever really steered him away from the conclusion he had come to terms with: He was going to be the first senator in history to vote to remove a president from his own party. But it was hard to square his personal beliefs with what he could no longer deny the party had become. He was still just as uncomfortable with what he saw as the performative, outrage-fueled brand of politics that got rewarded with cable news coverage and votes in Republican primaries—and that was now the lifeblood of Trump's presidency. He already had a sense of the ugliness that was coming his way if he voted to convict Trump. Someone had called him "a traitor" recently when he was at the grocery store. Another person accosted him at an airport, shouting that the senator ought to be ashamed of himself. The organizers of CPAC told him he wasn't welcome to speak at their annual conference that year.

In the days before the final vote in Trump's Senate trial, Romney's mind was focused on one question: Was he, a duly elected United States senator, being faithful to the oath of office he swore under God to uphold to "defend the Constitution of the United States against all enemies, foreign and domestic"? It was the kind of penetrating question that put conscience above the pursuit of political power—a question that exceedingly few Republicans were willing to entertain in the open in 2020. And yet, Romney was a politician. By no means was he naïve or unconcerned about the reverberations that would follow. Romney understood—just like every other elected Republican did—that his future in the party that had chosen him as its standard bearer eight years earlier might now rise or fall on whether voters liked what he was saying about Trump. He and his staff were already working on a plan for how to smooth things over with Republican lawmakers and voters back home in Utah who would be calling for retribution. Still, until the night before the vote, Romney was reserving judgment, waiting for evidence from someone "in the room" with Trump, as he told his aides, who could clear him. But that never came.

On February 5 at 2:01 P.M., Romney stood at his desk at the back of the Senate chamber where the most junior members are assigned seats and began speaking. He didn't make it a minute before he started struggling to retain his composure. "I am profoundly religious. My faith is at the heart of who I am," he said, looking down at his notes and swallowing hard several times before he could continue. No one in the chamber moved—not the pages near the rostrum or the reporters in the press gallery. The stillness was more apparent because none of Romney's Republican colleagues were at their desks when he began speaking. A handful of Democratic senators looked on. Some were visibly emotional. The only Republican to show up was Senator Roger Wicker of Mississippi, who walked in after Romney started speaking. Romney's voice quavered as he regained his composure. "I knew from the outset that being tasked with judging the president, the leader of my own party, would be the most difficult decision I have ever faced. I was not wrong," he said. But Romney believed that Trump had violated the promise he made before God and committed an egregiously self-serving wrong. "Corrupting an election to keep oneself in office is perhaps the most abusive and destructive violation of one's oath of office that I can imagine," he went on. When he was finished, Romney and two aides who had accompanied him into the chamber slipped out a side door to avoid the more crowded corridors where reporters would be waiting. They made their way down a long corridor in the Capitol basement where senators have small, private offices without saying a word. The silence broke only momentarily as they were about to step into an elevator and the senator's chief of staff turned to his boss and insisted that he go first. "After you."

Romney made a point of mentioning in his speech that he expected to hear abuse from angry constituents, Trump supporters, and the president himself immediately. He was not wrong. Within hours of the vote, Republicans in the Utah state legislature started moving against him. A freshman state representative named Phil Lyman, who kept a Trump-autographed MAKE AMERICA GREAT AGAIN hat in a Plexiglas case in his office, drafted a resolution to censure Romney. The speaker of the state house called for a separate resolution that he said would be Utah's way of "paying tribute" to Trump, but would also spare the senator from rebuke. Romney, who had been elected in 2018 with 62 percent of the vote, hopped on a flight to Salt Lake City to contain the damage. He met with lawmakers at the state capitol the next day, not as the political titan he once was in a state that revered him but as the deposed leader of his party asking for a pardon. Some of the legislators accused him of trying to settle scores with the president. "You're out to get Trump," one of them said. "How are we supposed to think this isn't just another way to get even with him?" asked another. Some conservatives had also started talking about another way to retaliate: by reviving controversial legislation to give Utah voters the unprecedented power to recall Romney and any other U.S. senator. It was an audacious attempt to rewrite the rules of the electoral process and almost certainly unconstitutional, as only the Senate has the power under the law to expel its members.

After a few days, the censure resolution died as legislative leaders said they were eager to get past the rancor of impeachment. Republicans dropped their talk of pushing the recall bill. But Romney hardly got a totally reprieve. Elsewhere, Republicans would continue to try to write Romney into the history books as a traitor and a sore loser in Trump's party. "Romney," declared Lou Dobbs of *Fox Business*, "is going to be associated with Judas, Brutus, Benedict Arnold. Forever." The president's son Donald Jr. called on Romney to be expelled from the Senate, something that hadn't happened since the chamber removed members from the South during the Civil War for supporting the Confederacy. Trump, who still fumed in private that Romney had "blown it" in the 2012 election and gloated that he had accomplished what Romney could not, spoke at the National Prayer Breakfast in Washington the day after his acquittal. He used the event, a bipartisan tradition, to settle scores with Romney by questioning his religious conviction. "I don't like people who use their faith as justification for doing what they know is wrong," he said. Even Romney's niece, the Republican National Committee chair Ronna McDaniel, twisted the knife. "This is not the first time I have disagreed with Mitt, and I imagine it will not be the last," she said. "The bottom line is President Trump did nothing wrong, and the Republican Party is more united than ever behind him." On her last point, McDaniel wasn't spinning. In February, Gallup said it recorded its highest approval rating yet for Trump among Republicans: 94 percent. Among Democrats, just 7 percent approved. Gallup said the partisan polarity was the largest it had measured "in any Gallup poll to date."

By creating a distinct world in which his followers took in information that largely confirmed what they already believed, Trump usually excluded mention of inconvenient truths. His tribute to Limbaugh at the State of the Union went on for about three minutes. That was far more time than he devoted in his speech to an emerging threat to all Americans and to the world: a deadly new coronavirus strain that had officially killed 490 people in China and was spreading rapidly across Asia. In the weeks and months that followed, Trump would claim repeatedly that the virus "came out from nowhere," blindsiding him and his administration. But that revisionist account of what was known at the time is plainly at odds with the facts—not only facts uncovered in private email exchanges between administration officials and confidential White House memos, but facts that were readily apparent to anyone who glancingly followed the news. The February 5 front page of *The New York Times,* which led with news of Trump's address to the nation, also prominently featured a story about the Chinese government's failures to get a handle on the rapidly escalating situation. The paper cited a statement from the Communist Party leadership that said the virus was putting incredible strain on the nation and would be "a major test of China's system and capacity for governance." Inside the White House, a top official had already warned that a crisis of similar scale was possible in the United States, with enormous potential costs in dollars and lives. Peter Navarro, a brusque, hard-charging adviser on trade and economics, wrote a memo dated the week before the president's State of the Union that projected more than half a million deaths because the nation was effectively "defenseless" in the event of a full-blown outbreak. After Navarro failed to get Trump to heed his warnings, he wrote a second memo that contained even grimmer projections for the country. "As many as 1–2 million souls," Navarro wrote, could perish. The memos struck an alarmist tone, which Navarro was known for taking in almost any situation regarding China. But they also provided a detailed analysis of how to apply the lessons of other recent pandemics to the present and data on how many people each person infected with the virus appeared to spread it to. Much of what was in the memos was prescient.

The alarm bells that Trump aides like Navarro were ringing in January raise many questions about Trump's timidity in approaching the coronavirus and whether he could have brought his base around to seeing the threat for what it was if he'd acted on the information available to him at the time. Navarro was an unapologetic economic nationalist and China hawk, placing him in a camp with conservative Trump allies like Bannon who had helped sever the Republican Party from decades of orthodoxy on free trade. Trump's base had come around to seeing China as an untrustworthy adversary, as had many other Americans who found Trump distasteful. Trump had a logical and politically viable argument to make to his base. The playbook had already been written by Navarro and like-minded allies like Tucker Carlson of Fox News and Senator Tom Cotton of Arkansas: An adversarial, totalitarian government had systematically and violently tried to suppress information about the virus, they argued, and now that we know how dangerous it is, Americans need to work together to protect themselves. But Trump was unable to see it this way, so his supporters wouldn't either. His thoughts clouded by rage over the impeachment, he did not understand the virus to be a collective threat. He saw only a threat to him and his reelection—another "hoax" that his enemies had cooked up to hurt him. And most of his protectors in the conservative media were happy to feed and promulgate this story. In those early days before fearful Americans would shut themselves in their homes and stay there for a year or more, the virus had already become another flashpoint in the culture war that Trump supporters waged against his perceived enemies.

Fox News's Laura Ingraham was among the loudest voices in the president's ear telling him that the virus was not a dangerous public health crisis but hype—a false narrative, she said, pushed by "Trump haters" who needed a problem to pin on him. "It seemed like some of the Trump haters were actually relishing in this moment," Ingraham said in late February on her prime-time program. "A new avenue it was: a coronavirus. That's a new pathway for hitting President Trump," Ingraham claimed. She did some math for her viewers. If eighty thousand people were infected worldwide, she told them, consider that eighty thousand people also died of what she called "regular old influenza" in the United States alone in 2017.

Two days later, Hannity began his program with an especially rageful monologue. To emphasize how little concern he had about the deadly respiratory illness, his producers flashed a giant white zero on the screen to emphasize the point that no one in the United

States had died. He sounded scornful and sardonic. "Tonight, I can report the sky is absolutely falling. We're all doomed. The end is near. The apocalypse is imminent. And you're going to all die, all of you, in the next forty-eight hours. And it's all President Trump's fault." When Trump flew to South Carolina later that week to hold a rally outside Charleston, where some people slept in tents and huddled under blankets all night outside the venue, he expressed the same kind of disbelief and denial to the crowd. He attacked the press for being in "hysteria mode" while offering false reassurances to his supporters. "One of my people came up to me and said, 'Mr. President, they tried to beat you on Russia, Russia, Russia.' That did not work out too well. They could not do it. They tried the impeachment hoax." Now, Trump said, this person told him that his enemies were trying to pin the virus on him. "This is their new hoax," the president declared. In a normal year, thirty-five thousand people die from the flu, he said. Sometimes it "goes up to a hundred thousand people." And then he noted the nonexistent death toll: "So far we have lost nobody to coronavirus in the United States. Nobody." The crowd cheered. But it would take only one day to prove him wrong. On Saturday, February 29, news of the first confirmed coronavirus death in the United States was reported in Washington State.

What Trump and many of his supporters never seem to have considered very seriously was the fact that treating a public health crisis as if it was just another one of Trump's political grudge matches might result in large-scale death. And so tens of millions of Americans who got their information from pro-Trump sources like Ingraham and Hannity heard in those early days that a once-in-a-lifetime pandemic was actually downright ordinary, possibly keeping many of them from taking precautions that could have slowed the rate of infection and saved lives.

Research later emerged showing how Fox's coverage contributed to the spread. A study published by the University of Chicago in late 2020 found that *Hannity*'s viewers took an average of four to five days longer than viewers of other Fox News programs to start washing their hands more frequently, limiting their contact with others, or taking other mitigating steps. The researchers said that difference of just a few days, while seemingly insignificant, was critical because other studies estimated that roughly half of the deaths in the early stages of the pandemic could have been prevented if distancing and stay-home orders had been implemented just a week earlier.

The Chicago study also examined county-level data on COVID infections and death and established a link between higher COVID spread and *Hannity* viewers compared with people who watched Tucker Carlson's show, which initially took a much more serious tone with its virus coverage and warned viewers in late February that more than one million Americans could eventually die. The study concluded that "greater local viewership of *Hannity* relative to *Tucker Carlson Tonight* is associated with a greater number of COVID-19 cases starting in early March and a greater number of deaths resulting from COVID-19 starting in mid-March." Eventually, Carlson did as any ratings-conscious host would who relied on the sustained affection of Trump supporters and didn't maintain his cautious posture for long. By the fall, as experts were warning that a second, deadlier wave of infections was imminent, Carlson was blaming Democrats and the media for inciting "politically motivated hysteria." Even when Trump caught the virus himself, the Fox host claimed that the president's enemies were exploiting the situation to keep the country living in fear. "They need you to be afraid," Carlson said. "Perpetually. Otherwise, you won't obey them."

It became common in right-wing media to mock and attack the experts who urged people to stay home and limit contact with others— just as if they had been Trump's pursuers in the Justice Department or the Democratic House conference. When Limbaugh weighed in on February 28, he dismissed concern over the virus as hateful hype. He cited for his audience as proof a publication with a troubling history of distorting scientific facts called *The Western Journal*. It had recently reported that the virus "appears far less deadly" than the flu. As Limbaugh read from the article, he sounded as certain of what it said as if the information had come from the Mayo Clinic. In fact, *The Western Journal* was a clearinghouse for right-wing misinformation that had been blacklisted the year before by *Apple News* for promoting articles that the tech giant determined were "overwhelmingly rejected by the scientific community." Had Limbaugh been up-front with his audience about the available research at the time, as limited as it was, he could have informed them that COVID-19 was believed to have a death rate that was about ten times higher than that of the common flu.

People who were taking precautions to protect themselves and urging others to do so became something else in the eyes of Trump defenders: emblems of a weak, overly feminized country of snowflakes that couldn't tough it out. They brushed off the alarmingly high mortality rate for older Americans, mocking those who think "it's novel that 80 year olds are dying at a high rate from a flu." Those were the words of Candace Owens, a conservative YouTube personality, in a tweet to her two million followers on Twitter. The demean-and-deflect attitude from people like Owens, who dismissed the lockdowns and public health warnings as part of a "mass global mental breakdown," was just the kind of hardheaded defense Trump loved. And when he held a reception at the White House to honor African American History Month in late February, he invited Owens and then praised her as "a real star." The blasé attitude became another expression of Trump tribalism. And it flourished on social media, where Trump supporters shared memes that scorned those who weren't as dismissive of the threat. One was an image of a red T-shirt that said I SURVIVED CORONAVIRUS 2020. And the poohpoohing continued on Fox News. A guest on *Fox & Friends* on March 13 was a sixty-five-year-old woman who claimed to have caught the virus but said it was nothing—she claimed to have barely felt ill.

By the end of March, there wasn't any question about the truth. The United States surpassed China as the country with the most known coronavirus cases. The pathogen was ravaging New York City, the epicenter of the outbreak where hundreds of people were dying every day. At Elmhurst Hospital Center in Queens, a short distance from Trump's boyhood home, some patients died while waiting for a bed. The scene, as described by one doctor, was "apocalyptic." Two city hospitals reported that their morgues had already reached capacity. On March 31, Drs. Anthony Fauci and Deborah

Birx, two of the leading health experts coordinating the government's response, issued a shocking estimate for how many Americans could eventually fall to the disease: between 100,000 and 240,000.

Trump had occasional, fleeting moments of empathy, concern, and fear. The death of a friend from New York in April, a businessman named Stanley Chera, hit him especially hard. In private, Trump seemed unnerved and surprised that the virus had taken his life since he believed that Chera, who was just a few years older than him, was a physically strong man—"a bull" as Trump described him. There was another time when Trump saw on television how dire the situation was at Elmhurst, a scene that quite literally drove it all home for Trump. At a press conference, he spoke with a sense of anguish, recalling how he could picture the way Elmhurst looked as a child, down to the color of the paint outside and the size of its windows. "I've seen things that I've never seen before," Trump said, describing the freezer trucks brought in to store the quickly accumulating dead. "I mean, these are trucks as long as the Rose Garden, and they are pulling up to take out bodies. And you look inside and you see the black body bags. What's in there?" he said in disbelief. "Must be supplies. It is not supplies. It's people."

But more often he was focused on petty, self-aggrandizing pursuits. He not only demanded that his name be printed on the $1,200 economic relief checks that Americans started receiving in April, he wanted it stamped on the government-issued public health guidance too. The oversized postcards that the Centers for Disease Control and Prevention sent out with tips on how to slow the spread of the virus were slapped with the label PRESIDENT TRUMP'S CORONAVIRUS GUIDELINES FOR AMERICA. He was, as usual, fixated on appearances. So he wouldn't put on a mask once the CDC started recommending them for more than just frontline workers.

His pollster Tony Fabrizio showed him data that indicated he would suffer no meaningful backlash from his supporters if he wore one in public. Over the span of five years of polling Republicans in the Trump era, Fabrizio had observed that the president's voters behaved differently than any other political constituency he'd studied.

They granted him an extraordinary degree of leeway to behave crassly, to contradict himself, and to slaughter Republican sacred cows. He could change their opinions about people and issues. Their positions became his. He told Trump he was "a pied piper" who played for his supporters "the tune that they want to follow." Trump's most loyal voters wouldn't punish him for putting on a mask more often, Fabrizio argued. His voters could excuse almost any criticism or accusation against him, seeing what they wanted to see. Fabrizio had experienced this in his own family. When the Russian inquiry started, his own father immediately said that anything investigators turn up in Trump's finances was no big deal, reasoning that development was a business where everyone got their hands a little dirty. "A New York developer has to pay off people, big surprise," his father said. Fabrizio was amazed. "Are you preemptively excusing this?" Despite the widespread perception that Trump had mishandled the pandemic and the harm that was causing to his reelection chances, Fabrizio could see in his data that there were still enough swing voters who could be led to believe that Trump was capable of being a focused and serious leader. Plenty of Americans said Trump had done a good job when they were asked about his handling of individual COVID-mitigation measures such as getting medical supplies to states. They'd see a mask mandate in the same vein, Fabrizio told the president. Many supporters would probably write it off as if it wasn't really his choice. *Those Washington consultants told him to do it.* Another campaign pollster, John McLaughlin, agreed that Trump wouldn't hurt himself politically but also left him an out: "You have to be who you are," McLaughlin said.

Trump thought it would look "phony," he told aides. For someone whose entire professional and political life was oriented around having the right look, he still couldn't see why this particular look was good for his political prospects. "In other words, the sole purpose of doing a news conference would be to show up in a mask," he objected. Perhaps it would have seemed like an empty gesture to some supporters. More likely, it was the idea that allies like Bannon had put in his head, recalling Trump's statement that his supporters were so committed to him that he could shoot someone on Fifth

Avenue and get away with it: *If you put on a mask, there goes your superpower with your people. And if you did shoot someone on Fifth Avenue, they'd be calling the cops.*

Aides urged Trump to call off his scheduled campaign rallies, arguing that the media and much of the public would see them as super-spreader events. He reluctantly agreed. Deprived of his preferred outlet for communicating with and performing for his supporters, Trump started holding daily televised briefings from the White House. He had said to friends and staff alike that he was always intrigued by the idea of hosting "fireside chats" similar to what FDR had done with his periodic radio addresses to the nation as it struggled through depression and world war. The phrase, coined by a CBS station manager, invoked the reassuring image of the president inviting himself into every American home and taking a seat by the fireplace for a friendly conversation. Trump's daily briefings, by contrast, were short on warmth. They gave him the opportunity for an hour or more each day to vent, insult, brag, and congratulate himself. Often he showcased first responders, scientists, and executives of companies supplying medicine and equipment. But it was Trump who would return to center stage and commandeer the show. He cast himself as the hero of the pandemic—a wartime president, he said, who belonged in the pantheon of greats like Lincoln and Roosevelt. He spewed contempt at the news media, which he blamed for never acknowledging the hard work he put in and the successes that followed. "When you read the phony stories, you—nobody—nobody acknowledges this," he huffed during one briefing.

He indulged in excessive self-pity, credit-taking, and an audacious revision of history. When he praised members of his administration and others for their hard work, he often slipped in a compliment for himself. Acknowledging the work of the Food and Drug Administration commissioner, Stephen Hahn, Trump said, "He's worked, like, probably as hard or harder than anybody." Then he corrected himself. "Other than maybe Mike Pence. Or me," the president added. A *New York Times* analysis of more than 260,000 words spoken by the president over more than a month of briefings found that the most recurring utterances from Trump by far were self-congratulations—occurring roughly six hundred times. The briefings would last two and a half hours on some days. The cable news networks carried them live seven days a week without interruption. Historians could not recall any instance of any president in the television era seizing for himself a platform with such scope and reach. "It was thought that presidents were extraordinarily powerful at the height of the Cold War when they could ask the three networks for twenty minutes of TV time," Michael Beschloss, a presidential historian, observed. "But as far as a president's being able to exert influence, I think this is much greater than that." Trump supplemented the briefings with interviews with friendly hosts, usually on Fox News. And he received little pushback as he made himself out to be the most victimized leader in the nation's history. "It's so unfair. It's so unfair," he complained to Hannity in an interview in late March. "If we could only have a fair media in this country." In May during another Fox interview that was broadcast from the Lincoln Memorial, Trump claimed that he had been more abused than the sixteenth president, who was of course assassinated. "I believe I am treated worse," he said with the giant marble likeness of Lincoln looming over him.

Trump's self-indulgent wallowing grew even more disconnected from a nation in crisis on May 25 when a white Minneapolis police officer killed a Black man, George Floyd, after kneeling on Floyd's neck for eight minutes and forty-six seconds. The incident, caught on camera and broadcast to a nation whose nerves were frayed by the pandemic, caused even many conservative white Americans to reassess their thoughts on racial inequality. Such introspection eluded Trump. As with the coronavirus, the sensationalistic nature of cable news, and Fox News in particular, colored his perception of the seriousness of the problem and the motives of his critics. One day soon after Floyd's killing, Trump met with a group of Republican campaign officials and strategists at the White House and surprised many of them with what he was most focused on as cities across the country convulsed in protest: his seething anger at the media. Trump asked everyone in the room to air their grievances about the way news outlets covered stories and to say which cable news channel was worse, CNN or MSNBC. When lawmakers proposed taking the names of Confederate officials off institutions like military forts, Trump mocked the idea as a politically correct folly. "And then what are we going to name it? We're going to name it after the Reverend Al Sharpton?" he said when asked about renaming Fort Bragg, the North Carolina military installation named for a Confederate officer. He insisted against the advice of advisers that monuments to the South needed to be protected as a matter of preserving "a great American heritage," a dog whistle term that was often used to defend racist symbolism. He attacked protesters who knelt—a nod to how Floyd died, strangled under the officer's knee—as unpatriotic because he associated the gesture with the NFL players he went after on Twitter for kneeling during the national anthem. He boasted that he had done more for Black Americans "than any president since Abraham Lincoln." Asked about the pattern of officers killing unarmed Black people, Trump denied it was a big problem and attacked the interviewer. "What a terrible question to ask," he snapped at CBS News's Catherine Herridge. "So are white people. More white people, by the way."

Just like the virus, a national reckoning on racial inequalities became for Trump another culture war battle that he took as a personal attack. The belief system of the American conservative and the immense value it places on the ideal of the self-made man sees the failure of an individual before it sees the failures of the systems and institutions that are often biased against particular individuals. To acknowledge that the crime, poverty, and education problems endemic in many predominantly Black communities were the legacy of slavery and the century and a half of unequal treatment that followed was to acknowledge that there was something deeply flawed about America. People who believed in the nation's exceptionalism not only as an article of faith but as a defiant rejection of the doubt and cynicism they saw liberals often expressing about their country had a harder time seeing this. As far as many of them were concerned, America couldn't still be a racist country in 2020, whatever its past sins may have been. After all, it had *twice* elected a Black president and made Oprah one of the wealthiest businesswomen on earth, the thinking went. Trump continued lashing out. He threatened the "thugs" and "all other forms of Lowlife & Scum" at the demonstrations. "When the looting starts, the shooting starts," he warned on Twitter. He seemed trapped in the past—if not 1968 with his Nixonian talk of maintaining "law and order," then in his campaign four years earlier when he had spoken ominously of decrepit inner cities and festering crime. Frank Luntz, who had surveyed likely voters about Trump's messaging on the protests, shared his findings with Republicans on Capitol Hill: The effect of using the phrase "law and order" so often, he said, was to "conjure up images of people getting clubbed in the head." Luntz said it was a strategy doomed to fail. "He's talking to the people who show up at his rallies and who decided they were going to vote for him three and a half years ago." The weight of it all—the pandemic, millions of people out of work, millions protesting in the streets—was too much. Fabrizio met with the president in the Oval Office to brief him on his latest findings. At this rate, if Trump didn't make a more sincere attempt to tone it down, the election would be lost. "Mr. President, voters are just fatigued. They're tired," Fabrizio told him. Trump erupted. "They're fucking fatigued? They're tired? I'm fucking tired!"

By midsummer, Republican Party leaders in Washington had all the data they needed to know they should be prepared for a wipeout at the ballot box. Internal polling conducted on down-ballot races showed that voters were in the mood to punish Trump and the entire party, and that a repeat of the 2018 midterms was possible. Especially worrisome was the state of Georgia, where the early retirement of Senator Johnny Isakson meant that both of the state's Senate seats were on the ballot. Given that Republicans were already defending half a dozen other competitive seats and Democrats were well positioned to pick up a few of those, the possibility that control of the Senate could be decided in Georgia with those two races was remote but real enough to keep Mitch McConnell and his allies in Washington up at night. The senior senator, David Perdue, was a formidable incumbent who came from a brand-name political family in Georgia and was generally well regarded for a high-profile business career that included senior executive positions at Reebok and Dollar General. In July, private Republican polling showed that Perdue had dropped from being ahead by 7 points to down 2. But what was most worrisome wasn't that small deficit—a statistical tie, really—but the fact that voters said they didn't dislike Perdue. In fact, 44 percent said they approved of him and just 31 percent said they did not.

What this told party strategists, however, was alarming. And it was also clear statistical evidence pointing to the reality they couldn't deny any longer: The Republican Party was the party of Trump. The problem Republican candidates like Perdue were having didn't have anything to do with them. The problem was their association with Trump's party. Voters all across the country were taking out their frustrations with the president on other Republicans. Trump's unpopularity was costing Cory Gardner his seat in Colorado, who at that point was down 12 points. And in Michigan, where Republicans had one of their strongest and most dynamic candidates, a thirty-nine-year-old Black combat veteran and businessman named John James who spoke compellingly about the scourge of racist policing, they were still trailing by double digits. At one point, Trump was such a drag on his party's candidates that Republicans were forced to spend money to prop up Senator Dan Sullivan in Alaska, a state that hadn't voted for a Democrat for president since Lyndon Johnson. The executive director of the National Republican Senatorial Committee explained what was really happening with a candor that few in his party were willing to display: "I mean, it's not because of Dan Sullivan. I'm just telling you."

The antipathy that voters felt toward Trump was unlike anything Democrats had seen before either. Inside the Biden campaign, which was in the midst of narrowing down its vice presidential short list in late July, top strategists were looking to their research to help guide them on a pick. But what they found was that voters were not fixated on any individual potential number two. Instead, they wanted Biden to pick a running mate who would do no harm to his chances of defeating Trump. Anita Dunn, a senior Biden adviser, recalls how extraordinary it was that voters were thinking so strategically. "The only thing that voters care about is who can help you beat Donald Trump. It's all anyone wants to do. And I've never seen anything like this."

Friends noticed that the presidency had made Trump more bitter over the years. But the worst of it came that summer. "This was a guy who was celebrated most of his life," says Chris Ruddy, describing Trump's inability to make the transition from celebrity private citizen to the most powerful elected official on earth. He could not handle the criticism, scrutiny, demands for accountability, or pressure from the multiple investigations. "He was used to getting a lot of laudatory press, and he was not fully prepared. . . . Then suddenly, to be attacked. His code is to hit back. And then he starts punching back at everybody. Some part of the public likes that, and they think he's being real and honest." Of course, many Americans did not like it, and Ruddy and others looked at the closeness of the last election, and the demographic changes in the nation since then, and they knew Trump would lose if he didn't convince people he could lead them. In Ruddy's back-of-the-napkin analysis of the 2020 electorate, eight million whites over the age of fifty had died since 2016. That left Trump with about two million fewer voters. And since he had lost the popular vote by three million, Ruddy calculated Trump was behind by about five million overall—an almost certainly insurmountable deficit. "I talked to him about doing a five-trillion-dollar stimulus. I told him, 'You need to turn the cash on because the economy is in cardiac arrest.'" But Trump didn't buy it. He was living in the world where the people he believed were the ones telling him what he wanted to hear. "He's been told everything is coming back, we've got it under control, everybody is going to rehire."

Other allies were questioning his grip on reality. Tucker Carlson became so dismayed at Trump's evident self-destruction that he told friends half-jokingly that he was voting for Kanye West for president instead. Bannon, who had devoted his new podcast to vigorously defending the president during the impeachment and offering unsolicited communications strategy to West Wing staff he thought were clueless in the matter, worked his way back into Trump's good graces. By the summer, they were speaking again by phone, with Bannon riding out the pandemic on the 152-foot yacht of a Chinese dissident friend, Miles Kwok, and taking hydroxychloroquine prophylactically, the drug used to treat malaria that the Food and Drug Administration warned was ineffective and possibly dangerous as a COVID-19 treatment. Bannon usually found a way to look past his private doubts about Trump's seriousness and competence because he thought the president was the only political figure capable of uniting the fractious populist insurgency on the right that Bannon believed he could control himself one day. In private, he offered donors, senators, congressmen, political consultants, and journalists his honest assessment of Trump's flaws and strengths, which he was franker about than other Trump associates often were, many of whom Bannon denigrated as sycophants, like Corey Lewandowski. "Corey's the guy who wears the hats and buys the books," he said of Trump's first campaign manager, likening him to a Trump superfan. Roger Stone: "A fucking flake" and the kind of guy "you realize isn't crazy like a fox. He's just crazy." Bannon had a much higher regard for his own place in the hierarchy of Republican politics because, as he often claimed, he knew what he was getting with Trump—the good and the bad. He saw the president as "an instrument" or "a vessel" of discontent for tens of millions of Americans—"the deplorables" or "the hammerheads"—who felt sold out by both political parties. He also understood why Trump's opponents hated him so much. To suburban women: "He's the husband who cheated on you, the boss who sexually harassed you, and the dad who always forgot your birthday." Bannon warned the White House that Trump's need to overtake the news cycle was helping Democrats more than it was helping Trump: "You can't get him out of your head. He just dominates every day. It's like a nightmare. You'll do anything to get rid of it."

But Trump's inattentiveness to the pandemic alarmed Bannon.

And his response to George Floyd's death had him increasingly convinced that Trump had lost his mind. He complained to colleagues that Trump didn't seem interested in his job. "Being president and doing the job of president are two different things," he said. "He doesn't want to do the job of president of the United States." He told Rudy Giuliani at one point to relay a message to Trump that he evidently didn't have the stomach to deliver himself. Trump was not going to end up as a Roosevelt or a Lincoln in the history books, as he so often claimed. Instead, Bannon said, Trump would end up going down in history as one of the two or three worst presidents ever: "It'll be James Buchanan, Donald Trump, and Millard Fillmore." Having run Trump's successful underdog bid four years earlier during its final weeks, Bannon was openly critical of how the new team was running the reelection campaign. "Trump did not win in 2016. That's the one thing they never embraced and understood. Hillary Clinton lost. Trump did not win," he said. He complained that aides were showing Trump poll numbers that weren't real. "It's like showing Hitler fake armor divisions when the Reichstag is burning down," Bannon scoffed. Indeed, they were. To keep him from erupting in anger, aides often gave him selective slices of data that contained reasons for optimism from polls that otherwise were little reason to celebrate. They'd tell him he was improving in the Reno media market and with seniors in Phoenix. Said one aide, "They'd tell him he's up seventeen points with left-handed redheads in Pennsylvania."

Bannon agreed with the assessment of Trump strategists like Fabrizio that Biden's strategy of staying out of the public eye and doing very few public events was working by focusing all the attention on Trump and his inability to show the leadership that voters wanted. "All Biden needs to do," Bannon joked, "is issue a proof-of-life video every six weeks."

Here the country was struggling to overcome a pandemic and a recession, and the president was still complaining on Twitter. He shared with his eighty million followers posts that accused Pelosi of drinking "booze on the job" and ridiculed the weight of Stacey Abrams, the Georgia Democrat who was a rumored possible vice presidential pick for Biden. He praised Michelle Malkin, a far-right pundit who associated with anti-Semites, Holocaust deniers, and white nationalists. He spread false rumors that a talk show host who criticized him was involved in covering up the death of one of his interns. He posted a video of a supporter in New Mexico stating "the only good Democrat is a dead Democrat." And he didn't seem to care how badly he had mismanaged the White House response to the coronavirus. In mid-September, a new book from the veteran *Washington Post* journalist Bob Woodward came out, *Rage.* Based in part on eighteen interviews that Trump agreed to conduct with Woodward between December 2019 and July 2020, Woodward reported that Trump knew in early February how deadly and contagious the coronavirus was, even though publicly he was comparing it to an ordinary seasonal illness. The story blew up. Trump attacked Woodward and disputed the characterizations of the former administration aides quoted in the book who painted a picture of Trump as erratic, mean-spirited, and incompetent. "Made-up frauds, a con on the public," Trump insisted. But privately, he seemed pleased with himself when he talked to friends about the book. It was full of quotes from him and all anyone could talk about, he bragged. On October 19, fresh off his hospital stay after contracting COVID-19, he dialed in to a call for campaign staff and volunteers while he was in Las Vegas for a campaign event. At times, he slurred his words. Referring to early voting returns in Michigan, he claimed that he was so far ahead, "Nobody's ever seen a thing like that." Democrats, he said, had carried the early vote "for centuries." He then turned to his campaign manager, Bill Stepien, to back up his wild assertion. Stepien hedged, saying only that Trump was ahead of where the campaign expected him to be. Trump boasted about the reception he'd just had outside a fundraiser in Orange County, California, describing it as reminiscent of a true hero's welcome. "It looked like Lindbergh landed in the old days on Broadway," Trump said, a reference to Charles Lindbergh's ticker tape parade in 1917 to celebrate his record-breaking flight from New York to Paris—an event that an estimated four million people attended.

Bannon sometimes shared an observation about Trump that he seemed to find at once damning and deeply impressive: "He's the guy who'd pass the lie detector test. Like Bill Clinton. He believes it as soon as it comes out of his mouth."

The idea for what would become the biggest lie Trump ever told started to take shape that fall, as Bannon and Giuliani began talking about an election night bombshell. Trump would declare victory regardless of the outcome. Jonathan Swan of *Axios* first reported on the possibility on November 1, two days before the election. But for weeks before that, Bannon had been pushing the idea. Given the evidence the Trump campaign had in its internal polling, deciding to declare victory then with a few weeks still to go before Election Day was a farce. Bannon knew as much because he'd seen the polling himself. The campaign was nervous about losing Missouri, a state Trump had won by 18 points in 2016 but was now only up 2 or 3. Iowa and Ohio also looked too close for comfort—both must-win states. He was losing every battleground state in the Midwest and Arizona, which a Republican had lost only once since 1952.

Trump's tendency to doubt the credibility of elections whenever Republicans didn't win was not a new tactic. On the eve of the 2012 election, he tried to sow doubts about the integrity of the balloting ahead of Obama's reelection. He referenced a bizarre kind of election fraud, one that had not been covered much in the right-wing media's extensive body of work that dealt with election fraud. Trump claimed that votes for Mitt Romney had somehow been flipped in the counting process and tallied as votes for Obama. His fixation on the possibility that elections could be stolen did not end even after he won in 2016. He still claimed falsely that millions of immigrants had voted illegally, depriving him of a victory in the popular vote. By late September, Trump had begun asking friends and aides whether it might be a good idea to just declare victory on the night of the election regardless of what the vote count said. It was not an idea that he was sold on at first, but one that he found intriguing. It was also a move he assumed his conservative media allies would back. They'd demonstrated such little resistance to him after nearly four years in office. Why should they suddenly object now?

If Trump decided to go through with prematurely declaring victory on Election Day, there was only one network that could potentially pose a problem for him if it decided to rain on his parade. But Trump did not anticipate any trouble from Fox News, which was steering its voter fraud coverage in a favorable direction for him during the last few weeks of the campaign. Internal communications show that the network executive responsible for overseeing news gathering was encouraging staff to follow stories about minor election irregularities and hyping Trump's specious claims. On September 30, Tom Lowell, Fox's vice president and managing editor of news, announced the creation of a new endeavor called the "Election Integrity Project." Lowell, who had made a name for himself as Megyn Kelly's executive producer, said its purpose was to showcase "different stories where election integrity was potentially compromised." He would also describe the project as a "daily roundup/archive of voting ballot Irregularities." Fox reporters, editors, and producers received regular emails in the weeks before and after Election Day with reports about these alleged episodes, many of which would be disproven or cited misleadingly by Trump supporters to focus attention on run-of-the-mill election irregularities. In his email announcing the project, Lowell repeated a debunked claim of voter fraud as the kind of news the network would be tracking. These examples of supposed election malfeasance would be catalogued by state in a document that was updated every day and sent out to the staff, he said, writing that this included "E.g. erroneous NY ballots, ballots being thrown into rivers, etc." Of course, no errors would be significant enough to have potentially altered the outcome on November 3. There were no ballots dumped in a river, even if Trump had insisted otherwise during one of the debates. He appears to have been referring to a story from Wisconsin about the discovery of three trays of mail, which included several absentee ballots, on the side of a road near a ditch. Independent fact-checkers rated Trump's claim false, citing no evidence to suggest it was anything other than a coincidence that ballots happened to be in a larger batch of lost mail. Sometimes Lowell also directed Fox journalists to keep tabs on salacious, questionably sourced stories that other media were largely ignoring, like the accusations that Biden's son Hunter had used his family name to set up lucrative business deals in China. When Biden himself refused to address the allegations, Lowell urged his staff to keep on top of the story. "The Biden silent on Hunter angle is a great story," he wrote in an email that went out to the network's senior producers and politics team.

After four years of chipping away at the credibility of the institutions at the heart of a free and functioning republic—a press that keeps people informed about the workings of their government, a national security and law enforcement apparatus that protects them, a democratic system that ensures their votes will count—Trump, the Republican Party, and their allies in the conservative media had created an environment in which anything but a Trump victory would be viewed as illegitimate by his supporters. Trump didn't have to lie to them on election night. They already believed the other side was out to cheat him—and them.

But then on the night of the election, Fox News itself unexpectedly upended Trump's plans. It told the truth.

The decision that would pit Fox News against the president it helped create started with Rupert Murdoch. After the 2016 election, Murdoch was so unhappy with the arrangement the network had with the consortium that tabulated Election Day exit polls for the country's largest news organizations that he ordered Fox to pull out. Exit polls are notoriously noisy as data sets go. And Murdoch believed that the surveys, culled from interviews with voters across the country as they are exiting the voting booth, had misled him and Fox News forecasters into thinking Hillary Clinton was winning. Fox, along with the *Associated Press,* which also pulled out, created their own surveys of voters across the country that they could use to inform their decisions on calling races. It was a successful venture from the start. Fox demonstrated its willingness to go its own way in 2018 when it was the first to declare that the Democratic Party would win control of the House. The call angered Republicans at the time, who accused Fox of jumping the gun. But they were right.

The decisions inside Fox were made by a team that included the network's Washington managing editor, Bill Sammon, and Arnon Mishkin, an industry veteran who didn't work for Fox as a full-time employee. Mishkin didn't fit the Fox stereotype. He was a Democrat who lived on the Upper West Side. He understood his role as doing what Roger Ailes hired him to do: make the best calls and help Fox produce good television. And if that occasionally upset Republicans with calls on election night, all the better. He loved beating competitors and being right, which he usually was.

Before Election Day, Fox had been surveying a wide swath of 100,000 voters across the country who'd voted early in person and by mail. Then they compared that data with what they were seeing come back from Election Day surveys of voters at the polls. This much was clear: Donald Trump was losing. Arizona was looking especially bleak for the president. Other news outlets wouldn't call the state for days, but the data Mishkin was looking at from the pre-election polls, which matched up almost perfectly with the Election Day totals, meant that their modeling was correct. Just before 11:20 P.M., Sammon took a small step that he and other news executives had been doing as long as election forecasting had been a business. He scrolled the mouse on his computer over to the box that checked Biden as the winner in Arizona, a state the Democrats had only won once since Harry Truman in 1948. Sammon picked up the phone and was patched through to the control room and explained what was happening. It was Sammon's call alone to make, not Rupert Murdoch's or anyone else's in the Fox executive suite, who were aware of what was happening but did not stand in his way. That was a vestige of the way Ailes ran the network, preferring plausible deniability from the workings of his decision desk. "Roger wanted nothing to do with that," says Chris Stirewalt, who worked with Mishkin and Sammon on election nights. For days after the call, Fox anchors doubted the work of their colleagues on the air. Once, when the anchor Martha MacCallum questioned Mishkin with various "what if" scenarios implying that Trump still somehow had a chance, Mishkin made clear he was having none of it. "What if frogs had wings?" he asked sarcastically.

Mishkin's call short-circuited Trump's plan to declare victory. The president hesitated on going out to speak to the crowd that was waiting for him in the East Room of the White House. Biden would speak first, depriving the president of another opportunity to try to get out ahead of the unwelcome news. "Folks, the people of this nation have spoken. They've delivered us a clear victory, a convincing victory, a victory for we, the people," Biden declared. Trump was left to sulk, looking dour as he plodded out to the lectern set up for him in the East Room after 2 A.M. And despite the defiant tone he would take later, Trump at first sounded like a man defeated. He referred directly to Mishkin, conceding that "maybe" Arizona was lost after all. "The gentleman that called it, I watched tonight. He said, 'Well, we think it's fairly unlikely that he could catch up.' Well, fairly unlikely?" Trump said, sounding annoyed. As he wound down his remarks, he became angrier. "This is a fraud on the American public. This is an embarrassment to our country. We were getting ready to win this election," he said, catching himself and rephrasing. "Frankly, we did win this election."

Weeks passed. Trump still refused to concede, keeping false hope alive among his supporters with a flurry of weak lawsuits and his stubborn insistence that he'd been cheated. On November 20, one of them called in to Limbaugh's show. He said he had been at a Trump rally over the weekend that was full of people who refused to accept defeat. He explained how his son went with him and that he'd never seen such a massive crowd. "We saw more people than we've ever seen in our lifetime, ever—and we're season ticket holders for the Ravens, for gosh sakes. I've been in crowds of eighty thousand people," he said, growing more emotional as he continued. "I have never seen so many people. But were there any Republicans there? No. None. None!"

Limbaugh asked him to clarify. Was the man saying that the official Republican Party had turned its back on Trump? he asked. "You mean no elected Republicans? Is that what you mean?" The man said yes. "No one stands for us, Rush. Only you and Donald Trump." And then he appeared to cry. "I am not a revolutionary, Rush, but I would die for my president."

On the morning of January 6, Mitt Romney responded to an email from an old friend. The friend had seen video that had gone viral of a woman confronting the senator and demanding to know why he wasn't supporting Trump. Romney kept his cool and held firm. In the email, Romney's friend congratulated him and said he was proud. Romney responded by paraphrasing a quote Winston Churchill delivered in 1938 warning of the dangers of appeasing Adolph Hitler. "Republicans were given the choice between dishonor and defeat. They chose dishonor. And they will be defeated," Romney wrote.

Afterword

At first, some of the signs Liz Cheney was getting from fellow Republicans after January 6 were encouraging. There were the text messages she received from a county supervisor back home in Wyoming, who told her that morning he hoped she would object to the certification of the presidential election. But then, after he watched the assault unfold on television, the commissioner wrote her back and sheepishly recanted. *Never mind,* he said. Then there was the surprisingly candid rebuke of the president by one of his most steadfast allies in Congress, Kevin McCarthy, the House Republican leader. McCarthy, like nearly all members of Congress who were forced to flee to safety as the rioters overran the Capitol, had been deeply shaken by the attack. In a speech he gave on January 13, the day the House would vote to impeach Trump for a second time, McCarthy didn't go so far as to support the impeachment. But he did call on Trump to denounce the people who carried out the assault, and urged his colleagues to support a fact-finding commission and a censure resolution as the "prudent" course of congressional reproach. "The president bears responsibility for Wednesday's attack on Congress by mob rioters," McCarthy said. "Joe Biden will be sworn in as President of the United States in one week because he won the election, and his Presidency and this Congress will face immediate challenges that must be addressed. I stand ready to assist in that effort with good faith, goodwill, and an open hand."

Cheney, the third-ranking House GOP leader, was one of only ten Republicans who voted to impeach Trump that day. She had been single-mindedly defiant about confronting members of her own party who supported the president in his effort to push Congress and Vice President Pence to reject President-elect Biden as the rightful victor. Cheney, a trained lawyer and former State Department diplomat, did what came naturally as someone who took her work as a career civil servant seriously. She told other Republicans that what she saw in authoritarian countries—the cults of personality, the coups, the bloodshed—looked frighteningly close to what was happening in the Republican Party. She wrote a twenty-one-page memo laying out the legal and constitutional arguments against objecting to the election results, saying that it would "set an exceptionally dangerous precedent."

Then, after the attack, she called her friend and former colleague Denver Riggleman, who had been voted out of office after a rebellion by conservative activists in his district, and asked him to help her push back against the false claims by Trump and some of his allies that leftist, anti-Trump activists had staged it all. "Keep it short," she told Riggleman, reasoning that the only way some of Trump's most avid defenders in the Republican conference would read it was if it was simple and concise. The report that he produced on January 9 contained chilling revelations about the involvement of violent, pro-Trump vigilantes and right-wing hate groups in the attack. They had maps of the underground tunnels linking the Capitol to the office buildings in the larger Capitol complex where lawmakers and their staffs had their offices. On message boards they talked of bringing zip ties, handcuffs, and sniper rifles. "We will storm the government buildings, kill cops, kill security guards, kill federal employees and agents and demand a recount," wrote one commenter on a website that propagated the QAnon conspiracy theory.

Soon it became clear to Cheney that there was no amount of reason or logic that would work. In response to her efforts to bring the truth to light, members of the Republican conference shunned her and called for her to be removed from her leadership role. And McCarthy, whose remorse over the events of January 6 and Trump's role in inciting it proved fleeting, didn't stand in their way. Cheney heard her fellow Republicans—members of the party in which her family had been like royalty before Trump—calling for acts such as defying the courts; it sounded to her like sedition. She also was especially galled by lawmakers like Senator Ted Cruz, who was steeped in the meaning of the Constitution, for validating Trump's lies by arguing that it was appropriate to object to the election results. They had given people false hope that the outcome of the election could be reversed, she told colleagues. And when that hope didn't materialize, January 6 happened.

The violence of January 6 and the target the insurrectionists chose— the seat of American democracy—made it a singularly devastating moment in the country's history. But the emotions and fears that fed the attack were not unique, nor was it the first time that Republican politicians like Cruz had legitimized them. The gateway to the insurrection was opened in Texas in early 2015. That spring, lawmakers started getting a high volume of phone calls from constituents who were distressed about a training exercise the military was planning. The operation, known as Jade Helm 15, would be spread out over seven states in the South and West and last from July to September. It would involve more than twelve hundred troops from the Army Green Berets, Navy SEALS, and other elite, highly skilled forces. It was also somewhat of a mystery to the general public since the Pentagon kept details tightly held. Aware that some people would no doubt be unsettled by the sight of heavy military machinery and combat forces in their communities, federal officials had provided local governments with months of advance notice, hoping to head off any misinformation about what the troops would be doing.

Rather than telling Texans they had nothing to worry about, Cruz and other Republican lawmakers coddled the Jade Helm 15 conspiracy theorists. They argued that they had a duty to respond to legitimate questions their constituents had raised—no matter that these questions were untethered from reality. Cruz, who was running for president at the time, said that his office had reached out to the Pentagon for more information about the operation. He insisted that while he didn't personally doubt the government's explanation of the exercise, he didn't blame Texans who did. And he pointed a finger at the Obama administration, saying it had created the climate of mistrust in which Texans could be so fearful. "When the federal government has not demonstrated itself to be trustworthy in this administration, the natural consequence is that many citizens don't trust what it is saying," Cruz said. Governor Greg Abbott went further and directed the Texas State National Guard to monitor the military's movements. In a letter to the guard's commander that his office released to the media, Abbott implored the guard to respect the public's right to know they would be protected. "During the training operation, it is important that Texans know their safety, constitutional rights, private property rights and civil liberties will not be infringed," Abbott wrote.

It was a mistake to conclude, as many did at the time, that these groups of misinformed and misled Americans live in silos, where they only talked to one another and their fringe beliefs didn't infect those beyond these small online communities. But the Jade Helm 15 controversy illustrated how conspiracy theories nurtured on social media were metastasizing and jumping to the mainstream of the Republican Party. And the Republicans who indulged these fantasies of an Obama-directed invasion of Texas were adopting the model of the social media companies, which incentivized what was popular, not what was correct.

Six weeks after January 6, Tony Fabrizio conducted a survey of Republican voters to see where they stood on the question of Trump's role as the leader of the party and the issues that were motivating them. It was the first follow-up study he had done of the GOP electorate since his report in 2007 that identified the group he called "Dennis Miller Republicans," whose growing sense of cultural isolation and anger revealed the early contours of what would become the Trump movement. And what he found was proof of how Trump had thoroughly remade the GOP in his image.

The people who described themselves as the most committed Republicans were also the most likely to say they were committed to

Trump. Feelings about the former president, Fabrizio explained, were so intertwined with the understanding many voters had about what it meant to be a strong Republican that party fidelity and Trumpism were becoming one and the same. Still, a good number of them appeared to be willing to ditch the GOP affiliation if that's what Trump called for. Knowing what had happened on January 6, 49 percent of Republicans said they considered themselves to be more supportive of Trump than they were of the Republican Party. Subsequent surveys that asked the same question would find that this percentage remained steady in the months that followed. Asked whether they were more likely to support a Trump, Bush, or Reagan Republican, 51 percent said Trump while only 12 percent aligned themselves with the Bushes. Fabrizio also added a new subcategory of Republican voter to account for the growing number of people who openly embraced blatant falsehoods about the Democratic Party and Trump's opponents. He called them the "Infowars" Republicans, after the website run by the conspiracy theorist Alex Jones. These people, who said they believed in four or more conspiracy theories spread by QAnon, accounted for 10 percent of the GOP electorate, Fabrizio found.

Few conservatives are willing to say that January 6 will be a defining, sullying aspect of Trump's legacy. To many of them, it's another offense that seems small in the context of their larger pursuit of undoing decades of liberal social policy. And they may see their ultimate goal realized in 2022 when the Supreme Court—with three new conservative justices appointed by Trump—takes up a case that could do away with *Roe v. Wade.* "When I judge his legacy, as I would with any president, I take the bitter with the sweet," says Leonard Leo, who helped encourage and persuade Trump to appoint conservatives to the bench and devoted his career to pushing the federal courts further to the right. "The fact of the matter is when it comes to the courts, there isn't a whole lot of room for Joe Biden to make big changes in his first four years in office. And that's because of Donald Trump," he adds. "I can tell you, what the president achieved was not only very important but arguably at this particular moment in history, essential."

The Supreme Court that Trump put in place—six of the nine justices are conservatives—was a goal that conservative activists didn't believe they would achieve so soon. Frank Cannon, the social conservative, anti-abortion strategist, recalls the uneasiness among many people like him at the beginning of Trump's term. There was a lot of concern, he says, about whether Trump would keep his promises and, "if he did, was it worth it?" Cannon looks at how quickly the courts changed. "What was a longer-term project actually got collapsed into four years of changing the nature of the courts," he says. "So yeah, it was worth it." Marjorie Dannenfelser says Trump's fulfillment of his promises to conservatives forced people like her to shed their romantic notions about what kind of leader they should want. "What is politics? Is it anything other than transactional? Sometimes that's all you get," she says.

After leaving office, Trump became even more disparaging toward anyone and anything he believed hadn't shown him enough gratitude and deference. Trump spent time over the summer determined to ensure they played no role in the Republican Party of the future. He campaigned against Republicans like Cheney who voted to impeach him after January 6. Other party leaders like McCarthy so fear the sway he holds over Republican voters that they no longer voice their revulsion—if they still feel it—over the insurrection. McCarthy reversed his position on censuring Trump and creating a fact-finding commission. He tried but ultimately failed to block the creation of a congressional body with the power to investigate the attack. And he backed away from his assertion that Trump was responsible, making the demonstrably false claim in September that the former president had "no involvement" in it. Adam Kinzinger, who warned his colleagues of the danger of Trump's rhetoric and barricaded himself inside his office with a pistol on January 6, is retiring from Congress.

In interviews for this book, the subject that animated Trump the most was attacking disloyal Republicans. He keeps a long list of offenders. There's Fox News, which disappointed him with that early call declaring Biden the winner in Arizona. "They're doing poorly now, which is nice to watch," he says. There are the senators and members of the House he believes owe him their elections but have been insufficiently grateful. He is especially scornful of those who voted for impeachment after January 6 like Senator Susan Collins of Maine. "Don't forget I won. I won. I know I won Maine too, by a lot. By a lot," he says. "Had I gotten negative on Collins, she would have lost," he claims, adding, "I was thinking about it."

Of course he lost Maine by nine percentage points. But his repetition of the lie that he rightfully won in 2020 had a tremendous impact on his voters, large majorities of whom continue to deny Biden's legitimacy as president. It also left its mark on the nation's voting laws as Republican-led states rushed to enact new barriers and restrictions once he left office. These laws, versions of which Republicans had been passing for years as they exaggerated the prevalence of voter fraud, are among the most visible examples of how short the distance always was between Trump and the beating heart of the modern Republican Party. Conservative lawmakers hardly needed the encouragement. And in a sign of how full circle the GOP had come, the author of one resolution in the Arizona legislature that sought to award the state's eleven electoral votes to Trump—citing "irregularities so significant as to render it highly doubtful whether the certified results accurately represent the will of the voters"—had worked with Trump when he was promoting the Obama birther conspiracy theory. Kelly Townsend, a state senator, was a Tea Party activist when she met Trump in his office at Trump Tower in 2011 to discuss legislation that would have required politicians in Arizona to produce their birth certificates to get on the ballot. Townsend, like many pro-Trump lawmakers across the country who proposed similarly dubious measures that ultimately went nowhere, was following the playbook of Rudy Giuliani and Steve Bannon, who were pushing Republican legislators and members of Congress into darker and more dangerous territory. Compared with conservative gambits of the past that posed the risk of economic catastrophe, such as refusing to raise the nation's debt limit, this was even worse. "This makes the Tea Party look like a church social," Bannon told people. He understood that voter fraud and the 2020 election would become the next litmus test for Republicans. "Any 2024 hopeful that doesn't sign on. Dead," he said.

In the defeat he refused to acknowledge, Trump saw the beginnings of his next campaign. This is his new "Build the Wall." He acknowledges as much. "There is more anger now than there ever has been," he says. "In my opinion, the single biggest issue today is not the border, it's the scam election of 2020. That's the single biggest issue."

Trump also wants credit for the success of those Republicans who are often mentioned as possible GOP presidential contenders—a concept he seems unable to come to terms with because in his mind he is the present and future leader of the party. "Look, I helped Ron DeSantis at a level that nobody's ever seen before," he says of the Florida governor who won his race in 2018 with Trump's support. "I endorsed Ron, and he ended up winning in a landslide." He adds, "I give the candidate a lot of credit. But I'm just saying, I've taken people that didn't have a chance. Like, I could name twenty of them, I can name thirty of them. And they ended up winning the races easily." He believes this puts him in a league that even the most beloved modern Republican president before him cannot compete in. "If you got a Ronald Reagan endorsement, it was nice to have. But it didn't mean anything in terms of points," he says.

Trump's critics inside and outside the party have taken to calling the GOP the "Trump Party" as an epithet. His supporters throw out the nickname with pride. Some Republicans have tried to downplay his dominance with unconvincing results. Senator Rick Scott of Florida, for instance, was asked in an interview a few weeks after January 6 if the GOP was still Trump's. He responded that it belonged to the people.

Trump offers a clarification to Scott's comment. "But the people like me the best, by far."

Acknowledgments

A *New York Times* colleague once encouraged me to think about journalism as a passport into worlds that most people are never allowed to see. For nearly twenty years, the *Times* has been my passport to new experiences and knowledge I never imagined could be so enriching. This book would not have been possible without the *Times,* in more ways than I can possibly convey. There were doors that opened for me because I was lucky enough to be able to append that suffix at the end of my name when I approached sources: "Hi, I'm Jeremy Peters, from *The New York Times.*" The insights I gained into the Republican Party over the course of covering three presidential campaigns for the paper are on every page of this book.

There are many *Times* journalists who helped me along the way. Carolyn Ryan has been a generous friend and an editor who's helped me see stories I didn't know I could tell, even though they were right there in my notebook. Frank Bruni and Rick Berke helped me navigate a new life and career in New York when I was still very green and taught me what a truly well-rounded journalist is. Michael Barbaro, Rachel Dry, and Julie Bloom have helped me become a better storyteller and synthesizer of news. Carl Hulse, Bill Hamilton, Elisabeth Bumiller, Maureen Dowd, Peter Baker, Julie Davis, Adam Nagourney, Adam Liptak, Dick Stevenson, Mark Leibovich, Amy Chozick, Ashley Parker, Yamiche Alcindor, and Jonathan Martin all gave me a deeper understanding of the White House, Congress, and the campaign trail, and a clear-eyed sense of what I was getting into with this book. Michael Schmidt, Matt Rosenberg, and Adam

Goldman were reassuring and always good for a laugh when I needed one.

There were people who helped me catch early breaks at the *Times* or looked out for me along the way, including Micki Maynard, Jodi Rudoren, Bruce Headlam, Larry Ingrassia, Mary Suh, Patrick Healy, David Halbfinger, Gail Collins, Rebecca Blumenstein, and Danny Hakim, whose dog I will always be happy to walk even though I moved beyond my intern days long ago. And there is Maggie Haberman, whose insight into Donald Trump and encyclopedic knowledge of his history in New York has been an invaluable asset to me. Without the generations-long commitment of the Sulzberger family to preserving what's special about the *Times* and the leadership of A. G. today, I wouldn't have been able to undertake this project. Dean Baquet and Joe Kahn continue to be inspiring, thoughtful stewards and the reason our journalism has thrived in this uncertain era.

I also owe a great debt to journalists outside the *Times* who have guided me. Charles Bierbauer of CNN gave me my first job in Washington, where I caught the political reporting bug. Had Jesse Rodriguez not started putting me on television, I never would have met the incredibly dedicated professionals at MSNBC who helped me introduce my work to a whole new audience. Joe Scarborough, Mika Brzezinski, Alex Korson, and the *Morning Joe* team have always had my back. Andrea Mitchell and her crew of producers led by Michelle Perry have been incredible to work with, as have Brian Williams, Chris Matthews, Hallie Jackson, Katy Tur, and the network's all-star hosts who were kind enough to make me a repeat guest. Elise Jordan has always been a rock.

There are journalists whose work I've admired and relied on as I wrote: Joshua Greene, Robert Costa, Jake Sherman, Anna Palmer, Jonathan Darman, Jonathan Allen, Phil Rucker, and Brian Stelter—who have all been through the harried, lonely, but intensely rewarding journey of writing a book before and offered great insights and tips. Thanks to the earlier writing and reporting of other experts in their fields, I saw how it's done. I returned frequently as I wrote this to the work of Jane Mayer, Gabriel Sherman, Geoffrey Kabaservice, Nicole Hemmer, Bob Woodward, George Packer, John Heilemann,

Mark Halperin, and Sam Tanenhaus. Their reporting and scholarship has helped us all have a richer understanding of American politics.

I had ample personal and professional support from friends and colleagues who helped me fact-check and organize these pages, let me stay in their homes for long stretches while I wrote, and offered other forms of essential support. Karen Donfried and the German Marshall Fund of the United States gave me an office and early encouragement. Hilary McClellan, Rachael Brown, and Sue Carswell read behind me and saved me from errors I surely wouldn't have caught myself. Marc Serber and Jim Oberman helped with critical research and digging. Matthew Cullen was always fast and reliable at synthesizing the news, helping me to add important context and better organization. Tom Sheridan and Vincent Walsh helped me recharge my creative batteries when I needed a writing getaway. Matt Ullian, Stephen Friedfeld, Travis Jackson, Pat and Ashley Schmidt, Ari and Lisa Himmel, and Stephen and Julia Reitman, thank you for being such generous hosts and friends.

There would be no book without the foresight of my literary agent, David Kuhn. David saw the potential for a book in me before I did and kept the project moving along from beginning to end, all the while in the highly capable hands of the professionals at Crown. Molly Stern saw the value of this project early on, and David Drake and Gillian Blake have been invested in its success in ways for which I will always be deeply grateful. Kevin Doughten has been far more than an editor but a true partner since he saw what this book could be in the fall of 2017. Kevin, a true big-picture thinker whose enthusiasm and patience never waned, has helped strengthen the arguments and reporting on these pages more than anyone.

I owe a lot to my family—and not only because they were forgiving of me whenever I had to shut myself in a room and write over several Thanksgivings and Christmases. My two brothers, Ryan and Brendon, have tolerated me as their bossy older brother more than they probably should have. My parents knew I'd never be the athlete in the family, so they encouraged my pursuit of writing from my days as an aspiring film critic for my high school newspaper. No one checks in on my work more than my mom, who always wants to know the reason if I haven't been in the paper lately and when I'll be on television so she can tell all her pickleball friends. My dad has been a careful reader and shadow editor all along, offering advice and support since he drove me to see all those movies in high school.

I can't imagine having seen this to the end without my partner of thirteen years, Brendan Camp. Through three presidential campaigns, seven years in Washington, and seemingly endless manuscript revisions, Brendan kept me grounded. And while he always helped me see how lucky I've been with the opportunities that led to this book and to my career, what he helped me realize most of all was how lucky I am to have him in my life.

Notes

Introduction

xi **chasing the man down** Scott Richardson, "Former Local Board Member Stops Knife Attack," *The Pentagraph,* Aug. 17, 2006, pantagraph.com/news /former-local-board-member-stops-knife-attack/article_7503fa1d-772d-50eb -8866-88742b0a455a.html.

xiii **people were stabbed** Emily Davies et al., "Multiple People Stabbed After Thousands Gather for Pro-Trump Demonstrations in Washington," *The Washington Post,* Dec. 12, 2020, washingtonpost.com/local/trump-dc-rally -maga/2020/12/11/8b5af818-3bdb-11eb-bc68-96af0daae728_story.html.

xiv **erupted around 2 P.M.** "Examining the U.S. Capitol Attack: A Review of the Security, Planning and Response Failures on January 6," United States Senate, June 1, 2021, p. 24.

xiv **"Let's walk down"** Remarks of President Donald Trump, Rally on Electoral College Vote Certification, C-SPAN.org, Jan. 6, 2021.

xv **Congress at 1:03 P.M.** "Examining the U.S. Capitol Attack," p. 23.

xv **"Remain quiet"** "Examining the U.S. Capitol Attack," p. 27.

xv **locking the doors** "Rep. Jackson Describes Making Makeshift Weapons as Capitol Rioters Overran Police," FoxNews.com, Jan. 8, 2021.

xvi **"Deep State traitor"** Annie Karni, "Ronny Jackson, Ex-White House Doctor, Wins Texas Runoff," *The New York Times,* July 14, 2020.

xvi **Jackson came under fire** Ronny Jackson (@RonnyJacksonTX), Twitter, May 14, 2020, 3:37 P.M., twitter.com/RonnyJacksonTX/status/12610177722 44467721.

xvi **Right before heading up to the Capitol** Ronny Jackson (@RonnyJacksonTX), Twitter, Jan. 6, 2021, 12:51 P.M., twitter.com/RonnyJacksonTX/status/13468 77167733530624.

xvii **They broke legs off chairs** Jonathan Tilove, "These Texas Congressmen Fought off the Mob. Then They Voted with Trump," *Texas Monthly,* Jan. 7, 2021.

xvii **ripped the base off a hand sanitizer dispenser stand** Brittney Cottingham (@bbcott), Twitter, Jan. 7, 2021, 2:41 P.M., twitter.com/bbcott/status/13472 67130346106882.

xvii *This should not be happening* "Rep. Jackson Describes Making Makeshift Weapons as Capitol Rioters Overran Police," FoxNews.com, Jan. 8, 2021.

xvii **Gonzales had a similarly disturbing thought** Henry Ramos, "Congressman Says Military Instincts Kicked in amid Capitol Riots," KENS 5, Jan. 8, 2021.

xviii **"If we are wrong"** Remarks of Rudolph W. Giuliani, Rally on Electoral College Vote Certification, C-SPAN.org, Jan. 6, 2020.

xix **They put bumper stickers** Richard Brody, "A TV Documentary Shows the Deep Roots of Right-Wing Conspiracy," *The New Yorker,* Jan. 14, 2021, newyorker.com/culture/the-front-row/a-tv-documentary-shows-the-deep-roots -of-right-wing-conspiracy.

xx **co-founded a group** Statement of Organization, Women Vote Trump, Federal Election Commission, May 10, 2016, docquery.fec.gov/pdf/623/20160 5109015398623/201605109015398623.pdf#navpanes=0.

xxi **She earned attention** Remarks of Amy Kremer, *The Sean Hannity Show,* April 6, 2017, youtube.com/watch?v=iTp2fUH10Dk.

xxi **And she made headlines** Petra Cahill, "Amy Kremer Offers Supporters Chance to Win AR-15 Rifle in Raffle," NBC News, March 7, 2017, nbcnews.com /politics/congress/amy-kremer-offers-supporters-chance-win-ar-15-rifle-raffle -n729971.

xxi **she beseeched the crowd** Remarks of Amy Kremer, "Rally on Electoral College Vote Certification," C-SPAN.org, Jan. 6, 2021.

xxi **what he'd just seen on *Breitbart*** Andrew Egger and Audrey Fahlberg, "The Storming of the Capitol," *The Dispatch,* Jan. 7, 2021.

xxii **"He has betrayed us!"** Lena V. Groeger, Jeff Kao, Al Shaw, Moiz Syed, and Maya Eliahou, "What Parler Saw During the Attack on the Capitol," ProPublica, Jan. 17, 2021, projects.propublica.org/parler-capitol-videos/.

xxii **The hasty exit** Remarks of Sen. Pat Toomey, *The Journal Editorial Report,* Fox News, Jan. 9, 2021.

xxii **an urgent demand** Remarks of Tom Cotton, *The Hugh Hewitt Show,* Jan. 7, 2021, hughhewitt.com/show-archive/page/18/.

xxiii **"After all the things I've done"** Randy Krehbiel, "'This Was Really a Riot,' Inhofe Says, Watching His Capitol Desk Invaded During Breach," *Tulsa World,* Jan. 6, 2021, tulsaworld.com/news/state-and-regional/govt-and-politics /this-was-really-a-riot-inhofe-says-watching-his-capitol-desk-invaded-during -breach/article_439af4ae-5082-11eb-96b1-53cf9e218598.html.

xxiii **"The problem with conservatives"** David Grann, "Robespierre of the Right," *The New Republic,* Oct. 27, 1997, newrepublic.com/article/61338 /robespierre-the-right.

xxv **"The Big Steal: 1952"** Phyllis Schlafly, *A Choice Not an Echo* (Washington: Regnery, 1964).

xxvi **"They were masquerading as Trump supporters"** Steve Contorno, "How Matt Gaetz Spread a Falsehood About Antifa Infiltrating the Mob That Attacked Congress," *Tampa Bay Times,* Jan. 7, 2021.

xxvi **"a con game"** Liam Stack, "Trump and the 'Rigged' Emmy Awards: A History of Snubs," *The New York Times,* Oct. 20, 2016.

xxvii **"a phony deal"** Jeremy W. Peters and Jonathan Martin, "Donald Trump, Losing Ground, Tries to Blame the System," *The New York Times,* nytimes .com/2016/04/13/us/politics/donald-trump-losing-ground-tries-to-blame-the -system.html/.

xxvii **"We don't know"** Remarks of Sarah Palin, *Fox News Primetime,* Fox News, Jan. 6, 2021.

xxvii **"quit makin' things up"** "Palin Steps Down as Alaska Governor," CNN.com, July 27, 2009, cnn.com/2009/POLITICS/07/26/palin.resignation/.

xxviii **attacked the Bush family** Ben Smith, "Palin Dismisses 'Blue-Blood' Bush criticism," *Politico,* Nov. 24, 2010, politico.com/blogs/ben-smith/2010/11 /palin-dismisses-blue-blood-bush-criticism-030991.

xxviii **Brian Kilmeade asked on *Fox & Friends*** *Fox & Friends,* 7:26 A.M., Jan. 7, 2021.

Chapter 1: The Tip of the Spear

3 **One in twelve people in Alaska** Alaska Department of Labor, "Alaska Population Overview 2007–2008 Estimates," Feb. 2010.

4 **"These have been tough times"** George W. Bush, "Remarks to Military Personnel and Families at Eielson Air Force Base, Alaska," The American Presidency Project, Aug. 4, 2008.

5 **a "whack job" and a "diva"** Dana Bash, "Palin's Off-Script Comments Irk McCain Aides," CNN, Oct. 27, 2008, cnn.com/2008/POLITICS/10/25/palin .tension/; Mike Allen, "7 Days—One Week Out—Republicans Expect to Be Crushed in Historic Landslide: Buy Emergency Time in Montana and West Virginia," *Politico,* Oct. 28, 2008.

5 **"hardened" version of her son** Doug Stanglin, "Sarah Palin: Arrested Son Was 'Hardened' by War," *USA Today,* Jan. 20, 2016.

6 **high concentration of evangelical Christians** Nathan Thornburgh, "Mayor Palin: A Rough Record," *Time,* Sept. 2, 2008.

6 **"valley trash" in an email** Megan Holland, "'Valley Trash': Senator Says He Used Wrong Words in Moment of Anger," *Anchorage Daily News,* Aug. 1, 2019, adn.com/alaska-news/2019/08/01/valley-trash-senator-says-he-used -wrong-words-in-moment-of-anger/.

6 **As Palin would explain** Tom Bell, "Alaskans Line Up for a Whiff of Ivana," *Anchorage Daily News,* April 3, 1996.

7 **victory in the Wasilla mayor's** Regular Election results, City of Wasilla, Dec. 6, 1992.

7 **Her opponent, John C. Stein,** "Palin's Start in Alaska: Not Politics as Usual," *The New York Times,* Sept. 2, 2008, nytimes.com/2008/09/03/us/politics /03wasilla.html.

7 **She promptly fired the police chief** Stephanie Komarnitsky, "Wasilla Mayor Fires Police, Library Chiefs," *Anchorage Daily News,* Jan. 31, 1997.

7 **She was intrigued** Ben Spiess, "Murkowski Whittles Senate Picks," *Anchorage Daily News,* Dec. 18, 2002.

7 **She returned the movie** Ibid.

8 **eventually forcing him to resign** Sean Cockerham, "Ruedrich Resigns Post as Regulator on State Oil and Gas Commission," *Anchorage Daily News,* Sept. 2, 2008.

8 **Palin claimed the Republican machine** Amanda Coyne, "How Palin Turned on Her Own Party and Became Governor," *Anchorage Daily News,* Aug. 29, 2006.

8 **by more than thirty points** Official Results, State of Alaska—2006 Primary Election, Aug. 22, 2006, elections.alaska.gov/06prim/data/results.htm.

9 **"one of us"** "Letters from the people," *Anchorage Daily News,* Aug. 31, 2006.

9 **Three months before the November general election** Coyne, "How Palin Turned on Her Own Party and Became Governor."

9 **She ended the speech with a promise** Remarks of Sarah Palin, "Alaska Gubernatorial Inauguration," C-SPAN.org, Dec. 4, 2006.

10 **Alaska's first "lady governor"** William Yardley, "Alaska Governor Concedes Defeat in Primary," *The New York Times,* Aug. 23, 2006, nytimes.com/2006 /08/23/washington/24alaskacnd.html.

10 **juggling a number of requests** "The Palin E-Mails," *The New York Times,* June 11, 2011, nytimes.com/interactive/projects/palin-emails.

11 **"agents of intolerance"** John Harwood and Dennis Farney, "McCain Calls Conservative Leaders 'Agents of Intolerance' in Risky Move," *The Wall Street Journal,* Feb. 29, 2000.

11 **"She reminded me of my aunt Jo"** "Letters from the people," *Anchorage Daily News,* Dec. 9, 2006.

12 **Palin and her allies tried** Dan Joling, "Move to Oust Ruedrich as Party Chairman Fails; GOP: Delegates Table the Resolution for Resignation as Convention Winds Down," *Anchorage Daily News,* March 16, 2008.

13 **reaching her on her BlackBerry** Sarah Palin, *Going Rogue: An American Life* (New York: HarperCollins, 2009), p. 6.

13 **Mark Salter, a longtime aide** John Heilmann and Mark Halperin, *Game Change* (New York: Harper Perennial, first paperback, 2010), p. 363.

15 **By 2007, Fabrizio had concluded** Document provided by source.

15 **"Listen, Billy"** Igor Volsky, "Bill O'Reilly and Dennis Miller Turn Hysterical over Gay Penguins," *ThinkProgress,* Nov. 17, 2011.

16 **But his surprisingly strong showing** Andrew Rosenthal, "The 1992 Campaign: Republicans; Bush Considering a Shift in Tactics to Fight Buchanan," *The New York Times,* Feb. 20, 1992.

16 **He endorsed a conservative proposal** Maria L. La Ganga, "Dole Endorses Prop. 187 Limits on Schooling," *Los Angeles Times,* June 20, 1996.

16 **repudiated affirmative action programs** Adam Nagourney, "Dole Sees Failure of Three Decades in Anti-Bias Fight," *The New York Times,* Oct. 29, 1996.

18 **"There is not a liberal America"** "Barack Obama's Remarks to the Democratic National Convention," *The New York Times,* July 27, 2004.

19 **"Obama, he's a piece of shit"** Elizabeth Goodman, "Ted Nugent Threatens to Kill Barack Obama, Hillary Clinton During Vicious Onstage Rant," *Rolling Stone,* Aug. 24, 2007.

19 **Follow-up reporting showed that the school** Bill Carter, "Rivals CNN and Fox News Spar over Obama Report," *The New York Times,* Jan. 24, 2007.

19 **Liz Trotta, a former *Washington Times* editor** Michael Calderone, "Fox Analyst Apologizes for Obama Assassination Joke," *Politico,* May 26, 2008.

20 **"terrorist fist jab"** Mark Sweney, "Fox News Anchor Taken Off Air After Obama 'Terrorist Fist Jab' Gaffe," *The Guardian,* June 13, 2008.

20 **That year was something of a watershed** Martin Tolchin, "For Some, Low Road Is the Only Way to Go," *The New York Times,* Oct. 28, 1984.

20 **Obama said he didn't** "Obama Stops Wearing American Flag Pin," Associated Press, Oct. 4, 2007.

21 **In the spring of 1992, Quayle** Dan Quayle, "Address to the Commonwealth Club of California," May 19, 1992, vicepresidentdanquayle.com.

22 **"I wear their scorn like a badge"** R. W. Apple, Jr., "Dan Quayle Steps Front and (Right of) Center," *The New York Times,* June 14, 1992.

22 **44 million viewers** Elizabeth Kolbert, "'Murphy Brown' Feud: When Art Replaces Life," *The New York Times,* Sept. 23, 1992.

22 **She had hired** Jane Mayer, "The Insiders," *The New Yorker,* Oct. 19, 2008.

23 **Barnes brought his wife** "Fred Barnes Explains How Sarah Palin Was 'Discovered' on a *Weekly Standard* Cruise," C-SPAN.org, July 27, 2017.

23 **And in July, the magazine published** Fred Barnes, "The Most Popular Governor; Alaska's Sarah Palin Is the GOP's Newest Star," *The Weekly Standard,* July 16, 2007.

24 **"The establishment's weakness has been exposed"** David Brooks and William Kristol, "The McCain Insurrection," *Washington Examiner,* Feb. 14, 2000.

24 **These were people who usually voted Republican** Jeffrey M. Jones, "In U.S., New Record 43% Are Political Independents," *Gallup,* Jan. 7, 2015.

26 **"The American Right has just died"** Patrick J. Buchanan, "Thoughts of War Crash the Party in St. Paul," syndicated column, Sept. 6, 2008.

26 **"Dudes for Sarah" and "Palin's Pit Bulls"** Julie Bosman, "Palin Plays to Conservative Base in Florida Rallies," *The New York Times,* Oct. 7, 2008.

26 **"She's more like one of us"** Dieter Bradbury, "Palin Touches Base," *Portland Press Herald,* Oct. 17, 2008.

26 **"The most refreshing thing"** David McGrath Schwartz, "Palin Connects in Northern Nevada," *Las Vegas Sun,* Sept. 15, 2008.

27 **"just a real woman"** Anthony Man, "Coral Springs Woman Goes Online to Promote Palin," *South Florida Sun-Sentinel,* Sept. 12, 2008.

27 **"she's a Mary Kay lady"** Anna Scott, "In Palin, Hockey Moms See Challenges," *Sarasota Herald-Tribune,* Sept. 15, 2008.

27 **"This is not a man who sees America"** Michael Cooper, "Palin, on Offensive, Attacks Obama's Ties to '60s Radical," *The New York Times,* Oct. 4, 2008.

28 **The two were casually** Scott Shane, "Obama and '60s Bomber: A Look Into Crossed Paths," *The New York Times,* Oct. 3, 2008.

29 **Dana Milbank reported** Dana Milbank, "Unleashed, Palin Makes a Pit Bull Look Tame," *The Washington Post,* Oct. 7, 2008, washingtonpost.com/wp-dyn/content/article/2008/10/06/AR2008100602935.html.

29 **according to *The New York Observer*** Jason Horowitz, "Black Congressmen Declare Racism in Palin's Rhetoric," *The New York Observer,* Oct. 8, 2008.

29 **in their comprehensive account** Dan Balz and Haynes Johnson, *The Battle for America: The Story of an Extraordinary Election* (New York: Penguin Books, 2009), pp. 333–34.

31 **Kathleen Parker wrote** Kathleen Parker, "Palin Problem," *National Review,* Sept. 26, 2008, nationalreview.com/2008/09/palin-problem-kathleen-parker/.

32 **Reports documented people shouting** "Anti-Obama Anger Erupts at McCain Events," *The Associated Press,* Oct. 10, 2008. https://www.nbcnews.com/id/wbna27123224.

Chapter 2: Winning Is Losing

35 **"I can hear you doubting"** John Batchelor, "GOP R.I.P.," *The Daily Beast,* April 10, 2009.

35 **North Carolina and Virginia both had new Democratic senators** David M. Herszenhorn, "Democrats Widen Senate Edge to Solid Majority," *The New York Times,* Nov. 5, 2008.

36 **Once the outcome of the contested race** Todd Melby, "Franken Declared Senate Winner, Coleman Concedes," Reuters, June 30, 2009.

38 **That included a surprising number** "The No Votes," *The New York Times,* Sept. 29, 2008.

39 **"The politics of fear, it's not going to work"** Jeremy W. Peters, "In Bid for House Seat, an Identity Crisis for New York Republicans," *The New York Times,* Aug. 6, 2009.

40 **"The Democrat is basically"** Remarks of Glenn Beck, *The Glenn Beck Program,* Fox News, Oct. 26, 2009.

40 **Robocalls in the district** Jason Horowitz, "Political Eyes on Republican Scozzafava After Conservatives Urge her to Quit," *The Washington Post,* Nov. 10, 2009.

40 **at a pizzeria in Potsdam** Mark Weiner, "GOP Picks Candidate for Congressional Seat, Attacks Likely Democratic Hopeful," Syracuse.com, July 23, 2009.

41 **Long vowed "to do everything"** Jeremy W. Peters, "Assembly Passes Gay Marriage Bill in New York; Senate Fight Awaits," *The New York Times,* May 12, 2009, nytimes.com/2009/05/13/nyregion/13marriage.html.

42 **"The No. 1 victory will be"** Jeremy W. Peters, "Scozzafava Is G.O.P. Candidate, but the Right Likes Hoffman," *The New York Times,* Oct. 26, 2009, nytimes.com/2009/10/27/nyregion/27upstate.html.

43 **a CD of holiday tunes** Jason DeParle, "GOP Receives Obama Parody to Mixed Reviews," *The New York Times,* Dec. 27, 2008.

44 **The title of the song was taken** David Ehrenstein, "Obama the 'Magic Negro,'" *Los Angeles Times,* March 19, 2007.

44 **"This columnist is black"** "Barack the Magic Negro, Explained," *The Rush Limbaugh Show,* March 23, 2007.

44 **Hughley asked Steele** Jonathan Martin, "Limbaugh Blasts Steele, the GOP," *Politico,* March 2, 2009, politico.com/story/2009/03/limbaugh-blasts-steele-the-gop-019498.

44 **"Why do we have to accept"** Remarks of Rush Limbaugh, "I Hope Obama Fails," *The Rush Limbaugh Show,* Jan. 16, 2009, rushlimbaugh.com/daily/2009/01/16/limbaugh_i_hope_obama_fails/.

46 **The crowd chanted his name** Jack Kuenzie, "Thousands Attend Tax Day 'Tea Party,' Sales Tax Rally," WIS News 10, April 15, 2009.

46 **In Salt Lake City, demonstrators jeered** Liz Robbins, "Tax Day Is Met with Tea Parties," *The New York Times,* April 15, 2009.

46 **But in a sign of the low regard** "Tax Protesters Take to the Streets of Bakersfield," *The Bakersfield Californian,* April 15, 2009.

46 **"Their heart is in the right place"** GOP staffer interview with author.

48 **After the January 6 riots** Rob "NZ" Neppell (@rneppell), Twitter, Jan. 8, 2021, 12:18 P.M., twitter.com/rneppell/status/1347593424669532161.

48 **"If you want polish"** Naftali Bendavid, "Tea-Party Activists Complicate Republican Comeback Strategy," *The Wall Street Journal,* Oct. 16, 2009.

48 **For the location** Ibid.

51 **Being in the opposition was also more suited** Clyde Haberman, "Roger Ailes, Who Built Fox News into an Empire, Dies at 77," *The New York Times,* May 18, 2017.

52 **"Do you think if you win"** *Glenn Beck,* Fox News, Oct. 22, 2009, youtube .com/watch?v=0jZ28NHx2Ek.

52 **"Sir, prove to me"** Alia Malek, "Muslim-American Groups Protest GMA's Hiring of Glenn Beck," *Columbia Journalism Review,* Jan. 26, 2007.

52 **Fox sent Beck to broadcast his show** *Glenn Beck,* Fox News, April 15, 2009, youtube.com/watch?v=nuzIMgJ-WPc.

53 **Alaska's liberal ethics laws** Andy Barr, "Palin Fights Back Against Ethics Charge," *Politico,* July 21, 2009.

53 **A *PolitiFact* analysis** Angie Drobnic Holan, "PolitiFact's Lie of the Year: 'Death panels,'" *PolitiFact,* Dec. 18, 2009, politifact.com/article/2009/dec /18/politifact-lie-year-death-panels/.

54 **"Best of all"** Andy Barr, "Palin Backs Hoffman in NY-23," *Politico,* Oct. 22, 2009.

55 **In late October** *The Glenn Beck Program,* Fox News, Oct. 26, 2009.

57 **The SBA List's founders ignored** Harper D. Ward, "Misrepresenting Susan B. Anthony on Abortion," The Official Susan B. Anthony Museum & House, Feb 15, 2018, susanb.org/misrepresenting-susan-b-anthony-on-abortion/.

58 **Ultimately she relented** "More Right-Wing Agita in NY-23," *The Village Voice,* Oct. 18, 2009.

59 **Hoffman lost on Election Day** Statement of Canvass, 23rd Congressional District, State of New York Board of Elections, elections.ny.gov/NYSBOE /Elections/2009/Special/23rdCDSpecialVoteResults.pdf.

59 **"This is healthy"** Adam Nagourney, "Energized GOP Looks to Avoid Party Feud," *The New York Times,* Nov. 4, 2009.

59 **"It might be a blow"** Observer Staff, "Hoffman, and His Movement, Sputter Out," *The New York Observer,* Nov. 4, 2009, observer.com/2009/11/hoffman -and-his-movement-sputter-out/.

59 **"This is probably the most"** Jeremy W. Peters, "House Race in New York's 23rd District Goes to the Democrat," *The New York Times,* Nov. 3, 2009, nytimes.com/2009/11/04/nyregion/04district.html.

Chapter 3: The Popularist

61 **There was a strip club** Clyde Haberman, "Near Ground Zero, the Sacred and the Profane," *The New York Times,* May 27, 2010, nytimes.com/2010 /05/28/nyregion/28nyc.html.

62 **"We as New York Muslims"** Ralph Blumenthal and Sharaf Mowjood, "Muslim Prayers Fuel Spiritual Rebuilding Project by Ground Zero," *The New York Times,* Dec. 8, 2009.

62 **And when he went public** Ibid.

62 **"I don't know which is more grotesque"** Pamela Geller, *Atlas Shrugs* (blog), Dec. 8, 2009.

62 **She became a regular commenter** Anne Barnard and Alan Feuer, "Pamela

Geller—Blogger, Provocateur, Lightning Rod," *The New York Times,* Oct. 8, 2010.

62 **She referred to Muslims as savages** Pamela Geller, *Atlas Shrugs* (blog), Dec. 8, 2009.

63 **One piece Geller posted** "Conservative Blogger 'Proves' Obama's Birth Certificate Forged," History Commons, July 20, 2008.

63 **"sharpening their machetes"** Pamela Geller, "It's Holocaust Day, and Another Holocaust Is Looming," *Breitbart,* April 12, 2010.

63 **"Islamic supremacism"** Pamela Geller, "Mayor Bloomberg Submits, Sanctions 911 Mega Mosque," *Breitbart,* May 30, 2010.

64 **"The Ground Zero Mosque story"** Pamela Geller, "It's Official: Ground Zero Mosque Defeated!" *Breitbart,* Sept. 26, 2015.

65 **Cordoba House received a favorable nod** Cristian Salazar, "Building Damaged in 9/11 to Be Mosque for NYC Muslims," Associated Press, May 7, 2010.

65 **Columnist Andrea Peyser** Andrea Peyser, "Mosque Madness at Ground Zero," *New York Post,* May 13, 2010.

65 **saw Peyser's piece and booked Geller** "Hannity Show Podcast: Atlas vs. Muslim America Congress," *Atlas Shrugs,* May 13, 2010.

65 **He would keep up with it** *Hannity,* Fox News, May 20, 2010.

66 **"This man is an extremist"** *Hannity,* Fox News, July 15, 2010.

66 **In Tennessee, Geller was invited** Pamela Geller, "Unindicted Co-Conspirator CAIR Tries to Ban Free Speech at Tennessee Tea Party," *Breitbart,* May 21, 2010.

66 **the Staten Island Tea Party** "Thousands Attend SIOA Rally Against Islamic Supremacist Mosque at Ground Zero," PR Newswire, June 8, 2010.

66 **"That place is going to be a house of evil"** Douglas Feiden, "You Betcha There's a Bunch of 'Em Here. News Finds a Wide Streak of Conservatives in Liberal City," New York *Daily News,* June 13, 2010.

66 **a fight almost erupted** Kristen Saloomey, Al Jazeera, June 20, 2010.

66 **they were Coptic Christians** Mike Kelly, "On This Ground, Zero Tolerance," *The Record,* June 7, 2010.

67 **draw tens of millions of readers** "Breitbart Traffic up 28% from All-Time Record–Set Last Month," *Breitbart,* Aug. 7, 2016.

67 **Huffington would later bring him back** Jeremy W. Peters, "Andrew Breitbart, the Right's Frenetic Blogger Provocateur," *The New York Times,* June 26, 2011.

68 **As *The New Yorker* described his work** Rebecca Mead, "Rage Machine," *The New Yorker,* May 17, 2010.

68 **offered to donate $10,000** Andrew Breitbart, "2010: A Race Odyssey-Disproving a Negative for Cash Prizes, or How the Civil Rights Movement Jumped the Shark," BigGovernment.com, March 25, 2010.

69 **Geller made him** Press Release from Freedom Defense Initiative, "FDI/SIOA 9/11 Rally of Remembrance: Yes to Freedom, No to Ground Zero Mosque," PR Newswire, Sept. 7, 2010.

69 **In fact, Fox chief** Brian Stelter, "Fox Canceled Hannity's Attendance at Tea Party Rally," *The New York Times,* April 16, 2010.

69 ***The New York Times Magazine* found Lazio so bland** James Traub, "The Ingratiator," *The New York Times Magazine,* July 30, 2000.

70　**He told a newspaper**　"Carl Paladino: Turn Prisons into Dorms for Welfare Recipients," syracuse.com, Aug. 21, 2010.

70　**He suggested using the state police**　It's A Free Country (podcast), "Where They Stand: Immigration," WNYC, Sept. 28, 2010.

70　**His advisers included**　Danny Hakim, "Roger Stone Plays Role in Two Opposing Campaigns," *The New York Times,* Aug. 11, 2010, nytimes.com/2010/08/12/nyregion/12stone.html.

71　**The foundation of Finkelstein's approach**　Craig Shirley, "Arthur Finkelstein, Republican Consultant Extraordinaire," *National Review,* Jan. 26, 2017.

72　**In 1994, he helped George Pataki**　Sam Roberts, "Arthur Finkelstein, Innovative, Influential Conservative Strategist, Dies at 72," *The New York Times,* Aug. 19, 2017.

72　**Explaining how he viewed American politics**　CERVO Institut Forum, May 16, 2011, youtube.com/watch?v=IfCBpCBOECU.

73　**Lazio, more measured**　Deb Geyerick, Julian Cummings, Ed Payne, Mark Morgenstein, and Steve Kastenbaum, "In Battle to Build Mosque Near Ground Zero, Opponents Ask 'Why There?' " CNN.com, July 21, 2010, cnn.com/2010/US/07/14/new.york.ground.zero.mosque/index.html.

73　**One compared the construction to defiling a battlefield**　"Islamic Center Near Ground Zero Sparks Anger," *All Things Considered,* NPR, July 15, 2010.

73　**founded by Justice Clarence Thomas's wife**　Kathleen Hennessey, "Justice's Wife Launches 'Tea Party' Group," *Los Angeles Times,* March 14, 2010.

73　**Liberty Central organized a petition**　Brian Beutler, "Federally Funded Religious Freedom Commission Packed with Anti-'Mosque' Members," *Talking Points Memo,* Aug. 23, 2010.

73　**Franklin Graham, the evangelical leader**　Elizabeth Dias, "Most U.S. Religious Leaders Support 'Ground Zero Mosque,' " *Time,* Aug. 18, 2010.

74　**Sarah Palin, now a Fox News contributor**　Sarah Palin (@SarahPalinUSA), Twitter, July 18, 2010, 2:57 P.M., twitter.com/sarahpalinusa/status/18858128918?lang=en.

74　**Newt Gingrich sat down with *Fox & Friends***　Andy Barr, "Newt Compares Mosque to Nazis," *Politico,* Aug. 16, 2010.

74　**He wrote a $1 million check**　Ben Smith, "Hedge Fund Figure Financed Mosque Campaign," *Politico,* Jan. 18, 2011.

74　**Another backer of conservative causes**　"Campaign Cash Follows Lazio's Fight over Mosque," Associated Press, Sept. 4, 2010.

75　**Seventy people were injured**　Homer Bigart, "War Foes Here Attacked by Construction Workers," *The New York Times,* May 9, 1970.

75　**They presented him with his own hard hat**　Robert B. Semple, Jr., "Nixon Meets Heads of 2 City Unions; Hails War Support," *The New York Times,* May 27, 1970.

77　**"Islam is peace"**　"Remarks by the President at Islamic Center of Washington, D.C.," George W. Bush White House Archives, Sept. 17, 2001.

78　**"Some Republicans gave up on winning"**　Anne E. Kornblut, "Bush and Party Chief Court Black Voters at 2 Forums," *The New York Times,* July 15, 2005.

78　**Sekulow had recently taken up the case**　"ACLJ Expresses Concern About

Planned Islamic Mosque Near Ground Zero in NYC," American Center for Law and Justice, Aug. 3, 2010.

79 **Political parties were like wives** "Bush Says Trump Was a Democrat Longer Than a Republican 'in the Last Decade,'" *PolitiFact,* Aug. 24, 2015.

79 **He boasted that one of the displays** Verena Dobnik, "Passions Rise at Dueling Rallies on NYC 'Mosque' Plan," Associated Press, Aug. 23, 2010.

80 **An evangelical pastor in Gainesville** Damien Cave, "Pastor's Plan to Burn Korans Adds to Tensions," *The New York Times,* Aug. 25, 2010.

80 **Jones called off his bonfire only after** Josh Gerstein and Jen DiMascio, "Florida Pastor 'Suspends' Quran Burning," *Politico,* Sept. 9, 2010.

80 **the pastor's plans had provoked** Ewen MacAskill, Richard Adamsin, and Kate Connolly, "Pastor Terry Jones Calls Off Qur'an Burning," *The Guardian,* Sept. 10, 2010.

80 **On September 1, he sat down for an interview** Brent Baker, "To Letterman's irritation, Trump Denounces Ground Zero Mosque as 'Insensitive,' 'Somebody Knocked Down the World Trade Center,'" Media Research Center, Sept. 1, 2010.

80 **On September 9, two days before** Letter from Donald J. Trump to Hisham Elzanaty, tmz.vo.llnwd.net/o28/newsdesk/tmz_documents/0909_trump.pdf.

81 **"We weren't prepared"** "When Donald Trump Tried to Buy Out Sharif's Building," *The Safina Society Podcast,* Jan. 20, 2020.

Chapter 4: The Paranoid Style

82 **The ad ran in several** Jason Linkins, "Fox News Newspaper Ad Makes False Claims About Tea Party Coverage," *The Huffington Post,* Nov. 18, 2009.

82 **The other networks hadn't missed the story** "Rival Networks Fire Back over Fox News Ad," Associated Press, Sept. 18, 2009.

82 **The demonstration on September 12** Jeff Zeleny, "In Washington, Thousands Stage Protest of Big Government," *The New York Times,* Sept. 12, 2009.

83 **waved Confederate flags** Ibid.

83 **It was such a big story** "Networks Respond to False Fox Ad," CNN, Sept. 18, 2009.

85 **suggested that the Obama administration** "Glenn Beck Says Government Will Stage False Flag Terror to Discredit Opposition," *InfoWars,* Nov. 11, 2010.

85 **said that the government** *Glenn Beck,* "Collapsing the System," Fox News, Oct. 28, 2009.

85 **When he was called** Brian Stelter and Bill Carter, "Fox News's Mad, Apocalyptic, Tearful Rising Star," *The New York Times,* March 29, 2009.

86 **The responding officer** Abby Goodnough, "Harvard Professor Jailed; Officer Is Accused of Bias," *The New York Times,* July 20, 2009.

86 **The president had accurately pointed to what he described** "Obama: Police Who Arrested Professor 'Acted Stupidly,'" CNN.com, July 22, 2009.

86 **Rush Limbaugh called** Remarks of Rush Limbaugh, "President Obama Comes Alive When the Topic Turns to Racism," *The Rush Limbaugh Show,* July 23, 2009, rushlimbaugh.com/daily/2009/07/23/president_obama_comes _alive_when_the_topic_turns_to_racism/.

86 **Rudy Giuliani gave an interview** Tom Namako, "Rudy's Open-and-Shut (Your Mouth!) Case," *New York Post,* Aug. 1, 2009.

86 **But it was Beck who went the furthest** *Fox & Friends* clip of Glenn Beck, July 2009, youtube.com/watch?v=2K8R2PdmbmA.

86 **"Glenn Beck expressed a personal opinion"** Chris Ariens, "FNC Responds to Glenn Beck Calling Pres. Obama a 'Racist,'" *TVNewser*, July 28, 2009.

87 **"Who are they?"** Remarks by Glenn Beck, *The Glenn Beck Program*, Aug. 26, 2009.

88 **previous presidents as far back as Calvin Coolidge** Justin S. Vaughn and José D. Villalobos, *Czars in the White House: The Rise of Policy Czars as Presidential Management Tools* (Ann Arbor: University of Michigan Press, 2015).

89 **(He would later claim)** Ben Smith, "Trutherism-lite, and a Second Jones Tie," *Politico*, Sept. 4, 2009.

89 **One particularly ambitious congressman** Garance Franke-Ruta and Anne E. Kornblut, "Embattled Environmental Aide Resigns," *The Washington Post*, Sept. 6, 2009.

89 **It all became too much** John M. Broder, "White House Official Resigns After GOP Criticism," *The New York Times*, Sept. 6, 2009.

90 **He helped put Al D'Amato of New York in office** Larry McCarthy, "The Roger Ailes I know," *Politico Magazine*, May 24, 2017.

91 **There were segments** Jeremy W. Peters, "'Fox & Friends' Finds Ratings and Controversy," *The New York Times*, June 20, 2012.

91 **He snapped at the headmaster** Tom Junod, "Roger Ailes on Roger Ailes: The Interview Transcripts, Part 2," *Esquire*, Jan. 27, 2011, esquire.com/news -politics/news/a9302/roger-ailes-quotes-5072437/.

92 **He thought that liberals coddled** Remarks of Roger Ailes, "Interview with Roger Ailes, president of Fox News Channel," Hoover Institution, Feb. 26, 2010, youtube.com/watch?v=lHYa9IupxRs.

92 **"A voter registration plan"** Ibid.

92 **He once told a group of college students** Remarks of Roger Ailes, Roy H. Park Distinguished Lecture, UNC Hussman School of Journalism and Media, April 12, 2012, jomc.unc.edu/events/roger-ailes-park-lecture-april-12-2012 -transcript.

92 **"A lot of what we do at Fox"** Tom Junod, "Roger Ailes—Esquire Transcripts of Roger Ailes Interview," *Esquire*, Jan. 25, 2011.

93 **Hofstadter described paranoiac tendencies** Richard Hofstadter, "The Paranoid Style in American Politics," *Harper's Magazine*, November 1964.

93 **Its coverage of the 2008 election** "News Corporation Reports Second Quarter Adjusted Operating Income of $818 Million on Revenue of $7.9 Billion," News Corporation, Feb. 5, 2009.

93 **He earned $19 million** Paul J. Gough, "Fox News Chief Roger Ailes Extends Contract," Reuters, Nov. 21, 2008.

94 **The reason, which Ailes later explained** Marc Ambinder, "Going Viral on Conservative Websites Today," *The Atlantic*, Feb. 27, 2008.

95 **"Senator, I just watched"** Zev Chafets, *Roger Ailes: Off Camera* (New York: Sentinel, 2013), p. 196.

95 **Corsi found the Obama video** Jerome R. Corsi, *The Obama Nation: Leftist Politics and the Cult of Personality* (New York: Threshold Editions, 2008), p. 1.

96 **"I literally chat with Hannity"** Remarks of Joseph Farah, *The Bill Cunningham Show*, March 2011, youtube.com/watch?v=sKE4spE6evw.

96   **"There's been good analysis"**   Eric Hananoki and Matt Gertz, "Corsi's Claim That Obama Posted 'False, Fake Birth Certificate' Flatly Rejected by Hawaii Health Department," *Media Matters for America,* Aug. 15, 2008.

96   **It was the kind of publication**   Jim Rutz, "Soy Is Making Kids 'Gay,' " *World-NetDaily,* Dec. 12, 2006.

97   **"If John Kerry loses"**   Susannah Meadows, " 'Unfit for Command': Hostile Fire," *The New York Times,* Oct. 10, 2004.

98   **Hume praised Corsi's book**   Howard Kurtz, "Moving to the Right: Brit Hume's Path Took Him from Liberal Outsider to the Low-Key Voice of Conservatism on Fox News," *The Washington Post,* April 19, 2006.

98   **Its manifesto read like the mission statement**   Glenn Beck, "The 9/12 Movement: The Four-Part Series," *The Glenn Beck Program,* Sept. 16, 2016.

98   **for recovering alcoholics, which Beck was**   Glenn Beck, "Glenn Beck: How He Recovered His Life and His Free Will," *Today.com,* Jan. 18, 2011.

98   **On Saturday, August 28, 2010**   Kate Zernike, Carl Hulse, and Brian Knowlton, "Glenn Beck Leads Religious Rally at Lincoln Memorial," *The New York Times,* Aug. 28, 2010.

99   **He put up a page on his Fox website**   Brian Stelter, "Glenn Beck Stakes Out a More Activist Role in Politics," *The New York Times,* Nov. 21, 2009.

99   **Ailes objected**   Hoover Institute interview with Ailes.

100   **He posted a list he called**   "28 Founding Principles of the United States," Joe Walsh for Congress, 2010.

101   **Harrison, a Texan**   Mike Allen, "GOP Committees Expect Big Wins," *Politico,* Oct. 27, 2010, politico.com/story/2010/10/gop-committees-expect-big-wins-044198.

101   **They won sixty-three**   Election Results 2010, House Map, *The New York Times,* nytimes.com/elections/2010/results/house.html.

101   **When the Congressional Research Service**   Membership of the 112th Congress: A Profile, Jennifer E. Manning Information Research Specialist November 26, 2012, Congressional Research Service.

102   **Thirty-two of them had never been elected**   Charles Pope, "Rep. Greg Walden Says Nearly Half the Incoming Republicans Are Newcomers to Politics," *PolitiFact,* Jan. 17, 2011.

102   **They often told themselves**   "The Federalist Papers: No. 52, The House of Representatives, From the New York Packet, Feb. 8, 1788: Hamilton or Madison," avalon.law.yale.edu/18th_century/fed52.asp.

102   **close to twenty Republican freshmen**   Phil Hirschkorn and Wyatt Andrews, "One-Fifth of House Freshmen Sleep in Offices," CBSNews.com, Jan. 22, 2011.

103   **ninety-two in all**   NRCC Young Guns About page, gopyoungguns2020.com/about/.

104   **Part of his job had included writing memos**   U.S. Department of the Treasury, Debt Limit webpage, home.treasury.gov/policy-issues/financial-markets-financial-institutions-and-fiscal-service/debt-limit.

105   **Just after 8:30, the results**   *Politico* Staff, "Election Day 2010 Live Updates," *Politico,* Nov. 2. 2010.

105   **Morgan Griffith, the first Republican since 1983**   Liana Bayne, "Morgan Griffith Unseats Incumbent Rick Boucher," *Collegiate Times,* Nov. 2, 2010.

105 **Across the border in western Pennsylvania** U.S. House of Representatives: History, Art & Archives, Kathleen A. Dahlkemper.

105 **Nearly half of the Blue Dog coalition** "Midterm Losses Bite Blue Dog Democrats," NPR *Weekend Edition,* Saturday, Nov. 6, 2010.

106 **But by 2011, Republicans would enjoy full control** "2010 Post-Election Control of Legislatures," National Conference of State Legislatures.

106 **The 2010 wave was so powerful** "Republicans Exceed Expectations in 2010 State Legislative Elections," National Conference of State Legislatures.

107 **"our Cuban Barack Obama"** Damien Cave, "Marco Rubio Is Pushed to Limelight by Expectant Conservatives," *The New York Times,* Nov. 3, 2010.

107 **"On principle and policy"** James Warren, "Surprise Representative Plans Surprises of His Own in Washington," *The New York Times,* Dec. 25, 2010.

Chapter 5: The Executive

108 **her political action committee** SARAH PAC, Report of receipts and disbursements on file with the Federal Election Commission, amended Jan. 31, 2012.

109 **They compiled a list** David A. Graham, "Piper Palin's 5 Best Antics on Sarah Palin's One Nation Bus Tour, More," *The Daily Beast,* June 7, 2011.

110 **They had to trap** Katharine Q. Seelye, "Palin's Parents Aided in Sept. 11 Cleanup," *The New York Times,* Sept. 25, 2008.

110 **"She'd love me to get back in the race"** "Trump Says Palin Wants Him to Run," *UPI,* June 1, 2011.

112 **"It's not the capitalism"** Charlie Spiering, "Transcript: Sarah Palin's Iowa speech," *Washington Examiner,* Sept. 4, 2011.

112 **In a speech in the spring** Ron Devito, "5-Point Military Doctrine—Sarah Palin—SEE IT," U.S. for Palin, May 3, 2011.

112 **The time had come** Tony Lee, "9 Ways Sarah Palin Was a Trailblazer for Donald Trump," *Breitbart,* July 15, 2017.

112 **"They just make stuff up!"** Margaret Wente, "The Importance of Seeing Sarah Palin," *The Globe and Mail,* Oct. 1, 2010.

112 **She belittled the Bush family** Brian Montopoli, "Sarah Palin Hits George and Barbara Bush as Elite 'Blue Bloods,'" CBS News, Nov. 24, 2010.

113 **Haley Barbour, the governor of Mississippi** Peter Hamby, "Barbour Calls on Republicans to Unite Behind Eventual Nominee," CNN, June 17, 2011.

114 **Among Republicans who didn't go to college** Jeffrey M. Jones, "Huckabee, Palin, Romney Tie for Lead in GOP '12 Preferences," *Gallup,* Feb. 23, 2011.

114 **The Palins had recently** Catherine Reagor, "Sarah Palin Sells Scottsdale Mansion for $2.275 Million," azcentral.com, Sept. 19, 2016.

115 **"You know why"** Remarks of Stephen K. Bannon, "Conservatives4Palin /Grizzly Coalition meet-up," Conservative Political Action Conference, Feb. 10, 2012, youtube.com/watch?v=HYDiSKpz7N8.

117 *The New York Times* **noted in its coverage** Michael D. Shear, "Romney Launches Campaign," *The New York Times,* June 2, 2011.

117 **"the establishment has to be paid its due"** Alexander Burns and Dan Hirschhorn, "Palin Tour Leaves GOP Cold," *Politico,* June 3, 2011.

117 **"We have to get back to what made America great"** Seema Mehta, "Palin,

Giuliani Steal Some Romney Thunder in New Hampshire," *Los Angeles Times,* June 3, 2011.

117 **The state's largest newspaper** Nick Ramsey, "Paper Headlines Palin, Bumps Romney," MSNBC.com, June 3, 2011.

118 **He had tried to distance himself** Elspeth Reeve, "Romney's Task Today: Distance Himself from RomneyCare," *The Atlantic,* May 12, 2011.

118 **terminal medical condition** Molly Ball, "A 'Severely Conservative' Romney Tries to Woo CPAC," *The Atlantic,* Feb. 10, 2012, theatlantic.com/politics /archive/2012/02/a-severely-conservative-romney-tries-to-woo-cpac/252941/.

119 **scoffed, "Corporations are people"** Ashley Parker, "'Corporations Are People,' Romney Tells Iowa Hecklers Angry over His Tax Policy," *The New York Times,* Aug. 11, 2011, nytimes.com/2011/08/12/us/politics/12romney.html.

120 **As governor, he once declared** "George W. Romney—Businessman, Politician, Volunteer, and Civil Rights Hero," Michigan Civil Rights Commission Resolution Honoring George Romney, July 20, 2015.

120 **Romney turned down bonuses** David Leonhardt, "Two Candidates, Two Fortunes, Two Distinct Views of Wealth," *The New York Times,* Dec. 23, 2007.

120 **would have been called socialist** David Leonhardt, "When the Rich Said No to Getting Richer," *The New York Times,* Sept. 5, 2017.

122 **He used the debates** Jeremy W. Peters, "Republican Debates Put Moderators in Hot Seat, Too," *The New York Times,* Nov. 21, 2011. https://www.nytimes .com/2011/11/22/us/politics/republican-debates-put-moderators-in-hot-seat .html.

122 **poor children could improve** Elicia Dover, "Gingrich's NAACP, Food Stamp Remarks Stir Controversy," ABCNews.com, Jan. 6, 2012. https://abcnews .go.com/blogs/politics/2012/01/gingrichs-naacp-food-stamp-remarks-stir -controversy.

122 **"No. I don't see that"** Jeremy W. Peters, "Inside Debate Prep at Fox News, a Discussion Over Race Question," *The New York Times,* Jan. 18, 2012. https:// thecaucus.blogs.nytimes.com/2012/01/18/inside-debate-prep-at-fox-news-a -discussion-over-race-question/.

123 **According to a biography of the Fox News chief** Marianne Garvey, Brian Niemietz, Lachlan Cartwright, and Molly Friedman, "In New Biography, Roger Ailes Dumps on Conservative Darlings Gov. Chris Christie, Mitt Romney, Sean Hannity and more," New York *Daily News,* Jan. 12, 2014.

125 **In their 1995 interview** Remarks of Roger Ailes, "Straight Forward with Roger Ailes," NBC, December 1995.

126 **On March 28, Trump went on** *Fox & Friends* "Fox Goes Birther: Trump Tells Unquestioning Co-hosts, 'I'm Starting to Wonder . . . Whether or Not [Obama] Was Born in This Country,'" *Media Matters for America,* March 28, 2011.

126 **"Bold, brash and never bashful"** Frances Martel, "You Saw This Coming: Fox News Announces 'Mondays with Trump' on *Fox & Friends,*" March 31, 2011.

126 **"They went wild"** Interview with Donald J. Trump, *Fox & Friends,* April 18, 2011.

127 **It wasn't the most flawless** Remarks of Donald J. Trump, Conservative Political Action Conference, C-Span.org, Feb. 10, 2011, c-span.org/video/?297 952-12/donald-trump-remarks.

128 **"They cannot believe"** Remarks of Donald J. Trump, NBC News Transcripts, *Today,* NBC, April 7, 2011.

128 **But when *Newsmax* published it** Ben Smith, "Trump Fails to Produce Birth Certificate," *Politico,* March 28, 2011.

128 **"Hardworking, unbelievable, salt-of-the-earth people"** *The Laura Ingraham Show,* March 30, 2011, youtube.com/watch?v=WqaS9OcoTZs.

128 **Could it have to do with religion?** Sean Hannity, "Exclusive: Donald Trump Rips into President Obama's Past," Fox News, April 15, 2011.

130 **"I believe the president was born in the United States"** Kasie Hunt, "Mitt: Obama Born Here, Period," *Politico,* April 12, 2011.

131 **He made a beeline for the elevator** Molly Ball, "Trump Endorses, and Mitt Romney Grins and Bears It," *The Atlantic,* Feb. 2, 2012.

131 **"There are some things"** Mark Leibovich, "Trump Endorses Romney in Las Vegas," *The New York Times,* Feb. 2, 2012, nytimes.com/2012/02/03/us/politics/trump-endorses-romney-in-las-vegas.html.

134 **On November 19** Filing of Donald J. Trump with the United States Patent and Trademark Office, Nov. 19, 2012, https://tmsearch.uspto.gov/bin/showfield?f=doc&state=4804:d57g1l.2.62.

Chapter 6: The Autopsy

135 **left office with the lowest approval** Gerhard Peters, "Final Presidential Job Approval Ratings," American Presidency Project, 1999–2021.

136 **voters had rolled the dice** Jeff Zeleny, "New Face and a Call for Change Shake Up the Democratic Field," The New York Times, Jan. 4, 2008.

136 **"the substantial majority of our people"** Sam Tanenhaus, "The Promise of Polarization," *The New Republic,* October 29, 2018, https://newrepublic.com/article/151612/promise-polarization-book-review-sam-rosenfeld-the-polarizers.

136 **And when Goldwater suffered a crushing loss** Donald Janson, "Rightists Buoyed by TBE Election," *The New York Times,* Nov. 23, 1964.

136 **the "great silent majority"** Richard Nixon, Address to the Nation on the War in Vietnam, The National Archives via The Miller Center, Nov. 3, 1969.

136 **"Mitt Romney will win big tonight"** Steve Forbes, "Romney Will Win Decisively," *Forbes,* Nov. 6, 2012.

137 **"Something old is roaring back"** Peggy Noonan, "Romney's Quiet Rise," *The Wall Street Journal,* Nov. 5, 2012.

138 **"creation science"** Susan J. Demas, "Mitt Romney is clearly winning, if you ignore the polls," *MLive.com,* Sept. 27, 2012 https://www.mlive.com/politics/2012/09/polls_romney_winning.html.

138 **"the polls are skewed"** *Hannity,* Fox News Network, 9 p.m., Sept. 25, 2012.

138 **Then he created a new website** David Weigel, "From the Maker of Unskewed Polling Comes: The Obama Voter Fraud Map," *Slate,* Nov. 20, 2012.

138 **But when the Republican on the commission** "What's Behind Fears of Voter Fraud?" *PBS NewsHour,* Nov. 4, 2016.

139 **Then he called for people** Kimberly Nordyke, "President Obama Re-Elected: Donald Trump Goes on Twitter Rant," *The Hollywood Reporter,* Nov. 6, 2012.

140 **Many told Fleischer** Notes provided by source.

141 **The Romney campaign's analysis** Document provided by source.

142 **The second report** Document provided by source.

144 **In a 1990 interview** Rush Limbaugh to Michael Harrison, *Talkers Magazine*, Aug. 20, 1990, audio accessed via *The Michael Harrison Interview* podcast, Feb. 23, 2021.

146 **So were many of the people** Notes provided by source.

147 **these "lapsed Republicans"** Document provided by source.

149 **Rebranded as the "Growth & Opportunity Project"** "Growth & Opportunity Project," Republican National Committee, March 18, 2013.

149 **"Our message was weak"** "Reince Priebus on the Future of the Republican Party," C-SPAN.org, March 18, 2013.

150 **"This is a very different party"** Thomas B. Edsall, "Bush Abandons 'Southern Strategy,'" *The Washington Post*, Aug. 6, 2000, washingtonpost.com /archive/politics/2000/08/06/bush-abandons-southern-strategy/0ed90167-d1ac -4b91-ba9d-c543b7c98bbc/.

151 **It accused Republicans** Francis Cannon, Maggie Gallagher, and Rich Danker, "Building a Winning GOP Coalition: The Lessons of 2012," American Principles in Action, 2013.

152 **"Every one of those eleven million people"** "Transcript of Donald Trump's Remarks," 2013 Conservative Political Action Committee, March 15, 2013.

152 **The memo ... discussed** Document provided by source.

153 **On the radio, Limbaugh rejected** Rush Limbaugh, "The GOP's Real Problem Is Simple," *The Rush Limbaugh Show*, March 18, 2013.

153 **Mark Levin called for Priebus** "Mark Levin: 'The Republican Party Is Going to Split, and There's Going to Be Two Parties,'" *RealClearPolitics*, March 18, 2013.

153 **The response Nunberg crafted** Donald J. Trump (@realdonaldtrump), Twitter, March 19, 2013, 2:47 P.M.

153 **And at 3:19 P.M. he weighed in again** Donald J. Trump (@realdonaldtrump), Twitter, March 19, 2013, 3:19 P.M.

Chapter 7: America First, Second, and Third

155 **Sessions attacked the bill** Eliana Johnson, "Amnesty's Worst Enemy," *National Review*, Aug. 6, 2014, nationalreview.com/2014/08/amnestys-worst -enemy-eliana-johnson.

155 **senators had scrambled** Robert Pear and Carl Hulse, "Immigration Bill Fails to Survive Senate Vote," *The New York Times*, June 28, 2007, nytimes .com/2007/06/28/washington/28cnd-immig.html.

156 **Even Sean Hannity seemed amenable** Rachel Weiner, "Sean Hannity: I've 'Evolved' on Immigration," *The Washington Post*, Nov. 8, 2012, washington post.com/news/post-politics/wp/2012/11/08/sean-hannity-ive-evolved-on -immigration/.

157 **with roughly 5 percent** "The Contributions of New Americans in New Hampshire," The Partnership for a New American Economy report, August 2016.

157 **3 percent of the population was Hispanic** "New Hampshire Economic Conditions," New Hampshire Employment Security, Economic and Labor Market Information Bureau report, February 2014.

158 **Brown proposed legislation that would** Scott Brown, op-ed, *The Boston Herald,* July 14, 2006.

159 **In his ad, Brown accused** Brown campaign ad youtube.com/watch?v=WQi4WBSc-hk&feature=youtu.be.

160 **It drew so many people** Jeremy W. Peters, "David Brat Was Aided by Influential Figures Like Laura Ingraham," *The New York Times,* June 11, 2014.

161 **"Eric Cantor doesn't represent you"** Olympia Meola, "Right, Left Rip Cantor on Immigration," *Richmond Times-Dispatch,* May 28, 2014.

161 **He asked in one piece** Stephen Miller, "The Case for Christmas," *The Chronicle,* Dec. 4, 2006, dukechronicle.com/article/2006/12/case-christmas.

161 **complained that Hollywood** Stephen Miller, "Hollywood and the Culture War," *The Chronicle,* Jan. 11, 2006, dukechronicle.com/article/2006/01/hollywood-and-culture-war.

161 **Occasionally he put politics** Stephen Miller, "Making Duke Perfect: Part II," *The Chronicle,* Oct. 23, 2006, dukechronicle.com/article/2006/10/making-duke-perfect-part-ii.

162 **"a nation paralyzed"** Stephen Miller, "Duke Lacrosse: A Call to Action," *The Chronicle,* Nov. 6, 2006, dukechronicle.com/article/2006/11/duke-lacrosse-call-action.

162 **He tried to draw attention** Stephen Miller, "Racial Hypocrisy," *The Chronicle,* Feb. 26, 2007, dukechronicle.com/article/2007/02/racial-hypocrisy.

162 **In 1991, a few days before Christmas** Patrick J. Buchanan, "Announcement of Candidacy," CNN.com, March 20, 1995.

163 **already vetoed one bill** Stephen A. Holmes, "President Vetoes Bill on Job Rights; Showdown Is Set," *The New York Times,* Oct. 23, 1990.

163 **signed a second** Andrew Rosenthal, "Reaffirming Commitment, Bush Signs Rights Bill," *The New York Times,* Nov. 22, 1991, nytimes.com/1991/11/22/us/reaffirming-commitment-bush-signs-rights-bill.html.

163 **In an unpublished manuscript** PJB manuscript provided to author.

164 **"a tiny and closed fraternity"** Buchanan, *Nixon's White House Wars* (New York: Crown Forum, 2017), p. 71.

165 **Buchanan announced** Patrick J. Buchanan, "America First—and Second, and Third," *The National Interest* 19 (Spring 1990), pp. 77–82.

165 **"the most visible and maybe the most important"** Howard Kurtz, "Pat Buchanan: The Jewish Question," *The Washington Post,* Sept. 20, 1990.

166 **his ten-point border security plan** "Buchanan Zeroes In on 'Illegals,'" *The Christian Science Monitor,* May 15, 1992.

167 **had not been able to replicate the jolt** Robin Toner, "New Hampshire; Bush Jarred in First Primary; Tsongas Wins Democratic Vote," *The New York Times,* Feb. 19, 1992.

167 **he delivered a fiery speech** "Migrants Hear Buchanan Pitch a Tighter Border," *Los Angeles Times,* May 13, 1992.

167 **Barr had provided an estimate** Paul R. Wieck, "The Problems Still Faced by Unskilled Workers," *The Christian Science Monitor,* May 28, 1992.

167 **Standing outside a jail** Ronald Brownstein, "Buchanan Links Riot to Border Problem," *Los Angeles Times,* May 14, 1992.

168 **spoke fondly of what immigrants contributed** "Labor Day Speech at Liberty State Park, Jersey City, New Jersey," Reagan Library, Sept. 1, 1980.

168 **Gallup in fact would not record** Jeffrey M. Jones, "New High in U.S. Say Immigration Most Important Problem," *Gallup,* June 21, 2019.

168 **Proposition 187, a ballot initiative** B. Drummond Ayres, Jr., "Californians Pass Measure on Aliens; Courts Bar It," *The New York Times,* Nov. 10, 1994.

168 **Buchanan's results on primary day** "Statement of Vote, Primary Election June 2, 1992," California Secretary of State, elections.cdn.sos.ca.gov/sov /1992-primary/sov-complete.pdf.

169 **one of the most memorable convention addresses** PJB, "Culture War Speech: Address to the Republican National Convention," *Voices of Democracy,* Aug. 17, 1992.

170 **"The fringe has taken over"** Garry Wills, "George Bush, Prisoner of the Crazies," *The New York Times,* Aug. 16, 1992.

171 **But the local paper** "In Salem, Scott Brown Talks Immigration, and His Continued Opposition to the ACA," *New Hampshire Union Leader,* Aug. 6, 2014.

171 **"I'm sure the polling is on his side"** Seth McLaughlin, "Scott Brown Uses Border Fight in New Hampshire Senate Push," *The Washington Times,* Aug. 4, 2014.

171 **A group with ties to the pro-immigration organization** Seung Min Kim, "Facebook-linked Group Drops $1M on Shaheen," *Politico,* Oct. 10, 2014.

172 **nineteen-hundred-word manifesto** Document provided by source.

173 *Breitbart* **noted Brown's shift** Matthew Boyle, "Scott Brown Nails Shaheen on Immigration: 'I Want to Fight for Jobs for New Hampshire' over Jobs for Illegal Aliens," *Breitbart,* Oct. 21, 2014.

174 **And she explained why it was so important** *The Laura Ingraham Show,* accessed from *Breitbart,* breitbart.com/clips/2014/10/22/ingraham-scott-brown -gets-it, October 22, 2014.

174 **or 3 percentage points** "New Hampshire Election Results," *The New York Times,* Dec. 17, 2014.

174 **Dave Bossie, president of the conservative group** "After Obama's Immigration Action, a Blast of Energy for the Tea Party," *The New York Times,* Nov. 25, 2014.

Chapter 8: "That's Hitler!"

176 **they had compiled a list** Document provided by source.

176 **When it came time** "Donald Trump at the Freedom Summit," C-SPAN.org, April 12, 2014.

178 JEB BUSH WAS PUBLIC ENEMY NO. 1 Brett LoGiurato, "Jeb Bush Booed by Conservatives in NH," *Business Insider,* April 14, 2014.

178 *The Washington Post:* Jaime Fuller, "Donald Trump Mentions Jeb Bush at Tea Party Event, Gets Boos from the Audience," *The Washington Post,* April 12, 2014.

179 **"The 'Serious' Question"** Document provided by source.

179 **And more than anything else** Document provided by source.

179 **Trump rarely got more than 5 percent** "National Republican Primary Polls," *FiveThirtyEight,* July 1, 2016.

179 **As journalists chronicled his exploits** Laura Italiano, "Trump Calls Romney a 'Choker,' Says Jeb Is 'Total Fool,'" *New York Post,* May 22, 2015.

179 **In December 2014, a column** James Warren, "President Trump (Made You Look)," New York *Daily News,* Dec. 20, 2014.

179 **In January 2015, Chuck Todd said on NBC** *Meet the Press,* transcript, NBC News, Jan. 25, 2015.

180 **In February 2015, the *Los Angeles Times*** Michael A. Memoli, "Jeb Bush Tells Conservative Skeptics He Hopes to Be Their 'Second Choice,'" *Los Angeles Times,* Feb. 27, 2015.

180 **"The man can only ride ya"** Loulla-Mae Eleftheriou-Smith, "Sarah Palin Delivers Bizarre and Rambling Speech at Iowa Freedom Summit—and Her Teleprompter Freezing Is Only Partly to Blame," *The Independent,* Jan. 26, 2015.

181 **At Bossie's Iowa Freedom Summit** Alex Hanson and Makayla Tendall, "Updates from the Iowa Freedom Summit," *Iowa State Daily,* Jan. 24, 2015.

182 **"They said that was like the Wharton School"** Donald J. Trump, "Donald Trump Reflects on His Beginnings, Ventures, and Plans for the Future," Economic Club of Washington, Dec. 15, 2014.

183 **Trump offered George the seat** Letter from Donald J. Trump to George Conway, April 13, 2006, *The Washington Post.*

184 **"Romney had one thing going for him"** Italiano, "Trump Calls Romney a 'Choker.'"

184 **conducted a survey in 2017** Document provided by source.

185 **A complaint later filed** First General Counsel's Report, Federal Election Commission, March 7, 2016, eqs.fec.gov/eqsdocsMUR/17044405316.pdf.

187 **Bush and Walker were tied** Anderson Robbins Research and Shaw & Company Research, "Fox News Poll: Bush, Walker, Carson Top GOP Pack, Support for Clinton Down," FoxNews.com, June 4, 2015.

187 **"I actually laughed"** "Donald Trump running for President," Fox News, June 17, 2015.

188 **The Spanish-language network Univision** "Univision Ends Miss Universe Business Deal over Trump Mexico Comments," NBC News, June 25, 2015.

188 **The network said on June 29 that it was severing** Paul Farhi, "Donald Trump Talks Himself Right Out of NBC's Plans," *The Washington Post,* June 29, 2015.

188 **On July 1, Macy's said** Alan Rappeport, "Macy's Drops Donald Trump's Fashion Line over Immigrant Remarks," *The New York Times,* July 1, 2015.

188 **Then José Andrés, the Spanish-born celebrity chef** Emily Heil, "José Andrés Backs Out of Restaurant in Donald Trump's Hotel," *The Washington Post,* July 8, 2015.

189 **And ESPN ditched its plans** "ESPN Moves Celebrity Golf Tournament Course," ESPN.com, July 6, 2015.

189 **When Fox News went into the field** Paul Singer, "Bush, Trump See Bump in new Fox News Poll," *USA Today,* June 24, 2015.

189 **"Go back to Univision"** Chris Cillizza, "Donald Trump's Jorge Ramos News Conference, Annotated," *The Washington Post,* Aug. 26, 2015.

190 **(After seeing it, she tweeted)** Ann Coulter (@AnnCoulter), Twitter, Aug. 16, 2015, 2:47 P.M., twitter.com/anncoulter/status/632987034320261120.

190 **threatening to impound wages** Sean Sullivan, "Donald Trump: Undocumented Immigrants 'Have to Go,'" *The Washington Post,* Aug. 16, 2015, washingtonpost.com/news/post-politics/wp/2015/08/16/donald-trump-undocumented-immigrants-have-to-go/.

191 **"clutching their pearls"** Sarah Palin, "Palin: Trump Stumps Media Kingmakers," *Breitbart,* July 31, 2015.

191 **Bannon consulted with Nunberg** Document provided to author.

191 *Breitbart* **had opened** Leslie Kaufman, "Breitbart News Network Plans Global Expansion," *The New York Times,* Feb. 16, 2014.

192 **"I believe in what he's throwing out there"** James Hohmann, "Donald Trump Makes a Texas-Size Splash with Visit to Mexican Border," *The Washington Post,* July 23, 2015.

192 **In September, when Jeb Bush questioned** Patricia Mazzei, "In Miami—and en Español—Jeb Bush Punches Back at Donald Trump's 'Blah Blah Blah,'" *Miami Herald,* Sept. 2, 2015.

192 **The lead quote from Trump** Matthew Boyle, "Donald Trump Fires Back at Jeb Bush," *Breitbart,* Sept. 2, 2015.

193 **"The excitement for him"** William J. Feltus, Kenneth M. Goldstein, and Matthew Dallek, *Inside Campaigns: Elections Through the Eyes of Political Professionals* (Washington, D.C.: CQ Press, 2016), p. 6.

194 **two thousand people were waiting** Kathleen Gray, "A Lovefest for Donald Trump in Birch Run," *Detroit Free Press,* Aug. 11, 2015.

Chapter 9: A Death in Texas

196 **This was an old trick** Jeremy W. Peters, "Conservatives Hone Script to Light a Fire over Abortion," *The New York Times,* July 24, 2014.

197 **"I am pro-choice"** "Trump in 1999: 'I Am Very Pro-Choice,'" NBCNews .com, July 8, 2015.

197 **"No cursing"** Document provided by source.

197 **"I will be the greatest"** Julia Limitone, "Donald Trump: I Will Be the Greatest Jobs President God Ever Created," *Fox Business,* Jan. 9, 2017.

198 **Once, during a speech** Maggie Haberman, "Trump at Liberty U: Vengeance and Prenups," *Politico,* Sept. 24, 2012, politico.com/blogs/burns-haberman /2012/09/trump-at-liberty-u-vengeance-and-prenups-136558.

199 **But the sentiment of "Never Trump"** "Pro-life Women Sound the Alarm: Donald Trump Is Unacceptable," Susan B. Anthony List, Jan. 26, 2016.

201 **Trump swore when** "Presidential Candidate Donald Trump at the Family Leadership Summit," C-SPAN.org, July 18, 2015.

204 **At fifteen, he began preaching** "From Pulpit to Politics, U.S. Senate Hopeful Is Comfortable with Both," *New Orleans Times-Picayune,* Oct. 9, 2002.

204 **"It's been a long day"** John MacCormack, "Cibolo Creek Ranch Owner Recalls Scalia's Last Hours in Texas," *My San Antonio,* Feb. 14, 2016.

204 **a thirty-thousand-acre retreat** Cibolo Creek Ranch's website, cibolocreek ranch.com.

205 **roughly seven hundred members** International Order of St. Hubertus website, iosh-usa.com.

205 **when Scalia still hadn't appeared** U.S. Marshals Service correspondence, fixthecourt.com/wp-content/uploads/2018/03/FixTheCourt_Segment3_Final -Scalia.pdf.

206 **"Please keep this information confidential"** Ibid.

207 **In an interview on Monday** Caitlin Yilek, "Trump Flirts with Suggestion That Scalia Was Murdered," *The Hill.com,* Feb. 16, 2016. https://thehill.com/blogs /ballot-box/presidential-races/donald-trump-justice-antonin-scalia-murdered -pillow-conspiracy-theory.

207 **A president of this party would fill** "Justices 1789 to Present," Supreme Court of the United States, Supremecourt.gov.

208 **(It all seemed too much)** Michael O'Donnell, "Eisenhower vs. Warren: The Battle over Brown," *The Atlantic,* April 2018.

209 **"President Reagan had three vacancies"** Phyllis Schlafly, "America's 'Last Chance,'" *The Phyllis Schlafly Report,* Feb. 2016.

209 **She warned of an alleged Communist infiltration** Phyllis Schlafly, *A Choice Not an Echo: The Inside Story of How American Presidents Are Chosen* (Alton, Ill.: Pere Marquette Press, 1964), p. 60.

209 **was as "phony"** Schlafly, *A Choice Not an Echo,* p. 57.

209 **she refused to accept the results** Geoffrey Kabaservice, *Rule and Ruin: The Downfall of Moderation and the Destruction of the Republican Party, From Eisenhower to the Tea Party* (Oxford: Oxford University Press, 2012), p. 206.

210 **One of her favorite senators** Brandon Moseley, "Eagle Forum Endorses Jeff Sessions," *Alabama Political Reporter,* March 18, 2020.

210 **"They try to tell you they're very pro-family"** Scott Greer, "Schlafly: Immigration Is Killing the American Family," *The Daily Caller,* Oct. 26, 2014.

210 **She warned that any immigration reform bill** Katie McHugh, "Phyllis Schlafly: Republicans Are 'Fools' to Back 'Any Kind of Amnesty,'" *The Daily Caller,* March 6, 2014.

212 **"deeply religious Catholic"** Jeffrey Toobin, "The Conservative Pipeline to the Supreme Court," *The New Yorker,* April 10, 2017.

213 **"It is sad to see"** Robin Cook, "Confirmation of High Court Justices Akin to Political Campaign, Leo Says," University of Virginia School of Law, Sept. 20, 2006.

213 **When he goes on the road** Jay Michaelson, "The Secrets of Leonard Leo, the Man Behind Trump's Supreme Court Pick," *The Daily Beast,* July 9, 2018.

213 **He saved the titanium rods** Melissa Quinn, "Inside the Mind of Leonard Leo, Trump's Supreme Court Right-Hand Man," *Washington Examiner,* Jan. 28, 2018.

213 **"No one has been more dedicated"** Ed Whelan, "Mistaken Attack by Andy Schlafly on Leonard Leo," *National Review,* Dec. 9, 2016, nationalreview .com/bench-memos/schlafly-attack-leonard-leo/.

215 **Trump released his list** Alan Rappeport and Charlie Savage, "Donald Trump Releases List of Possible Supreme Court Picks," *The New York Times,* May 18, 2016.

215 **As Bob Woodward described in his retelling** Bob Woodward, "Origin of the Tax Pledge," *The Washington Post,* Oct. 4, 1992.

216 **It committed politicians—in writing** "About the Taxpayer Protection Pledge," Americans for Tax Reform," March 15, 2014.

Chapter 10: No More Bushes

218 **Buchanan then promised** "Iowa Republican Straw Poll," C-SPAN.org, Aug. 14, 1999.

219 **"He'll never be president"** Sasha Issenberg, "Interview with Mike Murphy of Pro-Jeb Bush Super-PAC Right to Rise Part 1," *Bloomberg,* Oct. 20, 2015.

219 **"He's doing this to inflame and incite"** Jacob Koffler, "Donald Trump Shares, Then Deletes, Tweet About Jeb Bush's Wife," *Time,* July 6, 2015.

219 **"To make these"** Ibid.

221 **Murphy helped produce** "New Bush Ad Attacks Buchanan's Mercedes," Associated Press, March 14, 1992.

221 **Jeb would "dominate"** John Cassidy, "Who Killed Jeb Bush's Campaign? Jeb Did," *The New Yorker,* Feb. 22, 2016.

221 **An NBC News/*Wall Street Journal* poll** Mark Murray, Chuck Todd, and Andrew Rafferty, "First Read: Jeb Bush Leads the GOP Pack," NBC News, June 22, 2015.

221 **Murphy convinced donors** "Report of Receipts and Disbursements," Federal Election Commission, Jan. 31, 2016, docquery.fec.gov/pdf/742/201601 319005190742/201601319005190742.pdf.

221 **Bush's apparatus was taking in** Eli Stokols, "Jeb's Shock-and-Awe Number," *Politico,* July 9, 2015.

222 **Less than two weeks before he formally announced** Nick Gass, "Jeb Bush to Announce 2016 Bid on June 15," *Politico,* June 4, 2015.

222 **His announcement, which he delivered** Michael Barbaro and Jonathan Martin, "Jeb Bush Announces White House Bid, Saying 'America Deserves Better,'" *The New York Times,* June 15, 2015.

222 **Bush broke into Spanish** Patricia Mazzei and Amy Sherman, "With Pressure on, Jeb Bush Delivers Forceful Speech Confirming 2016 Presidential Candidacy," *Miami Herald,* June 15, 2015.

223 **the personification of Bush's 2014 comment** "Jeb Bush: GOP Nominee Should Be Willing to 'Lose the Primary to Win the General,'" NBC News First Read, Dec. 1, 2014.

223 **"Way too many people believe Republicans are"** Jon Ward, "Jeb Bush CPAC Speech Says GOP Must Stop Being 'Anti Everything' Party," *The Huffington Post,* March 15, 2016.

224 **(Trump offered a snide response)** Michael Barbaro, "Jeb Bush Takes a Cue from Donald Trump's Playbook: Punch Back," *The New York Times,* Aug. 24, 2015.

225 **"He's almost too polite"** Susan Page, "Barbara Bush Blames Trump for Heart Attack, GOP Exit in The Matriarch," *USA Today,* March 27, 2019.

225 **After starting the summer** Carrie Dann, "Donald Trump Surges in New NBC News Poll," NBC News, Aug. 2, 2015.

225 **"We don't have time"** "GOP Debate 2015: Transcript of the Prime-time Debate," CBS News, Aug. 7, 2015.

226 **Kasich had sent so many items** John R. Kasich Collection, Westerville Public Library, inventory of items accessed from westervillelibrary.org/kasich-search.

227 **The narrator concluded** Ed O'Keefe, "Bush Super PAC's New TV Ad: 'If Trump Wins, Conservatives Lose,'" *The Washington Post,* Feb. 12, 2016.

227 **Kochel, who spent much of his time in Iowa** McKay Coppins, "Jeb Bush, 2016's Gay-Friendly Republican," *BuzzFeed News,* Feb. 26, 2015.

228 **Bush had already gone to extraordinary lengths** Adam C. Smith and Alex Leary, "Revisiting Jeb Bush and the Terri Schiavo Case," *Miami Herald,* Jan. 17, 2015.

228 **"The notion puzzles Floridians"** Brian E. Crowley, "Five Myths About Jeb Bush," *The Washington Post,* June 19, 2015.

229 **By then Jeb was rumored to be interested** Eun Kyung Kim, "Barbara Bush

on Jeb Run: 'We've Had Enough Bushes' in White House," *Today.com*, April 25, 2013.

230 **recommended a course of action** Correspondence provided by source.

231 **he said it was imperative** Remarks of Jeb Bush, South Carolina Primary Night Speech, C-SPAN.org, Feb. 20, 2016, c-span.org/video/?405022-1/jeb -bush-primary-night-speech.

Chapter 11: Meet Me in St. Louis

233 **which she had first played** Allegations of Clinton Marital Infidelity, C-SPAN, Jan. 27, 1992.

235 **"a glorified synagogue newsletter"** Josh Hasten, "Airing Controversy," *Jerusalem Post*, May 3, 2012.

236 **The thefts caught the attention** Karen W. Arenson, "Yeshiva Students Say the University Is Behind Removal of Campus Paper," *The New York Times*, Dec. 15, 1999.

236 **who told Klein that the militant group** "Is Hamas Backing Obama for President?," *Factcheck.org*, May 31, 2008.

236 **questioned his rival's commitment** Larry Rohter, "On McCain, Obama and a Hamas Link," *The New York Times*, May 10, 2008.

237 **Klein interviewed a Hamas co-founder** S. A. Miller, "Hamas Nod for Ground Zero Mosque," *New York Post*, Aug. 16, 2010.

238 **"Donald Trump is not about that"** "Pence Says Gennifer Flowers Will Not Attend Trump, Clinton Debate," Fox News, Sept. 25, 2016.

239 **twenty cents a copy** "Extremist Book Sales Soar Despite Criticism in GOP," *The New York Times*, Oct. 4, 1964.

239 ***The Texas Observer* recognized** Sarah T. Hughes, "The Crisis in the Cities," *The Texas Observer*, Sept. 18, 1964.

239 **writers like David Brock** David Brock, "His Cheatin' Heart," *The American Spectator*, Sept. 7, 2012, spectator.org/his-cheatin-heart/.

240 **who shot himself in a park** Stephen Labaton, "A Report on His Suicide Portrays a Deeply Troubled Vince Foster," *The New York Times*, Oct. 11, 1997.

240 **But Bossie's overly zealous** Eric Schmitt, "Top Investigator for House Panel Leaves Under Fire," *The New York Times*, May 7, 1998.

240 **deceptively edited transcripts** George Lardner, Jr., and Juliet Eilperin, "Burton Apologizes to GOP," *The Washington Post*, May 7, 1998.

241 **referring to it in conservative code** Karen Hosler, "Dole Calls Clinton Morally Unfit to be President," *The Baltimore Sun*, Oct. 9, 1996.

241 **He nudged them to unload on Hillary** Aaron Klein, "Broaddrick, Willey, Jones to Bill Clinton's Defenders: 'These Are Crimes,' 'Terrified' of 'Enabler' Hillary," *Breitbart*, Oct. 9, 2016.

242 **one of the most explosive stories** David A. Fahrenthold, "Trump Recorded Having Extremely Lewd Conversation About Women in 2005," *The Washington Post*, Oct. 8, 2016.

243 **Trump sent out a tweet with an excerpt** Aaron Klein, "Video Interview: Bill Clinton Accuser Juanita Broaddrick Relives Brutal Rapes," *Breitbart*, Oct. 9, 2016.

246 **"four very courageous women"** "Ahead of Debate, Trump Holds News Conference with Bill Clinton Accusers," *The Washington Post*, Oct. 9, 2016.

247 **they threatened to have the women** "Trump Campaign Tried to Seat Bill Clinton's Accusers in VIP Box," *The New York Times*, Oct. 10, 2016.

249 **dropped only thirty minutes after** Aaron Sharockman, "It's True: WikiLeaks Dumped Podesta Emails Hour After Trump Video Surfaced," *PolitiFact*, Dec. 18, 2016.

249 **as many as thirty** "Inside Story: How Russians Hacked the Democrats' Emails," Associated Press, Nov. 4, 2017.

249 **On October 4, Assange** Andrea Shalal, "WikiLeaks' Assange Signals Release of Documents Before U.S. Election," Reuters, Oct. 4, 2016.

249 **he believed more was coming** Robert S. Mueller III, "Report on the Investigation into Russian Interference in the 2016 Presidential Election, Volume I," March 2019, p. 54.

250 **code for "child pornography"** "Dissecting the #PizzaGate Conspiracy Theories," *The New York Times*, Dec. 10, 2016.

250 **"Do you know about this online conspiracy theory"** Burt Helm, "Pizzagate Nearly Destroyed My Restaurant. Then My Customers Helped Me Fight Back," *Inc.*, July 2017.

251 **fierce, warrior-like masculinity** Adam Goldman, "The Comet Ping Pong Gunman Answers Our Reporter's Questions," *The New York Times*, Dec. 7, 2016.

251 **On the morning of December 4** Marc Fisher, John Woodrow Cox, and Peter Hermann, "Pizzagate: From Rumor, to Hashtag, to Gunfire in D.C.," *The Washington Post*, December 6, 2016.

251 **Earlier he had tried to** Special Agent Justin Holgate, Affidavit in Support of a Criminal Complaint, United States District Court for the District of Columbia, Dec. 12, 2016.

Chapter 12: "Give Them What They Want . . ."

254 **He did not dwell** Emily McFarlan Miller, "After Lewd Tape Release, Ralph Reed Lays Out Evangelical Case for Trump," *Religion News Service*, Oct. 10, 2016.

255 **Falwell said, describing what he expected** Ibid.

257 **in a tweet he later deleted** "Popular Christian Author Eric Metaxas Stands by Donald Trump," *Religion News Service*, Oct. 12, 2016.

257 **With Election Day approaching, he agreed** Trump Letter to Pro-life Leaders, Sept. 2016.

258 **Falwell Jr. shared a concern** Yousef Saba, "Falwell Censored Anti-Trump Column, Liberty U Student Editor Says," *Politico*, Oct. 18, 2016.

259 **Palin weighed in almost immediately** "Sarah Palin Says She's Heard 'Much Worse' in Locker Rooms Than Trump's Lewd 2005 Remarks," New York *Daily News*, Oct. 9, 2016.

259 **Cissie Graham Lynch** "Billy Graham's Granddaughter 'Unapologetically' Endorses Donald Trump," *Christian Post*, Nov. 2, 2016.

260 **Trump would go on to win 81 percent** "How the Faithful Voted: A Preliminary 2016 Analysis," Pew Research Center, Nov. 9, 2016.

261 **it called the next big battleground** "Calling the Presidential Race," Associated Press, Nov. 9, 2016.

262 **He spoke for only** "Donald Trump Victory Speech," C-SPAN.org, Nov. 9, 2016.

265 **steered more money to Pompeo** Megan Janetsky and Matthew Kelly, "Trump Picks Top Koch Recipient for Secretary of State," *OpenSecrets.org*, March 14, 2018.

266 **"These guys are really on fire"** "Pence Helped Pick Christians from Congressional Bible Studies for Trump Admin., Ralph Drollinger Says," *Christian Post*, May 8, 2018.

267 **In the sixteen-minute speech** Peter Baker and Michael D. Shear, "Donald Trump Is Sworn In as President, Capping His Swift Ascent," *The New York Times*, Jan. 20, 2017.

268 **"His appeal skyrocketed"** "America First: Immigration and Nationalism Unite Donald Trump's Coalition," *National Review*, April 27, 2016.

269 **on the night that Trump announced his decision** "Conservative Groups Unify to Push Neil Gorsuch's Confirmation," *The New York Times*, Feb. 1, 2017.

270 **But Trump, he said, actually picked up** Jeremy W. Peters, "For Religious Conservatives, Success and Access at the Trump White House," *The New York Times*, Feb. 13, 2017.

270 **"I've been to the White House"** Jeremy W. Peters, "Trump Keeps His Conservative Movement Allies Closest," *The New York Times*, Aug. 2, 2017.

271 **Trump became the first** Jeremy W. Peters, "Trump Tells Anti-Abortion Marchers 'We Are With You All The Way' and Shows It," *The New York Times*, January 19, 2018.

271 **a busy week** Ibid.

Chapter 13: Holy War

274 **the headline screamed** Aaron Klein, "After Endorsing Democrat in Alabama, Bezos's Washington Post Plans to Hit Roy Moore with Allegations of Inappropriate Relations with Teenagers," *Breitbart*, Nov. 9, 2017.

274 **Within a few days** Hunter Schwartz, "More Than 20 Republicans Have Called for Roy Moore to Step Aside," CNN, Nov. 13, 2017.

277 **when he spoke publicly about Moore** "Trump Defends Roy Moore, Citing Candidate's Denial of Sexual Misconduct," *The New York Times*, Nov. 21, 2017.

278 **After a seven-day trial** "Alabama's Chief Judge Ordered to Remove Ten Commandments Monument from Courthouse," American Civil Liberties Union of Alabama press release, Nov. 18, 2002.

278 **and denounce the judge's conduct** Peggy Wallace Kennedy, "Roy Moore Is More Dangerous Than My Father," Al.com, Jan. 7, 2016.

279 **"Roy Moore for Senate!"** Jeffrey Gettleman, "Alabama Panel Ousts Judge over Ten Commandments," *The New York Times*, Nov. 14, 2003.

279 **with shouts of "Amen"** Kim Chandler, "Roy Moore Wins Chief Justice Race," Al.com, Nov. 7, 2012.

279 **taken off the bench** "Roy Moore, Alabama Chief Justice, Suspended over Gay Marriage Order," *The New York Times*, Sept. 30, 2016.

279 **compared it to being sworn in** Roy Moore, "Muslim Ellison Should Not Sit in Congress," *WorldNetDaily,* Dec. 13, 2006.

280 **"One of our attorneys is a *Jee-yew*"** Alan Blinder, "Roy Moore's Wife Says Some of the Couple's Friends Are Black or Jewish," *The New York Times,* Dec. 12, 2017.

280 **"There's this disjunction"** "GOP, Once Unified Against Obama, Struggles for Consensus Under Trump," *The New York Times,* March 26, 2017.

280 **no less than 15 percent of the time** "House to Vote Yet Again on Repealing Health Care Law," *The New York Times,* May 14, 2013.

281 *Politico* **noted how the conservatives' defiance** Rachael Bade, Josh Dawsey, and Jennifer Haberkorn, "How a Secret Freedom Caucus Pact Brought Down Obamacare Repeal," *Politico,* March 26, 2017.

283 **"I'll be honest"** "President Trump Remarks at Senator Strange Campaign Rally," C-SPAN.org, Sept. 22, 2017.

284 **Moore won by 9 points** "Alabama Election Results: Roy Moore Advances in Race for U.S. Senate Seat," *The New York Times,* Sept. 27, 2017.

284 **in his concession speech** Jonathan Martin and Alexander Burns, "Roy Moore Wins Senate GOP Runoff in Alabama," *The New York Times,* Sept. 26, 2017.

284 **tweets he had posted about Strange** "Trump Deletes Tweets Supporting Luther Strange," *The New York Times,* Sept. 27, 2017.

284 **"The swamp is trying to steal the victory"** Julie Hirschfeld Davis and Jonathan Martin, "At Alabama Rally, Trump Toggles Between Republican Loyalists," *The New York Times,* Sept. 22, 2017.

285 **who Bannon said regarded Moore supporters** Alex Isenstadt, "Bannon to Alabama: 'They Think You're a Pack of Morons,'" *Politico,* Sept. 25, 2017.

286 **the explanations Moore gave** "Roy Moore Interviewed by Hannity; 'Generally' Didn't Date Girls in Late Teens, Accusations 'Never Happened,'" *RealClearPolitics,* Nov. 10, 2017.

287 **he thundered from the stage** "Bannon Finds New Fight Backing Roy Moore, but Risks Are High," *The New York Times,* Dec. 5, 2017.

287 **"I believe in innocent until proven guilty"** Jenny Jarvie, "The Roy Moore Controversy Is a Thorny Issue for Alabama Baptists," *Los Angeles Times,* Nov. 15, 2017.

288 **"It would be a very dangerous precedent"** Nicholas Fandos, "Trump Officials Urge Caution on Judging Roy Moore as Senators Pull Support," *The New York Times,* Nov. 12, 2017.

288 **endorsement of Moore on Twitter** "Roy Moore Gets Trump Endorsement and RNC Funding for Senate Race," *The New York Times,* Dec. 4, 2017.

288 **"Assume you were a person of the left"** Peter Wehner, "Why I Can No Longer Call Myself an Evangelical Republican," *The New York Times,* Dec. 9, 2017.

289 **Fox officially called the race** "Doug Jones Wins Alabama Senate Seat," video .foxnews.com, Dec. 13, 2017.

289 **when all the ballots were counted** "Alabama Election Results," *The New York Times,* Dec. 12, 2017.

291 **According to an account his accuser** Emma Brown, "California Professor,

Writer of Confidential Brett Kavanaugh Letter, Speaks Out About Her Allegation of Sexual Assault," *The Washington Post,* Sept. 16, 2018.

292 **"This is about Donald Trump getting in one of his guys"** Jeremy W. Peters and Susan Chira, "Kavanaugh Borrows from Trump's Playbook on White Male Anger," *The New York Times,* Sept. 29, 2018.

Chapter 14: The Party

296 **"You in?"** " 'If Trump Loses, I'm Grabbing My Musket,' Former Congressman Tweets," *USA Today,* Oct. 26, 2016.

296 **giving him a nationally syndicated show** "Salem Radio Network to Launch The Joe Walsh Show," Salem Radio Network press release, Feb. 8, 2017.

296 **had a staff of fifteen** Ibid.

297 **warning that Trump's loss** "Beck to Hannity: 'We Are Officially at the End of the Country as We Know It' If Trump Loses in 2020," *The Hill,* March 19, 2019.

297 **As an affiliated foundation** Peters, "A Popular Political Site Made a Sharp Right Turn. What Steered It?" *The New York Times,* Nov. 17, 2020.

298 **40 percent of Trump's supporters cited Fox News** "Trump, Clinton Voters Divided in Their Main Source for Election News," Pew Research Center, Jan. 18, 2017.

298 **Sixty percent of Republicans** "Americans Are Divided by Party in the Sources They Turn To for Political News," Pew Research Center, Jan. 24, 2020.

298 **one anonymous member** Paul McLeod, "Democrats Still Hope Mitt Romney Will Take On Trump," *BuzzFeed News,* Sept. 25, 2019.

298 **Buchanan seemed quite satisfied** Patrick J. Buchanan, "It's Trump's Party Now," *RealClearPolitics,* March 3, 2017.

299 **"appear to exist in their own"** Leigh Bradberry and Gary Jacobson, "Does the Tea Party Still Matter? Tea Party Influence in the 2012 Elections," *Electoral Studies* 40, Dec. 2015, pp. 500–508.

299 **"the Four Corners of Deceit"** *The Rush Limbaugh Show,* transcript, April 29, 2013.

299 **"I feel like I'm back in school"** *The Rush Limbaugh Show,* transcript, Jan. 24, 2017.

300 **Ayres put together a deck of slides** Document provided to author.

301 **Trump once told Sean Hannity** "Trump on Kim Jong Un: 'Why Shouldn't I Like Him?' " *The Washington Post,* March 1, 2019.

301 **as long as Trump was** Information provided to author by source with access to survey.

304 **Republicans would lose forty seats** "U.S. House Election Results 2018," *The New York Times,* May 15, 2019.

304 **"We are the party of Donald J. Trump!"** "Republican Voters Embrace Trump-Style Candidates," *The New York Times,* June 12, 2018.

306 **"pure, raw hatred"** "Limbaugh: Impeachment Driven by 'Raw Hatred' of Trump and 'People Who Elected Him,' " *The Hill,* Dec. 6, 2019.

306 **Sean Hannity described the people** "Hannity: Hate-Trump Media Is Just Lies, Noise," video.foxnews.com, May 30, 2019.

306 **"still can't get over"** "Kellyanne Conway Claims 'We Never Talk About Hill-

ary Clinton' As Donald Trump Repeatedly Talks About Hillary Clinton," *Yahoo! News,* Jan. 11, 2018.

307 **"we are in a coup d'état"** "Franklin Graham Asserts That Trump Could Be Toppled in a Coup," *Baptist News Global,* Jan. 30, 2018.

308 **"like the Woodward and Bernsteins"** "Life, Liberty & Levin," Fox News transcript, March 31, 2019.

309 **called out his favorite media personalities** "Donald Trump Thanks God for Fox News, Mocks Journalists Who Win Pulitzer Prizes," Newsweek.com, Oct. 12, 2019.

309 **colleagues complained about his reliance** Maxwell Tani and Justin Baragona, "Leaked Memo: Colleagues Unload on John Solomon, the Journo Who Kicked Off Trump's Ukraine Conspiracy," *The Daily Beast,* Sept. 28, 2019.

309 **Giuliani revealed** Ken Vogel and Jeremy W. Peters, "The Man Trump Trusts for News on Ukraine," *The New York Times,* Nov. 12, 2019.

309 **later admitted in an interview with Hannity** "Trump: Claim of Obama Wiretapping Based 'on a Little Bit of a Hunch,'" *The Hill,* April 25, 2019.

310 ***The Hill* announced that it had completed a review** "The Hill's Review of John Solomon's Columns on Ukraine," *The Hill,* Feb. 19, 2020.

Chapter 15: Dishonor and Defeat

314 **at 2:01 P.M., Romney stood at his desk** United States Senate Press Gallery daily log, dailypress.senate.gov/?p=36239.

314 **"I am profoundly religious"** "Romney Delivers Remarks on Impeachment Vote," Senator Mitt Romney's prepared text, Feb. 5, 2020.

315 **a resolution to censure Romney** "Mitt Romney Is a 'Judas' to Many Republicans. But Not in Utah," *The New York Times,* Feb. 10, 2020.

315 **called for a separate resolution** "Romney Returns to Utah to Explain Vote as Lawmakers Talk Censure of Senator," *Deseret News,* Feb. 6, 2020.

315 **by reviving controversial legislation** "U.S. Senator Recall Bill Picks Up Steam in Utah After Mitt Romney Votes to Convict Trump," *Deseret News,* Feb. 5, 2020.

316 **declared Lou Dobbs of *Fox Business*** "Fox News Stars Rail Against Romney for Trump Impeachment Vote: 'Going to Be Associated with Judas,'" *TheWrap,* Feb. 6, 2020.

316 **something that hadn't happened** List of Senate expulsions, "U.S. Senate: About Expulsion," Senate.gov, senate.gov/about/powers-procedures/expulsion .htm.

316 **"I don't like people who use their faith"** "Trump Lashes Out at Impeachment Foes and Pelosi Hits Back," *The New York Times,* Feb. 6, 2020.

316 **"This is not the first time"** @GOPchairwoman Twitter account, Feb. 5, 2020.

316 **its highest approval rating yet** Jeffrey M. Jones, "Trump Job Approval at Personal Best 49%," Gallup, Feb. 4, 2020.

317 **The paper cited a statement** Li Yuan, "Coronavirus Crisis Shows China's Governance Failure," *The New York Times,* Feb. 4, 2020.

317 **projected more than half a million deaths** Maggie Haberman, "Trade Adviser Warned White House in January of Risks of a Pandemic," *The New York Times,* April 6, 2020.

317 **"As many as 1–2 million"** Jonathan Swan and Margaret Talev, "Peter

Navarro Memos Warning of Mass Coronavirus Death Circulated West Wing in January," *Axios,* April 7, 2020, axios.com/exclusive-navarro-deaths -coronavirus-memos-january-da3f08fb-dce1-4f69-89b5-ea048f8382a9.html.

333 **Jonathan Swan of *Axios* first reported** Jonathan Swan, "Trump Plans to Declare Premature Victory If He Appears Ahead on Election Night," *Axios,* Nov. 1, 2020, axios.com/trump-claim-election-victory-ballots-97eb12b9-5e35 -402f-9ea3-0ccfb47f613f.html.

Afterword

339 **urged his colleagues to support** "GOP Leader McCarthy Says President Trump 'Bears Responsibility' for Capitol Attack, Favors Censure over Impeachment," C-SPAN.org, Jan. 13, 2021.

339 **one of only ten** Roll Call 17 on H. Res. 24, "On Agreeing to the Resolution Impeaching Donald John Trump, President of the United States, for high crimes and misdemeanors," Jan. 13, 2021.

340 **She wrote a twenty-one-page** Document provided by source.

340 **contained chilling revelations** "Violent Actors and Ideologies Behind the Events of January 6, 2021," Network Contagion Research Institute," Jan. 9, 2021.

341 **It would involve** Dan Lamothe, "Jade Helm 15, Heavily Scrutinized Military Exercise, to Open Without Media Access," *The Washington Post,* July 8, 2015.

342 **"When the federal government has"** David Weigel, "Ted Cruz Says He Has Asked Pentagon for Answers on Jade Helm 15," *Bloomberg News*, May 2, 2015.

342 **And what he found** Documents provided by source.

343 **Subsequent surveys that asked** Verified Voter Omnibus Survey of 1,016 registered voters, Echelon Insights, Aug. 13–18, 2021.

344 **"no involvement"** Amy B. Wang, "Jan. 6 Committee Leaders Blast McCarthy's 'Baseless' Claim About Trump's Innocence," *The Washington Post*, Sept. 4, 2021.

345 **That sought to award** Text of SCR 1002, Arizona State Senate, Fifty-fifth legislature, first regular session, 2021. https://www.azleg.gov/legtext/55leg/1R /bills/scr1002p.pdf.

346 **Senator Rick Scott** Quint Forgey, "Rick Scott: GOP Is 'Voters' Party,' Not Trump's," *Politico*, Feb. 28, 2021.

Index

ABOUT THE AUTHOR

JEREMY W. PETERS is a correspondent for *The New York Times* who has covered the last three presidential elections.

@jwpetersNYT

ABOUT THE TYPE

This book was set in Sabon, a typeface designed by the well-known German typographer Jan Tschichold (1902–74). Sabon's design is based upon the original letter forms of sixteenth-century French type designer Claude Garamond and was created specifically to be used for three sources: foundry type for hand composition, Linotype, and Monotype. Tschichold named his typeface for the famous Frankfurt typefounder Jacques Sabon (c. 1520–80).